LAND OF STARK CONTRASTS

Land of Stark Contrasts

FAITH-BASED RESPONSES TO HOMELESSNESS
IN THE UNITED STATES

Manuel Mejido Costoya, Editor

NEW YORK   2021

Fordham University Press has no responsibility for the persistence or accuracy
of URLs for external or third-party Internet websites referred to in this
publication and does not guarantee that any content on such websites is,
or will remain, accurate or appropriate.

Fordham University Press also publishes its books in a variety of electronic
formats. Some content that appears in print may not be available in electronic
books.

Visit us online at www.fordhampress.com.

Library of Congress Cataloging-in-Publication Data

Names: Mejido Costoya, Manuel, editor.
Title: Land of stark contrasts : faith-based responses to homelessness in
 the United States / Manuel Mejido Costoya, editor.
Description: New York : Seattle University Center for Religious Wisdom and
 World Affairs and Fordham University Press, 2021. | Includes
 bibliographical references and index.
Identifiers: LCCN 2021001964 | ISBN 9780823293957 (hardback) | ISBN
 9780823293964 (paperback) | ISBN 9780823293971 (epub)
Subjects: LCSH: Church work with the homeless—United States.
Classification: LCC BV4456 .L36 2021 | DDC 362.5/925750973—dc23
LC record available at https://lccn.loc.gov/2021001964

Printed in the United States of America

23 22 21   5 4 3 2 1

First edition

Contents

PART II – RELIGIOUS WORLDVIEWS AND THE COMMON GOOD REIMAGINED

PART III – THEOLOGICAL INSIGHTS FOR HOMELESS MINISTRIES

LAND OF STARK CONTRASTS

Introduction

Manuel Mejido Costoya

What can I know?
What ought I do?
What may I hope?

— IMMANUEL KANT

A Land of Stark Contrasts

The wandering poor, sturdy beggars, and masterless men of the colonial epoch; the vagrants and great army of tramps of the Gilded Age; the train-riding
vagabonds and hobohemians of the Progressive Era; the transients and migrants of the Dust Bowl and Great Depression; the skid row bums and freight-
riding beats and hippies of the postwar period; the deinstitutionalized unhoused
of the 1960s and '70s; and the more racially diverse and younger street people
of our late-modern epoch.[1] In its different instantiations, homelessness has
been with us since the beginning, as a symptom of social crisis and as the opportunity for community responses, evoking both our inner demons and "the
better angels of our nature."[2]

Though almost certainly an undercount,[3] according to the latest estimates
from the federal government, on any one night in January of 2019, 567,715
people were homeless in the United States, approximately one-third (37 percent)
of which were unsheltered.[4] This represents a one-year increase of 3 percent,
or 14,885 more people that were experiencing homelessness. Driving this national increase is the rise in the number of homeless individuals and families
in major urban centers, like New York, Los Angeles, and Seattle. Furthermore,
minority populations are disproportionately impacted by homelessness. While

1

African Americans make up 13.3 percent of the country's population, they represent 40.6 percent of people experiencing homelessness. Hispanics and Native Americans, too, are disproportionately impacted by this social problem. Indeed, as noted in a 2020 United Nations report, "Homelessness is one of the crudest manifestations of poverty, inequality and housing affordability challenges. . . . It is a failure of multiple systems that are supposed to enable people to benefit from economic growth and lead a safe and decent life."[5]

Another recent United Nations report focusing on extreme poverty and human rights in the United States succinctly captures the disparities that need to frame any attempt to grapple with the issue of homelessness in America:

> The United States is a land of stark contrasts. It is one of the world's wealthiest societies, a global leader in many areas, and a land of unsurpassed technological and other forms of innovation. Its corporations are global trendsetters, its civil society is vibrant and sophisticated and its higher education system leads the world. But its immense wealth and expertise stand in shocking contrast with the conditions in which vast numbers of its citizens live. About 40 million live in poverty, 18.5 million in extreme poverty, and 5.3 million live in Third World conditions of absolute poverty. It has the highest youth poverty rate in the Organisation for Economic Co-operation and Development (OECD), and the highest infant mortality rates among comparable OECD states. Its citizens live shorter and sicker lives compared to those living in all other rich democracies, eradicable tropical diseases are increasingly prevalent, and it has the world's highest incarceration rate, one of the lowest levels of voter registrations among OECD countries and the highest obesity levels in the developed world. . . . It has one of the highest poverty and inequality levels among the OECD countries, and the Stanford Center on Inequality and Poverty ranks it 18th out of 21 wealthy countries in terms of labour markets, poverty rates, safety nets, wealth inequality and economic mobility.[6]

Why these "stark contrasts"? A principal reason no doubt is that in America long-term societal objectives tend to be framed narrowly in terms of economic growth. While economic prosperity is important, a society also needs to be oriented by values such as social inclusion, care for the planet, and good governance.[7] Consider, for example, that while the U.S. ranks fourth among the 33 richest countries in terms of GDP per capita, it ranks twenty-first in terms of the Sustainable Development Goals (SDGs), a broader framework for thinking about societal objectives, unanimously adopted by the 193 member states of the United Nations in 2015.[8]

Consider also that while GDP per capita has more than doubled since 1972, life satisfaction, or happiness, has not risen. In fact, in recent years measured happiness has actually been on the decline, reaching a ten-year low in 2016.[9] Behind this paradoxical trend are factors that include the decline in social trust; the rise of mega-dollars in U.S. politics; soaring income and wealth inequality; the decrease in social mobility; and the deterioration of America's health and educational systems.[10] As the economist Jeffrey Sachs has observed,

> The United States offers a vivid portrait of a country that is looking for happiness "in all the wrong places." The country is mired in a roiling social crisis that is getting worse. Yet the dominant political discourse is all about raising the rate of economic growth.[11]

Homelessness in the United States needs to be understood against this backdrop. It is a symptom of an American Dream that is increasingly being cast principally or exclusively in terms of economic growth, with the assumption that the desired social outcomes will follow.

Though it is increasingly being recognized as an important issue throughout rural America,[12] homelessness is largely an urban problem, exemplifying the economic and social challenges facing U.S. cities in the post-industrial age. The fifty largest American cities experienced a 5 percent increase in unhoused individuals and an 11 percent increase in unsheltered homelessness between 2018 and 2019.[13] The prevalence of homelessness across these cities, moreover, is not proportional to population size, suggesting that what is driving homelessness is not simply the scale of urbanization. Though ranked among the five most populous cities, Chicago, Houston, and Phoenix, for example, do not have the largest homeless population. By contrast, Seattle is the eighteenth-most-populous city and has the third-largest number of homeless individuals. Among the five major cities with the largest homeless population, four are on the West Coast, a region that is experiencing a housing crisis, and two—San Jose and Seattle—are also considered pacesetting high-tech urban hubs.[14]

An important story told about American cities is that of the "Great Divergence".[15] With the emergence of the information economy, some cities have become prosperous innovation hubs, favoring knowledge-intensive industries that attract highly educated workers, while other cities, in the throes of deindustrialization, continue to be linked to a manufacturing sector that generates mainly low-income jobs and fails to attract the skills needed for innovation. This growing inequality *between* cities is an important dynamic, no doubt, especially in light of the populist politics that has come to the fore recently.[16] Yet, concerning specifically the issue of homelessness, there is another dynamic that is perhaps more germane—namely, the growing inequalities *within* cities.[17]

The inequalities that plague most American cities, and especially those booming technology hubs, have been well documented.[18] The structural determinants of these persistent—and even increasing—inequalities can be found in the new forms of urban marginality that crystallized in the most advanced societies in and through the information technology revolution, the restructuring of capitalism, and the end of the Cold War.[19] Three mutually reinforcing dynamics generate these "regimes of advanced urban marginality": first, class fragmentation and labor flexibilization brought about by market deregulation, deindustrialization, the growing rate of inner-city dislocations, and weakening of unions;[20] second, the racialization and penalization of poverty brought about by increasing unemployment and labor-force nonparticipation among the urban underclass, the implosion of the protective communal ghetto, and the rise of mass incarceration;[21] and third, the dismantling of protective welfare brought about by the rise of mandatory workfare and the punitive management of poverty.[22] These transformations of class, race, and state, which constitute the neoliberal city, provide the backdrop against which to situate common risk factors for homelessness, like unaffordable housing, job insecurity, and incarceration.

One of the principal determinants of homelessness is unaffordable housing. Especially in the wake of the Great Recession of the late 2000s and early 2010s, more and more individuals and families are being pushed out of the housing market as a result of the commodification of housing, rent hikes, forced eviction, lack of rental housing, (re-)gentrification, and social and spatial exclusion.[23] Demand for rental properties in the United States, for example, has increased across age and socioeconomic groups over the last decade, due largely to the decline in homeownership, which peaked in 2004 at 69 percent and declined to 63 percent by 2015.[24] Poignantly captured through the growth and financialization of single-family rental housing,[25] as a larger share of American households turn to renting to meet long-term housing needs, rent increases have outpaced income growth. The impact of this housing crisis on low-income families, furthermore, has been truly shocking, both from a historical and an international perspective: 52 percent of all poor renting families today spend over half of their income on housing, and a quarter of these families spend more than 70 percent on rent and utilities.[26]

This relationship between affordable housing and homelessness is particularly apparent in the West Coast, where a housing crisis driven by the tech boom has led to the proliferation of homeless encampments from San Diego to Seattle.[27] Housing insecurity, moreover, disproportionately affects minority populations through the mechanisms of residential racial segregation and eviction.[28] Matthew Desmond has brought to national attention eviction as a

cause of housing instability and homelessness that is especially pernicious at
the intersection of race and gender. He provides a poignant analogy: Eviction
has become common in the lives of women from impoverished black neighborhoods, just like incarceration has become common in the lives of men from
these neighborhoods.[29]

It has been well documented that the working poor, and in particular minorities and those with less formal education, experience a "double precarity"
of insecure employment and insecure housing. Studies, however, have tended
to focus on housing instability and homelessness as consequences of unemployment. Yet, the causal relationship runs in the other direction, as well: Research
has found that the probability of experiencing job loss among low-income renters was higher for those workers who had previously experienced an eviction,
landlord foreclosure, or housing condemnation.[30] Moreover, the close link between homelessness and the criminal justice system, especially among minority
populations, has also been well established. A disproportionate number of
homeless individuals have criminal records, and individuals who have experienced homelessness are overrepresented among the incarcerated. While individuals with criminal records face barriers to finding stable housing, unhoused
individuals may be prosecuted for attempting to survive in the streets.[31]

Deeply entrenched in our liberal market societies, the social stigma associated with homelessness further exacerbates these risk factors. Homelessness is
often perceived to be the result of an individual character flaw rather than the
consequence of certain structural conditions associated with, for example, the
neoliberal city.[32] The homeless individual is discredited and excluded, labeled a
deviant and an outcast, and even—as social neuroscientific research has found—
dehumanized.[33] In fact, it has been suggested that, shaping collective definitions
of poverty, charity, and public welfare, this stigmatization played an important
role in structuring the emergence of homelessness as a public problem during
the Reagan era.[34] Given the ubiquity of this social stigma and the neoliberal
turn to the punitive management of poverty as a strategy for governing problem
areas and populations,[35] it is not surprising that there has been an upward trend
in the criminalization of homelessness in the United States.[36]

Interventions to address homelessness need to be understood in terms of
three dynamics that have been transforming public policy and community revitalization efforts across the country for well over a quarter of a century: First, the
paradigm shift from the "staircase" approach to service delivery, which requires
individuals to demonstrate "housing readiness," to Housing First, where the
rapid provision of housing without preconditions is seen as the key to stabilization
and reintegration.[37] Second, the devolution of welfare programs and social services—
that vertical pivot downward from national to state and local governments, as

evidenced, for example, in the expansion of block grant funding under the Personal Responsibility and Work Opportunity Reconciliation Act of 1996.[38] And third, the growing sway of network governance—that horizontal pivot outward from government to business and civil society in and through which have emerged a plethora of community-based, cross-sectoral or multi-stakeholder initiatives, including public-private partnerships.[39]

These three dynamics converged in the Homeless Emergency Assistance and Rapid Transition to Housing (HEARTH) Act of 2009, the first and only major reauthorization of the McKinney-Vento Homeless Assistance Act of 1987, the largest source of funding for homeless assistance programs.[40] In addition to accelerating the paradigm shift to Housing First by, for instance, authorizing federal funds for rapid re-housing assistance, HEARTH also attempted to leverage the local multi-stakeholder planning bodies—Continuums of Care—by charging these units with creating "coordinated entry systems," a standard, but polycentric process for assessing service and housing needs and connecting individuals with available resources. These place-based efforts, which aim to better address the complexity of the causes of homelessness and the heterogeneity and flexibility of the responses needed,[41] represent both opportunities and challenges to faith-based organizations (FBOs) that are seeking to address this social problem.

Religion and Homelessness: Three Approaches

Having just situated the issue of homelessness as a symptom of the disparities that define our late-modern age, I would now like to tease out three approaches to the relationship between religion and homelessness that will serve as a frame of reference for this volume. One approach grapples with the role of public religion—FBOs—in community revitalization efforts. A second approach considers how religious worldviews and precepts inform those conceptions of justice and the common good that ground our duties toward individuals experiencing homelessness and the institutional arrangements that ensure that all members of society flourish. And a third approach focuses on how the adherents of a faith tradition understand and address the suffering of unhoused individuals in light of their convictions and hopes.

Public Religion and Community Revitalization

Alexis de Tocqueville's classic thesis about religion in America provides a point of departure to understand the important role that FBOs play in the welfare system of the United States and specifically in responding to homelessness.[42] In contradistinction to the European case, it was the twin clauses of disestablishment and free exercise—paradoxically the "separation of church and state"—that made religion the premier political institution:[43] at the individual level by cultivating civic virtues that foster volunteering, philanthropy, and social engagement;[44] at the organizational level, through a system of denominational pluralism that made voluntary religious congregations schools of citizenship, prototypical civil society organizations;[45] and at the societal level, through a civil religion that transcends historical and ideological differences.[46]

From the American Anti-Slavery Society and the Woman's Christian Temperance Union, through the social gospel, the Southern Christian Leadership Conference, and the Interreligious Committee Against Poverty, up to the Sanctuary movement and the White House Office of Faith-Based and Community Initiatives—religion has been at the heart of American civic life, negotiating contrary ideals of faith in public and the good society: "reformer" or "charitable donor," "prophetic witness" or "helping hand," "social activist" or "volunteer," "conscientious advocate" or "social entrepreneur."[47] One tradition of public religion, grounded in mainline Protestantism and resonating with the positive rights of civic republicanism, can be traced through the social progressivism of the settlement movement, the New Deal, and the War on Poverty, up to the New Poor People's Campaign.[48] Grounded in the holiness movement and resonating with the liberal democratic pursuit of negative rights, the other tradition of public religion can be traced through the premillennialism of evangelical urban revivals and rescue missions, the Scopes Trial, and the Moral Majority, up to compassionate conservatism.[49] These different approaches to faith in public and the good of government provide justifications for the variety of visions and strategies of faith-based responses to homelessness and other social problems.

America's exceptional anti-statist tradition,[50] moreover, can be cast in terms of the country's unique process of secularization: The model of free exercise of religion protected from state intervention generated a pluralistic, self-organized, and privately regulated civil society, on the one hand, and a weak welfare state, on the other.[51] Religion was from the outset an integral part of attempts to address the social problems associated with, for example, urbanization, industrialization, and Jim Crow, because America's liberal welfare regime presupposed a role for the private sector and voluntary associations.[52] Amplified by the aforementioned dynamics of devolution and network governance, the conditions of post-secularism, the problematizing of the "political overgeneralization of the secularized worldview,"[53] has led to the increasing sway of FBOs in community revitalization efforts.

The Charitable Choice provision of the 1996 Welfare Reform Act and the different iterations of the 2001 White House Office of Faith-Based and Community Initiatives were the culmination of this enduring legacy.[54] Should the federal government seek to increase the flow of funds to FBOs in an effort to expand the scope of "charitable choice" and "level the playing field" in the competition for public grants? Or is such legislative and administrative action inconsistent with the separation of church and state?

In the context of this polarizing and politically charged debate between the Religious Right and the Secular Left, starting in the mid-1990s and peaking in about 2003,[55] an important body of literature emerged in an attempt to better understand the role of FBOs in community development and social protection.[56] Some of this literature has been criticized for its misguided assumptions about public religion, social welfare, or voluntary associations in the United States,[57] while critics of other literature have suggested that too little is still known about the different challenges FBOs face as they strive to build capacity and implement specific initiatives at the local level.[58] Regardless of the position one takes, it is clear that faith-based responses to homelessness need to be understood in light of the intense debate that was stoked by the Charitable Choice movement at the close of the twentieth century, and that only confirmed the contested nature of faith in public in America.

Perhaps more important than religious tradition (for instance, Jewish/Christian/Muslim), denominational distinction (for instance, Catholic/Mainline/Evangelical), or ideals of faith in public (for instance, "social activist"/"helping hand"),[59] as civil society organizations that are grappling with how to effectively respond to homelessness, FBOs are, first and foremost, attempting to navigate two organizational settings: namely, the "caring communities" model of local congregations and the service-organizational model of arm's-length faith-based nonprofits.[60] The first category includes local churches, mosques, and temples, while the second category includes what has been referred to as "para-church" or "para-denominational" organizations[61]—that is, faith-based special-purpose or service agencies—both those that are incorporated as a 501(c)(3)[62] and those that are under the auspices of a congregation, but operating at arm's length—as well as denominational, ecumenical, or interreligious advocacy and lobbying organizations.[63]

Caring communities are grounded in a "thick" set of shared values that are developed and nurtured over a long period of time and over a wide range of activities. Having as their primary function prayer and worship, these organizations are relatively ill-equipped to pivot from soul work to social work—that is, from accompaniment of anomic individuals to addressing the material condition of not having shelter. Caring communities often lack the specialized knowledge and resources needed to effectively scale up from volunteering and philanthropy to the provision of social services and the transformation of unjust systems.

Over 80 percent of the approximately 300,000 congregations across the United States are involved in some type of community development effort. Over half of all these houses of worship cited feeding the hungry among their four most important social initiatives, while close to 20 percent of these mentioned providing housing or shelter and 12 percent mentioned addressing homelessness as one of their top activities.[64] There is wide consensus that the most valuable capacity congregations bring to social issues is mobilizing volunteers. This said, the majority of resources marshaled by congregations do not occur through formal programs, but through the informal activities of "caring communities."[65]

In contrast to caring communities, service organizations are oriented by "thin" arm's-length or contractual understandings where social interaction is defined through the circumscribed roles of "providers" and "recipients" or "professionals" and "clients." As they professionalize, bureaucratize, and develop their reach and effectiveness, arms-length FBOs come to face a growing tension between efforts to operationalize their religious beliefs and the pressures of instrumental rationality driven by the isomorphisms that structure the field of nonprofit organizations.[66]

Though more numerous, as social service providers, congregations are trumped by arms-length faith-based nonprofits like, for example, Catholic Charities, Jewish Family Services, and the Salvation Army. Estimates suggest that there are approximately 6,500 faith-based service agencies across the country, contributing about one-fifth of all private social service provision.[67] One national study found that faith-based service agencies provide 30 percent of emergency shelter beds and have the capacity to house more than 150,000 people a night in different types of housing.[68] And research conducted in eleven U.S. cities found that the share of emergency shelter beds provided by faith-based nonprofits varied significantly by municipality, with a range of 90 percent and 78 percent FBO-provided emergency shelter beds in Omaha and Houston to 37 percent and 33 percent in San Diego and Portland, respectively.[69]

Aligned with classical sociological oppositions such as community and society,[70] lifeworld and system,[71] each of these two models—the caring communities model and the service-organizational model—gives pride of place to a particular understanding of public religion, civil society, and community development, not to mention a specific formulation of the problem domain— homelessness. Because of methodological and theoretical distinctions between, for instance, the sociology of religion and the policy sciences, most of the scholarship has tended to focus exclusively on one of these two models, tacitly or explicitly restricting the term "faith-based organization" to either congregations or arms-length nonprofits.[72]

Religious Worldviews and the Common Good Reimagined

The fall; banishment; a paradise that has been lost and will be regained, perhaps, one day; the homelessness of a people; migration and displacement; exile from the homeland; being out-of-joint in the world; nonbelonging; unnatural excommunication and alienation; the absence of home as wholeness, center, hearth; striving to return to the place of origin; *nostos* and nostalgia; a homeward journey; a safe return; the wisdom of the other, the stranger, the homeless wanderer; one's rightful place in a community, the polis, the just city. Metaphorically, the opposition between *homelessness* and *home* is a recurring archetype among religious worldviews, an essential trope in cosmic narratives and etiological myths, imbued at times with apocalyptic imagery.[73] This opposition has also been framed in terms of an existential interpretation of the hermeneutical circle as the predicament of the finitude of the human being.[74]

Not surprisingly, then, care for the unhoused person—the sojourner, the outcast, the disenfranchised—is a central precept across religious worldviews and faith traditions. Grounded in an archetypal opposition, caring for the individual experiencing homelessness is never simply a brick-and-mortar issue. Providing shelter is always linked to the ultimate value of "home" in and through, for instance restoring right relationship, enabling human flourishing, love of neighbor, filial piety, compassion, and the like. This material and symbolic gesture, as ritual and not a utilitarian calculus, transforms a group of individuals into a community, making social bonds sacred.[75] Unconditional hospitality toward the unhoused person—the stranger, the foreigner—is a radical and dangerous responsibility that obfuscates doors and borders, transcends ethical systems, destabilizes the force of law, revealing the limitations and violence of particular constructions of "homelessness" as a contemporary social problem.[76] As such, the religious precept to welcome the unhoused person fulfills a utopian function: namely, reimagining a society where homelessness has been eradicated.[77]

As manifested by the tensions between substantive and procedural justice and "thick" and "thin" conceptions of the good, duties to homeless individuals oriented by religious worldviews tend to be broader than the responsibilities that are required of the citizen in liberal democracies like the United States.[78] Whether it is because of the classical concern for violent conflict or the more nuanced contemporary attempt to address the problem of pluralism, historically, liberalism has tolerated religious worldviews in the privately regulated sphere of civil society, but has excluded them from public discussions about law, the welfare state, and the like. As the communitarians have long argued, this exclusion is problematic because it is based on an atomistic individualism that undercuts the bonds of community, stifling a dialogical and culturally rich understanding of citizenship, justice, and the good life.[79] This idea of a socioculturally embedded self short-circuits the voluntaristic ethic of personal responsibility that views homelessness as the result of individual failure as well as the correlated "not-in-my-back-yard" ethos—NIMBYism—that suffuses municipal ordinances, legal frameworks, and policy responses to homelessness in liberal democracies. Religiously anchored duties to unhoused individuals, like the communitarian critique of the autonomous self, presupposes and opens a space for a society oriented by an active commitment to the common good, to social justice and not just fairness.[80]

Closely aligned with communitarianism, drawing on the Tocquevillian perspective alluded to in the previous section, an influential school of American social thought has argued that religion provides an important corrective to the methodological individualism and overly formalized contractualism that underpin liberalism.[81] In contemporary societies, this school of thought maintains, religious conceptions of the world and the practices of communities of faith can effectively mediate between the freedom of the ancients and freedom of the moderns,[82] between positive and negative liberties.[83] They view the failure to appreciate this positive role of faith in public to be a symptom of the dominant language of radical individual autonomy that is rooted in expressive and utilitarian moral traditions associated with liberal theories of justice and the logic of the market. They call for a retrieval of the biblical and republican moral traditions that view individuals as interconnected in their commitment to the good society. Unlike democratic liberalism, this civic republican perspective acknowledges the significant role of, for instance, civil religion in framing the ultimate values that transcend our cultural and ideological differences and public theology in articulating these ultimate values in particular moments in history.[84]

With communitarianism and civic republicanism, religious conceptions of human flourishing and the good life, then, can contribute to framing homelessness in a manner that challenges liberal—minimalist—institutional arrangements. Marshaling notions of charity and hospitality, for example, faith traditions can contribute to the unfinished project of a "Second Bill of Rights."[85] Indeed, communities of faith can contribute to the efforts of a number of legal scholars and civil society actors in advocating for a Homeless Bill of Rights that, in addition to statutory commitments to "negative rights," such as the right to use and move freely in public spaces and the right to be free from employment discrimination based on housing status, should also contain "positive rights," such as the right to shelter, nourishment, and medical attention.[86]

The important contributions religious worldviews make to understandings of the culturally situated self, positive rights, and the common good is receiving increased legitimacy under the late-modern conditions of post-secularism. Generated by the postmodern deconstruction of knowledge and the post-Westphalian decentering of the West, "post-secularism," according to Richard Falk, "fundamentally challenges in different forms the dominant idea of a universalizing modernity that is forever linked to science, instrumental rationality and the Enlightenment tradition."[87] And, for Charles Taylor, the "post-secular" is not necessarily a reversal in the decline of beliefs and practices, but a time in which the "hegemony of the mainstream master narrative of secularization will be more and more challenged."[88] Insofar as it takes issue with the European narrative of secularization understood as the privatization of religion,[89] post-secularism has been most closely associated with the European context.[90] Yet, this concept is also analytically useful in North America to the extent that it reflectively problematizes what, as was suggested in the previous section, Jürgen Habermas has referred to as the "political overgeneralization of the secularized worldview." That is, in post-secular societies there is increasing parity between secular and religious claims in the public sphere. "Insofar as they act in their role as citizens," argues Habermas, "secularized citizens may neither fundamentally deny truth-potential to religious worldviews nor deny the right of believing citizens to make contributions to public discussion in religious language." Indeed, he continues, "a liberal political culture can even expect that secularized citizens take part in efforts to translate relevant contributions from the religious language into a publicly accessible language."[91]

Whether it is in the name of progressive multi-stakeholder governance or the neoliberal dismantling of the welfare state, one of the manifestations of the greater legitimacy of religious language in the post-secular public sphere is the increasing sway of faith-based engagement in community development initiatives discussed in the previous section.[92] Yet, perhaps more significant than the greater impact that communities of faith and their organizations are having on emergency and social services for unhoused individuals, for example, in a post-secular context, religious conceptions of the world are increasingly contributing to addressing the systemic causes of homelessness by envisioning new societal objectives and development paradigms as alternatives to "universalizing modernity" and its secular, liberal, and market components. The Gross National Happiness principle of the Himalayan Buddhist Kingdom

of Bhutan,[93] the *Suma Qamaña* (Living Well) development model from Bo-
livia and the indigenous peoples of the Andean region,[94] a papal encyclical
aligned with the United Nations SDGs,[95] and Islamic financing as a catalyst
for shared prosperity[96]—these are just a few examples of development paradigms and initiatives anchored in religious conceptions of the world that could
contribute to reimagining a city, nation, and world where all individuals have
a house and home.

Theological Insights for Homeless Ministries

A theology of homelessness grapples with the predicament faced by unhoused
individuals, given the convictions and hopes of a particular faith tradition.
Christianity, for example, is oriented by the conviction that the suffering of
homeless individuals cannot be reduced to the material condition of lacking
shelter. It is also a spiritual condition of brokenness—a lack of home, ecclesia.
This is precisely why, for the Christian, the act of responding to homelessness
involves both the social work of providing a house through philanthropy and
justice and the soul work of creating a home through love, mercy, accompaniment, and bearing witness. For Christianity, moreover, addressing homelessness is anchored in the hope that this act of compassion is redemptive, an
eschatological sign of the triumph of life over death. Understood thus, in the
North American context, a Christian theology of homelessness is caught betwixt and between two traditions: One tradition is rooted in the social gospel
theology of the Progressive era and runs through the integral humanism of
the new Christendom and the liberationist paradigm. The other is rooted in
a revivalist evangelical and pietistic understanding of social reform and runs
through Christian realism, postliberalism, and radical orthodoxy. These two
traditions offer contrasting accounts of the relationship between, for example,
church and culture, hope and history, faith and social action, justice and redemption, theology and the social sciences. From these accounts emerge the
different theological rationales and strategies that orient Christian urban ministries related to addressing homelessness as well as theological justifications
for conceptions of faith in public, justice, the common good, and the like.

One theological rationale for homeless ministries is oriented by the ideal
of prophetic transformation through "this-worldly" engagement with institutions and social systems; millennialism and an emphasis on eschatological
hope in and through historical change; an attempt to overcome an individualistic interpretation of Christian doctrines by an emphasis on social solidarity, in particular with the disenfranchised; a social, structural, or institutional
understanding of sin; and a correlationist approach to the relationship between

theology and the social sciences. The social gospel movement interpreted this perspective in light of an optimistic view of institutions and social change that defined the Progressive Era and the Keynesian New Deal as well as the pragmatist principle that, through reform and social engineering, homelessness, poverty, and the other ills of industrialization and urbanization would gradually be eliminated. This view was buttressed by a social theoretical reading of the doctrine of the Kingdom of God[97] and a Christian ethics that attempted to move from the voluntarism of philanthropy to the social solidarity of justice.[98]

Through the lens of a European corporatist—tripartite—model of cooperation, the new Christendom of Roman Catholicism, too, shared in the reformist optimism of social gospel theology.[99] Occupying the sphere of civil society, the church would be the steward of transcendental values, and the state, through the sphere of politics, would be the overseer of worldly power. The resulting Integral Humanism would fuse the spiritual and material realms through a Bergsonian dynamism whereby the church—the laity in particular— would transform secular society and history as exemplified by Christian democracy, Catholic Action, and the Catholic Worker movement, with its houses of hospitality for the homeless.[100]

Important theological resources for homeless ministries grounded in prophetic transformation became available when optimistic reformism gave way to revolutionary rupture with the emergence of Latin American liberation theology in the late 1960s. With the liberationist paradigm shift, neo-Kantianism, pragmatism, and the philosophy of action gave way to Hegelian-Marxian dialectics;[101] soteriology framed in terms of social engineering and the *élan vital* of historical change gave way to soteriology as the "historical praxis" of liberation understood as the making—and not interpreting—of history, of transcendence;[102] gradualism and corporatism gave way to a contestatory and social-movement model of church exemplified by base ecclesial communities;[103] and eschatological hope in and through a Christian humanist synthesis gave way to the agonistic tension—the negative dialectic—between prophecy and utopia.[104] Two liberationist doctrines in particular, which are in many ways in continuity with the more radical interpretations of the social gospel and Catholic Worker movements, are especially germane to a theology of homelessness: first, the "preferential option for the poor," according to which ministerial practices and theological reflection need to take as their point of departure the emancipatory interest of homeless individuals.[105] And second, the doctrine of "social sin," "institutionalized injustice," or "sinful structures," according to which ministerial action needs to be directed to the systemic determinants of homelessness and not just to the immediate needs of unhoused individuals.[106] The variety of liberation theologies that emerged in the North American context, in response to the different symbolic-cultural dynamics of oppression,[107] provide a wealth of resources for homeless ministries that are attempting to navigate the complex intersections of race and housing insecurity, ethnicity, and poverty, as well as accompany unhoused individuals from minority populations in their everyday struggle for home—that is, as they struggle with the predicament of being caught betwixt and between, for example, the dreams of the Christian religion and the nightmares of black consciousness[108] or the real and imaginary border-lands that separate Anglo and Hispanic America.[109]

The other theological rationale for homeless ministries is oriented by an emphasis on human fallibility and sinfulness; a tragic and ironic understanding of institutions and social change; a paradoxical understanding of the relationship between history and the Kingdom; a focus on being a witness to the "other-worldly"—kerygmatic—sign rather than on "this-worldly" transformation; an emphasis on ecclesiology over eschatology—that is, on being a church rather than on transforming the world; the primacy of forgiveness over justice, redemption over liberation; an attempt to overcome the historical relativism of liberal interpretations of Christian doctrines by stressing the existential predicament—the radical finitude—of modern human life; and a fideism that gives pride of place to theology over the social sciences. This perspective took form in and through the rescue work that emerged from the holiness revivals of the Gilded Age. Organizations like the Christian and Missionary Alliance and the Salvation Army, with their focus on personal piety and their pessimistic—premillennialist—social views emphasized rescue and redemption of broken and lost individuals over the quixotic goal of social transformation. Yet, this engagement with the urban homeless and poor, which preceded the more liberal and secular social gospel, was pacesetting in an epoch when social reform was not popular.[110]

With his Christian realism, Reinhold Niebuhr provided a comprehensive and nuanced account of the ambiguity that, according to this theological rationale, undergirds the Christian "social task." Only when the false presuppositions of the liberal worldview have been unmasked and the correlation between, for example, historical growth and moral progress sundered does it become evident that it is impossible to overcome the chasm that separates love and social justice.[111] The taking to scale of love—prophetic transformation—is always bound to fail because of the incommensurability between individuals and society.[112] Soul work and social work exist in a paradoxical tension. This tension is what reveals that systems and principles of justice are always incomplete.[113]

Emerging in the last decades of the twentieth century, and in many ways the culmination of this second tradition, postliberal theology and radical orthodoxy have important implications for thinking about the theological foundations of homeless ministries. Whether considered Protestant and Anglican or American and British analogues,[114] or whether the latter is considered to be a subset— the political-theological program—of the former,[115] both schools draw on postmodernist thought to overcome the liberal interpretation of Enlightenment-Modernity and in particular the unity of the ego cogito and the paradigm of secularization. Postliberal theology and radical orthodoxy are, in this sense, theological expressions of the post-secular condition alluded to in the two previous sections. Both schools aim to reenchant the world through a linguis-tified or poststructuralist fideism that, by destabilizing classical dichotomies like grace and nature, faith and reason, spirit and matter, church and world, opens a space for a more robust ecclesiology against pernicious individual-ism, technoscience, the surveillance state, militarism, globalized capitalism, and the like.

An exponent of postliberalism, Stanley Hauerwas, for example, has argued that liberal theology's accommodationist Constantinianism undermines the tension between faithful witness and social engagement and consequently fails to appreciate the fact that "the Church is constitutive of the kingdom"—that is, that eschatology always needs to be articulated within an ecclesiology.[116] And drawing on the continental tradition, John Milbank, who is considered the leading figure of radical orthodoxy, has maintained that only a Christian social theory, which must first and foremost be understood as an ecclesiology, can counter the hegemony of neoliberalism.[117]

This Volume's Contribution

Corresponding to social-scientific, ethical, and theological domains of inquiry, the three approaches to religion and homelessness I have just presented cor-relate with the three questions posed in the epigraph at the beginning of this introduction that, according to Immanuel Kant, critical thinking should ac-commodate: "What can I know? What ought I do? What may I hope?"[118] As a heuristic,[119] this schema has been used to organize the thirteen chapters that constitute this volume.[120] Let me now outline these chapters in terms of the three approaches.

Part I

Drawing on, for example, the sociology of religion, critical theory, urban stud-ies, public policy, and nonprofit management, one approach to the relation-ship between religion and homelessness understands FBOs as civil society actors and as stakeholders in local development efforts. What is and ought to be the role of religion in the public life of liberal democracies? What resources do FBOs marshal in addressing homelessness? What capacity constraints do they face? How do the different types of FBOs—congregations and faith-inspired nonprofits, for instance—contribute to community problem solving around homelessness? Are FBOs more effective than nonsectarian organizations in addressing this issue? How do FBOs balance providing for the immediate needs of unhoused individuals and addressing the systemic determinants of this social problem? How do they integrate religious elements into their programs and services? How can FBOs better leverage partnerships with government and business and other civil society organizations, and vice versa? These are some of the key questions with which the five chapters that constitute Part I of this volume are grappling.

In "Talking About Homelessness: Shifting Discourses and the Appeal to Religion in America's Seventh-Largest City," James Spickard traces the discourses surrounding San Antonio's Haven for Hope, one of the most comprehensive homeless transformation sites in the United States, paying particular attention to the shifting ways in which homelessness has been locally conceived and the roles that FBOs have been asked to play in its solutions. He considers how these conceptions have limited the city's ability to solve the structural problems that generate homelessness—and have even limited its view of public responsibility. As a manifestation of "neoliberal" discourse and policies, Spickard shows how the city has outsourced compassion to faith-based and other private sector organizations to help improve people's lives.

In "Becoming More Effective Community Problem Solvers: Faith-Based Organizations, Civic Capacity, and the Homelessness Crisis in Puget Sound," Manuel Mejido Costoya and Margaret Breen report on the two phases of an initiative that explored how FBOs could more effectively respond to the homelessness crisis in the Puget Sound region. They begin by documenting the study they conducted, in and through which emerged a picture of FBOs as community problem solvers—that is, as civil society organizations that are experimenting with new modalities of catalyzing effective social change in collaboration with governmental and nongovernmental actors. They then take stock of a capacity-building pilot they rolled out in an effort to enhance the civic capacity of nineteen local FBOs and three nonsectarian organizations seeking stronger collaboration with FBOs.

In "Disenfranchising the Unhoused: Urban Redevelopment, the Criminalization of Homelessness, and the Peril of Prosperity Theology in Dallas and Beyond," Michael Fisher examines the social, political, and economic elements that enable the criminalization of unhoused people in cities undergoing extensive redevelopment. Although urbanization and the criminalization of the homeless are two separate processes, Fisher considers how they converge in an entrepreneurial approach to urban development. Through a case study of the city of Dallas, the author explores how the criminalization of homelessness has been legitimized by the religious discourse of prosperity theology.

In "Religious Responses to Homelessness in the San Francisco Bay Area: Addressing White Supremacy and Racism," Laura Stivers argues that FBOs need to better understand the relationship between structural racism and housing insecurity if they are to more effectively address homelessness. She situates this argument by examining specific policies that have caused racial disparity in relation to housing in the San Francisco Bay Area, focusing specifically on African Americans. Stivers next proposes an ethics of societal transformation rather than one of individual responsibility, drawing on the values of solidarity and interdependence as well as on the theological notion of God's movement for freedom of all humans. She concludes by considering how several Bay Area congregations have developed this ethic of societal transformation as they aim to address the intersection of structural racism and housing insecurity.

In "Homelessness and Health in Seattle: Challenges and Opportunities of Faith-Based Services," Lauren Lawson argues that it is essential for FBOs to adequately understand the connection between health and housing insecurity if they are to effectively respond to homelessness. Focusing on Seattle, she begins by providing an overview of the role of FBOs in the provision of social services and teasing out the relationship between health and homelessness. Against this backdrop, Lawson then identifies conceptual models for incorporating health into services for unhoused people. She concludes with a case study of a faith-based program that successfully integrated a health perspective in its work with individuals experiencing homelessness.

Part II

Oriented by, for example, the comparative study of religion, cultural anthropology, social theory, and ethics, a second approach to religion and homelessness considers how religious worldviews and precepts inform those conceptions of justice and the common good that ground our duties toward individuals experiencing homelessness and the institutional arrangements that ensure that all members of society flourish. How do exchanges and mutual understanding across denominations and faith traditions inform these religious duties and correlated arrangements? What normative insights are gleaned from the historicization of homelessness? How do indigenous knowledge and forms of life challenge contemporary strategies to address this social problem? How can the aspirational and utopian impetus of religious worldviews—reimagining a better world—be operationalized into sustainable solutions to homelessness, rights-based frameworks, and alternative or post-development paradigms? How do religious claims take form in the public sphere of our liberal, pluralistic, and unequal society? What is the status of these religious claims in a post-secular setting, in a context where the secular paradigm has been decentered? These are some of the questions explored by the four chapters included in Part II of this volume.

In "Homelessness and Coast Salish Spiritual Traditions: Cultural Resources for Programmatic Responses in British Columbia," Bruce Miller examines aspects of the spiritual practices of the Pacific Northwest's Coast Salish peoples that could be used to address the contemporary problems related to homelessness among the Indigenous populations of North America. He examines how concepts such as "claiming," "covering," and kinship, as well as, for example, longhouse events, contribute to a culture of inclusion and belonging that can be extended beyond blood and affinal kin to a larger Indigenous world. He considers how several Coast Salish spiritual leaders have already begun to operationalize these concepts and practices, and he addresses their potential integration into outreach services and other relevant community-based programs.

In "In these United States, Homelessness Is Who You Are: Examining a Socially Constructed Category through the Lens of an Interfaith Encounter in Downtown Boston," Nancy Khalil grapples with how the category "homeless" is constructed as an identity in the United States and how this status stigmatizes individuals in a way that is similar to how social markers like race, religion, ethnicity, and sexual identity marginalize individuals. Through an ethnographic account of a unique relationship between an Episcopal cathedral in downtown Boston and an Arab-immigrant, Muslim-owned café next door, Khalil explores how homelessness emerges as an identity-based analytical category that is nationally particularized. She argues that while in the United States homelessness is bureaucratically treated as a condition, in parallel, this category has also been socially constructed in a manner that is distinctly imagined in the American context.

In "Religion and Civic Activism Reconsidered: Situating Faith-Based Responses to Homelessness," John Coleman reviews the three decades of research he has conducted on the links between FBOs, social service, and citizen activism and applies these findings to the issue of homelessness. He begins by considering the tension that exists between religion and liberal societies, which he formulates in terms of the relationship between discipleship and citizenship.

He then, from a sociological lens, recaps the work he did on religion and social capital, drawing on his earlier studies of para-church organizations like
Bread for the World and Focus on the Family, as well as his later work on the
Jesuit Refugee Service, Pax Christi, and Catholic Charities U.S.A. He concludes his chapter with some reflections on the correlations between his earlier
research and faith-based groups addressing homelessness.

In "On the Passionality of Exile in Medieval Kabbalah: An Invitation to
Historicize Contemporary Religious and Public Discourses on Homelessness,"
Jeremy Brown engages with the Hebrew writings of the thirteenth-century sage
R. Ezra ben Solomon of Gerona and selections from subsequent Iberian kabbalists writing in the same tradition. He argues that these documents disseminate a mystical discourse of homelessness, fashioned in both theosophic and
historiosophic terms, that offer a compelling vision of social ethics. In his reflections, Brown considers the extent to which ancient theological constructions of exile structure the contemporary human experience of homelessness
and how religious conceptions of charity continue to inform even post-
confessional approaches to faith-based advocacy.

Part III

Anchored in, for instance, constructive and practical theology, religious ethics and biblical hermeneutics, a third approach to the relationship between
religion and homelessness considers how the adherents of a faith tradition understand and address the suffering of unhoused individuals in light of their
doctrinal system and practices. How does a homeless ministry duly integrate
spiritual and material care for unhoused individuals? What are the theological and doctrinal justifications for this work? How does one collaborate with
nonsectarian stakeholders without instrumentalizing religious convictions?
How does one apply the social and policy sciences to relevant programs and
initiatives without reducing faith work to social work? How does a homeless
ministry negotiate acts of charity to the individual and the pursuit of more just
social structures? How does one negotiate the work of justice and the work of
redemption? These are some of the principal questions that are explored by
the four chapters in Part III of this volume.

In "Wounds of Love: Spiritual Care and Homelessness in the Streets of Seattle," Paul Blankenship examines the relationship among housing insecurity, suffering, and Christian spirituality in the streets of Seattle. He begins by
describing the homeless street ministry of a local FBO. Next, by engaging the
work of modern Christian theologians and contemporary social scientists who
study Christianity, he explores why people who are homeless motivate a housed

Christian's desire for God and make their practice of love possible. And he concludes his chapter by considering the difference a housed Christian's spiritual love makes in the lives of people who are homeless and reflects on what it will take for that love to become more loving.

In "Making Spirits Whole: Homeless Ministries as a Tool for Integral Development," María Teresa Dávila draws on the Roman Catholic notion of integral human development to explore the challenges and possibilities of addressing the spiritual and material as well as the personal and systemic dimensions of homeless ministries. She argues that the soul work of homeless ministries—attending to the deep spiritual wounds that accompany the precarious life of individuals experiencing homelessness or housing insecurity—is a key element to bringing wholeness where a combination of life circumstances and systemic forces has led to socioeconomic uncertainty and psychic and spiritual harm resulting in a lack of self-worth and shame. At the same time, Dávila stresses that a proposal that takes homeless ministries seriously for the task of integral human development must also consider systemic challenges impacting a person's or a community's ability to acquire or access adequate housing.

In "'And I Saw Googleville Descend from Heaven': Reading the New Jerusalem in Gentrified Latinx Communities of Silicon Valley," Roberto Mata examines John's rhetorical portrayal of the New Jerusalem in the book of Revelation through the struggles of Latinx communities against gentrification in Silicon Valley. Drawing from research on the continued gentrification of Latinx neighborhoods in the city of San Jose and Google's plan to build a second headquarters there, Mata maps the rhetoric of revitalization undergirding the portrayal of Googleville and the New Jerusalem. He argues that, like Googleville, the New Jerusalem promises wealth, health, and security to those who buy into its rhetoric of progress and revitalization of the ancient world, while, at the same time, such projects marginalize, displace, and exclude groups of people deemed unworthy to enter the new spaces. Mata submits that this exclusion is reflected not only in the violent representations of the Other but also in the socioeconomic displacement and policing of boundaries that accompany the descent of the earthly Googleville and the heavenly New Jerusalem.

In "Offensive Wisdom: Homeless Neighbors, Bible Interpretation, and the Abode of God in Washington, D.C.," Sathianathan Clarke proposes to do biblical interpretation and constructive theology from below by examining the nine years he participated in a bible study group with unhoused individuals at the Church of the Epiphany in Washington, D.C. He begins by considering this study group as a dialogical alternate space for seeking biblical meaning, noting how this relational space forges a kinship around the word of God to practice equality and experience human dignity. Next, Clarke elaborates upon two motifs that emerged through the study group discussions: the identity and mission of Jesus and the subjectivity of homeless neighbors. He argues that in this "offensive wisdom" there are traces of the kingdom of God as a structural domain in the real world. Finally, Clarke constructively engages with this wisdom, developing a number of theological insights to orient the work of homeless ministries.

Overarching Themes

Taken together, these thirteen chapters challenge us to move beyond narrow ways of understanding and responding to homelessness. Indeed, perhaps this is what is most significant about approaching our most pressing social problems from the point of view of religious conceptions of the world and the practices of faith communities. Before bringing this introduction to a close, I propose to sketch five overarching themes that capture the comprehensive frame of reference presented in this volume.

Public Religion, Neoliberalism, and Social Change

A number of authors take issue with the framing of homelessness in terms of individuals and markets, personal responsibility, and the private sector. Public religion, FBOs, and congregations, rather, must give pride of place to and seek to transform the systemic determinants of this social problem, it is argued across several chapters. Neoliberalism's "emphasis on markets," suggests Spickard, "leads it to think private activity is more efficient; its focus on individuals leads it to favor helping people personally rather than changing social systems. The result is a discourse primed to encourage religious involvement in charity work but not in social change." Dávila, for her part, juxtaposes the Roman Catholic doctrine of integral human development to a "neoliberal anthropology" that casts persons as individual consumers in a free market that makes them solely responsible for their material well-being. This dominant anthropology, she maintains, "is not concerned with whether a person has the ability to enter and nourish meaningful relationships that empower her to be productive in her life, as part of communities of support, faith communities among them."

Reflecting on the potentially pernicious voluntarism that has long been associated with liberalism, Coleman reminds us that "religiously motivated volunteers are more likely to employ a communitarian language to describe their involvements and appeal to some sense of the common good, rather than rely on merely individualistic language to explain their behavior." He links this ethic of civic engagement to the "social capital" that is generated by congre-

gations and that "spills over, beyond their members, into whole neighborhoods."
Observing how the voluntaristic ethos impacts the social scientific study of religion, Mejido and Breen argue that there is a "tendency for the dominant
legacy of methodological individualism in the analysis of religion and civic
activity in American public life to eclipse the organizational-institutional approach to the role of FBOs in revitalizing local communities." Their research
shows that, once we move past the question of individual social action, it becomes apparent that FBOs are aspiring to proactively enhance social safety
nets and address the systemic causes of homelessness, including precarious employment and unaffordable housing.

Fisher is critical of a prosperity theology that, by sanctifying private property and reifying personal piety, is blind to the "entrepreneurial posture" of
urban redevelopment in and through which city space becomes a territory for
market-oriented economic growth and elite consumption practices. "Although
the current capitalist social order individualizes social problems so as to deflect from the interlocking structural forces that generate them," he argues,
"our theologies, and by extension our religious communities, must not." In a
similar vein, Stivers submits that most congregations and faith-based nonprofits do not deploy an analysis of structural racism in their responses to homelessness and housing insecurity. "While it is individuals who experience
homelessness," she maintains, "the phenomenon of homelessness is a social
problem related to poverty and factors that contribute to poverty, such as low-
wage work, lack of affordable housing, high medical costs, and more."

Human Flourishing and Substantive Conceptions of the Good

Several chapters propose frameworks for understanding human flourishing and
substantive conceptions of the good life. Seeking to go beyond the reduction-
istic individualism—homo oeconomicus paradigm—of neoliberalism, these
frameworks map out the duties, practices, and institutional arrangements that
would be required to tackle the systemic determinants of homelessness. Stivers, for instance, grounds her "ethics of societal transformation" in the idea
of the "solidarity economy" where "the burden for success would not rest
primarily on the backs of individuals but on economic and social policies that
create the foundations for human well-being and sustainability: policies that
support the sacredness of each human being and encourage interdependence
over competition in a capitalist system of winners and losers." In marshaling
a Catholic vision of human dignity and integral development, Dávila draws on
the "capabilities approach," which integrates a number of dimensions, including
"human participation and a sense of belonging, the exercise of imagination

and engagement of emotions, play, and other nonmaterial dimensions" that are essential for the development of persons, communities, and nations.

Lawson develops a "social-ecological model" for understanding the complex relationship between health and homelessness. This model, she explains, is depicted as four concentric rings, corresponding to distinct levels that impact a person's well-being—namely, the individual, interpersonal, communal, and societal levels. "The social-ecological model not only helps to identify potential risk factors, it can determine protective factors, as well." Miller argues that, in a context where "contact-induced problems" serve as a primary driver of homelessness among the Indigenous communities of North America, the forms of life and spiritual practices of Coast Salish peoples support the aid and recognition of the intrinsic worth of the unhoused. Thus, for instance, "cleansing and welcoming ceremonies open people, including the unhoused, to transformation and to overcoming alienation." These cultural precepts of caring for others and seeing the unhoused as inherently valuable, Miller suggests, can be taken to scale as programmatic responses to homelessness.

Coleman proposes the "Christian moral ideal of discipleship"—a substantive vision of human life, society, and the human good—to relativize the minimalist duties of liberal democracies. "Notoriously," he argues, "modern democracies are agnostic about the good. Democratic citizenship, it is usually argued, must be relatively blind to all substantive arguments concerning social goods," like housing, for example. Indeed, disciples, Coleman argues, contribute three elements to citizenship—a utopian imagination, countercultural judgments, and the vocation to construct a new social order. And against an otherworldly and interiorized understanding of eschatology, Clarke offers a world-transforming and tangible conception of "the abode of God"—the kingdom of God (*Basileia tou Theou*) that fuses with the tradition of positive rights, "since an abode brings to mind house, residence, shelter, and habitat." "Perhaps yearning and praying for 'the abode of God,'" he maintains, "will make the Christian community work toward God's transformed world that provides the 'least of these' among us with 'the right to a standard of living adequate for the health and well-being of himself and of his family, including food, clothing, *housing* and medical care and necessary social services, and the right to security,'" as articulated in the Universal Declaration of Human Rights.

Hermeneutics, Deconstruction, and Other Interpretive Strategies

Several authors offer strategies that aim to either hermeneutically broaden understandings of the relationship between religion and homelessness or deconstruct dominant conceptions of this social problem, traditional theological interpretations, or established paradigms of biblical studies. Brown, for instance, correlates medieval kabbalistic constructions of exile and contemporary public discourses of homelessness with the aim of developing an original assessment of both past and contemporary horizons. "By facilitating a nuanced understanding of how one particular historically situated religious discourse of homelessness has been constructed," he argues, "I invite contemporary advocates of social change to submit the historical, cultural, theological, and ethical presuppositions of their own discourses to a comparable degree and mode of criticism." Thus Brown's chapter "moves within a hermeneutical circle, wherein the critique of present social conditions potentiates a historically grounded analysis, and reciprocally, a lucid interpretation of religious history contributes to the refinement of present-day advocacy."

Distancing herself from what she argues has been the dominant approach by scholars and advocates of attempting to explain the causes of this social problem, Khalil sets out to "question the idea of homelessness itself and how we as an American society have come to define and understand what that means." Rather than working within this empirical field, by tracing the polysemic nature of homelessness, she subverts the universality and rigidity of the category that unifies and gives closure to the field. "For some it is the lack of permanent housing; for others, it is understood as a lifestyle resulting from poor choices or illnesses; and yet for others, it can be an indication of lack of safety, not resources. The category of 'homelessness' that can encompass such a range of situations to create and capture a type of person emerges distinctly in the United States." To bring forth the limits and particularity of the concept of homelessness in the United States, she also draws on an ethnographic account of perceptions of this social problem in the country of birth of one of her informants: "Egypt did not have homeless, not because it was devoid of people living in the streets, but because, according to him, society there did not leave individuals forgotten and in despair." For Khalil, this perception effectively captures how the concept of "'a homeless' in the United States emerges and develops into a socially constructed category neither easily defined nor bounded, nor, given the national epidemic currently confronting the nation, dispensable."

Although it is not developed in this direction, with Khalil, Miller's chapter can also potentially be read as a poststructuralist, postcolonial, or postdevelopmentalist appropriation of anthropological research. Rather than analyzing Coast Salish spiritual and cultural practices as existing at the margins of a post-contact society, such an interpretive strategy understands these indigenous forms of life as normatively disruptive of late-modern—liberal democratic and market-based—nation-states like Canada and the United States. As Miller points out, save banishment, which was commonly short, Coast Salish society had no homelessness. "It is the very absence of homelessness that creates the grounds on which Coast Salish cultural practices have relevance today." "One might ask," he continues, "why did they not have homelessness historically? How did they conceive of home and the relations of people to territory such that people were housed?"

Using Latino communities in San Jose that are undergoing gentrification as a reading lens, Mata disrupts the established scholarship on the New Jerusalem of Revelation 21. "While these interpretations are attentive to John's rhetoric of revitalization insofar as they highlight the positive dimensions of the New Jerusalem's descent," he submits, "they hardly critique its negative implications and risk embracing the author's point of view, as well as his silencing of the inscribed marginalized voices." Situating himself within an emancipatory rhetorical approach to biblical studies, which stresses the role of sacred texts in the struggles for social justice, Mata brings forth the underside of the rhetoric of revitalization. "While they are often cast as a solution to the world's problems and overly wealthy and secure spaces, projects of revitalization also contain their own sets of exclusions. As with the New Jerusalem, the rhetorical construction of Googleville as a solution to the city's problems with traffic, housing, and homelessness is hardly neutral. The vision of Googleville may mask the interests of city officials, real estate investors, and Google itself."

Blankenship puts his ethnographic fieldwork on the spirituality of homelessness at the service of a hermeneutic phenomenology that aims to enrich traditional theological issues—like the problem of theodicy—by casting these as existential dilemmas faced by street ministers. By drawing on the mystical trope of the "wounds of love," he argues that "Christians have a problem of presence that people who are homeless help resolve," without this implying the instrumentalization of the "suffering poor." "I propose that people who are homeless wound some housed Christians with love," submits Blankenship. He provides two justifications: "First, the relationship some housed Christians have with people who are homeless is spiritual. The relationship is spiritual because it is where some housed Christians indicate that they find, experience, and pursue God. Second, it is precisely the alternating presence and absence of God's love amongst the homeless that establish, motivate, and enrich the relationship."

In an attempt to avoid the "overspiritualization" of Catholic social teaching, Dávila proposes a reconstruction of the spiritual works of mercy—like instructing the ignorant, counseling the doubtful, and bearing wrongs patiently—in terms of what she refers to as the "soul work of homeless ministries." From this perspective, "instruction and counsel," for example, are cast

as "fostering opportunities for self-reflection and reviewing one's story and journey in a process of accompanying each other in the task of learning from our
past and perhaps our shared vulnerabilities and shared blessings toward
wholeness in the future"; while "patience," she argues, is reimagined as "ensuring the constancy and continuity of the programming needed to attend to
the spiritual integrity of the unhoused."

Reflecting on the interpretive method used by the homeless individuals that
participated in the collaborative bible study group he coordinated, Clarke notes
that it "subverted conventional hermeneutical categories and yet reconfigured
them creatively." The common denominator among the reading approaches
was that "there was always a push to make the Word come down to become
entwined with their struggles and strivings for human dignity and freedom."
He refers to this interpretive approach as "collectively interested eclecticism,"
which cannot be reduced to but is in a creative tension with the more traditional methods, like the biblicist, constructivist, and liberationist strategies. "In
such an approach," argues Clarke, "mostly homeless neighbors with some securely housed collaborators participate in a process of biblical meaning-seeking
and meaning-making by shrewdly and calculatingly employing all modes of
interpretation while keeping an eye on how such interpretations can enhance
the worth and dignity of all human beings, especially those who are cast out
by society."

Expanding the Evidence Base through Qualitative Research Methods

A variety of qualitative research methods are deployed throughout this volume
in an effort to develop thick descriptions of the experience of homelessness
and expand the evidence base on faith-based responses to this social problem.
Oriented by the Thomas theorem—"If men define situations as real, they are
real in their consequences"—and symbolic interactionism and the sociology
of knowledge more generally, Spickard adopts the method of discourse analysis to examine how neoliberalism has come to structure perceptions or "talk"
of homelessness as well as proposed solutions in San Antonio. Fisher, too, privileges this social-scientific method. Emphasizing "the representational aspects of discourse and its role in knowledge production," his variant of discourse
analysis, however, is indebted to the poststructuralism of Michel Foucault and
the neo-Marxist cultural theory of Stuart Hall. Not surprisingly, then, Fisher's chapter is framed in terms of an archaeological and genealogical examination of the disenfranchisement of the unhoused, understood as a discursive
formation that can be traced back to the work ethic of nascent capitalism in
late-medieval Europe, he argues, and that, in the contemporary United States,

is being shaped by contested religious discourses—a legitimating prosperity theology and a potentially counter-hegemonic public theology.

The study of faith-based responses to homelessness in Greater Seattle and the capacity building pilot with local FBOs that Mejido and Breen document in their chapter are anchored in grounded theory and community-based participatory research, respectively. The purpose of the study was "the discovery of theory from data systematically obtained from social research." It comprised two stages: "We began," the authors explain, "by deploying a theoretical sampling strategy, in and through which emerged a picture of Puget Sound FBOs as community problem solvers. We then conducted a series of case studies with the aim of achieving greater depth in our theory building." Grounded in the action research paradigm, the capacity building pilot was more closely aligned with community-based participatory research (CBPR) than with participatory-action research (PAR). "With the risk of oversimplifying," Mejido and Breen note, "PAR emphasizes the empowerment of disenfranchised groups through radical democratic practices, while CBPR emphasizes the capacity building of local stakeholders for community improvement." The pilot, hence, was rolled out as a space where FBOs could develop the capacity to problem solve around how to more effectively implement responses to homelessness in partnership with local government and other stakeholders.

Lawson, too, draws on CBPR in her efforts to research and address the health concerns of unhoused people, as she examines in a case study at the end of her chapter. Collaboration between the Seattle University College of Nursing, the Seattle Mennonite Church, and a cohort of homeless individuals led to the development of a grant-funded medical respite initiative—JustHealth—that provided motel rooms, case management services, and follow-up medical assistance to homeless individuals who had been discharged from the hospital with no safe place to stay. Both the community assessment that was used to identify this particular risk factor and the support system that was rolled out, which included scholars and practitioners, students, and volunteers, exemplify the kind of usable knowledge that is generated by action research.

Coleman applies qualitative sociological analysis in order "to test the democratic potential of discipleship"—that is, in other words, to "inspect the evidence of how discipleship creates social capital—those bonds of reciprocity and trust—and its wide democratic input and influence." Over a several-year period, he and his reach team used a mixed-methods approach—which included archival research, semi-structured interviews, and participant observation, for example—to collect data on six FBOs: Habitat for Humanity, the Pacific Institute for Community Organizing (PICO), Bread for the World, Pax Christi, Focus on the Family, and the African Methodist Episcopal Church. This research program, which made an important contribution to the analysis of public religion in the United States, is used to think about the potential role of FBOs in addressing homelessness. Thus, for example, guided by the notion of "social capital," Coleman points out that "local communities often show more trust in FBOs working on homelessness than their secular counterparts, typically if they have had longstanding histories and involvement in the local community." This is the case especially in distressed neighborhoods, he argues, where FBOs have earned "moral capital" for leading community development efforts "when other local institutions have left."

Ethnographic research techniques are the most common qualitative methods used throughout the volume, though. Khalil, for example, conducted interviews, including with the owner of the Black Seed Café and Grill in downtown Boston. Miller, who has been working with Coast Salish communities since the 1970s, explains some of his fieldwork experience in this way: "Living in the longhouse, the site of spirit dancing in the winter, gave me a chance to understand firsthand the role of leaders . . . in their dealings with the disadvantaged, unhoused, or spiritually disturbed people in their own communities, and on several occasions unhoused people resided in the longhouse along with me." In addition to this participant observation, Miller also conducted in-depth interviews with Coast Salish spiritual leaders where he explored how they understood the relationship between their cultural practices, the homeless, and the unhoused.

Blankenship conducted fieldwork in Seattle for two-and-a-half years with Christian "street ministers" from an FBO—Operation Nightwatch—as well as with people who are chronically homeless and insecurely housed. "I am a Christian theologian and an ethnographer," he explains. "What this means is that I spend a lot of time learning about worlds that are different than my own through, among other things, participant observation, semi-structured interviews, and historical research. That is the nature of ethnography." And, in order to collect data from the bible study group with unhoused individuals, Clarke applied autoethnography, "a self-conscious yet self-critical mode of research and writing," where "subjectivity is readily conceded without sacrificing commitment to the rigorous, adequate, and reliable representation of the others that are also the subjects of the narrative."

The Potential of Faith-Based Responses to Homelessness

Throughout the volume, authors assess the limits and possibilities of faith-based responses to homelessness, often casting the potential role of FBOs in addressing this social problem as a dilemma. It is perhaps Spickard who, approaching it from the point of view of the process of secularization, best captures this dilemma in its most general terms when he muses that "it is now normal for people to think of religious groups running public welfare programs. . . . This puts religions back in the public sphere." And yet, communities of faith and their organizations, he continues, "cannot change social systems. They lack the power to address the structural conditions that produce homelessness in the first place." Indeed, FBOs "may be in the public sphere, but they cannot shape the public world."

Some authors more specifically understand this dilemma as the challenge of articulating an adequate framework—normative or theological language— for orienting modes of intervention, strategies, and programs. For Fisher, this is precisely the role of public theology, which "must contest and dismantle the religious rationalizations that undergird the social and political-economic elements that shape the public discourse on homelessness and incite efforts of criminalization." For Dávila it is about fusing the spiritual and corporal works of mercy, on the one hand, and the struggle for justice, for systemic change, on the other. "Efforts to address the material needs of the unhoused, of providing adequate shelter, the sense of permanency and routine that are key to feeling safe and thriving as persons and communities," she maintains, "must go hand in hand with attending to the deep spiritual wounds, both personal and systemic, that accompany the precarious life of homelessness and housing insecurity." And, grounded in his exposition of "offensive wisdom," for Clarke it is about FBOs adopting a complementary approach: "While keeping one eye on cultivating personal dignity and individual transformation, the other eye must pay attention to critically disassembling a system that creates homelessness while putting together a social and political order in which no one will be unsheltered." This bifocal analysis and course of action, he continues, "takes homeless neighbors as distinct persons with intrinsic worth even as it deals with transforming societal structures that create homelessness."

Other authors approach the dilemma of faith-based responses to homelessness in terms of the variety of types of FBOs and the different capacity constraints they face. "We can ask, as I did in my own earlier study of FBOs," writes Coleman, "whether congregations, as such, are as effective as the separately incorporated denominational units and the interfaith ones in dealing with homelessness." And Mejido and Breen propose the paradigm of "community problem solvers" in order to frame "the local revitalization efforts of these organizations in terms of the civic capacity to experiment with new modalities of catalyzing effective social change." Leveraging opportunities and negotiating constraints, faith-based nonprofits and congregations, they argue, "in different ways, strive to blend local knowledge and professional knowledge, the adaptability of bottom-up civic engagement, and the complexities of top-down programming to rethink homelessness interventions."

Notes

1. Cf. Nels Anderson, *The Hobo: The Sociology of the Homeless Man* (Chicago: University of Chicago Press, 1923); Todd Depastino, *Citizen Hobo: How a Century of Homelessness Shaped America* (Chicago: University of Chicago Press, 2003); Kenneth L. Kusmer, *Down and Out, On the Road: The Homeless in American History* (New York: Oxford University Press, 2002); Henry Miller, *On the Fringe: The Dispossessed in America* (Lanham, Md.: Lexington, 1991); Peter H. Rossi, *Down and Out in America: The Origins of Homelessness* (Chicago: University of Chicago Press, 1990); Forrest Stuart, *Down, Out, and Under Arrest: Policing and Everyday Life in Skid Row* (Chicago: University of Chicago Press, 2016); Vincent Lyon-Callo, *Inequality, Poverty, and Neoliberal Governance: Activist Ethnography in the Homeless Sheltering Industry* (Toronto: University of Toronto Press, 2004); Jason Adam Wasserman and Jeffrey Michael Clair, *At Home on the Street: People, Poverty and a Hidden Culture of Homelessness* (Boulder, Colo.: Lynne Rienner, 2010); David Snow and Leon Anderson, *Down on Their Luck: A Study of Homeless Street People* (Berkeley: University of California, 1993); Christopher Jencks, *The Homeless* (Cambridge, Mass.: Harvard University Press, 1995); Anthony Marcus, *Where Have All the Homeless Gone? The Making and Unmaking of a Crisis* (New York: Berghahn, 2006); Joel John Roberts, *How to Increase Homelessness: Real Solutions to the Absurdity of Homelessness in America* (Los Angeles: Loyal, 2004); and Robert R. Desjarlais, *Shelter Blues: Sanity and Selfhood Among the Homeless* (Philadelphia: University of Pennsylvania Press, 1997).

2. Abraham Lincoln, "First Inaugural Address," in *Collected Works of Abraham Lincoln*, ed. Roy P. Basler (New Brunswick, N.J.: Rutgers University Press, 1953), 4:263–71.

3. See, for instance, this methodological assessment of the Greater Los Angeles Homeless Count: Economic Roundtable, "Who Counts? Assessing Accuracy of the Homeless Count," by Daniel Fleming and Patrick Burns (Los Angeles: November 2017). See also James V. Spickard's analysis in Chapter 14 of *Research Basics: Design to Data Analysis in Six Steps* (Thousand Oaks, Calif.: Sage, 2019), 320–47.

4. United States Department of Housing and Urban Development, "The 2019 Annual Homeless Assessment Report," by Meghan Henry, Rian Watt, Anna Mahathey, Jullian Ouellette, and Aubrey Sitler, Abt Associates (Washington, D.C.: January 2020).

5. United Nations Economic and Social Council, "Report of the Secretary-General on Affordable Housing and Social Protection Systems for All to Address Homelessness," E/CN.5/2020/3, Commission for Social Development Fifty-Eighth Session, New York, February 10–February 19, 2020, 2.

6. United Nations General Assembly, "Report of the Special Rapporteur on Extreme Poverty and Human Rights on His Mission to the United States of

America," A/HRC/38/33/Add.1, Human Rights Council Thirty-Eighth Session, New York, June 18–July 6, 2018.

7. Jeffrey D. Sachs, *The Age of Sustainable Development* (New York: Columbia University Press, 2014).

8. Sachs, Guido Schmidt-Traub, Christian Kroll, David Durand-Delacre, and Katerina Teksoz, *SDG Index and Dashboards: Global Report* (New York: Bertelsmann Stiftung/Sustainable Development Solutions Network, 2016). See also Sachs, *Building the New American Economy* (New York: Columbia University Press, 2017).

9. Sachs, "Restoring American Happiness," in *World Happiness Report 2017*, ed. John Helliwell, Richard Layard, and Jeffrey D. Sachs (New York: Sustainable Development Solutions Network, 2017), 178–84.

10. Cf. Anne Case and Angus Deaton, *Deaths of Despair and the Future of Capitalism* (Princeton, N.J.: Princeton University Press, 2020); Robert Reich, *The System: Who Rigged It, How We Fix It* (New York: Knopf, 2020); Robert Putnam, *The Upswing: How America Came Together a Century Ago and How We Can Do It Again* (New York: Simon & Schuster, 2020); and Joseph Stiglitz, *People, Power, and Profits: Progressive Capitalism for an Age of Discontent* (New York: W.W. Norton, 2019).

11. Sachs, "Restoring American Happiness," 183.

12. United States Interagency Council on Homelessness, *Strengthening Systems for Ending Rural Homelessness: Promising Practices and Considerations* (Washington, D.C.: June 2018).

13. United States Department of Housing and Urban Development, *2019 Annual Homeless Assessment Report*.

14. Ibid..

15. Enrico Moretti, *The New Geography of Jobs* (New York: First Mariner, 2013).

16. Thomas Piketty, "Brahmin Left vs. Merchant Right: Rising Inequality and the Changing Structure of Political Conflict (Evidence from France, Britain and the US, 1948–2017)," World Inequality Lab Working Paper Series no. 2018/7 (Paris School of Economics, March 2018); and Ronald F. Inglehart and Pippa Norris, "Trump, Brexit, and the Rise of Populism: Economic Have-Nots and Cultural Backlash," Faculty Research Working Paper Series RWP16-026 (Cambridge, Mass.: Harvard University Kennedy School, August 2016).

17. According to Richard Florida and Charlotta Mellander, "Americans have become increasingly sorted over the past couple of decades by income, education, and class. A large body of research has focused on the dual migrations of more affluent and skilled people and the less advantaged across the United States. Increasingly, Americans are sorting not just between cities and metro areas, but within them as well. . . . It is not just that the economic divide in America has grown wider; it's that the rich and poor effectively occupy different worlds, even when they live in the same cities and metros"; Florida and Mellander, *Segregated City: The Geography of Economic Segregation in America's Metros* (Toronto: Martin Prosperity Institute, February 2015), 8–9. Consult also Paul Taylor and Richard Fry, *The Rise of*

Residential Segregation by Income (Washington, D.C.: Pew Research Center, August 1, 2012).

18. Alan Berube, *City and Metropolitan Income Inequality Data Reveal Ups and Downs Through 2016* (Washington, D.C.: Brookings Institution, February 5, 2018).

19. Manuel Castells, *End of Millennium*, The Information Age: Economy, Society, and Culture, vol. 3 (Oxford: Basil Blackwell, 2000).

20. See, for instance, Robert Castel, *Les Métamorphoses de la question sociale: Une chronique du salariat* (Paris: Fayard, 1996); and William Julius Wilson, *The Truly Disadvantaged: The Inner City, the Underclass, and Public Policy*, 2nd ed. (Chicago: University of Chicago Press, 2012).

21. Loïc Wacquant, *Urban Outcasts: A Comparative Sociology of Advanced Marginality* (Malden, Mass.: Polity Press, 2008). See also Wilson, *When Work Disappears: The World of the New Urban Poor* (New York: Vintage Paperback Edition, 1997).

22. Wacquant, *Punishing the Poor: The Neoliberal Government of Social Insecurity* (Durham, N.C.: Duke University Press, 2009).

23. United Nations Economic and Social Council, "Report of the Secretary-General on Affordable Housing and Social Protection Systems for All to Address Homelessness," 3 and 7.

24. Since the start of the millennium, gross rent has on average increased 3 percent annually, while income has declined by an average of 0.1 percent per year, falling from $56,531 in 2001 to $56,516 in 2015; Pew Charitable Trusts, *American Families Face a Growing Rent Burden: High Housing Costs Threaten Financial Security and Put Homeownership Out of Reach for Many* (Philadelphia and Washington, D.C.: April 2018).

25. Profiting off the historic decline in homeownership, a number of large institutional investors have, in the aftermath of the 2008 recession, increased their sway in the single-family rental housing (SFR) industry. These real estate investment trusts (REITs) have created a new asset class by securitizing the rental income of foreclosed homes they converted into rental properties. These speculative and oligopolistic dynamics have resulted in the channeling of potentially disruptive global capital into local housing markets across the country. The teaser of a March 2020 *New York Times* feature article casts what is at stake in the financialization of SFR in these terms: "Hundreds of thousands of single-family homes are now in the hands of giant companies—squeezing renters for revenue and putting the American dream even further out of reach"; Francesca Mari, "A $60 Billion Housing Grab by Wall Street," *New York Times Magazine*, March 8, 2020, accessed March 6, 2020, www .nytimes.com. The 2017 thematic report of the United Nations Special Rapporteur on adequate housing nicely frames the human rights implications of the issue thus: "The 'financialization of housing' refers to structural changes in housing and financial markets and global investment whereby housing is treated as a commodity, a means of accumulating wealth and often as security for financial instruments that are traded and sold on global markets. It refers to the way capital investment in housing increasingly

disconnects housing from its social function of providing a place to live in security and dignity and hence undermines the realization of housing as a human right"; United Nations General Assembly, "Report of the Special Rapporteur on Adequate Housing as a Component of the Right to an Adequate Standard of Living, and On the Right to Non-Discrimination in this Context," A/HRC/34/51, Human Rights Council Thirty-Fourth Session, New York, February 27–March 24, 2017, 3. For an investigative account of this issue in the United States, see Aaron Glantz, *Homewreckers: How a Gang of Wall Street Kingpins, Hedge Fund Magnates, Crooked Banks, and Vulture Capitalists Suckered Millions Out of Their Homes and Demolished the American Dream* (New York: HarperCollins, 2019). For a more technical analysis, consult, for instance, Suzanne Lanyi Charles, "The Financialization of Single-Family Rental Housing: An Examination of Real Estate Investment Trusts' Ownership of Single-Family Houses in the Atlanta Metropolitan Area," *Journal of Urban Affairs* 42, no. 8 (2020): 1321–41; and Desiree Fields, "Constructing a New Asset Class: Property-Led Financial Accumulation after the Crisis," *Economic Geography* 94, no. 2 (2018): 118–40.

26. Matthew Desmond, "Heavy Is the House: Rent Burden Among the American Poor," *International Journal of Urban and Regional Research* 42, no. 1 (2018): 160–70.

27. National Law Center on Homelessness & Poverty, *Tent City, USA: The Growth of America's Homeless Encampments and How Communities are Responding*, A Report by the National Law Center on Homelessness & Poverty (Washington, D.C.: December 2017). For example, as Mejido Costoya and Breen explain in their contribution to this volume, a recent study found that in Seattle the number of individuals experiencing homelessness has increased directly with the fair-market rent, which correspondingly has risen in line with the region's real GDP, driven by the growing number of high-income digital workers; Maggie Stringfellow and Dilip Wagle, "The Economics of Homelessness in Seattle and King County," McKinsey, May 2018. Another study found that half of the households in California cannot afford the cost of housing in their local market and that practically no low-income households can afford the cost of housing; Jonathan Woetzel, Jan Mischke, Shannon Peloquin, and Daniel Weisfield, *A Tool Kit to Close California's Housing Gap: 3.5 Million Homes by 2025*, report by McKinsey Global Institute, October 2016. This helps explain why in 2017 the share of the homeless population in California was greater than 6 percent and why, between 2016 and 2017, it was the Golden State that recorded the largest increase in homelessness—13.7 percent—among the fifty states; United States Department of Housing and Urban Development, *The 2017 Annual Homeless Assessment Report*.

28. Richard Rothstein has thoroughly documented how segregated neighborhoods, with their poverty, violence, and inequality traps, was the result of racially explicit policies of federal, state, and local governments, and how other causes of segregation, such as white flight, real estate steering, and bank redlining, were effective only because of these government policies and laws; Rothstein, *The Color of Law: A Forgotten History of How Our Government Segregated America*

(New York: W. W. Norton, 2017). See also this important collection of essays on the geography of housing choices: Xavier de Souza Briggs, ed., *The Geography of Opportunity: Race and Housing Choice in Metropolitan America* (Washington, D.C.: Brookings Institution Press, 2005).

29. Desmond, *Evicted: Poverty and Profit in the American City* (New York: Penguin Random House, 2017). Desmond has found that poor women, and especially low-income African American women, are at high risk of eviction. For example, women living in black neighborhoods in Milwaukee represent 9.6 percent of the population, but 30 percent of evictions. Among renters, over one in five black women report having been evicted sometime in their adult life. The same is true for roughly one in twelve Hispanic women and one in fifteen white women; Desmond, "Unaffordable America: Poverty, Housing, and Eviction," *Fast Focus*, no. 22, Institute for Research on Poverty, University of Wisconsin, Madison (March 2015).

30. Desmond and Carl Gershenson, "Housing and Employment Insecurity among the Working Poor," *Social Problems* 63 (January 2016): 46–67.

31. One study of public shelters in New York City found that 23.1 percent of the shelter population had had an incarceration within a two-year period; Stephen Metraux and Dennis P. Culhane, "Recent Incarceration History among a Sheltered Homeless Population," Departmental Papers, School of Social Policy and Practice, University of Pennsylvania, July 2006. Data from a national survey of jail inmates found that inmates were between 7.5 and 11.3 times more likely than the general adult population to have been homeless within a year of incarceration; Greg A. Greenberg and Robert A. Rosenheck, "Jail Incarceration, Homelessness, and Mental Health: A National Study," *Psychiatric Services* 59, no. 2 (February 2008): 170–77.

32. John R. Belcher and Bruce R. DeForge, "Social Stigma and Homelessness: The Limits of Social Change," *Journal of Human Behavior in the Social Environment* 22 (2012): 929–46.

33. Research has found that people tend to dehumanize homeless individuals, classifying them as members of extreme out-groups, while they perceive in-groups or moderate out-groups as fully human; Lasana T. Harris and Susan Fiske, "Social Groups That Elicit Disgust Are Differentially Processed in mPFC," *Scan* 2 (2007): 45–51; and Harris and Fiske, "Dehumanizing the Lowest of the Low: Neuroimaging Responses to Extreme Out-Groups," *Association for Psychological Science* 17, no. 10 (2006): 847–53.

34. Mark J. Stern, "The Emergence of the Homeless as a Public Problem," *Social Service Review* 58, no. 2 (June 1984): 291–301.

35. Wacquant, *Punishing the Poor*.

36. Based on the analysis of municipal codes in 187 cities between 2011 and 2014, the National Law Center on Homelessness & Poverty found that there was, for example, a 119 percent increase in the number of cities that ban sleeping in vehicles; a 60 percent increase in the number of cities that prohibit camping; and a 25 percent increase in the number of cities that forbid begging in public. Measures and ordinances that penalize life-sustaining activities, such as sleeping and bathing, are based on

the dubious legal theory that they are necessary for protecting the public interest. The constitutionality of these criminalization laws has been questioned for violating the First, Eighth, and Fourteenth Amendments as well as international human rights treaties such as the International Covenant on Civil and Political Rights; National Law Center on Homelessness & Poverty, *No Safe Place: The Criminalization of Homelessness in U.S. Cities* (A Report by the National Law Center on Homelessness & Poverty, Washington, D.C., 2015).

37. Deborah Padgett, Benjamin Henwood, and Sam Tsemberis, *Housing First: Ending Homelessness, Transforming Systems, and Changing Lives* (New York: Oxford University Press, 2016).

38. Thad Kousser, "How America's 'Devolution Revolution' Reshaped Its Federalism," *Revue Française de Science Politique* 64, no. 2 (2014): 265–87. Consult also Kenneth Finegold, Laura Wherry, and Stephanie Schardin, "Block Grants: Historical Overview and Lessons Learned," in *New Federalism: Issues and Options for States* (Washington, D.C.: Urban Institute, April 2004).

39. Bruce Katz and Jeremy Nowak, *The New Localism: How Cities Can Thrive in the Age of Populism* (Washington, D.C.: Brookings Institute Press, 2018).

40. Joseph Leopold, "Five Ways the HEARTH Act Changed Homelessness Assistance," Urban Wire, Urban Institute, May 9, 2019, accessed December 3, 2020, www.urban.org.

41. Patrick Fowler, Peter Hovmand, Katherine Marcal, and Sanmay Das, "Solving Homelessness from a Complex Systems Perspective: Insights for Prevention Responses," *Annual Review of Public Health* 40 (April 2019): 465–86.

42. Alexis de Tocqueville, *Democracy in America* [1835 and 1840] (London: University of Chicago Press, 2000).

43. José Casanova, "The Religious Situation in the United States 175 Years after Tocqueville," in *Crediting God: Sovereignty and Religion in the Age of Global Capitalism*, ed. Miguel Vatter (New York: Fordham University Press, 2011), 253–72.

44. Robert Putnam and David Campbell, *American Grace: How Religion Divides and Unites Us* (New York: Simon & Schuster, 2010).

45. Casanova, "Exploring the Postsecular: Three Meanings of 'the Secular' and Their Possible Transcendence," in *Habermas and Religion*, ed. Craig Calhoun, Eduardo Mendieta, and Jonathan VanAntwerpen (Malden, Mass.: Polity, 2013), 52–91.

46. Robert N. Bellah, *The Broken Covenant: American Civil Religion in Time of Trial* (Chicago: University of Chicago Press, 1992).

47. Steven M. Tipton, *Public Pulpits: Methodists and Mainline Churches in the Moral Argument of Public Life* (Chicago: University of Chicago Press, 2007).

48. Steven Stritt, "The First Faith-Based Movement: The Religious Roots of Social Progressivism in America (1880–1912) in Historical Perspective," *Journal of Sociology and Social Welfare* 41, no. 1 (March 2014): 77–105.

49. George M. Marsden, *Fundamentalism and American Culture* (New York: Oxford University Press, 2006).

50. Seymour Martin Lipset, *American Exceptionalism: A Double-Edged Sword* (New York: W. W. Norton, 1996).

51. Casanova, "Exploring the Postsecular."

52. Casanova, "Rethinking Secularization: A Global Comparative Perspective," *Hedgehog Review* (Spring and Summer 2006): 7–22.

53. Jürgen Habermas, "Equal Treatment of Cultures and the Limits of Postmodern Liberalism," *Journal of Political Philosophy* 13, no. 1 (2005): 27.

54. Tipton, *Public Pulpits*; and Robert Wuthnow, *Saving America: Faith-Based Services and the Future of Civil Society* (Princeton: Princeton University Press, 2004).

55. Wolfgang Bielefeld and William Suhs Cleveland, "Defining Faith-Based Organizations and Understanding Them through Research," *Nonprofit and Voluntary Sector Quarterly* 42, no. 3 (2013): 442–67.

56. See, for instance, Sheila Suess Kennedy and Wolfgang Bielefeld, *Charitable Choice at Work: Evaluating Faith-Based Job Programs in the States* (Washington, D.C.: Georgetown University Press, 2006); John Bartkowski and Helen Regis, *Charitable Choice: Religion, Race, and Poverty in the Post-Welfare Era* (New York: New York University Press, 2003); Robert Wineburg, *A Limited Partnership: The Politics of Religion, Welfare, and Social Service* (New York: Columbia University Press, 2001); Ram Cnaan and John DiIulio, *The Invisible Caring Hand: American Congregations and the Provision of Welfare* (New York: New York University Press, 2002); and Ram Cnaan, with Robert J. Wineburg, and Stephanie C. Boddie, *The Newer Deal: Social Work and Religion in Partnership* (New York: Columbia University Press, 1999).

57. Cf. Theda Skocpol, "Religion, Civil Society, and Social Provision in the U.S," in *Who Will Provide? The Changing Role of Religion in American Social Welfare*, ed. Mary Jo Bane, Brent Coffin, and Ronald Thiemann (Boulder: Westview, 2000), 21–50; and Mark Chaves, "Debunking Charitable Choice: The Evidence Doesn't Support the Political Left or Right," *Stanford Social Innovation Review* 1, no. 2 (Summer 2003): 28–36.

58. Michael Lee Owen, "Capacity Building: The Case of Faith-Based Organizations," in *Building the Organizations That Build Communities: Strengthening the Capacity of Faith- and Community-Based Development Organizations*, ed. Roland V. Anglin (Washington, D.C.: United States Department of Housing and Urban Development, 2004), 127–64; and Elliot Wright, "Religion's Investment and Involvement in Community-Based Economic Development: An Overview," in Anglin, *Building the Organizations That Build Communities*, 27–42.

59. Tipton, *Public Pulpits*.

60. Wuthnow, *Saving America*.

61. Consult, for example, John A. Coleman, "Religious Social Capital: Its Nature, Social Location, and Limits," in *Religion as Social Capital: Producing the Common Good*, ed. Corwin Smidt (Waco, Tex.: Baylor University Press, 2003), 33–47; Coleman, "Religion and Public Life: Some American Cases," *Religion* 28

(1998): 155–69; and Coleman, "Under the Cross and the Flag: Reflections on Discipleship and Citizenship in America," *America: The Jesuit Review* 174, no. 16 (May 11, 1996): 6–14.

62. That is, a nonprofit or charitable organization that is exempt from federal income tax under Section 501(c)(3) of the United States Internal Revenue Code.

63. Richard L. Wood and Brad R. Fulton, *A Shared Future: Faith-Based Organizing for Racial Equity and Ethical Democracy* (Chicago: University of Chicago Press, 2015); Pew Research Center, *Lobbying for the Faithful: Religious Advocacy Groups in Washington, D.C* (Washington, D.C.: Pew Forum on Religion & Public Life, May 2012); and Tipton, *Public Pulpits*, in particular Chapter 7, "Religious Lobbies and Public Churches: Ecclesiology Matters."

64. The type of activity and the intensity of involvement included under these categories vary considerably, though. For instance, food assistance includes supplying volunteers to serve dinner at a homeless shelter about once a month, operating a food pantry, and donating money to a local food bank. Congregations specifically addressed housing needs by, for example, organizing volunteers to participate in a Habit for Humanity project or collaborating with the municipal government to build affordable housing; Mark Chaves and Alison J. Eagle, "Congregations and Social Services: An Update from the Third Wave of the National Congregations Study," *Religions* 7, no. 55 (2016).

65. These informal activities include, for instance, fostering the value of caring for others through sermons and small groups; creating civic spaces for advocacy and lobbying efforts; and fostering social capital through interactions that cut across status and other markers of identity; Wuthnow, *Saving America*. See also Chaves and Eagle, "Congregations and Social Services."

66. Robert Wuthnow nicely captures this "iron-cage"-like dilemma when he observes that, while these service organizations contribute positively to the cultural norms underpinning civil society, "they communicate ideals of unconditional love far less often than might be supposed from thinking about these ideals only within the context of religious teachings"; Wuthnow, *Saving America*, xvii. Consult also Stephen Mosma, *Putting Faith in Partnerships: Welfare-to-Work in Four Cities* (Ann Arbor: University of Michigan Press, 2004); and Paul DiMaggio and Walter Powell, "The Iron Cage Revisited: Institutional Isomorphism and Collective Rationality in Organizational Fields," *American Sociological Review* 48, no. 2 (1983): 147–60.

67. Wuthnow, *Saving America*, 141.

68. National Alliance to End Homelessness, "Faith-Based Organizations: Fundamental Partners in Ending Homelessness" (Washington, D.C.: May 2017).

69. Byron Johnson, William Wubbenhorst, and Alfreda Alvarez, *Assessing the Faith-Based Responses to Homelessness in America: Findings from Eleven Cities* (Waco, Tex.: Baylor University Institute for Studies of Religion, 2017). Spearheaded by the Baylor Institute for Studies of Religion, this research also found that there was an inverse correlation between the share of FBO-provided emergency shelter beds and the share of unsheltered homeless individuals.

70. Ferdinand Tönnies, *Community and Society* [1887] (New York: Basic Books 1980).

71. Habermas, *The Theory of Communicative Action*, vol. 2, *Lifeworld and System: A Critique of Functionalist Reason* (1981; repr. Boston: Beacon Press, 1989).

72. Thus, for instance, the authors of the aforementioned Baylor study on FBOs and homelessness in eleven U.S. cities acknowledge at the outset of their report that while their research "focuses on the reach of faith-based organizations, it is worth noting that it does not include the work of many churches, temples, synagogues, and mosques throughout each city, to provide meals, clothing, furniture, counseling, childcare, transportation and more"; Johnson, Wubbenhorst, and Alvarez, *Assessing the Faith-Based Responses to Homelessness in America*, 15. By methodologically excluding congregations, this study misses an important dimension of faith-based response to homelessness. Years ago, in response to what he lamented was the lack of research on the linkages between congregations and para-church groups, the social ethicist and sociologist of religion John A. Coleman conducted a multiyear study that included an exploration of the symbiotic relationship between these caring communities and faith-based service organizations. Reflecting on his research findings, Coleman writes: "Few studies of para-church groups . . . and their relationship to local congregations currently exist at the national and even the regional and local levels. . . . Congregations and para-church organizations may need each other to generate an effective public church in America. . . . Many local congregations do not really know how to use the social capital they generate in more public settings. . . . To build their own networks, para-church organizations both depend on and add to the social capital they find in congregational settings. . . . It seems clear what congregations do for para-church groups: they provide the initial network of social friendships and reciprocity on which to build. What do para-church groups give to congregations in return? The same people who say that their sense of discipleship inculcated in local congregations primarily moved them to civic action wax enthusiastic about how it was the para-church group, rather than the parish, that taught them how to put their faith into concrete action and have larger civic consequences"; Coleman, "Religious Social Capital: Its Nature, Social Location, and Limits," 39–41. See also Coleman's chapter in this volume.

73. Northrop Frye, *Anatomy of Criticism* (Princeton: Princeton University Press, 1957), 141–46.

74. For example, reflecting on his lecture on Friedrich Hölderlin's poem "Homecoming," Martin Heidegger writes, "The essence of the homeland . . . is . . . mentioned with the intention of thinking the homelessness of contemporary man from the essence of Being's history. . . . Homelessness so understood consists in the abandonment of Being by beings. Homelessness is the symptom of oblivion of Being"; Martin Heidegger, "Letter on Humanism" (1946), in *Basic Writings*, ed. David Farrell Krell (San Francisco: Harper Collins, 1993), 241–42. And, arguing that having a *home* cannot be reduced to having a *house*, that we must distinguish between the brick-and-mortar "building" and the existential predicament of

"dwelling" understood as "the stay of mortals on the earth," Heidegger writes, "On all sides we hear talk about the housing shortage, and with good reason. Nor is there just talk; there is action too. We try to fill the need by providing houses, by promoting the building of houses, planning the whole architectural enterprise. However hard and bitter, however hampering and threatening the lack of houses remains, the proper plight of dwelling does not lie merely in a lack of houses. The proper plight of dwelling is indeed older than the world wars with their destruction, older also than the increase of the earth's population and the condition of the industrial workers. The proper dwelling plight lies in this, that mortals ever search anew for the essence of dwelling, that they must ever learn to dwell. What if man's homelessness consisted in this, that man still does not even think of the proper plight of dwelling as the plight? Yet as soon as man gives thought to his homelessness, it is a misery no longer. Rightly considered and kept well in mind, it is the sole summons that calls mortals into their dwelling"; Heidegger, "Dwelling Building Thinking" [1954], in *Basic Writings*, 363.

75. Emile Durkheim, *The Elementary Forms of Religious Life* [1912] (New York: Free Press, 1965); Marcel Mauss, *The Gift: The Form and Reason for Exchange in Archaic Societies* [1925] (1950; repr. London: Routledge, 2002).

76. Emmanuel Levinas, *Totality and Infinity: An Essay on Exteriority* (1961; repr. Pittsburgh: Duquesne University Press, 1969); Jacques Derrida, *Of Hospitality: Anne Dufourmantelle Invites Jacques Derrida to Respond* (Stanford, Calif.: Stanford University Press, 2000); and Derrida, "Force of Law," in *Deconstruction and the Possibility of Justice*, ed. Drucilla Cornell, Michael Rosenfeld, and David Gray Carlson (New York: Routledge, 1992), 3–67.

77. Ernst Bloch, *The Principle of Hope*, vol. 3 (1959; repr. Cambridge, Mass.: MIT Press, 1986).

78. See, for example, John Rawls's Introduction to *Political Liberalism* (New York: Columbia University Press, 1993). Consult also the collection of essays in Paul J. Weithman, ed., *Religion and Contemporary Liberalism* (Notre Dame, Ind.: University of Notre Dame Press, 1997).

79. See, for instance, Michael Sandel, *Liberalism and the Limits of Justice* (Cambridge: Cambridge University Press, 1982); Michael Walzer, *Spheres of Justice* (Oxford: Blackwell, 1983); and Charles Taylor, *Sources of the Self: The Making of the Modern Identity* (Cambridge: Cambridge University Press, 1989).

80. David Hollenbach, S.J., has argued that "social justice" rather than "fairness" is a more adequate guiding principle for a flourishing city insofar as it is concomitant with enabling participation in the common good: "Social justice requires an overall institutional framework that will enable people both to participate actively in building up the common good and to share in the benefits of the common good. . . . The 'subject' of social justice, therefore, is the major institutions that enhance or impede people's participation in creating and benefiting from the common good. To bring justice to the urban poor, metropolitan-wide institutions must be reformed so that the barriers to their participation are reduced"; Hollenbach, *The Common*

Good and Christian Ethics (Cambridge: Cambridge University Press, 2002), 201. See also Martha Nussbaum's Aristotelian approach to the human capability framework and her proposition for a "thick vague theory of the good"; Nussbaum, "Human Functioning and Social Justice: In Defense of Aristotelian Essentialism," *Political Theory* 20, no. 2 (1992): 202–46, and "Nature, Function and Capability: Aristotle on Political Distribution" (Working Paper 31, World Institute for Development Economics Research, United Nations University, Helsinki, 1987).

81. Bellah, Richard Madsen, William M. Sullivan, Ann Swidler, and Steven M. Tipton, *Habits of the Heart: Individualism and Commitment in American Life* (Berkeley: University of California Press, 1985), and Bellah, Madsen, Sullivan, Swidler, and Tipton, *The Good Society* (New York: Vintage, 1991).

82. Benjamin Constant, "The Liberty of the Ancients Compared to That of the Moderns," in *Political Writings*, ed. Biancamaria Fontana (Cambridge: Cambridge University Press, 1988), 309–28.

83. Isaiah Berlin, "Two Concepts of Liberty," in *Four Essays on Liberty*, ed. Henry Hardy (New York: Oxford University Press, 1969), 118–72.

84. Bellah, "Religion and the Legitimation of the American Republic," *Society* 15, no. 4 (1978): 16–23, and *Broken Covenant*. As Steven Tipton has cogently argued, from these competing understandings of the individual in society emerge two contrasting interpretations of the First Amendment's religion clauses: While the biblical and republican strands emphasize the Free Exercise Clause, the expressive and utilitarian strands give pride of place to the Establishment Clause. In other words, the moral traditions that view the individual as embedded in community understand the expression of religion as playing a constitutive role in public life. By contrast, the moral traditions that stress the autonomy of the individual understand religion as potentially destabilizing for the social order and therefore must be circumscribed in civic life, but tolerated in the private sphere as a negative liberty; see Tipton, *Public Pulpits*, 34–39.

85. Cass R. Sunstein, *The Second Bill of Rights: FDR's Unfinished Revolution and Why We Need It More Than Ever* (New York: Basic Books, 2004).

86. Sara K. Rankin, "A Homeless Bill of Rights (Revolution)," *Seton Hall Law Review* 45 (2015): 383–434.

87. Richard Falk, "The Post-Secular Divide," in *Power Shift: On the New Global Order* (London: Zed, 2016), 20–21.

88. Taylor, *A Secular Age* (Cambridge, Mass.: Harvard University Press, 2007), 534.

89. Casanova, "Exploring the Postsecular," 52–91.

90. See, for example, Peter Nynäs, Mika Lassander, and Terhi Utriainen, eds., *Post-Secular Society* (New Brunswick, N.J.: Transaction, 2015), and Justin Beaumont and Christopher Baker, eds., *Postsecular Cities: Space, Theory and Practice* (London: Continuum, 2011).

91. Habermas, "Equal Treatment of Cultures and the Limits of Postmodern Liberalism," 27. Elsewhere, Habermas formulates this post-secular principle thus: "For the liberal state has an interest in unleashing religious voices in the political public

sphere, and in the political participation of religious organizations, as well. It must not discourage religious persons and communities from also expressing themselves politically as such, for it cannot know whether secular society would not otherwise cut itself off from key resources for the creation of meaning and identity; Habermas, "Religion in the Public Sphere," *European Journal of Philosophy* 14, no. 1 (2006): 10.

92. See, for example, Justin Beaumont, "Introduction: Faith-Based Organisations and Urban Social Issues," *Urban Studies* 45, no. 10 (2008): 2011–17.

93. Karma Ura, Sabina Alkire, and Tshoki Zangmo, "Gross National Happiness and the GNH Index," in *World Happiness Report*, ed. John Helliwell, Richard Layard, and Jeffrey Sachs (New York: Earth Institute, 2012), 108–58.

94. Manuel Mejido Costoya, "Latin American Post-Neoliberal Development Thinking: The Bolivian 'Turn' Toward *Suma Qamaña*," *European Journal of Development Research* 25, no. 2 (2013): 213–29.

95. Pope Francis, *Laudato Si': On Care for Our Common Home* (Vatican City: Libreria Editrice Vaticana, 2015).

96. Zamir Iqbal and Abbas Mirakhor, eds., *Economic Development and Islamic Finance* (Washington, D.C.: World Bank, 2013).

97. In a neo-Kantian vein reminiscent of Ernst Troeltsch, Walter Rauschenbusch, for example, argues for the retrieval of an eschatology that had been eclipsed by the methodological individualism of liberal Protestant Theology: "When the doctrine of the Kingdom of God is lacking in theology, the salvation of the individual is seen in its relation to the Church and the future life, but not in its relation to the task of saving the social order"; Rauschenbusch, *A Theology for the Social Gospel* (New York: Abingdon, 1917), 137.

98. Before he became a detractor of social gospel theology, a young Reinhold Niebuhr described thus the failure of Christianity to authentically engage in what he called "social work" and what today we would probably call "community development" or "local revitalization": "The most obvious weakness of religion in social action is that it seems always to create a spirit of generosity within terms of a social system, without developing an idealism vigorous or astute enough to condemn the social system in the name of a higher justice"; Niebuhr, *The Contribution of Religion to Social Work* (New York: Columbia University Press, 1932), 19.

99. Jacques Maritain, *Integral Humanism: Temporal and Spiritual Problems of a New Christendom*, in *The Collected Works of Jacques Maritain*, vol. 11 (1936; repr. Notre Dame, Ind.: University of Notre Dame Press, 1996).

100. Dorothy Day, *House of Hospitality* (New York: Sheed and Ward, 1939).

101. At the outset of what is considered the foundational text of Latin American liberation theology, Gustavo Gutiérrez writes, "What Hegel used to say about philosophy can likewise be applied to theology: it rises only at sundown. The pastoral activity of the Church does not flow as a conclusion from theological premises. Theology does not produce pastoral activity; rather it reflects upon it"; Gutiérrez, *A Theology of Liberation: History, Politics, and Salvation* (1971; repr. Maryknoll, N.Y.: Orbis, 1988), 9.

102. Gustavo Gutiérrez writes, "To speak about a theology of liberation is to seek an answer to the following question: what relation is there between salvation and the historical process of human liberation?"; Gutiérrez, *Theology of Liberation*, 29. In the conclusion to his posthumously published magnum opus, Ignacio Ellacuría submits that when "dynamically and concretely considered, historical reality has a character of praxis that, together with other criteria, leads to the truth of reality and to the truth of the interpretation of reality. This is not so much [Giambattista] Vico's equivalence between the 'verum' and the 'factum.' It is rather the equivalence between the 'verum' and the 'faciendum': The truth of reality is not what is already made. This is only a part of reality. If we do not return to what is being made, and what still needs to be made, then the truth of reality will escape us. Indeed, the truth needs to be made; but this does not simply mean that we need to implement or realize what is already known. It means, rather, that we need to make that reality which, through the interplay of praxis and theory, manifests itself as the real truth. That reality and truth need to be made and discovered, and that they need to be made and discovered in the collective and successive ensemble of history—of humanity—is to suggest that historical reality is the object of philosophy"; Ellacuría, *Filosofía de la realidad histórica* (San Salvador: UCA Editores), 602 (my translation).

103. Taking issue with Maritain's ecclesiology, Gutiérrez writes, "For some time now, we have been witnessing a great effort by the Church to rise out of this ghetto power and mentality and to shake off the ambiguous protection provided by the beneficiaries of the unjust order which prevails on the continent. Individual Christians, small communities, and the Church as a whole are becoming more politically aware and are acquiring a greater knowledge of the current Latin American reality, especially in its root causes. The Christian community is beginning, in fact, to read politically the signs of the times in Latin America"; Gutiérrez, *Theology of Liberation*, 58. See also Leonardo Boff, *Church, Charism and Power: Liberation Theology and the Institutional Church* (1981; repr. New York: Crossroad, 1985).

104. In an important essay, Ignacio Ellacuría writes, "Utopia and prophecy, if presented separately, tend to lose their historical effectiveness and become idealist escapism; and so, instead of becoming forces for renewal and liberation, they are at best reduced to functioning as a subjective solace for individual persons"; Ellacuría, "Utopia and Prophecy in Latin America," in *Mysterium Liberationis: Fundamental Concepts of Liberation Theology*, ed. Igancio Ellacuría and Jon Sobrino (Maryknoll, N.Y.: Orbis, 1993), 289.

105. This doctrine was endorsed by the hierarchy of the Catholic Church during the second Conference of Latin American Bishops (CELAM), held in Medellín, Columbia in 1968. Consult Alfred T. Hennelly, ed., *Liberation Theology: A Documented History* (Maryknoll, N.Y.: Orbis, 1990).

106. This doctrine was endorsed by the Catholic Church hierarchy during the third Conference of Latin American Bishops (CELAM), held in Puebla, Mexico in 1979; see ibid.

107. Cf. James H. Cone, *A Black Theology of Liberation*, 40th anniversary ed. (Maryknoll, N.Y.: Orbis, 2010), and Virgilio Elizondo, *Galilean Journey: The Mexican-American Promise*, rev., expanded (Maryknoll, N.Y.: Orbis, 2000).

108. James H. Cone, *Martin and Malcolm and America: A Dream or a Nightmare* (Maryknoll, N.Y.: Orbis, 1991).

109. Gloria Anzaldúa, *Boderlands/La Frontera: The New Mestiza* (San Francisco: Aunt Lute, 1987).

110. Marsden, *Fundamentalism and American Culture*, 85.

111. In his treatment of "The Kingdom of God and the Struggle for Justice," Niebuhr takes issue with the ostensibly "irrefutable proofs" of the liberal and progressive view of the social task: "The 'Kingdom of God' seemed to be an immanent force in history, culminating in a universal society of brotherhood and justice. The secular and liberal-Protestant approaches to the socio-moral problem, based upon this presupposition, are too numerous to mention. Modern sociological treatises are practically unanimous in assuming this view of history. The Marxist interpretation of history deviates from it. But the deviation is only provisionally radical. Its catastrophism is finally subordinated to a progressive and utopian concept of history. The liberal-Protestant version has added little but pious phrases to the interpretation"; Niebuhr, *The Nature and Destiny of Man: A Christian Interpretation*, vol. 2, *Human Destiny* (1943; repr. Louisville, Ky.: Westminster John Knox Press, 1996), 245.

112. Niebuhr, *Moral Man and Immoral Society: A Study in Ethics and Politics* (1932; repr. Louisville, Ky.: Westminster John Knox Press, 2013).

113. See Niebuhr's example of "unemployment benefits" in *Nature and Destiny of Man: A Christian Interpretation*, 2:249–51.

114. Sometimes referred to as the Yale School, postliberal theology can be traced back to the cultural-linguistic approaches of Hans Frei and George Lindbeck, while radical orthodoxy is associated with John Milbank, Graham Ward, and Catherine Pickstock. Consult, for example, George A. Lindbeck, "Foreword to the German Edition," *The Nature of Doctrine: Religion and Theology in a Postliberal Age*, 25th anniversary ed. (1984; repr. Louisville, Ky.: Westminster John Knox Press, 2009), xxix–xxxii; and John Milbank, Graham Ward, and Catherine Pickstock, "Introduction: Suspending the Material; The Turn of Radical Orthodoxy," in *Radical Orthodoxy: A New Theology*, ed. John Milbank, Catherine Pickstock, and Graham Ward (London and New York: Routledge, 1999), 1–20.

115. Daniel M. Bell Jr., "Postliberalism and Radical Orthodoxy," in *The Cambridge Companion to Christian Political Theology*, ed. Craig Hovey and Elizabeth Phillips (Cambridge: Cambridge University Press, 2015), 110–32.

116. Assessing Rauschenbusch's "Why Has Christianity Never Undertaken the Work of Social Reconstruction?," Hauerwas writes, "Rauschenbusch's inadequate ecclesiology was a correlative of his identification of the kingdom of God with progressive accounts of history that ironically meant his position could lead to the loss of the eschatological tension between Church and world that is a characteristic

of Constantinianism"; Stanley Hauerwas, "Repent—The Kingdom Is Here," in *Christianity and the Social Crisis in the 21st Century*, ed. Paul Raushenbush (New York: HarperCollins, 2007), 174. See also Stanley Hauerwas and William H. Willimon, *Resident Aliens: A Provocative Christian Assessment of Culture and Ministry for People Who Know That Something Is Wrong* (Nashville, Tenn.: Abingdon, 1989).

117. Toward the end of his important work, Milbank argues, "There can only be a distinguishable Christian social theory because there is also a distinguishable Christian mode of action, a definite practice. The theory explicates this practice, which arose in certain precise historical circumstances, and exists only as a particular historical development. The theory, therefore, is first and foremost an ecclesiology, and only an account of other human societies to the extent that the Church defines itself, in its practice, as in continuity and discontinuity with these societies. As the Church is already, necessarily, by virtue of its institution, a 'reading' of other human societies, it becomes possible to consider ecclesiology as also a 'sociology.' But it should be noted that this possibility only becomes available if ecclesiology is rigorously concerned with the actual genesis of real historical churches, not simply with the imagination of an ecclesial ideal"; Milbank, *Theology and Social Theory: Beyond Secular Reason*, 2nd ed. (Malden, Mass.: Blackwell, 2006), 382.

118. Immanuel Kant, *Critique of Pure Reason* [1781/1787] (Indianapolis: Hackett, 1996), A805/B833, 735.

119. A discussion of the epistemological—and possibly ontological—implications of this schema for framing interdisciplinary exchanges around religion and social problems falls outside the scope of this introduction. Suffice it to say that this Kantian or neo-Kantian framework challenges the one-sidedness of the nomological sciences and the hermeneutical sciences, or of positivism and postmodernism. Religious phenomena, for example, should not be reduced to their instrumental role in addressing social problems, while social problems are not texts to be interpreted.

120. Chapters were classified based on the disciplines and research questions they were deemed to prioritize. This said, while some of the chapters clearly align with one of the three approaches, other chapters—being more intentionally interdisciplinary, for example—could fit within more than one of these approaches.

PART I
Public Religion and Community Revitalization

Talking About Homelessness

Shifting Discourses and the Appeal to Religion in America's Seventh-Largest City

James V. Spickard

Talk matters. This is not news. Scholars from Epictetus to W. I. and Dorothy Thomas have argued that "if men define situations as real, they are real in their consequences."[1] How we frame a social problem shapes how we try to solve it. This is as true for homelessness as it is for racial and ethnic conflicts, a country's tendency to go to war, or environmental change. The terms we use to grasp these problems shape the solutions we consider.

A decade ago, Anthony Marcus noted that "the social problems that drove men and women to beg for change or just pass idle days in public could have been understood . . . in a variety of . . . ways."[2] People could have noticed a lack of affordable housing, in which case providing housing would have been an obvious answer. People might have focused on an employment crisis, which would have recommended public works jobs. The situation could equally have been read as a crisis of public health, or of education, or indeed as a combination of all of these (which is surely the case).

However, none of this happened. Instead, the dominant discourse presented homelessness as a crisis of individuals. It focused on their addictions, their mental health, their disabilities, their work difficulties, their fractiousness, their lack of skills, or their personal bad luck. The result was a series of individual solutions: drug rehab, A.A., mental health programs, medical care, job skills training, résumé writing, or helping unhoused people fill out applications for public assistance. Though these all aided individuals, none addressed the systemic problems that increased homelessness in the first place. As Vincent Lyon-Callo pointed out in his case study of a homeless shelter in Northampton, Massachusetts, training individuals to write applications for jobs that do not exist can distract even shelter workers from identifying sources of housing that are readily available.[3]

Like all discourses, talk about homelessness changes from time to time and place to place. Some elements are relatively stable, such as the distinction between the "worthy" and the "unworthy" poor, between "locals" and "transients," or between those "ready to help themselves" and those "trying to milk the system." These ideas have dominated much of American history.[4] They portray homelessness as a matter of flawed individuals, typically vagrant, on whom government aid was wasted.

In contrast, the 1930s Great Depression produces a different view. A crashed economy, massive unemployment, and capitalism's seeming inability to restore prosperity prompted government action. Public works projects, income support, and a host of new financial regulations were intended to stabilize markets while aiding the poor. Later federal spending on the G.I. Bill, defense and aerospace, and the Interstate Highway system stimulated the economy and created a new, professionally based middle class.[5] Keynesian management produced a stable economy, decreased social inequality, and created a decades-long dearth of street homelessness. It was not until the economic crises of the early 1980s that homelessness again became a major part of American city life.[6]

By then, however, Ronald Reagan had been elected president on a platform that saw government as the problem, so government solutions were not forthcoming. Administration officials argued that deregulated markets are the best means for distributing goods and services in all times and places.[7] Michael Burawoy has called this ideology "third-wave marketization."[8] The periods 1775–1830, 1914–33, and 1980–present each used "market fundamentalism" to dismantle worker protections, shred social safety nets, and deregulate businesses.[9] Each one also increased poverty and social inequality, and each ultimately resulted in an economic crash. The first two waves aroused considerable working-class and religious push-back, exemplified by the Chartist, trade union, and social gospel movements. Despite the economic crises that followed financial deregulation—1989–91, 1997–98, 2001, 2007–8, 2010–12—third-wave marketization has not given those movements much traction.[10]

Burawoy's term "marketization" is attractive, but it leaves out one key element of the contemporary discourse about homelessness: an emphasis on individuals. The term "neoliberalism" does a better job. That ideology combines a belief in the sanctity of markets with a focus on the individual roots of social problems.[11] Prime Minister Margaret Thatcher's famous "There is no such thing as society" quote is typical: neoliberalism emphasizes personal responsibility and the role of the private sector in helping those in need. In Thatcher's words, "The quality of our lives will depend upon how much each of us is prepared to take responsibility for ourselves and each of us [is] prepared to turn round and help by our own efforts those who are unfortunate."[12] Government, in this view, should play at best a minor role.

Thatcher did not talk about religious involvement in helping others, but Americans certainly do. Polling data show stable support for religious groups helping the poor, and those polled even think they are best at doing some of the needed tasks. A 2009 Pew study, for example, showed that 52 percent of Americans thought religious organizations were more effective than private organizations and government at feeding homeless people.[13] Sixty-nine percent said they favored allowing religious groups to apply for government funding to provide social services. Other polls have shown similar support for private-sector charities' involvement in tasks that from the '30s to the '60s were seen as government responsibilities.[14] Neoliberalism prefers such private action. Its emphasis on markets leads it to think private activity is more efficient; its focus on individuals leads it to favor helping people personally rather than changing social systems. The result is a discourse primed to encourage religious involvement in charity work but not in social change.[15]

Jason Hackworth has studied the effects of neoliberal discourse on both city planning and on the work of religious charities. He reminds us that the picture is inevitably complex. "Neoliberalism, like many other '-isms,' is a highly contingent process that manifests itself, and is experienced differently, across space."[16] In this chapter, I shall examine a specific space—San Antonio, Texas—to show the shifts in this city's discourse surrounding homelessness and the effect that discourse has had on its proposed solutions. Please remember: this is a study of discourse, not an evaluation of the San Antonio organizations working to help homeless people. In both discourse and programs, religion plays an important role.

San Antonio, Texas

With a population of nearly 1.5 million, San Antonio is the nation's seventh-largest city. It is, however, only the twenty-fourth-largest metropolitan area because it has annexed almost all of its suburbs, including the wealthy suburbs on its northern tier. The city sprawls across 465 square miles, nearly as many as Los Angeles, which has three times its population. Transportation depends on cars. An inner ring of elevated freeways circles the downtown business district, separating it from heavily Latino neighborhoods to the west and south and a traditionally Black neighborhood to the east (see Figure 1). Those neighborhoods are largely working class and have long been the source of the low-wage labor that serves the city's light industry.[17]

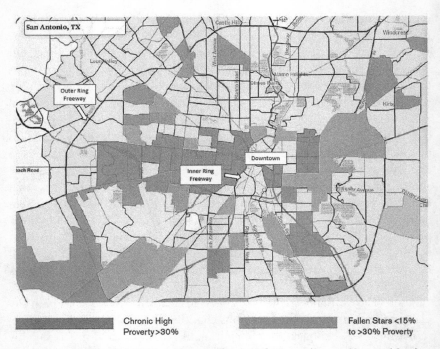

Figure 1. San Antonio Neighborhood Poverty Trends, 1980–2010 (Source: Heywood Sanders, "Cityscrapes: Lands of the Lost," *San Antonio Current*, December 17, 2014, accessed December 6, 2020, www.sacurrent.com)

Whites and upper-income Latinos live to the north and commute to the city center over a series of ring-and-spoke freeways. Housing there is newer, and those areas have the best schools and city services. What little crosstown bus service there is travels north during the morning and back south during the afternoon—carrying maids, cleaners, and others to and from their North Side workplaces. The result is the most income-segregated city in the U.S.[18] and the third-most-economically segregated large city, when one combines income, education, and occupational measures.[19] This inequality primes the city for homelessness.

As in many cities, homeless people have long congregated downtown. They found services and transportation there, and many had previously lived in the chronically poor neighborhoods immediately to the east and west. City leaders have openly worried that having visible homeless in that area would interfere with tourism, the city's third-largest industry.[20] There was thus some pressure to find another place for them. There was, however, also resistance to using a "leaf blower mentality" to force homeless people to move without solving their problems.[21]

In the summer of 2003, San Antonio's then-mayor, Ed Garza, established a Task Force on Hunger and Homelessness to come up with solutions. Chaired by council member Patti Radle, the homelessness subcommittee filed a report in January 2005 that recommended a series of programs for people who are temporarily or episodically homeless, plus a Ten-Year Plan to end chronic homelessness.[22] These plans focused on both systemic and individual risk factors. They involved a combination of emergency shelters, transitional housing programs, permanent supportive housing, and increased public housing, plus "safe havens" for those who cannot follow restrictive program rules. The city council adopted the plan by unanimous vote on January 27, 2005.

This plan is striking, given the neoliberal discourse prominent at the time. Rather than seeing homelessness as a matter of broken individuals, it identified five systemic factors that contribute to homelessness. The first of these was the city's lack of affordable housing, which the report noted had been exacerbated by "a significant reduction in public housing units" in recent years.[23] Other factors were "low-wage jobs that do not pay enough for a worker to afford decent housing," "limited or non-existent transportation to better-paying jobs," and "an educational system that leaves many unprepared for the job market."[24] The only systemic factor that spoke to individual behavior was a "fragmented, under-funded mental health and substance abuse treatment system"—and even that focused on the system, not on persons.[25] The report did list the typical individual risk factors—addiction, mental illness, low education levels, poor financial management, and so on—but it clearly set these in the context of a lack of housing, education, transportation, and jobs.

Moreover, three of the four major Ten-Year Plan elements focused on providing housing rather than just services to meet individuals' needs. The task force had already convinced the city to invest in a Homeless Management Information System (HMIS) to provide one-stop intake wherever a homeless or precariously housed person interacted with police or social service agencies. Plan element 1 involved using that system to match people with the services they need, then expanding those services that incoming data showed were most important. Element 2 was homeless prevention: providing services for those in danger of losing their shelter and rapid rehousing for those who had recently lost theirs. This included measures to ensure that people discharged from hospitals, mental health facilities, jails, and prisons would have somewhere to go other than the street. Element 3 called for use of a Housing First model to tame chronic homelessness. Element 4 involved expanding infrastructure of all kinds: low-cost housing, shelters, treatment programs, and so on. All such services needed to be better coordinated and easier for homeless and marginally housed people to obtain.

This was no individualistically oriented neoliberal document. It called on government to produce systemic solutions, not just focus on individual change.

Systemic solutions cost money, of course, and the task force proposed several ideas for raising it. The city put up its share, but the state legislature denied the city the authority to raise taxes on downtown businesses and gentrifiers to cover the rest. That forced the city to focus on the final plan recommendation: to build a unified homeless services program that would save homeless people from having to walk from place to place and would allow the various service agencies to coordinate their activities. This has shaped San Antonio's subsequent efforts.

Haven for Hope

A year after the Ten-Year Plan's adoption, a new mayor, Phil Hardberger, tasked a new Community Council to End Homelessness with moving the unified services project forward. Chaired by local oil executive Bill Greehey, the Council reviewed homeless services in twelve states and the District of Columbia and visited over 200 homeless facilities throughout the country.[26] They decided to build a twenty-two-acre "campus" a mile and a half from downtown (see Figure 2). There, homeless people could find shelter and all the services they need. The land was available, and it was also far enough from downtown to gain tourist-industry support.

Built between November 2007 and August 2010, Haven for Hope is, according to its 2010 Impact Report,

> the largest, most comprehensive Homeless Transformation Campus
> in the United States. Its vision is to provide a range of social services
> addressing the needs of San Antonio's homeless community (25,000
> annually) by integrating many critical services into a single
> multiservice-campus setting.[27] Most importantly, it is specifically designed
> to tackle the root causes of homelessness. Seventy-eight nonprofit
> and government Partner agencies provide a wide array of critical
> services to the homeless and [the] surrounding community, including:
> education, job training, day care, substance abuse treatment, medical
> care, identification recovery, case management, and animal care
> services.[28]

(Note that the report identifies "the root causes of homelessness" with individuals' problems.)

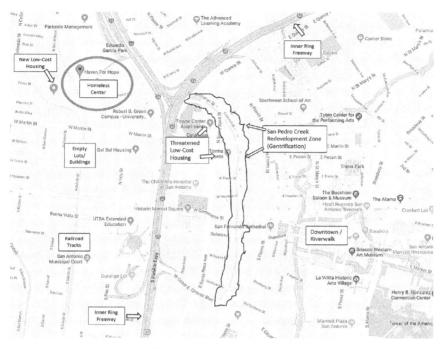

Figure 2. Location of Haven for Hope, 1.5 miles from San Antonio's Downtown

Haven for Hope was formed as an independent 501(c)(3) nonprofit organization in order, said the report, to keep it independent from politics. However, it has always received considerable city, county, and state funding. It has also received several large private donations, including from Greehey himself, who became the first chairman of the board of directors. Fundraising continues to be important, but from all I have been able to learn, the fundraising tail does not wag the programmatic dog. The organization remains resolutely mission-driven. That mission is "to transform and save lives." To do that, Haven's

> goal is to provide homeless individuals and families with the training, skills and assistance needed to help them become self-sufficient, and to do so in a cost-effective and sustainable manner.[29]

To do so, Haven currently partners with some ninety agencies to provide a full continuum of care. Over thirty-five of these agencies have space in Haven's campus. Some are faith-based, others are secular, and still others are governmental. The approach is ecumenical: a prominent current poster lists Haven's four core values as "radical compassion," "servant leadership," "driven by hope," and "pursuit of excellence." The religious tones are obvious, understated, and not at all sectarian.

Haven divides its services into two main programs. Homeless people who can prove nine months of county residence and are drug- and alcohol-free are eligible for the Transformational Campus, which includes shelter and a host of recovery programs and housing assistance. They "must be willing [to] commit to working with a case manager toward a goal of sustained, self-sufficient life."[30] Homeless who are not residents or are not drug- and alcohol-free may sleep on mats in the Courtyard (formerly Prospects Courtyard), where they get meals, communal showers, and basic health and psychiatric care. They must obtain a Texas state ID within thirty days to remain. Though spartan, the Courtyard was designed to be better than the streets. The Transformational Campus's personal recovery program is central to its operation.

Clearly, Haven is not a "Housing First" program, though it has built a 140-unit low-cost housing complex that is open to graduates of the Transformational program and to other low-income families who meet its entrance criteria. It is, instead, a rather traditional continuum-of-care program that seeks to move individuals step by step from the street to housing as they demonstrate their ability to stay sober, employed, and focused on their long-term goals. Though several studies have shown the effectiveness of a Housing First model for chronic homelessness,[31] and despite the mayor's task force's call for this approach, Haven did not take this path.

Indeed, early on (though not now), Haven had a decidedly paternalistic model of care. The 2010 Impact Report listed seven "guiding principles" to govern Haven's operation.[32] They were:

1. Move to a culture of transformation (versus the old culture of warehousing).
2. Co-location and virtual e-integration of as many services as possible.
3. Must have a master case management system that is customized [for each client].
4. Reward positive behavior.
5. Consequences for negative behavior.
6. External activities must be redirected or stopped.
7. Panhandling enables the homeless and must be stopped.

Numbers 1, 2, and 3 are program-oriented, but 4 and 5 assume that homeless people lack self-discipline and need fixing. About 4, the report stated that:

Positive behavior of individuals should be rewarded with increased responsibilities and additional privileges. Privileges such as higher quality sleeping arrangements, more privacy and elective learning opportunities should be used as rewards. It is important that these rewards be used as "tools" to approximate the "real world" in order to increase sustainable reintegration into society.[33]

Elaborating 5:

Too often there are no consequences for negative behavior of individuals. Unfortunately, this sends a message that bad behavior is acceptable. Within the transformational process, it is critical to have swift and proportionate consequences.[34]

These two principles present a distinct picture of homeless people. They portray them as children who are unable or unwilling to conform to ordinary society. The unwilling are excluded—exiled to the Courtyard until they "have decided to take the steps they need for recovery."[35] The willing are rewarded for doing what their caregivers want and punished for failing to do so. Ethnographers James Spradley and Robert Desjarlais have separately shown that street homeless, even mentally ill street homeless, have considerably more personal agency than this approach credits them.[36] Empirical studies of Housing First programs show that forcing homeless addicts to become sober prior to receiving housing does not make them any more housing-stable than does housing them immediately.[37] This paternalism does, however, correspond to the Elizabethan distinction between "worthy" and "unworthy" poor. It insists that poor people prove their virtue before they receive public aid.

In the program discussions that generated this volume, one of the participating scholars pointed out a structural parallel between Haven's approach and Christian images of the soul's final journey. If living on the streets is Hell, then the Courtyard is Purgatory, from which residents can potentially ascend—by way of the Transformational Campus—to the Heaven of being housed. None of Haven for Hope's literature uses such language. Haven does, however, treat residents as needing to purge themselves of their bad habits and attitudes. They need conversion before they are ready to be saved.

The Impact Report's final two principles were directed not toward Haven's clients but toward non-Haven service providers. Principle 6 urged a ban on independent programs to aid homeless people:

External activities such as "street feeding" must be redirected to support the transformation process. In most cases, these activities are well-intended efforts by good folks; however, these activities are very enabling and often do little to engage homeless individuals.[38]

Principle 7 urged a ban on personal charity:

> Unearned cash is very enabling and does not engage homeless
> individuals in job and skills training which is needed to end homeless-
> ness. Additionally, more often than not, cash is not used for food and
> housing but is instead used to buy drugs and alcohol which further
> perpetuates the homeless cycle. Homeless individuals who are panhan-
> dling should be engaged into the transformational process. Further-
> more, most panhandlers are not truly homeless but are preying on the
> good nature of citizens to get tax-free dollars.[39]

These "principles" were not unique to San Antonio but were part of a national movement to crack down on unsanctioned aid to homeless people.
On Los Angeles's Skid Row, for example, Forrest Stuart recorded how police
officers systematically harassed both homeless people and unsanctioned private aid groups in order to force the homeless into the area's three mega-
shelters.[40] They arrested or cited homeless people for jaywalking, sitting on
the sidewalk, and other "lifestyle crimes," dropping the charges if the arrest-
ees enrolled in a shelter program. Stuart pointed out that this did not work.
The church groups kept feeding, and the homeless dropped out of the mission programs a few days after joining. Police, however, thought that they
were doing the right thing. They described themselves to Stuart as "social
workers" dispensing "tough love" in order to force the homeless toward the
services they need.

A few years ago, San Antonio had its own scandal on this score. In 2015 the
city ordered police to ticket street-side feeding programs for violating health
ordinances, though only in the downtown and near-downtown. They made
the mistake of ticketing a licensed food truck operator for dispensing high-
quality meals out of the back of her covered pickup, an activity she had been
doing for years. She sued the city not just for selective enforcement—think
about all those uncited pizza delivery vans—but for the violation of her religious freedom. Texas had passed the Texas Religious Freedom and Restoration Act, which protected activities that were grounded in sincere religious
belief. Nationwide bad publicity made the city back down; they agreed to give
church groups free food-handling classes and to stop harassing homeless people
toward Haven and away from their regular haunts.[41]

Similarly, a year earlier San Antonio Police Chief William McManus had
proposed ticketing drivers who give money to people panhandling on San Antonio's street corners.[42] Bad publicity killed that initiative, too, though the
police department continued to ticket homeless people for lifestyle crimes in
the downtown area.[43]

Times have changed. By late 2015, Chief McManus told the local newspaper that "in the past, police would try to arrest it [homelessness] away, and that is an entirely ineffective approach. There has to be outreach."[44] The department now has a two-officer Homeless Outreach Positive Encounters (HOPE) team that connects homeless people with services.[45] If they can, they do so through Haven for Hope; if not, then they try other sources. The point is still to get homeless people off the streets and into treatment. The means have changed.

Attitudes have changed at Haven as well. The 2010 Impact Report's "guiding principles" are no longer on the center's website or in its literature. In their place are the four "core values" that I listed earlier.

Talking Efficiency

Still, neoliberal discourse has not vanished. It still permeates things said and things not said in San Antonio's homelessness talk. For example, at the time of this writing, Haven for Hope's website defines its mission as follows:

> Our mission is to offer a place of hope and new beginnings. We do this by providing, coordinating, and delivering *an efficient system of care* for people experiencing homelessness in Bexar County [emphasis added].[46]

Note the term "an efficient system of care." Today, as in 2010, Haven presents itself as a cost-effective way to coordinate homeless services. It brings together many different providers, making their work easier to coordinate; it is located near a satellite of the University Health System, which reduces transportation costs for medical emergencies. It simplifies policing. The 2010 Impact Report went into more detail about each of these elements, because it was written to convince "lenders/investors," "donors," "taxpayers," "government," "communities," and the "Community Development Financial Institutions Fund"[47] of Haven's fiscal responsibility and programmatic worth.[48] Even the "communities" category focused on the fiscal impact of building Haven a mile and a half from the downtown:

> The H4H campus is leading to an overall improvement in the downtown west-side San Antonio area. . . . The area was considered depressed and unsafe with vacant buildings and a high incidence of drug usage. H4H is dramatically improving the surrounding area through elimination of vacant, derelict properties and a former waste dump; all formerly frequented by homeless and substance abusers. H4H in essence serves as

a stabilizing anchor tenant for the community. The integration of San Antonio Police, new modern construction, and increased lighting serve to improve safety in the larger West-Side Downtown San Antonio Area.[49]

The point here is not to criticize the report's writers, Haven's management, or city and county officials for this economistic language. Much less is it to impugn Haven's service partners. The point is to note the dominance of this language itself.

That language is part of a bigger picture. In our anti-tax era, city governments cannot fund major social-service projects, and state and federal governments decreasingly do so. Cities must increasingly attend to their national credit ratings, which means they must justify social investments in economic terms.[50] Helping poor people doesn't happen without economic growth and a strict limit to local government debt. This either takes cities out of the public service business or it pushes them toward "public-private partnerships." Cities can grant tax credits to support affordable housing, but this is a finite resource. San Antonio's existing credits fall far short of the 153,000 affordable units that the city estimated were needed in 2013, so few units were built. Journalist Ben Olivo estimated that at its current rate of construction, it would take the city until 2294 to build enough affordable housing for its low-income population.[51]

Interestingly, high-end housing does not suffer the same limitations. It often receives large subsidies, with the expectation that such housing will attract high-income taxpayers. San Antonio recently awarded $10 million in tax abatements to an upscale condominium tower—about $173,400 per unit.[52] A few weeks later, city leaders found themselves scurrying to find alternative housing for people being gentrified out of two low-income downtown apartment complexes.[53] Those leaders did not suggest stopping the conversions, which their own efforts to redevelop the San Pedro Creek had set in motion (see Figure 2). They did not have the legal tools to do so—despite two city task forces that had examined the gentrification problem.[54]

Loss of these 380 low-income apartments will more than erase the gain in affordable units that Haven for Hope built for graduates of its Transformational program.

Haven Today

Today, Haven for Hope is a big operation, central to San Antonio's effort to move homeless people off the downtown streets and into ordinary society. In fiscal year 2016, it reported annual income of a bit under $22.5 million, mostly from donations and grants.[55] It spent $18.3 million on programs and $1.3 million on administration. The 2010 Impact Report's "guiding principles" are gone, and the organization has a more client-centered focus than was once the case. As Haven staff wrote:

> The initial service delivery on campus was based off of [sic] behavioral-based "best practices" in which services were delivered in a "one size fits all" approach. What we immediately learned was that this model of delivering services fostered positive changes for some but not all. The urgency of this problem called for the creation of a task force consisting of Haven for Hope staff and Partner staff. These meetings spearheaded multiple structural changes at Haven for Hope including a system for providing specialized services to different subsets of the homeless population, including veterans, seniors, those who have one or multiple disabilities and families.[56]

Haven embraced this notion of being "a learning organization":

> After extensive research and consultations with experts in the field of recovery, . . . Haven for Hope began to integrate a recovery model to all program services on campus. The recovery model has been used historically for treating symptoms of mental health and addictions, but the significant correlation between recovery, trauma, mental health, addictions, and homelessness provides Haven for Hope the opportunity to become a national pioneer for applying recovery-oriented systems of care to homelessness. These practices include integrating trauma-informed care and person/family-centered planning into our services on campus.[57]

That focus on "trauma-informed care" was evident in my interactions with Haven staff in the autumn of 2017. A senior administrator spoke movingly of the importance of finding out why clients resist Haven's help rather than (as formerly) punishing them for such resistance. He told of a rather argumentative client whom he was able to reach by simply asking him for his story. The trauma of childhood abuse had made him resist all authority. Once he could express this, he could work on it. Care and respect for individuals, the administrator said, can be a key that unlocks many doors.

Spiritual Services

A few pages back, I mentioned a prominent poster listing Haven's four "core values": "radical compassion," "servant leadership," "driven by hope," and "pursuit of excellence." I noted the religious tone of these values, particularly of

the first three. Haven is not an overtly religious organization, though it partners with congregations and faith-based groups. It does, however, have its own
religious components, which it is time to describe.

My first interaction at Haven was with members of the Spiritual Services
team—a core part of Haven's approach to helping homeless people. The team
leaders come from various "faith traditions" and are committed to "interfaith
activism." (These are Haven's preferred terms, though staff seem not to recognize their Christian origins.)[58] Their role, as the website describes it, is to
provide

> spiritual care [for Haven's clients] . . . in recognition that holistic
> healing and transformation include the Spirit, Body, and Mind.

Like the rest of Haven's program, this is a client-centered activity. Spiritual Services staff provide support for personal transformation, but they do not determine the direction that transformation will take. They are not seeking converts,
and at no time did I hear any Haven staffer claim that giving homeless people
religion would help them with their problems. Haven's Spiritual Services approach embodies the core values of radical compassion and servant leadership
just noted.

> Each person at Haven for Hope, whether they live here or work here,
> is prayerfully met in honor and respect for their Human Worth and
> Dignity with openness to their Religious Preference and Culture.[59]

To carry out this work the team solicits volunteers "from across the spectrum
of faith traditions." Activities range from simple contact with Haven residents
in both the Transformational Campus and the Courtyard to delivering Star-
bucks donations to Haven residents, deep listening to their concerns, and in
some cases the establishment of long-term relationships between residents and
a religious community. The last of these, called "Faith Homing,"

> is an opportunity for small groups from a faith community (churches,
> temples, etc.) to engage people staying at Haven, form relationships,
> and invite them into that faith community as a future faith and
> spiritual home.[60]

It is important to note that this is not traditional missionizing. The point is
not to change people's minds but to connect them to a community. As a member of the Spiritual Services team explained it to me, homeless people are cut
off. They lack resources and they lack connections. Giving them access to a
supportive community—of any sort—creates those connections. Haven works
by giving people skills to transform their lives, but they need social connec-

tions once they graduate from the program. Those social connections will steady them as they navigate the swells of everyday life.

San Antonio happens to be full of religious communities. Long-term community organizer Ernesto Cortés Jr. discovered this when he began work in the 1970s on San Antonio's heavily Latinx South and West sides. His training at the Industrial Areas Foundation taught him to begin in places where people are already connected.[61] In Chicago, where the IAF began, that meant neighborhood clubs, barber shops, fraternal organizations, schools, and churches. In San Antonio, the last two of these dominate. Cortés became adept at drawing on local churches' commitment to values to engage church people in the struggle to change San Antonio's civic priorities.[62]

Haven's staff also seek to engage religious congregations' values. As former Spiritual Services director Ann Helmke put it in a video posted on Haven's website, "Real long-term and instantaneous support begins when someone previously without shelter in their life connects with a faith community."[63] The Spiritual Services team member put it to me more strongly, saying that it was the Christian congregations' *duty* to connect with the less fortunate. This was not, in his telling, a matter of short-term charity. It was, he said, a matter of long-term commitment to the welfare of currently homeless individuals.

This notion of religious groups having special responsibility for the care of the less fortunate is a growing part of San Antonio's approach to social problems of all kinds. In 2017, for example, Helmke took a newly created post as the city government's first "faith liaison" and head of its new faith-based initiative. Reporter Elaine Ayala described this as a "new effort [that] promises to connect faith and secular groups, *improve efficiencies and effectiveness*, build capacity and—the initiative's central goal—build resiliency among the city's most vulnerable" [emphasis added].[64] The city provides Helmke's salary and gives her organizational support while she connects the city with faith and secular organizations that can serve public needs directly. These groups are, in Helmke's words, to "fill the gaps. . . . The [city's] goal is to partner more."

Given San Antonio's financial situation, with two-thirds of its budget taken up by police, fire, and other emergency services and years of delayed infrastructural repair needed in its poorer neighborhoods, it makes sense that the city would turn to private agencies. What is striking, however, is that no one seems to find this odd. City resources are spent on safety, utilities, and street repair, not on needy people. The dominant discourse sees poverty as an individual matter, to which charitable groups and individuals are supposed to respond. Governments can coordinate the activities of others, but they should not do most of the work and should certainly not provide most of the resources.

Is it fair to call this "neoliberalism"? For the most part, yes, while recognizing that the city has few alternatives in a low-tax, anti-government state and era. Neoliberalism stresses the importance of efficiency and presumes that private parties are more efficient than public ones. It focuses on individuals rather than on social structures. It treats markets as forces of nature rather than as something to be shaped for social ends. And it resolutely refuses to see markets' role in generating the growing inequality, of which pervasive street homelessness is a visible symptom.[65]

The neglect of structural factors is particularly striking. In none of my conversations with Haven staff did they speak about San Antonio's limited low-income housing. In none did they speak about homelessness's systemic causes. Some of the organization's literature does mention such causes, including a "lack of affordable housing, unemployment, [and] underemployment."[66] That same literature, however, lists programs that address individual, not system, issues, such as "mental illness and substance abuse." Haven's website stresses those as well. Yes, Haven has built some affordable housing, but it is a drop in the bucket compared to what San Antonio needs. It is not the organization's focus. Individuals are.

Interestingly, neoliberal theory does not mention religion or religious organizations. Neoliberal policies merely provide the structures within which religious and other groups operate, mainly by shrinking government and assigning its tasks to "the private sector." This originally meant businesses, whose profit motive was supposed to produce more goods for less money. Yet homelessness programs do not produce profit. Underfunded governments pawn these off to the religious sector, where charitable values are supposed to make profit unnecessary.[67] Either they step forward or no one does.

This has implications for how we understand religion's role in contemporary society. Fifty years ago, the British sociologist Bryan Wilson (1966) claimed that religion in the twentieth century had lost its former central place in society. In the long shift from medieval to modern times, governments had taken over and bureaucratized religions' former social tasks. The welfare office had replaced the poor box, the professional psychologist had replaced the pastoral counselor, and the secular hospital had replaced the houses of care run by monks and nuns. This, wrote Wilson, was the nature of our present era. He did not think that religious organizations would wither away. They would, however, retreat to the private sphere. They would continue to play a role in individuals' lives but not in society as a whole.

Does the contemporary use of faith-based organizations (FBOs) to solve social problems reverse this process of secularization? Does it indicate that religion is becoming more important in the public sphere, rather than less? Perhaps on one level. It is now normal for people to think of religious groups running public welfare programs. "Charitable choice" and various "faith-based initiatives" channel public money to religiously sponsored agencies, which people accept because religions are seen as upholding the common good. This puts religions back in the public sphere.

That's the positive side. At the same time, religious charities cannot change social systems. They lack the power to address the structural conditions that produce homelessness in the first place. They can do nothing to change markets. Unlike governments, which can do all these things, religious groups can at best put bandages on individuals' wounds. They may be in the public sphere, but they cannot shape the public world. This is part of what Wilson said religions once had done but no longer do.[68]

In fact, the turn to FBOs amounts to a shrinking of government rather than an expansion of religion. Like many cities, San Antonio has outsourced compassion. It has asked the nonprofit sector, including faith-based groups, to do what it no longer sees as its job.

Shifting Discourses

Jason Hackworth wrote that neoliberalism "manifests itself and is experienced differently" in various times and places.[69] San Antonio's talk about homelessness largely follows the neoliberal pattern, albeit with specific peculiarities.

The 2005 Mayor's Task Force report was no neoliberal document, in that it emphasized the structural causes of San Antonio's homeless crisis and proposed several government-based solutions. These included increasing the amount of public housing and establishing new streams of tax revenue dedicated to housing expansion, while simultaneously providing better care for those who needed personal support to get on their feet. This would amount, in the famous "river story" attributed to Saul Alinsky, to simultaneously rescuing people from drowning in the river and going upstream to stop whoever is throwing them in.[70]

Haven for Hope is, for the most part, dedicated to rescuing people. Though it began with a rather paternal, tough-love approach, it now speaks a language of compassion, servant leadership, and respect. It emphasizes the importance of identifying and solving people's traumas, which will help them get back on their feet. Yes, it still trains them to write résumés for jobs that might not exist and fill out applications for housing that is too scarce, and it orients its programs to transforming individuals rather than transforming the city in which those individuals live. It remains, to use Craig Willse's provocative term, part of the "homeless management industry."[71] But it plucks homeless people out of the river, as best it can, placing them on what passes for a safe shore.

That, of course, is the problem. San Antonio has less and less affordable housing, and the city's plan to raise the San Antonio's median income by attracting high-end tech workers will gentrify some existing housing away.[72] Efforts to establish Housing First programs founder on the city's low tax base, citizens' unwillingness to tax themselves for major improvements (and the state legislature's unwillingness to allow them to do so), and the city's inability to use the projected savings that Haven was supposed to bring to police and hospital budgets to buy, rent, or build the units that Housing First programs need.[73] Such collective actions attempt to sail against neoliberal headwinds. It is, it turns out, far easier to raise $100 million in charitable donations for an integrated homeless facility that treats individuals than it is for the city to solve its affordable housing crisis as a collective task.

I hope it works. Haven does, in fact, help individuals, often spectacularly. The problem is that pulling individuals out of the river cannot keep other people from falling (or being pushed) in.

Postscript

In the year since this chapter was written, San Antonio has made some progress toward a better way of talking about homelessness. Journalists and others have begun to question the neoliberal discourse that has dominated discussion over the last decades. For example, the establishment-oriented founder of a prominent local online news organization called for greater public funding for Haven, arguing that the city could and should not rely on the private sector to do the public's work. The local Housing First Community Coalition raised money for a seventeen-acre campus to house homeless seniors—and the city changed zoning to make that campus possible. The city hired HomeBase, a national organization with experience with Housing First programs, to develop its next homelessness plan. Most recently, the editorial board of the (rather conservative) local daily newspaper called for a better understanding of homelessness and explicitly cited Housing First as a best practice—a position seconded by a politically moderate local state representative.[74]

These are small but significant steps. They may be signs of change.

Notes

1. William Isaac Thomas and Dorothy Swain Thomas, *The Child in America: Behavior Problems and Programs* (New York: Knopf, 1928). Epictetus framed it

negatively: "What disturbs and alarms man are not actions, but opinions and fancies about actions"; cited in Robert K. Merton, "The Thomas Theorem and the Matthew Effect," *Social Forces* 74, no. 2 (1995): 382.

2. Anthony Marcus, *Where Have All the Homeless Gone? The Making and Unmaking of a Crisis* (New York: Berghahn, 2006), 2–3.

3. Vincent Lyon-Callo, *Inequality, Poverty, and Neoliberal Governance: Activist Ethnography in the Homeless Sheltering Industry* (Toronto: University of Toronto Press, 2004).

4. Kenneth L. Kusmer, *Down and Out, on the Road: The Homeless in American History* (New York: Oxford University Press, 2003).

5. Joseph Bensman and Arthur J. Vidich, *The New American Society: The Revolution of the Middle Class* (Chicago: Quadrangle, 1971).

6. Christopher Jencks, *The Homeless* (Cambridge, Mass.: Harvard University Press, 1994).

7. Neckties depicting Adam Smith became the Reagan Administration's unofficial uniform; see Clyde H. Farnsworth, "Neckties with an Economics Lesson," *New York Times*, July 7, 1982, A16, accessed December 6, 2020, www.nytimes.com; Adam Smith, *Inquiry into the Nature and Causes of the Wealth of Nations*, book 2 (London: W. Strahan, 1776), recounted dozens of historical incidents where government intervention caused economic damage.

8. Michael Burawoy, "From Polanyi to Pollyanna: The False Optimism of Global Labor Studies," *Global Labor Journal* 1, no. 2 (2010): 301–13; and Burawoy, "Facing an Unequal World," *Current Sociology* 63, no. 1 (2015): 5–34.

9. Joseph E. Stiglitz, *Globalization and Its Discontents* (New York: W. W. Norton, 2003).

10. James V. Spickard, "Où est passée la 'voix morale' de la religion? La troisième vague du marché et la montée de l'idéologie néolibérale," *Revue du M.A.U.S.S.* 49, trans. François Gauthier (2017): 148–66.

11. David Harvey, *A Brief History of Neoliberalism* (New York: Oxford University Press, 2007).

12. Margaret Thatcher, "Interview for Woman's Own ('no such thing as society')," September 23, 1987, Thatcher Archive (THCR 5/2/262): COI transcript, accessed December 6, 2020, www.margaretthatcher.org.

13. Pew Forum on Religion and Public Life, *Church-State Concerns Persist: Faith-Based Programs Still Popular, Less Visible* (Washington, D.C.: Pew Research Center, November 16, 2009).

14. Some of these were commissioned by the charity industry and are thus potentially biased—for instance, Philanthropy Roundtable, "Results of an Original 2015 National Poll," accessed December 6, 2020, www.philanthropyroundtable.org; and Independent Sector, *United for Charity: How Americans Trust and Value the Charitable Sector* (Washington, D.C.: 2016).

15. Jason Hackworth, *Faith Based: Religious Neoliberalism and the Politics of Welfare in the United States* (Athens: University of Georgia Press, 2012).

16. Hackworth, *The Neoliberal City: Governance, Ideology, and Development in American Urbanism* (Ithaca, N.Y.: Cornell University Press, 2007), 11.

17. Mark Warren, *Dry Bones Rattling: Community Building to Revitalize American Democracy* (Princeton, N.J.: Princeton University Press, 2001).

18. Richard Fry and Paul Taylor, *The Rise of Residential Segregation by Income* (Washington, D.C.: Pew Research Center, August 1, 2012), 6.

19. Richard Florida and Charlotta Mellander, *Segregated City: The Geography of Economic Segregation in America's Metros* (Toronto: Martin Prosperity Institute, February 2015), 56.

20. "Best Places for Business and Careers: San Antonio," 2017 Ranking, *Forbes Magazine*, accessed March 2, 2018, www.forbes.com.

21. Joel John Roberts, *How to Increase Homelessness: Real Solutions to the Absurdity of Homelessness in America* (Los Angeles: Loyal, 2004).

22. Mayor's Task Force on Hunger and Homelessness, "Ten-Year Plan to End Chronic Homelessness," City of San Antonio, Texas (January 13, 2005).

23. Ibid., 24.

24. Ibid.

25. Ibid.

26. Strategic Development Solutions, *Haven for Hope Impact Report* (San Antonio, Tex.: July 2010), 9.

27. This unattributed figure repeats Mayor Garza's Task Force report, which cited the U.S. Conference of Mayors' 2003 estimate from a survey of homeless providers. The impact report's accompanying claim of "almost 4,000 [homeless] on any given night" is considerably higher than any of the city's existing point-in-time counts (2011–18). For example, the 2018 count found 1,353 unsheltered adults and children, including 648 who were sleeping at Haven's outdoor Courtyard; see SARAH, *Summary Report: San Antonio / Bexar County 2018 Point in Time Count* (San Antonio, Tex.: South Alamo Regional Alliance for the Homeless, 2018), https://goo.gl/ii5pds. The local agency conducting the count does not report its counting method, which I suspect is not thorough. On the complexities of point-in-time counts, see Spickard, "Extended Example: Counting the Homeless," in *Research Basics: From Design to Data-Collection in Six Steps* (Thousand Oaks, Calif.: Sage, 2017), 326–53; and Daniel Fleming and Patrick Burns, *Who Counts? Assessing the Accuracy of the Homeless Count* (Los Angeles: Economic Roundtable, November 2017).

28. Strategic Development Solutions, *Haven for Hope Impact Report*, 3.

29. Ibid., 4, 8.

30. "Getting Help," on the website of Haven for Hope, accessed March 17, 2018, www. havenforhope.org.

31. Deborah Padgett, Benjamin Henwood, and Sam Tsemberis, *Housing First: Ending Homelessness, Transforming Systems, and Changing Lives* (New York: Oxford University Press, 2015); Jack Tsai, Alvin S. Mares, and Robert A. Rosenseck, "A Multi-Site Comparison of Supported Housing for Chronically Homeless Adults:

'Housing First' Versus 'Residential Treatment First,'" *Psychological Services* 74, no. 4 (2010): 219–32; Danielle Groton, "Are Housing First Programs Effective? A Research Note," *Journal of Sociology and Social Welfare* 40, no. 1 (2013): 51–63; but see Stefan G. Kertesz et al., "Housing First for Homeless Persons with Active Addiction: Are We Overreaching?" *Milbank Quarterly* 87, no. 2 (2009): 495–534.

32. Strategic Development Solutions, *Haven for Hope Impact Report*, 10.

33. Ibid., 45.

34. Ibid.

35. "Get Help," Haven for Hope, accessed August 1, 2017 (webpage since removed). This phase was on Haven for Hope's website in mid-2017 but is not there at the time of this writing (March 2018). Haven's website changes frequently and often radically, as the program changes its policies and emphases. The various page quotes are accurate as of the date they were collected.

36. James Spradley, *You Owe Yourself a Drunk: An Ethnography of Urban Nomads* (Boston: Little, Brown, 1970); and Robert Desjarlais, *Shelter Blues: Sanity and Selfhood Among the Homeless* (Philadelphia: University of Pennsylvania Press, 1997).

37. Sam Tsemberis, Leyla Gulcur, and Maria Najae, "Housing First, Consumer Choice, and Harm Reduction for Homeless Individuals with a Dual Diagnosis," *American Journal of Public Health* 94, no. 4 (2010): 651–56; Tsai, Mares and Rosenseck, "Multi-Site Comparison of Supported Housing for Chronically Homeless Adults," 219–32.

38. Strategic Development Solutions, *Haven for Hope Impact Report*, 45.

39. Ibid.

40. Forrest Stuart, *Down, Out, and Under Arrest: Policing and Everyday Life in Skid Row* (Chicago: University of Chicago Press, 2016).

41. Terrence McCoy, "What Happened When This Feisty Woman Got Fined $2,000 for Feeding the Homeless," *Washington Post*, April 20, 2015, accessed December, 6 2020, www.washingtonpost.com; Mark Reagan, "SAPD Ticketed Good Samaritan for Feeding Homeless People," *San Antonio Current*, April 14, 2015, accessed December 6, 2020, www.sacurrent.com; Iris Dimmick, "City Council to Consider Homeless Feeding Policy," *Rivard Report*, October 9, 2015, accessed December 6, 2020, www.sanantonioreport.org.

42. Josh Baugh, "McManus Proposes Plan to Ticket Drivers for Giving to Panhandlers," *San Antonio Express-News*, September 3, 2014, accessed December 6, 2020, www.mysanantonio.com.

43. Alexa Garcia-Ditta and Elaine Wolff, "SAPD Issues Thousands of Tickets for Homelessness," *San Antonio Current*, October 21, 2014, accessed December 6, 2020, www.sacurrent.com.

44. Baugh, "City to Change How It Handles Homelessness," *San Antonio Express-News*, December 8, 2015, accessed December 6, 2020, www.expressnews.com.

45. Josh Brodesky, "Hope for Homeless from a Pair of Cops: Where Typical Policing Failed, Officers Find Ways to Help Mend Lives," *San Antonio Express-News*, May 7, 2017, accessed December 6, 2020, goo.gl/EsCnp1.

46. "Mission Statement," Haven for Hope website, accessed March 17, 2018, www.havenforhope.org.

47. The fund sold the tax credits that Haven used to underwrite its construction.

48. Strategic Development Solutions, *Haven for Hope Impact Report*, 2.

49. Ibid., 35.

50. Hackworth, *Neoliberal City*, 17–39.

51. Ben Olivo, "San Antonio Is on Pace to Fill Its Affordable Housing Gap . . . by 2294," *Folo Media*, February 7, 2018, accessed December 6, 2020, www.folomedia.org.

52. Richard Webner, "City Awards $10M in Incentives for Luxury Condo Tower—$173,400 for Each Unit," *San Antonio Express-News*, January 26, 2018, accessed December 6, 2020, www.mysanantonio.com.

53. Dimmick, "Officials Seek Quick Fixes for Downtown Housing Affordability Issues," *Rivard Report*, February 26, 2018, accessed December 20, 2020, www.sanantonioreport.org.

54. The first of these task forces was created in the wake of the 2014 displacement of long-term residents of a southside mobile home park; see Marisol Cortez, *Making Displacement Visible: A Case Study Analysis of the "Mission Trail of Tears"* (San Antonio, Tex.: Vecinos de Mission Trails, May 2, 2017). The second is reporting to the city council as I write; see Dimmick, "Housing Task Force Recommends Sweeping Changes to Alleviate Market, Policy Shortfalls," *Rivard Report*, June 20, 2018, accessed December 6, 2020, www.sanantonioreport.org.

55. Guidestar, "Non-Profit Report: Haven for Hope of Bexar County," generated March 16, 2018, www.guidestar.org.

56. Ibid.

57. Ibid.

58. I am indebted to Lynn Davidman for reminding me that not all religions involve "faith" (personal communication, October 15, 2017).

59. "Spiritual Services," Haven for Hope website, accessed March 17, 2018, www.havenforhope.org.

60. Ibid.

61. The Industrial Areas Foundation (IAF) was founded in Chicago by Saul Alinsky. Its organizers attempt to build coalitions of neighborhood and other local organizations to advocate for ordinary people's needs; see Alinsky, *Reveille for Radicals* (New York: Random House, 1946).

62. Warren, *Dry Bones Rattling*; Lea Thompson, "COPS/Metro Alliance: 40 Years of Community Change," *San Antonio Report*, April 15, 2016, accessed March 17, 2018, www.sanantonioreport.org.

63. Haven for Hope, *"Haven for Hope—in Our City Final,"* Vimeo video, 6:40, December 10, 2014, accessed December 6, 2020, www.vimeo.com/114146395.

64. Elaine Ayala, "'In the City for Good,'" *San Antonio Express-News*, June 17, 2017, accessed December 6, 2020, www.expressnews.com.

65. There is considerable literature on America's growing inequality and its relationship to homelessness and to neoliberalism. Among the most readable is

Lyon-Callo, *Inequality, Poverty, and Neoliberal Governance*. Craig Willse, *The Value of Homelessness: Managing Surplus Life in the United States* (Minneapolis: University of Minnesota Press, 2015) is more radical and sometimes over-ideological.

66. Guidestar "Non-Profit Report: Haven for Hope of Bexar County," generated March 16, 2018, www.guidestar.org.

67. David Ashley and Ryan Sandefer, "Neoliberalism and the Privatization of Welfare and Religious Organizations in the United States of America," in *Religion in the Neoliberal Age: Political Economy and Modes of Governance*, ed. Tuomas Martikainen and François Gauthier (Farnham, Surrey: Ashgate, 2013), 109–28.

68. For more on religion and neoliberalism, see Martikainen and Gauthier, eds., *Religion and Neo-Liberalism: Political Economy and Governance*.

69. Hackworth, *Neoliberal City*, 11.

70. Randall Shelden and Daniel Macallair, *Juvenile Justice in America: Problems and Prospects* (Long Grove, Ill.: Waveland, 2008), 62.

71. Willse, *Value of Homelessness*.

72. City of San Antonio, *Comprehensive Housing Needs Assessment and Strategic Housing Plan* (San Antonio, Tex.: June 2013); Cortez, *Making Displacement Visible*.

73. Padgett, Henwood, and Tsemberis, *Housing First*.

74. Robert Rivard, "Haven for Hope Merits Greater Public Funding," *San Antonio Report*, December 9, 2018, accessed December 6, 2020, www.sanantonioreport.org; Dimmick, "Council Approves Zoning for Campus to House Homeless Seniors," *San Antonio Report*, November 9, 2019, accessed December 6, 2020, www.sanantonioreport .org; Editorial Board, "Wanted: A Better Conversation about Homelessness," *San Antonio Express-News*, January 8, 2020, accessed December 6, 2020, www.expressnews .com; and Ray Lopez, "Lopez: State Needs to Focus on Housing First Policy," *San Antonio Express-News*, January 8, 2020, accessed December 6, 2020, www .expressnews.com.

Becoming More Effective Community Problem Solvers

Faith-Based Organizations, Civic Capacity, and the Homelessness Crisis in Puget Sound

Manuel Mejido Costoya and Margaret Breen

Call it religion, patriotism, sympathy, love of humanity, or love of God. Call it what you will. There is a force that overcomes selfishness and drives it out. It is a force beside which all others are weak. Anywhere people have ever lived, it has shown its power. Today, as ever, the world is filled with it. The person who has never seen or never felt it is to be pitied.

This force of forces now goes to waste, or it assumes perverted forms. We may use it, if we but choose. All we have to do is give it freedom and scope. We are made for cooperation, like rows of upper and lower teeth. One thing alone prevents harmonious social development: the wrong that produces inequality.

—HENRY GEORGE, *PROGRESS AND POVERTY*

The Puget Sound region of the Pacific Northwest exemplifies the dilemmas of late-modern urban life in America, specifically as it relates to rising income and wealth inequalities, decreasing social mobility, and unequal access to housing, education, and health care.[1] Anchored by Amazon and Microsoft, Greater Seattle is one of the leading technology hubs in the United States.[2] It also has one of the highest minimum wages in the country;[3] a rapidly growing—tolerant, diverse, and innovative—millennial population;[4] and has long been considered a pacesetter in terms of sustainable development.[5]

Contrast this with the fact that the region has been in a homelessness state of emergency since at least 2015;[6] and, that among major U.S. cities, Seattle has the largest share of homeless individuals measured as a percentage of the total population.[7] Indeed, a recent study found that in Seattle and King County the number of individuals experiencing homelessness has increased directly with the fair market rent, which correspondingly has risen in line with the region's real GDP, driven by the growing number of high-income digital workers.[8] How can a region that is considered a bastion of progressive values and millennial culture, one that often tops the lists in terms of quality of life and environmental sustainability, a frontier of the innovation economy, and a gateway to the emerging center of gravity of the global economy, Asia-Pacific— how can such a region also have one of the most egregious homelessness problems in the country?

Furthermore, once considered an anomaly because of its relatively large "unchurched" population, the Pacific Northwest has come to exemplify the country's changing religious landscape as, increasingly, a growing proportion of individuals across the United States do not identify with any particular faith tradition.[9] We must not, however, confound the transformation in individual religiosity with accounts of religious decline.[10] It is not only that this change in individual religiosity—the increase in share of the religiously unaffiliated— could in the long run end up complementing and adding ferment to communities of faith and their organizations.[11] In addition, though the U.S. public is becoming less religious, an analysis of the role of faith-based organizations (FBOs) in American civic life could very well reveal that religion is as vibrant as ever, both in the Pacific Northwest and across the country.[12] Against simplistic accounts of religious decline, Puget Sound thus offers a natural experiment to study the civic engagement of FBOs in a context characterized by the prevalence of religious "nones"—indeed, a context that captures what at the national level is considered to be a transformation in individual religiosity.

Grappling with these dilemmas of late-modern life in Puget Sound, we launched a three-year initiative that sought to explore how FBOs could more effectively respond to the homelessness crisis in the region.[13] Oriented by the action research framework, our aim was to generate knowledge, in collaboration with local FBOs and other stakeholders, that could be used to strengthen the capacity of these same FBOs to be better problem solvers and, consequently, to be more effective catalyzers of social change. This knowledge base would then be made available in the classroom to train future religious leaders, urban planners, nonprofit executives, and policy analysts.

Our initiative comprised two phases: a study of faith-based responses to homelessness across the region and a capacity-building pilot with a cohort of local FBOs. Anchored in grounded theory, the study we conducted between the fall of 2016 and the fall of 2018 provided the conceptual underpinnings for the pilot we rolled out between the winter of 2018 and the fall of 2019, following a community-based participatory research (CBPR) approach. In this chapter we propose to take stock of our initiative. It is divided into two parts, corresponding to the two phases of our project. We will begin by documenting the key findings of our study. In the second part, we will examine the pilot rollout with an eye to the themes that emerged and the lessons that were learned.

Examining Faith-Based Responses to Homelessness

The purpose of our study was descriptive and not explanatory.[14] Our aim was not to test hypotheses, like, for example, "FBOs are more effective than nonsectarian organizations in the provision of emergency shelter." With Barney Glaser and Anselm Strauss,[15] our aim, rather, was "the discovery of theory from data systematically obtained from social research" on the opportunities and constraints faced by FBOs as they strive to address homelessness and revitalize communities around Greater Seattle. Our study comprised two stages: We began by deploying a theoretical sampling strategy, in and through which emerged a picture of Puget Sound FBOs as community problem solvers. We then conducted a series of case studies with the aim of achieving greater depth in our theory building. We consider now these two stages.

Theoretical Building Blocks

Between the fall of 2016 and the fall of 2017, we collected a variety of "slices of data" from the three counties that together constitute the Seattle–Tacoma–Bellevue metropolitan statistical area: namely, King County, which includes the city of Seattle; Snohomish County, to the north; and Pierce County, to the south. Following the established methodological principles of grounded theory,[16] we implemented a "multifaceted investigation" that included: (1) a compilation of data on the strategies to address homelessness of 139 local FBOs and twenty-nine government agencies and community stakeholders working closely with these FBOs; (2) site visits to seventy-eight of these organizations; (3) thirty-five informational interviews with leadership and staff from these organizations; and (4) a review of the literature on FBOs and community development in the United States.

The early stages of our research were marked by an "openness of inquiry" so as to initially gather as much data as possible across the entire field.[17] We catalogued the variety of faith-based responses to homelessness across Puget Sound, from vital direct services to broader support, ranging from community organizing and advocacy campaigns to leadership training and poverty immersion workshops. We also mapped out the government agencies and stakeholders that constitute the region's homelessness response systems, pay-ing particular attention to partnerships with FBOs.

Through weekly three-hour iterations of systematic coding and compara-tive analysis of the data we collected, as breadth gave way to depth, more substantively we found that, while FBOs across Puget Sound have tended to focus on how to provide for the immediate needs of unhoused individuals, in-creasingly, they are aspiring to proactively enhance social protection systems and address the systemic causes of homelessness, such as unaffordable hous-ing and precarious employment. Our sampling and analysis eventually yielded three core categories that proved to have the most descriptive power in rela-tion to what emerged as the main puzzle Puget Sound FBOs are grappling with: namely, how to achieve these more ambitious objectives given their limited resources and capacities. We outline here these three theoretical categories.

Organizational-Institutional Analysis

We submit that there is a tendency for the dominant legacy of methodologi-cal individualism in the analysis of religion and civic activity in American pub-lic life to eclipse the organizational-institutional approach to the role of FBOs in revitalizing local communities.

Through our theoretical sampling, we identified two broad approaches to FBOs and community development, both in the literature and on the ground: One approach considers the role of religious beliefs and practices in fostering civic engagement at the individual level. According to this perspective, reli-gion is positively correlated with volunteering, philanthropy, and being civi-cally active. Religious Americans, the evidence suggests, are more generous neighbors and more conscientious citizens. Intersubjective networks are the "secret ingredient" that explains the "religious edge."[18]

Another approach argues that, perhaps more than the examination of indi-vidual beliefs and practices and the dynamics of face-to-face interaction, the organizational-institutional analysis of FBOs gets to the core of the Tocquevil-lian thesis—namely, the idea that FBOs in the United States are exemplary civil and political associations and, as such, provide a counterfactual case to the European paradigm of secularization.[19] "The religious congregation, for Tocqueville," writes José Casanova, "is the prototype of all voluntary associa-tions of American civil society, and civil associations in turn are schools of democracy that pave the way for political associations, which on their part expand further the techniques and the purposes for more and wider associa-tion in a sort of virtuous circle."[20] Nancy Ammerman, too, echoes this push beyond methodological individualism when she suggests that "American religion has thrived not because it has freed each individual to pursue his or her own spiritual quest or because uniquely viable theological ideas have taken root here, but because American law and society have created a space for voluntary religious communities."[21]

Given the role of FBOs as civil society organizations (CSOs), it is germane, moreover, that the dominance of methodological individualism has also been lamented in the analysis of civic activity more broadly construed. Marshaling what she refers to as a "historical-organizational" perspective, Theda Skocpol, for example, has suggested that survey-based research and counting group membership do not suffice. One needs to inquire into the "organizational capacity" of the various kinds of associations that have flourished in the United States, she maintains.[22]

As our fieldwork progressed, we found that the Pacific Northwest is no exception to the Tocquevillian thesis. In this region, too, FBOs significantly contribute to public life. Yet, approaches to religion and society in the Pacific Northwest have tended to give pride of place to methodological individualism over organizational-institutional dynamics. That is, they have tended to focus on individual beliefs and practices in the context of a large "unchurched" population over the contributions the diverse types of FBOs have made and continue to make to civic life and to community development initiatives and the social welfare system, in particular. Working within the framework of methodological individualism, one important study, for example, provides a dubious distinction between "civic-minded mainline" and "evangelical entrepreneurs" in assessing the different expressions of faith in public in the region. While the first cluster "demonstrates an on-going vitality in its continuing work providing social services to the broader community and influencing social policy," faith communities from the second cluster "do not consider long-term civic involvement valuable"; rather, "they volunteer for community projects on a task- and time-circumscribed basis."[23] A number of the evangelical FBOs we interviewed and visited, like Seattle's Union Gospel Mission and Everett Gospel Mission, however, do not fit this typology, as they are engaged in homelessness-related social service provision, sometimes in partnership with local government, as we will see in the case studies that follow. This Weberian schema of correlating religious worldviews and individual social action, then, is flawed to the extent that it abstracts from the organizational imperatives and resource constraints that different types of FBOs must navigate as the institutional vehicles in and through which communities of faith address social issues.

In our focus group and interviews, moreover, we saw this methodological individualism manifest itself when discussions on the impact of faith-based responses to homelessness were cast by the leadership of FBOs, government agencies, and other stakeholders alike, in terms of, for instance, the importance of including a certain charismatic "influencer" in the meeting agenda; or the need to better leverage volunteers; or again, casting members of communities of faith as potential voters or advocates. While these are no doubt important aspects of faith-based initiatives, they should not eclipse the examination of the organizational contexts and dynamics in and through which these aspects take form.

Congregations and Faith-Based Nonprofits

We submit that the classification of FBOs in terms of two models—the caring communities model exemplified by congregations and the service-organizational model exemplified by arm's-length nonprofits—has much greater descriptive potential for examining the role of these organizations in community development than do other, more traditional typologies, such as religious tradition, denominational distinction, and the like.

As our sampling process advanced, we found that, in addition to, and perhaps more important than, religious doctrines and denominational distinctions, we needed to consider how FBOs, in seeking to address to homelessness, are navigating two distinct organizational settings: namely, the model of "caring communities," exemplified by congregations, and the service-organizational model, exemplified by faith-based nonprofits.[24] Already proposed in the introduction to this volume, the first category includes local churches, mosques, and temples, while the second category includes faith-based service agencies— both those that are incorporated as a 501(c)(3) and those that are under the auspices of a congregation, but operating at arm's length—as well as denominational, ecumenical, or interreligious advocacy and lobbying organizations.

Caring communities are grounded in a "thick" set of shared values that are developed and nurtured over a long period of time and over a wide range of activities. In contrast, service organizations are oriented by "thin" arm's-length or contractual understandings where social interaction is defined through the circumscribed roles of "providers" and "recipients" or "professionals" and "clients." Due to methodological and conceptual distinctions between, for instance, the sociology of religion and public policy studies, most of the scholarship, our review of the literature revealed, has tended to focus exclusively on one of these two models. Each model is correlated with the mobilization of specific resources and capacities to address homelessness. More importantly, perhaps, each model emphasizes a particular understanding of faith in public as well as a particular conception of civil society, not to mention a specific formulation of the "social problem" at hand. Indeed, this organizational distinction between congregations as caring communities and arms-length faith-based nonprofits is a more robust framework for grappling with the role of religion in public than, say, church-sect typologies, theological differences, and the like.

Civic Capacity

We submit that the impact that FBOs have in community development processes has tended to be cast in terms of wielding democratic power through contestation or fostering social capital through deliberative exchanges. Pride of place needs to be given to a third frame of reference: namely, the civic capacity to implement initiatives in collaboration with government and other stakeholders.

As our data collection, coding, and analysis homed in on the distinction between congregations and arms-length faith-based nonprofits from an organizational-institutional perspective, it became increasingly apparent that we needed a theoretical category that could capture the challenges these organizations faced as they attempted to address the region's homelessness crisis, given their capacity constraints, on the one hand, and their aspirations for social change, on the other. We found such a framework in the notion of "collective problem solving," an analytical tradition in the theory and practice of local democracy, inaugurated by Tocqueville[25] and developed by the pragmatist tradition, represented by John Dewey in particular,[26] that pushes beyond the important dynamics of contestation and deliberation and focuses on how FBOs deploy their "civic capacity" in collaboration with other stakeholders.[27]

When the frame of reference is democracy as a contest among interest groups, either in the form of elite control or pluralist bargaining,[28] the emphasis is on faith-based community organizing initiatives and coalitions as they strive to reshape government policy through the exercise of participatory democratic practices. As such, FBOs are understood first and foremost as critics of government and social policy rather than as channels for government-funded social services.[29] From this perspective, FBOs contribute to "democratic renewal"—to overcoming the democratic deficits and legitimation crisis associated with postindustrial society and the logic of neoliberal urban governance.[30] The community organizing and advocacy campaigns of scores of congregations and arms-length faith-based nonprofits throughout Puget Sound against the removal of unsanctioned encampments or for the sitting of permanent shelters we documented through our fieldwork are examples of this prophetic, contestatory role of FBOs.

By contrast, when the frame of reference is democracy as a collective process focused on advancing mutual understanding in and through dialogue, transcending strategic action and open to a process of social learning,[31] pride of place is given to FBOs as "schools of citizenship" that, teaching deliberative rather than purely competitive behavior, foster civic virtues and generate social capital, bonds of trust that are the building blocks of resilient communities.[32] Here, drawing on religious worldviews and precepts, with communitarianism and civic republicanism, FBOs contribute to framing homelessness in a manner that challenges liberal—minimalist—institutional arrangements.[33] Caring for the individual experiencing homelessness is never simply a brick-and-mortar issue. Providing shelter is always linked to the ultimate value of "home" in and through, for instance, restoring right relationship, enabling human flourishing, love of neighbor, filial piety, compassion, and the like. In this sense, FBOs also contribute to ensuring that the field of community development is not reduced to a matter of just, for example, creating employment or housing units. The numerous ecumenical and interfaith gatherings and vigils, testimonials, and statements against homelessness and in favor of affordable housing organized by FBOs throughout Greater Seattle we documented are examples of deliberative practices and consensus building.

Now, while the role of FBOs as sources of democratic power and social capital—contention and consensus—are vital, they do not get to the core of the practices and processes that constitute community development today. With Xavier de Souza Briggs, we argue that the idea of democracy as "collective problem solving" more accurately frames what is involved in community development, especially in the decentralized and rhizomatic context of devolution and network governance.[34] Encompassing the dynamics of contestation and deliberation, this frame of reference focuses on the "civic capacity" of FBOs, which is "not merely the capacity to set directions collectively but also to devise and implement the means of acting together more effectively, with and beyond government."[35]

Civic capacity blurs the traditional divide between direction setting and outcomes, policy making and implementation. It is about "effective public action," the fusion of legitimacy and productive capacity. While "legitimacy confers vital informal authority to be heard in the public square, to act on public problems, and to have other players respond to one's actions," "productive capacity is the means for learning, adapting, and operating to generate visible results."[36] The implementation of a tiny house village, an emergency shelter, or a safe parking initiative on church land and the rollout of a job insertion program for homeless individuals are manifestations of civic capacity.

We refer to FBOs as "community problem solvers" when framing the local revitalization efforts of these organizations in terms of the civic capacity to experiment with new modalities of catalyzing effective social change. As part of our theory building, with this concept we intend, then, to bring forth what emerged as the most systematic and significant feature of our sampling process: namely, that FBOs are exploring ways of coproducing, together with government and other stakeholders, innovative responses to homelessness. Leveraging opportunities and negotiating constraints through experimentation,[37] congregations, and faith-based nonprofits, in different ways, strive to blend local knowledge and professional knowledge,[38] the adaptability of bottom-up civic engagement, and the complexities of top-down programming to rethink homelessness interventions.[39] Structuring our field of study in this manner, we identified a number of types of interventions in and through which these innovation-driven efforts of FBOs are channeled, including community economic development strategies; social service provision; and the functioning as intermediaries between governmental and nongovernmental actors. The three case studies we will now consider examine the role of FBOs as intermediaries.

FBOs as Intermediaries—Three Case Studies

With the aim of deepening our emergent theory, between the winter of 2017 and the fall of 2018, we conducted three case studies of initiatives that were currently being rolled out by Puget Sound faith-based nonprofits in an effort to foster greater synergies between governmental and nongovernmental responses to homelessness. As is typical in small-N research, our sampling logic was guided by our analytical aims, the potential of "structured focused comparisons," and an emphasis on "extreme situations" where the process in question is "transparently observable."[40]

   In broad strokes, our sampling strategy was as follows: We began by selecting the most innovative of the Puget Sound faith-based initiatives we had catalogued during the first stage of our research. We then tabulated this subset of initiatives by the FBO typology (congregations and faith-based nonprofits) and intervention types (for instance, community economic development strategies; social service provision; and the functioning as intermediaries). From here we selected the most promising three cases: namely, the Network Builders program of Catholic Community Services of Western Washington, King County in particular; the interfaith and cross-sectoral campaign against family homelessness spearheaded by Associated Ministries of Tacoma-Pierce County; and the Para-Navigator partnership between Everett Gospel Mission and the municipal government of Snohomish County. Representing the three principal Christian denominations—Catholic, Mainline, and Evangelical—as well as the three counties covered in our study, these case studies, moreover, emphasize how the organizational and capacity dynamics we are seeking to describe here are fundamental and ubiquitous, cutting across religious doctrine and local policy and stakeholder contexts.[41] Cognizant of the limited space available, we will now sketch the main contours of these three case studies.

Catholic Community Services of Western Washington's Network Builder Initiative

In 1979, at the time of his appointment, Archbishop Raymond Hunthausen mandated the then and current president of Catholic Community Services of Western Washington (CCSWW)—Michael Reichert—to unite, organize, and develop the five Catholic Charities agencies across its jurisdiction.[42] These agencies had emerged from local efforts to aid the poor and, by the end of the 1970s, operated with a combined budget of $4 million and a staff of approximately 200 people.[43]

In the forty years since, these regional efforts have been developed into one of the most established and well-resourced FBOs in the state of Washington, if not the United States.[44] CCSWW and its sister agency, Catholic Housing Services (CHS), now employ 3,636 staff and 9,011 volunteers and command a total budget of $176 million, 76 percent of which originates from government contracts.[45] In terms of homelessness services in King, Snohomish, and Pierce counties, CCSWW-CHS operates 2,356 affordable housing units and five family centers that provide navigation to shelter and other services and is a primary partner in each county's mandated homeless response system through their joint administration and operation of the Coordinated Entry System, emergency shelters, and significant rapid rehousing dollars.

Despite having apparently fulfilled his mandate through this growth and consolidation of Catholic Charities, Reichert has, in recent years, begun to question the organization's impact. In the face of persistent and increasing homelessness across the region he has suggested that, in fact, the agency's development has come at the expense of vulnerable communities and their ability to solve problems at the local level. Accordingly, in the early 2000s, in an effort to develop more grassroots responses, Reichert instructed CCSWW leadership to figure out how they might bring organizational resources more effectively to bear in support of parish-led responses to problems like homelessness. The Network Builder initiative emerged in this context.

Mary Wahl, CCSWW network builder for the Northwest, assesses the particular value of parish-led responses this way:

> Parishes have historically proven to be champions for those needing emergency assistance and a safe, supportive environment. They are the

primary players within the Catholic system when it comes to creating responses to the poor and homeless, and must thus be at the community table for conversations and planning.

At the same time, she also notes that the particular skills CCSWW offers would be better leveraged if it could find a way to partner more effectively with parishes:

> CCSWW has proven skills for community project management, an understanding of community services coordination, experience providing services, knowledge of funding sources, and decades of being at the community table for conversations and collaboration.

But, notes Patty Repikoff, director of the Network Builder initiative, there is a problematic fragmentation between these two arms of the Catholic response to social problems: "CCSWW was formed out of parishes and out of parish need," she explains, "and over 100 years, [CCSWW] has gotten huge and . . . really lost contact with the parishes." Local church leaders and members express frustration, she reports, at the difficulties they experience accessing help when a need arises, and there is concern among parishes that CCSWW, with an increasingly non-Catholic staff, significant government funding, and secular feel, is not "really Catholic."

In response to these dynamics, CCSWW developed the role of network builder within a larger response called the Catholic Initiative for Poor Families and Communities. In November 2017, three regional network builders, recruited for their knowledge of the Catholic Church as much as their experience in social services, began their work rebuilding relationship with parishes. These network builders, Wahl suggests, "bring CCSWW skills and support to the local church as a technical adviser, an intermediary, a conveyer, and a facilitator in order to implement solutions rooted in the community."

Wahl's work at St. Pius X Church in Mountlake Terrace, Snohomish County, is held up by CCSWW as emblematic of the type of results this initiative aims to produce. Early in her tenure as network builder, Wahl met with Fr. Cal Christiansen, one of the priests at St. Pius X Church, who explained his congregation's desire to develop resources for parish volunteers struggling to help homeless and vulnerable neighbors within a chronically under-resourced social service system. The parish wanted to develop affordable housing on two acres of land next to the church, as well as renovate a large property to house critical support services. Wahl facilitated a planning and implementation process that encouraged the parish to look for partners outside of the Catholic system. Conversations ensued with representatives from the

local food bank, city and county government, Everett Gospel Mission, the local hospital district, and housing providers. Through these efforts the group
decided to embark upon the support services project as the most helpful first
step and developed a plan whereby St. Vincent de Paul and Pregnancy and
Parenting Support (PREPARES), two service providers within the Catholic system, would operate from the newly renovated building.

The CCSWW leadership believes that the network builder initiative will
be successful only if there is support from the wider Catholic system. CCSWW
understands that, without the backing and buy-in of local bishops, priests, and
Catholic partner agencies like St. Vincent de Paul, this effort cannot gain traction at the parish level. After focusing on securing early backing at the archdi-
ocesan level and then with local priests like Fr. Christiansen helping to generate
tangible projects, CCSWW is now starting to roll out new staff positions in
support of smaller clusters of parishes where energy and needs are presenting
themselves.

Associated Ministries of Tacoma-Pierce County's Campaign
to End Family Homelessness

Emerging out of the ecumenical movement over a century ago and incorporated as a nonprofit in 1969,[46] Associated Ministries (AM) has been exploring
for some time now leveraging its traditional role as convener of over 250 local
congregations through a campaign to end family homelessness in the city of
Tacoma, the seat of Pierce County.

During AM's early years, social programs were developed under the shared
ownership of member churches. Eventually, as these programs developed, they
would become independent nonprofits.[47] In the last few decades, however, AM
moved away from incubating nonprofits and instead intentionally developed
in-house programming. In the last ten years, the primary focus of this programming has been on homelessness. Accordingly, AM had to develop the specialized technical knowledge needed to support the funding and execution of
this model of service delivery. With 81 percent of their $3 million revenue in
2017 originating in contracts for four city and county government programs
integral to the countywide response to homelessness,[48] it would seem they
have reached some level of success in achieving this objective.[49]

In August 2015, AM's board of directors saw a troublesome disconnection
with their traditional base—the faith community—and instructed their new
executive director, Michael Yoder—ironically the first director not to be an ordained pastor—to strengthen the ties with local congregations. Yoder saw an
important opportunity to turn AM's attention toward their historical connections and deepen their commitment to interfaith work. He explains,

We are not correcting a wrong. AM's program development is not a problem that has to be fixed. In fact, it has built valuable expertise and stability and has given Associated Ministries a place at the table with government and other agencies.

But, he goes on to say,

if we [AM] could turn our hearts back to our historic role of conveying faith communities and add their voice and assets, their hidden muscle, to the community conversation, we would have the potential to really make a difference in ending homelessness.

AM has thus, in recent years, attempted to develop strategies to integrate local congregations into its work on homelessness. The most visible initiative is a quarterly meeting of faith communities, five of which have been convened by AM since 2017. The aim of these meetings is to educate congregations on issues related to homelessness, provide updates on current interventions, and generate possible projects. AM reports the presence of eighty local faith community members representing fifty-four communities, including a number from non-Christian traditions, at their March 2018 meeting.[50]

Beyond coordinating AM's more programmatic and visible efforts to strengthen ties with local communities of faith, Yoder spends time attending Ministerial Alliance meetings,[51] visiting congregations, and engaging in individual conversation with faith leaders. Based on these interactions, he reports that communities of faith see the potential for congregational revitalization if they could find a way to respond tangibly to homelessness in their neighborhoods. Yet, he says, these churches need support, a road map, and technical assistance. With a city council and press asking the church community to respond urgently and practically to homelessness,[52] and with the precedent of Graduate Tacoma, a campaign that brought the community around local schools to elevate Tacoma schools' graduation rates,[53] Yoder believes AM is well positioned as an intermediary that could mobilize local congregations around a cross-sector movement focused on ending family homelessness in Tacoma and Pierce County.

However, even with a plan on paper for a campaign structure, a budget, and possible funding sources, AM has not been able to fully implement this initiative. While CCSWW was able to leverage institutional infrastructure and resources to build bridges between the arm's-length and congregational energy, AM must rely on the looser ties of their ecumenical heritage and interfaith connections to bring religious communities around this initiative. AM knows that it needs a dedicated staff to communicate, build, and generate buy-in and shepherd projects at the congregational level. Yet, in contrast with CCSWW, it finds itself faced with arguably the more difficult task of having to develop new funds from nonsectarian community partners to put these staff in place.

Everett Gospel Mission and Snohomish County Partnership to Roll Out Para-Navigators

Opening its doors in 1961, a member of the Citygate Network (formally the Association of Gospel Rescue Missions),[54] Everett Gospel Mission (EGM) provides shelter and comprehensive recovery services to over 200 individuals each night. Its historical focus on personal piety and the rescue of "broken" souls manifests itself in EGM's funding and programming in a couple of important ways. In 2017, only 7 percent of EGM's $4.6 million revenue came from local government sources.[55] With this funding, EGM offers services primarily to chronically homeless adults, the demographic the leadership deems is most destitute and chronically underserved. While it has extended its services to include shelter, day services, and recovery programs for single men and women and single women with children, EGM remains dedicated to its original mission of rescuing homeless men.

In a departure from a pietistic understanding of social reform, EGM has chosen to train staff and volunteers in a way that challenges somewhat the assumption that poverty is all about individual responsibility. Sylvia Anderson, EGM's CEO, reports that she is not like other Gospel Mission leaders—not just, she says, as an African American woman, but also in her view on the causes of poverty and her rejection of what she refers to as a "bootstraps approach." She believes that the role of the mission is less to "save the lost" by asking for an individual recommitment to more pious practices and more to understand fully the stories of those the mission serves—the structural barriers they face as well as their personal challenges—and then to come alongside them to build strengths and develop strategies to overcome these barriers.

With this in mind, she and her director of strategic initiatives, John Hull, developed a training program that helps staff and volunteers understand more fully the experience of those without resources as they navigate banking, housing, education, and even social welfare systems. In the last five years, they have extended the reach of their training program and have delivered it to a number of churches alongside a secular version that has been delivered in Everett public schools, in local government, and with first responders. As they have been approached to run these trainings in the community, EGM has become a resource for municipal employees and officials.[56]

One of these officials is Alessandra Durham, a senior analyst for the Snohomish County Executive. In November 2017, Durham convened a faith leaders' roundtable with the initial purpose of "getting to know the faith
community and finding out from them what they needed." It was clear, Durham says, that there was a significant level of frustration at the lack of resources
and a desire to do something about the poor navigability of the resources that
were available as faith communities tried to help community members in need.
The group explored how local congregations might become better equipped,
and at that point, in early 2018, Snohomish County turned to EGM to ask them
to develop their existing training as a way to respond to this question.

Snohomish County asked EGM to prepare a proposal with a view to funding training sessions for the faith community and other interested groups that
would place para-navigators in congregations and other accessible community
spaces. These para-navigators would serve as community referral liaisons that
navigate homeless individuals and families through the human services system and toward the support and stability they need. The proposal develops
EGM's existing poverty immersion curriculum into a series of up to four half-
day workshops designed to train potential navigators about the factors causing
poverty, how to more effectively assess need, and then how to support system
navigation.

These workshops also provide more advanced sessions aimed at congregations who were considering the development of more programmatic responses.
These sessions are designed to help organizational leadership provide services
that align with their organizational goals as well as assess the relative value
and mechanics of programs that focus on providing immediate relief, housing, financial literacy support, and job insertion. The proposal presented also
notes the hope that, as this training builds a constituency of participants with
some common language and understandings, resiliency and the ability to problem solve locally in the face of limited resources will be increased.

John Hull suggests that EGM is especially well positioned to support this
work, not only because they had a curriculum ready to deliver or because they
had credibility as a front-line organization, but because, given their ties to the
Evangelical community, they could help extend the reach of this initiative to
more communities of faith. And as for Durham, she observes:

> This is about equipping and empowering the faith community
> because they know their people better than I ever will and they do this
> work every day. . . . But they have had to do it in a way that is incred-
> ibly frustrating . . . and so, it's about making sure the tools and educa-
> tion are in place for them to do their part.

Indeed, the Snohomish County government also appears to value EGM's role in channeling the participation of local congregations.

Enhancing the Effectiveness of Faith-Based Responses

Our capacity-building pilot was oriented by the action research approach to social-scientific investigation. Anchored in the elements of the emergent—grounded—theory we have just considered, the pilot was more closely aligned with community-based participatory research (CBPR) than with participatory-action research (PAR). The point of departure of action research is the idea that social-scientific inquiry should have an impact on real-life problems and serve as a catalyst for social change.[57] With the risk of oversimplifying, in operationalizing this idea of "usable knowledge," PAR emphasizes the empowerment of disenfranchised groups through radical democratic practices,[58] while CBPR emphasizes the capacity building of local stakeholders for community improvement.[59]

Oriented by CBPR, then, the pilot was designed as a space where FBOs could develop the capacity to problem solve around how to more effectively implement responses to homelessness in collaboration with local government and other community stakeholders. The usable knowledge generated through this exercise, in other words, sought both to increase the legitimacy of FBOs as community problem solvers and to provide them with the organizational capacity to generate concrete results in the fight against homelessness. Moreover, as a process, the pilot had an intentionally experimentalist design: FBOs would come together to learn from the comparison of good practices and develop strategies for their organizations that cannot be determined ex ante, but must instead be discovered in the course of problem solving.[60] As a community of practice, working-group members would pool local knowledge and professional knowledge, place-based "thick descriptions," and the technical model of scientific rationality, integrating the adaptive features of bottom-up civic engagement and the complexities of top-down programming to explore innovative ways of coproducing more effective responses to homelessness.[61]

The list of the twenty-three individuals representing twenty-two organizations that had been selected to participate in one of three working groups—encampments, tiny houses, and emergency shelter and permanent housing—was announced in the summer of 2018 (see Appendix 1).[62] About half of these individuals were either executive directors or congregational heads. Other positions included risk and compliance manager, regional network director, director of strategic initiatives, and homeless task-force lead. At the very least, working-group members had oversight over an initiative related to homelessness in her/his organization.

Fourteen out of the twenty-two organizations operated exclusively in King County, which, as stated earlier, encompasses the city of Seattle. Three operated in Pierce County to the south; two operated in Snohomish County to the north; and three of them operated in all three counties, which together constitute the Seattle–Tacoma–Bellevue metropolitan statistical area. Nineteen of the organizations were FBOs, and three of them were nonsectarian organizations. Of the nineteen FBOs, twelve were arms-length nonprofits, six were congregations, and one—the Episcopal Diocese of Olympia—was a denominational body. Furthermore, sixteen of these FBOs were Christian, two were Muslim, and one was Jewish. Among the sixteen Christian FBOs, seven were Mainline, six were Evangelical, and three were Catholic.

The twenty-two projects the three working groups examined were representative of the diversity of faith-based responses to homelessness we had sampled in our study throughout Greater Seattle.[63] These projects included building and situating tiny houses; advocacy campaigns; the development of emergency shelter and transitional and permanent housing on church land; outreach to unsanctioned encampments; a partnership with a local service agency to increase the resiliency of the newly housed; the rollout of community referral liaisons; a youth outreach and mentoring initiative; a reinsertion program; community organizing for religious land redevelopment; the training of volunteers; trauma-informed child-care and mental health-care services; a linguistically and culturally appropriate job placement program; and the creation of a social business to train and employ homeless youth (see Appendix 2).

There were a number of overarching challenges the working groups considered as they problem solved around how to fine-tune and implement these projects, a number of which we had already come across through our earlier fieldwork. These puzzles included: how to address the causes—and not just the effects—of homelessness; how to innovate around an inadequate social protection system and narrow conceptions of urban growth and social development; how to become more proactive contributors to homelessness responses; and how to navigate between providing for immediate needs and contributing to long-term solutions.

Some of the more specific puzzles the twenty-two organizations grappled with included: how to redevelop religious land for long-term housing solutions given limited resources and a lack of technical knowledge; how to function as a legitimate and effective intermediary between government and local stakeholders as well as between congregations; how to develop legitimate and productive partnerships with FBOs; how to blend local knowledge and professional knowledge to improve the targeting and delivery of social services along the continuum of care; and how to legitimately and effectively harness community resources and local knowledge to improve the quality, coherence, and effectiveness of interventions (see Appendix 2).

In what follows we present six themes that emerged in and through this capacity-building pilot. These themes can be understood as the pathways in and through which civic capacity began to be built; or, what might amount to the same thing, as the usable knowledge the working-group members fostered as they grappled with each other's projects and puzzles. Also integrated into these themes are some of the lessons we learned as we rolled out and supported this experimentalist process.

FBOs Are Turning to Community Economic Development Strategies

Two types of projects were explored in all three working groups as organizations considered, on the one hand, how to address the determinants—and not just the symptoms—of homelessness, and on the other, how to become more proactive contributors to addressing this social problem: namely, religious land redevelopment for long-term housing solutions and the creation of social enterprises to provide job opportunities for unhoused individuals.

For example, Alki United Church of Christ of West Seattle proposed to scale up a pilot program that builds and situates tiny houses in its land and in a nearby encampment, in partnership with encampments residents, government, and other local stakeholders. St. Luke's Episcopal Church in the gentrifying North Seattle neighborhood of Ballard explored how to redevelop their land in order to provide affordable housing and needed community services, including green space and gardening, rainwater capture, and community gardening, as well as providing subsidized rental space to support local social businesses. Seattle Mennonite Church in northern King County's Lake City, too, considered a plan to develop permanent affordable housing units on its land. And New Horizons Ministries, a faith-based nonprofit in downtown Seattle, considered expanding its social business, Street Bean Coffee Roasters, with its focus on job training and employment services for homeless youth.

By combining the market mechanisms and participatory practices of the social and solidarity economy,[64] these community economic development and social business strategies push beyond providing for the immediate needs of individuals experiencing homelessness through mere "assistance" and seek to create wealth, enhance assets, and expand the socioeconomic opportunities in poor or vulnerable neighborhoods in an effort to undercut the "double precarity"

of insecure employment and insecure housing disproportionately experienced by members of vulnerable groups, including the working poor.[65] These
types of projects, moreover, were perceived by working-group members as an
opportunity for FBOs to actively coproduce responses with government and
other stakeholders, as opposed to serving as mere channels of public and private funding or as passive implementing partners.[66]

Congregations and arm's-length faith-based nonprofits must negotiate different capacity and legitimation issues as they attempt to pivot to land redevelopment, social business creation, and other types of community economic
development strategies, like social impact investing and microfinancing, for
example. Lacking the resources and technical knowledge, congregations struggle to implement these types of projects. Alki United Church of Christ
seemed to depend on learning-by-doing to roll out its tiny houses initiative.
Moreover, it was uncertain about the scale or sustainability of its initiative. Having obtained feedback from parishioners and the wider community through
an appreciative inquiry process, the leadership of St. Luke's Episcopal Church
was considering what development options were financially viable and in align-
ment with the congregation's commitment to social justice. In exploring the
different options, however, the leadership had only been in contact with conventional contractors. They had not, for instance, explored alternative approaches to redevelopment or reached out to contractors specializing in
religious land development.[67] And Seattle Mennonite Church, which actually
aimed to engage in land redevelopment while expanding the services offered
to homeless individuals and families at their existing day center, had not yet
conducted a feasibility study of this ambitious project.

While arm's-length faith-based nonprofits do not face the capacity limitations of a congregation, they nevertheless must negotiate the legitimation
issue of whether community economic development strategies undercut
their values and mission. New Horizons Ministries grappled with whether to
expand its social business—Street Bean Coffee Roasters—or enhance its
support services and increase the capacity of its emergency and transitional
shelters to meet the more immediate needs of homeless youth. The tradeoff
this organization was grappling with was not about the legitimacy of market-
based approaches, though. This would be more of a mainline or "progressive" concern. With ties with the Evangelical community, New Horizons
Ministries had faith in markets as mechanisms for unleashing the compassionate engagement of individuals. The issue, rather, was whether addressing systemic causes of homelessness—unemployment—would lead to
entanglements with the quixotic goal of social transformation, which would
consequently distance this faith-based nonprofit from its mission to address

the immediate causes of brokenness and suffering through the rescue of anomic youth from the streets.

FBOs Are Attempting to Enhance the Delivery of Social Services

The working groups examined the challenges FBOs face because of their increasingly important role in patching what was perceived to be an inadequate and ineffective social safety net.[68] More specifically, the three groups problem solved around how congregations and faith-based nonprofits might be able to contribute to innovating Puget Sound's social protection system in order to better address the complexity of the causes of homelessness and the heterogeneity and flexibility of the responses needed.[69] Fourteen out of the twenty-two projects that were considered explored ways to improve the provision of social services along the continuum of care, from prevention and outreach to housing and employment.

Some of the congregations and faith-based nonprofits sought to improve the targeting and delivery of social services in the region. Puyallup Nazarene Church, for instance, proposed to scale up its pilot Wrap-Up initiative through a partnership with a local service agency—Network Tacoma—and Everett Gospel Mission to pair relationship-focused volunteers with professional social workers with the aim of increasing the resiliency of newly housed individuals and families. Seattle Union Gospel Mission examined developing a multiservice outreach team to bring support and resources to individuals living in unsanctioned encampments throughout the city who have been reluctant to accept services. Catholic Community Services of Snohomish County considered developing a plan, in partnership with Everett Gospel Mission and the Snohomish County government, to train community referral liaisons located in congregations—para-navigators—to accompany homeless individuals and families through the human services system and toward the support and stability they need. And Acres of Diamond proposed implementing an initiative to provide in-house trauma-informed childcare services with the aim of allowing residents with greater flexibility as they find employment and housing, while also providing quality, early childhood education.

Other congregations and faith-based nonprofits sought, rather, to enhance the quality, coherence, and effectiveness of social services across Puget Sound. Idris Mosque, for example, examined launching an outreach program, in partnership with its adolescent and young adult members, that seeks to address the educational and vocational needs of young people that are at risk of becoming homeless, especially those that are unemployed and not in school. The social outreach arm of Quest Church—The Bridge Care Center—explored taking to scale a reinsertion pilot program called Advocates Representing the Community, which provides unhoused individuals with the resources and support they need to move toward greater stability. Muslim Housing Services explored rolling out a culturally and linguistically appropriate job placement program in an effort to increase the stability and resiliency of the Seattle and King County homeless families it supports, the majority of which are refugees and first- or second-generation immigrants. And Compass Housing Alliance considered a plan to recruit and train volunteers from congregations in order to optimize the delivery of flexible and appropriate programming that meets the diverse needs of the unhoused population.

Whether they focused on improving targeting and delivery mechanisms or on enhancing the quality, coherence, and effectiveness of interventions, the discussions around this cluster of projects were driven by some variant of the question of how to bring local knowledge to bear on social service provision. By operationalizing religious worldviews and precepts, and as the institutional vehicles in and through which communities of faith address social problems, FBOs function as important catalyzers of local knowledge, understood as those place-based pictures and narratives—"thick descriptions"—used to make sense of the world that differ from professional ways of knowing and doing.[70] With the risk of overanalyzing, while congregations grappled with how to harness community resources and local knowledge to develop or sustain small-scale interventions, faith-based nonprofits grappled with how to enhance existing social services through the blending of local knowledge and professional knowledge. From their particular organizational contexts, each FBO type turned to local knowledge and its correlated bottom-up practices in an attempt to navigate the dilemmas faced by "street-level bureaucracies" and in particular the irresolvability of the "resource problem" and the tensions associated with the "myth of service altruism."[71]

FBOs Serve as Important Intermediaries

As they problem solved around the projects proposed by Associated Ministries of Tacoma Pierce County, Everett Gospel Mission, and the Church Council of Greater Seattle, the working groups gained an increasing appreciation for the important role that the larger, more established arm's-length faith-based nonprofits, in particular, can play as intermediaries among government, stakeholders, and congregations as well as among congregations. In this twofold go-between role, these organizations seek to enhance governmental and nongovernmental action as well as coordinate the structured participation of local communities of faith. These three projects were more about FBOs striving to become hubs of communities of practice than about their potential contribution to community economic development or social service innovation, for example.

As we noted earlier in the case studies, emerging out of the ecumenical movement over a century ago and incorporated as a nonprofit in 1969, Associated Ministries of Tacoma Pierce County explored leveraging its traditional role as convener of over 250 local congregations to spearhead a campaign to end family homelessness in the city of Tacoma, the county seat of Pierce County. Opening its doors in 1961, Everett Gospel Mission, which provides shelter and comprehensive recovery services to over 200 individuals each night, considered launching a community effort to respond to the unsanctioned encampments that regularly emerge adjacent to the organization's headquarters in a way that takes into account the divergent views and interests of the encampment's inhabitants, local businesses, and residents. And, tracing its roots to the Seattle Federation of Churches of the early twentieth century, the Church Council of Greater Seattle, a registered nonprofit organization with membership representing eighteen Christian denominations, considered a model of community organizing that brings together networks of technical knowledge and local support to develop a more integrated approach for congregations seeking to redevelop their land for affordable housing.

While their respective projects had to do more with service delivery and impact, the positions that the two working-group members from Catholic Community Services held within their organization exemplified the efforts by the official social outreach arm of the Catholic Church in Puget Sound and the second-largest faith-based nonprofit in the state of Washington to leverage its role as an intermediary and, in particular, as a networker of congregations or, more specifically, of Catholic parishes. As we noted earlier in the relevant case study, after decades of impressive organizational growth that, nevertheless, coincided with persistent and increasing homelessness in the region, the role of the network builder was created in the early 2000s in an effort to channel the resources of Catholic Community Services to Catholic parishes, with the aim of developing more effective and locally embedded responses to homelessness and related social problems. The projects that were presented in the working groups by the two network builders from Catholic Community Services—namely, the para-navigator initiative mentioned earlier and a plan to site an emergency shelter on a Catholic parish in Pierce County in order to force a change in the municipal government's permitting policy—were fruits of this strategic pivot of an arm's-length FBO to innovation through bottom-up adaptive responses, in an attempt to overcome the limitations of the service organizational model.

That civil society organizations play an important intermediary role in community improvement efforts has been well documented.[72] Yet, as it was acknowledged during the problem-solving sessions, the value added of the larger faith-based nonprofits as go-betweens is their capacity to, on the one hand, link government, civil society, business, and other stakeholders to the resources and knowledge rooted in local congregations; and on the other hand, network and pool congregational resources and knowledge to channel the structured participation of these faith communities into initiatives like enhancing social service provision, building affordable housing, creating social enterprises, and the like. The puzzle that Everett Gospel Mission, Catholic Community Services, Associated Ministries, the Church Council, and other working-group members grappled with, then, was how to continue to marshal the expertise and top-down programming that make them legitimate go-betweens across governmental and nongovernmental sectors while at the same time function as stewards of community resources and local knowledge in a way that is considered legitimate to rabbis, imams, pastors, priests, and other congregational leaders, not to mention the members of these respective faith communities.

At the cost of distancing themselves from congregations, these large FBOs have come to establish themselves as primary partners in homeless response systems throughout Puget Sound. The leaders of these FBOs are considered to be invaluable interlocutors by high-level municipal officials and grass-tops from across the region. Now the question these same leaders are exploring—indeed, the questions they explored during the problem-solving process—was how to become incubators of congregationally anchored responses that include, but cannot be reduced to, mobilizing volunteers or developing traditional advocacy campaigns. It was no doubt an encouraging sign that a number of promising conversations emerged during the working-group process between these larger FBOs and some of the participating congregations.

The Convening and Coordinating Role of Denominational Bodies Is Undervalued

As mentioned earlier, of the twenty-two organizations that participated in the problem-solving pilot, one was a denominational body. Stretching south from Canada to Oregon and west from the foothills of the Cascade Mountains to the Pacific Ocean, the Episcopal Diocese of Olympia, the regional judicatory of the Episcopal Church in western Washington, proposed a plan to assess its land use with an eye to leveraging opportunities for building emergency shelter and transitional and permanent—affordable—housing as well as other support services in the over 100 churches and ministries encompassing its jurisdiction.

As the pilot process advanced, this FBO contended with the lack of resources and expertise needed to implement its project, while working-group members gained appreciation for the untapped potential of denominational bodies as coordinators of congregational resources and knowledge.

A preliminary assessment conducted by the Episcopal taskforce on homelessness concluded that, though congregational buildings were not as underutilized as is sometimes claimed for many house small-scale programs and services for homeless individuals and families, there does exist excess property that might be appropriate for permanent long-term housing or temporary transitional housing. A number of obstacles to church land redevelopment were, moreover, identified. These included ecclesial politics, a skeptical hierarchy, zoning laws, and community attitudes (for instance, NIMBYism). The chief impediment, however, was a lack of technical knowledge at the congregational and diocesan levels. The two good practices that were examined as part of the assessment—namely, St. Margaret's Episcopal Church's Andrew's Glen community in Bellevue and Holy Family Catholic Church's New Bethlehem project in Kirkland—confirmed that partnerships with specialized agencies were essential to success. In this case it was Imagine Housing—a leading nonprofit affordable housing developer in East King County founded in 1997 out of St. Andrew's Lutheran Church in Bellevue—and Catholic Community Services in western Washington, respectively.

Most significantly from the point of view of the problem-solving process was that, as it learned about the complexity and fragmented nature of the issue at hand, the taskforce pivoted from a top-down strategy that sought to develop a set of protocols to guide local redevelopment efforts to a strategy that focused on the diocese as a broker of knowledge whose aim was to foster the sharing of germane information among the churches in its jurisdiction. Toward this end, the taskforce set out to map relevant assets and actors, disseminate educational material, and continue to compile good practices, with the objective of presenting a set of recommendations on homelessness and affordable housing at the November 2019 diocesan convention.

As working-group members grappled with this project, there was an increasing awareness that denominational bodies—dioceses, synods, annual conferences, conventions, and the like—are unrecognized and undervalued in efforts to address homelessness and other social problems. These ecclesial structures tend to frame matters of social justice and community revitalization in terms of deliberative practices and consensus building. That is, they give pride of place to promulgating social teachings, aspirational statements, and other moral benchmarks. One of the lessons learned through the problem-solving process was that there is also an opportunity for denominational bodies to enhance

the civic capacity of local congregations, in partnership with specialized nonprofits or government agencies, by structuring their participation in and
through communities of practice.

Nonsectarian Organizations Are Seeking to Foster Partnerships with FBOs

The three nonsectarian organizations that participated in the pilot process—
namely, the Housing Development Consortium, the U.S. Department of Veteran Affairs Puget Sound Health Care System, and Recovery Café—proposed
projects that aimed at fostering partnerships with FBOs. The three representatives of these organizations had an appreciation for the role of FBOs in community revitalization efforts as well as for the unique legacy of religion in
American civic life. One of the representatives had been an executive at Habitat for Humanity. Another had worked overseas for the U.S. President's Emergency Plan for AIDS Relief (PEPFAR), a pioneer and pacesetter in developing
partnerships with FBOs. And the third had collaborated with FBOs in the field
of mental health. These organizations thus acknowledged the importance of
collaborating with FBOs in the age of network governance and multi-
stakeholder initiatives. Yet, all three organizations began the working-group
process with a rudimentary understanding of the specific ways congregations
and faith-based nonprofits are attempting to address homelessness in the region. As corroborated by our preliminary study and reminiscent, perhaps, of
the ambivalence surrounding the most extensive and concerted effort to partner with FBOs—Charitable Choice,[73] these organizations tended to frame
faith-based responses to homelessness in terms of advocacy support or social
capital creation or as a source of volunteers. As the sessions advanced, though,
and as the three organizations gained a greater appreciation for the varieties
and complexities of faith-based responses to homelessness, their projects
evolved to accommodate a more robust understanding of what was meant by
partnering with FBOs. FBOs were now viewed more as problem solvers and
as coproducers and less as potential resources to be leveraged.

Founded in 1988 in Seattle, with over 175 member organizations from government, business, and civil society, the Housing Development Consortium
originally proposed a project that sought to integrate members of local congregations into its advocacy efforts around inclusive zoning and the financing
of redevelopment programs, like the Seattle for Everyone campaign and the
Community Package Coalition. To date, it was suggested, there had not been
a systematic effort in Puget Sound to mobilize communities of faith to take
action—contact their local representatives, attend public meetings, testify at

municipal hearings—in support of increasing the number of accessible homes for low-income families and individuals experiencing homelessness. As the problem-solving process unfolded, the Housing Development Consortium shifted its focus and considered partnering with other local stakeholders to create appropriate strategies and mechanisms for Puget Sound congregations interested in redeveloping their land for affordable housing. One idea that emerged in the working group was for this organization to roll out a "one-stop-shop" for faith-based housing efforts in the region.[74]

The U.S. Department of Veteran Affairs Puget Sound Health Care System proposed a pilot program that sought to foster collaboration between its Homeless Patient Aligned Care Teams (H-Pact) and local FBOs in order to more effectively provide homeless veterans medical care, case management, housing, and social services assistance necessary to help them obtain and stay in permanent housing and prevent a return to homelessness. Located in the Belltown neighborhood of Seattle's downtown waterfront and working at the intersection of homelessness, addiction, and mental health, Recovery Café explored implementing a plan to train select members of their recovery community to spearhead outreach efforts, in collaboration with local congregations and other stakeholders, in their new location in the city's SODO neighborhood, which is characterized by a large number of unsanctioned encampments. Both projects were oriented by the conventional wisdom regarding the positive correlation between FBOs and social capital and between social capital and social service delivery.[75] The actual initiatives, however, had not been operationalized. The working-group process helped identify potential FBO partners. It also helped flesh out the mechanisms of collaboration.

Collective Problem Solving Can Function as an Innovative Funding Model

Though we had suggested at the outset that the working-group sessions were an opportunity for the twenty-two participating organizations to fine-tune and enhance projects that they would be seeking public or private funding for in the near future, the pilot was, nevertheless, initially approached by most participants as a kind of professional development workshop where, in order to generate experiential learning, individuals take on different roles and interact through simulation-based modules and exercises. As the process unfolded, though, and the experimentalist approach to project development revealed the limits of traditional funding allocation methods, there was an increasing appreciation for this collective problem-solving process as an innovative funding model.

Exploring land redevelopment projects, social business creation, novel knowledge-sharing configurations, and new ways of delivering social services reinforced the realization among working-group members that there is practically no money available for such initiatives. This brought forth a fundamental tension between innovation through bottom-up attempts to harness community resources and local knowledge, on the one hand, and the top-down approach to funding where an agency or foundation stipulates objectives and sets the parameters of an initiative, on the other.

It was thus proposed that a future iteration of this problem-solving exercise should be carried out in partnership with a funding agency or foundation. In collaboration with the funder, the collective problem-solving cohort would determine the objectives and metrics of an initiative or a type of initiative. At the end of the process, the funder would award grants to the most promising projects. Functioning as an intermediary, the community of practice—the collective problem-solving cohort—could help ensure that funding resources will have a more effective impact and reach those FBOs that are doing innovative work. Different variations of this model are possible. For example, based on what we learned about large faith-based nonprofits serving as important intermediaries, these FBOs could partner with a funding agency and form a problem-solving cohort with a cluster of congregations. These congregations could be based on a particular geographic area or a specific religious tradition or denomination. Or a group of stakeholders—nonsectarian organizations, congregations, and faith-based nonprofits—interested in a specific type of response—say, religious land redevelopment—could approach a funder and propose a problem-solving cohort to develop affordable housing.

Conclusion

Aptly depicted by Henry George in the epigraph at the beginning of this chapter, communities of faith and their institutions have, from the beginning, been an important force in local revitalization efforts across the United States. It is remarkable that, given this legacy of public religion in America, we still know so little about the different organizational models in and through which FBOs operate and about the challenges FBOs face as they strive to solve social problems at the community level. This lacuna is especially evident to those who have attempted to build the capacity of FBOs to more effectively respond to the most pressing social problems impacting urban areas across the country.[76] Our chapter has documented the key findings and lessons learned of an initiative that attempted to make a modest contribution to this field of research and practice.

Appendix 1. An Overview of the Three Working Groups

Working Group	Organization	Type	Location	Religious Tradition	Denomination (Christian)
Encampments	Alki United Church of Christ	Congregation	King	Christian	Mainline
	Associated Ministries of Tacoma Pierce County	Nonprofit	Pierce	Christian	Mainline
	Catholic Community Services	Nonprofit	Pierce	Christian	Catholic
	Everett Gospel Mission	Nonprofit	Snohomish	Christian	Evangelical
	Puyallup Nazarene Church	Congregation	Pierce	Christian	Evangelical
	Recovery Café	Non-FBO	King	–	–
	Seattle Union Gospel Mission	Nonprofit	King	Christian	Evangelical
Tiny Houses	Catholic Community Services	Nonprofit	Snohomish	Christian	Catholic
	Episcopal Diocese of Olympia	Network of congregations	King Pierce Snohomish	Christian	Mainline
	Idris Mosque	Congregation	King	Muslim	–
	The Bridge Care Center	Nonprofit	King	Christian	Evangelical
	Temple De Hirsch Sinai	Congregation	King	Jewish	–
	U.S. Department of Veteran Affairs Puget Sound Health Care System	Non-FBO	King Pierce Snohomish	–	–
Emergency Shelter and Permanent Housing	Acres of Diamonds	Nonprofit	King	Christian	Evangelical
	Church Council of Greater Seattle	Nonprofit	King	Christian	Mainline
	Compass Housing Alliance	Nonprofit	King Pierce Snohomish	Christian	Mainline
	Jubilee Women's Shelter	Nonprofit	King	Christian	Catholic
	Muslim Housing Services	Nonprofit	King	Muslim	–
	New Horizons Ministries	Nonprofit	King	Christian	Evangelical
	St. Luke's Episcopal Church	Congregation	King	Christian	Mainline
	Seattle Mennonite	Congregation	King	Christian	Mainline
	Housing Development Consortium	Non-FBO	King	–	–

Appendix 2. Projects and Puzzles

Working Group	Organization	Project	Puzzle
Encampments	Alki United Church of Christ	A small, progressive and diverse Congregationalist church located near Alki Point in West Seattle, considered a program that builds and situates tiny houses in existing city supported encampments, in partnership with encampment residents, government and other local stakeholders, including congregations.	How to contribute to long-term housing solutions given limited resources and a lack of technical knowledge?
	Associated Ministries of Tacoma Pierce County	Emerging out of the ecumenical movement over a century ago, and incorporated as a nonprofit in 1969, this largely government-funded service agency explored leveraging its traditional role as convener of over 250 local congregations to spearhead a campaign to end family homelessness in the city of Tacoma, the county seat of Pierce County.	How to function as a legitimate and effective intermediary between the homeless population, government, and local stakeholders? How to function as a legitimate and effective intermediary between congregations?
	Catholic Community Services (Pierce County)	The Pierce County offices of the official human service outreach arm of the Catholic Church in western Washington, the second-largest faith-based nonprofit in the state in terms of operating budget, proposed developing a plan to site an emergency shelter on congregational land in order to, among other things, force a change in the city's permitting policy to allow greater discretion to religious organizations in the development of housing and homeless services.	How to marshal professional knowledge while serving as a steward of community resources and local knowledge? How to function as a legitimate and effective intermediary between government and congregations? How to marshal professional knowledge while serving as a steward of community resources and local knowledge?
	Everett Gospel Mission	Opening its doors in 1961, this member of the Association of Gospel Rescue Missions, which provides shelter and comprehensive recovery services to over 200 individuals each night, considered launching a community effort to respond to the unsanctioned encampments that regularly emerge adjacent to the organization's headquarters in a way that takes into account the divergent views and interests of the encampment's inhabitants, local businesses, and residents.	How to function as a legitimate and effective intermediary between the homeless population, government, and local stakeholders? How to marshal professional knowledge while serving as a steward of community resource and local knowledge?

	Description	Research question
Puyallup Nazarene Church	This large Nazarene congregation located in the city of Puyallup, east of Tacoma at the foot of Mount Rainier, considered scaling up its pilot Wrap-Up ministry by partnering with a local service agency—Network Tacoma—and Everett Gospel Mission to bring suitably trained, relationship-focused volunteers together with professional social workers with the aim of increasing the resiliency of newly housed individuals and families.	How to legitimately and effectively harness community resources and local knowledge to improve the quality, coherence, and effectiveness of social services?
Recovery Café	Founded in 2003 and located in the Belltown neighborhood of Seattle's downtown waterfront, this nonsectarian organization working at the intersection of homelessness, addiction, and mental health explored implementing a plan to train select members of their recovery community to spearhead outreach efforts, in collaboration with local congregations, Union Gospel Mission, and other stakeholders, in their new location in the city's SODO neighborhood, which is characterized by a large number of unsanctioned encampments.	How to develop legitimate and productive partnerships with FBOs? How to blend local knowledge and professional knowledge to improve the targeting and delivery of social services?
Seattle Union Gospel Mission	Opening its doors as a soup kitchen in 1932 to serve the local Hoovervilles of the Great Depression, the largest Gospel Mission in Puget Sound, which operates programs and facilities in over fifty sites throughout King County, examined developing a multi-service outreach team to bring support and resources to those living in unsanctioned encampments throughout the city, and who have been reluctant to accept services.	How to blend local knowledge and professional knowledge to improve the targeting and delivery of social services?
Tiny Houses		
Catholic Community Services (Snohomish County)	The Snohomish County offices of the official human service outreach arm of the Catholic Church in western Washington, the second-largest faith-based nonprofit in the state of Washington in terms of operating budget, considered developing a plan, in partnership with Everett Gospel Mission and the Snohomish County government to train para-navigators, community referral liaisons located in congregations that navigate homeless individuals and families through the human services system and toward the support and stability they need.	How to blend local knowledge and professional knowledge to improve the targeting and delivery of social services along the continuum of care?
Episcopal Diocese of Olympia	Stretching south from Canada to Oregon and west from the foothills of the Cascade Mountains to the Pacific Ocean, the regional judicatory of the Episcopal Church in western Washington proposed a plan to assess its land use with an eye to leveraging opportunities for building, emergency shelter, and transitional and permanent—affordable—housing as well as other support services in the over 100 churches and ministries encompassing its jurisdiction.	How to function as a legitimate and effective intermediary between congregations? How to contribute to long-term housing solutions given limited resources and a lack of technical knowledge?

(Continued)

Appendix 2. (continued)

Working Group	Organization	Project	Puzzle
Tiny Houses (*continued*)	Idris Mosque	Founded in 1981, this progressive and socially engaged Muslim community in Seattle's gentrifying Northgate neighborhood considered launching an outreach program, in partnership with its adolescent and young-adult members, that seeks to address the educational and vocational needs of young people who are at risk of becoming homeless, especially those who are unemployed and not in school.	How to legitimately and effectively harness community resources and local knowledge? How to blend local knowledge and professional knowledge to improve the targeting and delivery of prevention strategies linked to education and training?
	The Bridge Care Center	The social outreach arm of Quest Church, an evangelical congregation in the gentrifying North Seattle neighborhood of Ballard, explored taking to scale a reinsertion pilot program called Advocates Representing the Community, which provides unhoused individuals with the resources and support they need to move toward greater stability.	How to legitimately and effectively harness community resources and local knowledge? How to blend local knowledge and professional knowledge to improve the quality, coherence, and effectiveness of social services along the continuum of care?
	Temple De Hirsch Sinai	The largest Reform Jewish congregation in the Pacific Northwest considered developing an advocacy campaign in collaboration with Congregations for the Homeless, a network of twelve churches in East King County offering a range of services to unhoused individuals and families, to generate communitywide support for an unpopular permanent shelter for homeless men in the city of Bellevue, across Lake Washington from Seattle.	How to function as a legitimate and effective intermediary between the homeless population, government, and local stakeholders? How to function as a legitimate and effective intermediary between congregations?
	U.S. Department of Veteran Affairs Puget Sound Health Care System	This federal agency regional office proposed a pilot program that aims to foster collaboration between its Homeless Patient Aligned Care Teams (H-Pact) and local FBOs in order to more effectively provide homeless veterans medical care, case management, housing, and social services assistance necessary to help them obtain and stay in permanent housing and prevent a return to homelessness.	How to develop legitimate and productive partnerships with FBOs? How to legitimately and effectively harness community resources and local knowledge?

Emergency Shelter and Permanent Housing	Acres of Diamonds	This Christian nonprofit located in the township of Duvall, in sprawling northeastern Puget Sound, offering a safe place for homeless mothers and children to break the cycles of addiction, poverty, and abuse, proposed implementing a plan to provide in-house trauma-informed child care services with the aim of allowing residents to have greater flexibility as they find employment and housing, while also providing quality early childhood education.	How to blend local knowledge and professional knowledge to improve the quality, coherence, and effectiveness of social services along the continuum of care?
	Church Council of Greater Seattle	Rooted in the ecumenical movement and the Seattle Federation of Churches of the early twentieth century, this registered nonprofit organization with membership representing eighteen Christian denominations considered a model of community organizing that brings together networks of technical knowledge and local support to develop a more integrated approach for congregations seeking to redevelop their land for affordable housing.	How to function as a legitimate and effective intermediary between government and local stakeholders? How to function as a legitimate and effective intermediary between congregations? How to marshal professional knowledge while serving as a steward of community resources and local knowledge?
	Compass Housing Alliance	Founded in 1920 as the Lutheran Sailors and Loggers Mission in Seattle's Pioneer Square, this leading provider of services and developer of affordable housing for homeless individuals and families in twenty-three locations across Puget Sound explored rolling out a plan to recruit and train volunteers from congregations in order to optimize the delivery of flexible and appropriate programming that meets the diverse needs of the unhoused population.	How to legitimately and effectively harness community resources and local knowledge? How to blend local knowledge and professional knowledge to improve the targeting and delivery of social services along the continuum of care?
	Jubilee Women's Shelter	Founded in 1983 by the Sisters of St. Joseph of Peace, its main site located in the former convent of the Sisters of Holy Names in Seattle's Capitol Hill neighborhood, this nonprofit, which provides support services and community housing to very low-income women—including pregnant homeless women—of all faiths and cultures, considered an initiative to develop specialized services—especially mental health care—to support their higher-barrier residents transition from homelessness or situations of domestic violence to independent living.	How to blend local knowledge and professional knowledge to improve the quality, coherences, and effectiveness of social services along the continuum of care?
	Housing Development Consortium	Founded in 1988 in Seattle, with over 175 member organizations from government, business, and civil society, this nonsectarian association, which functions as an advocate, broker, and convener around issues related to affordable housing, considered partnering with FBOs and other local stakeholders to develop appropriate responses and tools for Puget Sound congregations that are interested in redeveloping their land for this purpose.	How to develop legitimate and productive partnerships with FBOs? How to blend local knowledge and professional knowledge to innovate around affordable housing?

(Continued)

Appendix 2. (continued)

Working Group	Organization	Project	Puzzle
Emergency Shelter and Permanent Housing (*continued*)	Muslim Housing Services	The largest Islamic housing assistance nonprofit in Puget Sound sought to roll out a culturally and linguistically appropriate job placement program in an effort to increase the stability and resiliency of the Seattle and King County homeless families it supports, the majority of which are refugees and first- or second-generation immigrants from East Africa, Eastern Europe, and the Middle East that have not been able to access mainstream services.	How to blend local knowledge and professional knowledge to improve the targeting and delivery of social services aimed at long-term solutions (for instance, employment)?
	New Horizons Ministries	Founded in 1978 by a Greek Orthodox priest outside a donut shop near Seattle's Pike Place Market, and today associated with the Evangelical community and operating in Belltown, this faith-based nonprofit explored the tradeoff between two plans: expand its social business—Street Bean Coffee Roasters—with its focus on job training for homeless youth; or enhance its support services and increase the capacity of its emergency and transitional shelters.	How to navigate between providing for immediate needs and contributing to long-term solutions (for instance, employment)? How to scale up a social business given a lack of technical knowledge?
	St. Luke's Episcopal Church	A mainline congregation in the gentrifying North Seattle neighborhood of Ballard proposed a plan to develop their land, in partnership with their denomination and the local community, in order to provide affordable housing and needed community services.	How to redevelop religious land for long-term housing solutions given limited resources and a lack of technical knowledge? How to blend local knowledge and professional knowledge to innovate around affordable housing and service delivery?
	Seattle Mennonite Church	Located in North Seattle's Lake City, with roots in the region going back five decades, this socially engaged Mennonite congregation considered a plan to develop permanent affordable housing units on its land while expanding the navigation services offered to homeless individuals and families at their existing day center.	How to navigate between providing for immediate needs and contributing to long-term solutions? How to redevelop religious land for long-term housing solutions given limited resources and a lack of technical knowledge? How to blend local knowledge and professional knowledge to innovate around affordable housing?

Notes

We would like to acknowledge the valuable research support provided by Hannah Hunthausen.

1. Compare, for example, Anne Case and Angus Deaton, *Deaths of Despair and the Future of Capitalism* (Princeton, N.J.: Princeton University Press, 2020); Robert Reich, *The System: Who Rigged It, How We Fix It* (New York: Knopf, 2020); Jeffrey D. Sachs, *Building the New American Economy* (New York: Columbia University Press, 2017); and Sachs, "Restoring American Happiness," in *World Happiness Report 2017*, ed. John Helliwell, Richard Layard, and Jeffrey D. Sachs (New York: Sustainable Development Solutions Network, 2017), 178–84.

2. With a score of 73.82, the Seattle metropolitan area was ranked second in CBRE's 2019 analysis of technology talent markets in North America, behind the San Francisco Bay Area (84.79), and in front of Toronto, Ontario (69.88) and Washington, D.C. (69.83). This index was constructed using thirteen metrics that gauged the competitive advantages of markets and their ability to attract and grow tech talent pools. Consult CBRE Research, "2019 Scoring Tech Talent," Los Angeles (July 2019).

3. In 2014, Seattle's city council passed an ordinance to incrementally raise the minimum wage to $15 per hour; cf. Michael Reich, Sylvia Allegretto, and Anna Godoey, "Seattle's Minimum Wage Experience 2015–16," Institute for Research on Labor and Employment, University of California, Berkeley (June 2017); and Ekaterina Jardim, Mark C. Long, Robert Plotnick, Emma van Inwegen, Jacob Vigdor, and Hilary Wething, "Minimum Wage Increases and Individual Employment Trajectories," National Bureau of Economic Research (NBER) Working Paper Series 25182, Cambridge, Mass. (October 2018).

4. Seattle has one of the fastest-growing millennial populations, defined as the generation born between 1981 and 1997. This cohort grew 10.8 percent between 2010 and 2015. Other cities with high growth rates among young adults include Denver (12.8 percent), Honolulu (12.2 percent) and Austin (11.8 percent); William H. Frey, "The Millennial Generation: A Demographic Bridge to America's Diverse Future," Metropolitan Policy Program at Brookings, Washington, D.C. (January 2018).

5. With a score of 66.0, the Seattle metropolitan area was ranked fourth according to the U.S. Cities Sustainable Development Index, behind San Francisco-Oakland-Hayward (69.7), San Jose-Sunnyvale-Santa Clara (67.9), and Washington-Arlington-Alexandria (66.7), and in front of Madison, Wisconsin (65.0). This index ranks the 105 most populous cities (metropolitan statistical areas [MSAs]), using the unanimously adopted 2015 United Nations Sustainable Development Goals (SDGs), a framework for action around shared prosperity, social inclusion, and care for the planet; Alainna Lynch, Anna LoPresti, and Caroline Fox, *The 2019 US Cities Sustainable Development Report* (New York: Sustainable Development Solutions Network, 2019).

6. For instance, in November of 2015, the mayor of Seattle, Edward Murray, issued a Proclamation of Civil Emergency, requesting disaster relief and funding from state and federal governments that, several years later, "never seem to come." And in May of 2017 the city council of Tacoma, Washington's third-largest municipality, declared a "public health emergency" around homeless encampments that was eventually extended through 2019; Danny Westneat, "The Politics of Our Homelessness Emergency: 'Extraordinary Measures' that Never Seem to Come," *Seattle Times*, January 22, 2020; and Matt Nagle, "Homeless Encampments and Public Perception, *Tacoma Weekly News*, November 8, 2019.

7. Seattle is the eighteenth-largest U.S. city in terms of population, but it has the third-largest number of individuals experiencing homelessness; 1.65 percent of Seattle's population is homeless. Los Angeles has the second-largest share of homeless individuals (1.39 percent), followed by Washington, D.C. (1.10 percent); U.S. Department of Housing and Urban Development, *The 2019 Annual Homeless Assessment Report to Congress*, by Meghan Henry, Rian Watt, Anna Mahathey, Jillian Ouellette, and Aubrey Sitler, Abt. Associates, Washington, D.C. (January 2020).

8. Maggie Stringfellow and Dilip Wagle, "The Economics of Homelessness in Seattle and King County" (New York: McKinsey, May 2018).

9. Comprising the states of Alaska, Washington, and Oregon, the Pacific Northwest has been dubbed the "none zone" because, historically, it has had the highest proportion of religious "nones"—individuals with no religious affiliation—than any other region in the country. Thus, nearly two decades ago, in 2000, the Polis Center's Religion by Region Project reported that the Pacific Northwest had a 38.1 percent religious adherence rate, in contrast to the national rate of 59.4 percent; Patricia O'Connell Killen and Mark Silk, eds., *Religion and Public Life in the Pacific Northwest: The None Zone* (Walnut Creek, Calif.: AltaMira, 2004). Once considered the exception, the region today, some have conjectured, provides a glimpse into the future of religion in America, as across the country the number of religious "nones" is rapidly on the rise, especially among the generation born between 1981 and 1996, who are far more likely to identify as religious "nones" compared to other generational cohorts; Pew Research Center, *U.S. Public Becoming Less Religious* (Washington, D.C.: Pew Research Center, 2015). Indeed, according to the Pew Research Center, millennials who do not identify with a religion (35 percent) are double the share of unaffiliated baby boomers (17 percent) and more than three times the share of members of the silent generation (11 percent); Michael Lipka, "Millennials Increasingly Are Driving Growth of 'Nones,'" Fact Tank, Pew Research Center, Washington, D.C. (May 12, 2015). And yet, confirming that the region's moniker still holds true, among the seventeen major U.S. metropolitan areas, Seattle has the largest share of religious "nones" (37 percent), followed by San Francisco (35 percent), and Boston (33 percent); and it has the second-smallest share of Christians (52 percent), just behind San Francisco (48 percent), and followed by Boston (57 percent); Michael Lipka, "Major U.S. Metropolitan Areas Differ in their Religious Profiles,'" Fact Tank, Pew Research Center, Washington, D.C. (July 29, 2015).

10. Both the historically large share of religiously nonaffiliated in the Pacific Northwest and the rapid increase of this cohort across the United States are consistent with that modern manifestation of "individual mysticism," of spiritual or "invisible" religion; Ernst Troeltsch, *The Social Teachings of the Christian Churches*, 2 vols. (1912; repr. Louisville, Ky.: Westminster John Knox, 1992); and Thomas Luckmann, *The Invisible Religion: The Problem of Religion in Modern Society* (London: Macmillan, 1967). Indeed, in America—if not in late-modern Western societies—the individual is condemned to live in a "paradigmatically Jamesian" world: s/he must tarry with polytheistic and polymorphic meaning systems; José Casanova, "Rethinking Secularization: A Global Comparative Perspective," *Hedgehog Review* (Spring and Summer 2006): 7–22.

11. Casanova, "The Religious Situation in the United States 175 Years after Tocqueville," in *Crediting God: Sovereignty and Religion in the Age of Global Capitalism*, ed. Miguel Vatter (New York: Fordham University Press, 2011), 253–72.

12. It might seem intuitive that the fallout in traditional religious beliefs and practices is having a negative impact on the social engagement of certain types of FBOs—for example, mainline congregations—in a way that is analogous to the negative impact that this transformation in individual religiosity is having on, say, graduate theological schools; Ian Lovett, "Seminaries Reflect Struggles of Mainline Churches: Storied Institutions are Shutting their Doors as Enrollment Shrinks," *Wall Street Journal*, August 10, 2017, accessed December 6, 2020, at www.wsj.com. Yet, three waves of data from the National Congregations Study (NCS) found that the share of congregations involved in service-related activities increased from 70.8 percent in 1998 to 78.2 percent in 2012; Brad R. Fulton, "Trends in Addressing Social Needs: A Longitudinal Study of Congregation-Based Service Provision and Political Participation," *Religions* 7, no. 51 (2016): 1–16. Furthermore, in addition to congregations, today specialized faith-based service organizations like Catholic Charities, Jewish Family Services, and the Salvation Army, which are significantly more detached from the dynamics of individual beliefs and practices, make important contributions to America's welfare system. One study, for instance, found that there are approximately 6,500 faith-based service agencies across the country, contributing about one-fifth of the share of all private human service provision; Robert Wuthnow, *Saving America: Faith-Based Services and the Future of Civil Society* (Princeton, N.J.: Princeton University Press, 2004). And another study estimated that faith-based service agencies provide 30 percent of emergency shelter beds and have the capacity to house more than 150,000 people a night in different types of housing; National Alliance to End Homelessness, "Faith-Based Organizations: Fundamental Partners in Ending Homelessness," National Alliance to End Homelessness, Washington, D.C., May 2017. The Charitable Choice provision of the 1996 Welfare Reform Act and the different iterations of the 2001 White House Office of Faith-Based and Community Initiatives, which were designed to increase the flow of public funds to FBOs, highlight the important role that

FBOs have been perceived to play in American civic life; Stephen V. Monsma, *Putting Faith in Partnerships: Welfare-to-Work in Four Cities* (Ann Arbor: University of Michigan Press, 2004). Indeed, even the argument that Charitable Choice did not change much on the ground because FBOs have always been involved in social service provision supports the thesis that these organizations make important contributions to community revitalization efforts; Mark Chaves, "Debunking Charitable Choice: The Evidence Doesn't Support the Political Left or Right," *Stanford Social Innovation Review* 1, no. 2 (Summer 2003): 28–36. In addition to faith-based service agencies, since the 1960s there has also been a proliferation across the country of hundreds of FBOs dedicated to governmental and public affairs; Steven M. Tipton, *Public Pulpits: Methodists and Mainline Churches in the Moral Argument of Public Life* (Chicago: University of Chicago Press, 2007). Ranging from the Faith and Freedom Coalition, on the "religious right," through the Interfaith Alliance, along the religious mainline, to the Poor Peoples Campaign, on the "religious left," these "para-church groups" have far outpaced the growth of denominational churches. Corroborating this trend, a study by the Pew Research Center found that the number of FBOs engaged in religious lobbying or religion-related advocacy inside the Beltway has increased roughly fivefold in the past four decades, from fewer than forty in 1970 to more than 200 today; Pew Research Center, *Lobbying for the Faithful: Religious Advocacy Groups in Washington, D.C.* (Washington, D.C.: Pew Forum on Religion & Public Life, May 2012). And even in the realm of "from below" contestatory politics, there has also been an explosion of FBOs. Thus, for instance, according to one study, the PICO National Network, the faith-based community organizing coalition, currently has 4,500 member organizations, which represent a 12.5 percent increase in the number of chapters, compared to 1999; Richard L. Wood and Brad R. Fulton, *A Shared Future: Faith-Based Organizing for Racial Equity and Ethical Democracy* (Chicago: Chicago University press, 2015). Indeed, it seems that any attenuating effect that America's changing religious landscape is having on the civic engagement of FBOs is being offset by the conditions of the so-called "new localism" and "post-secularism." On the one hand, the vertical pivot downward from national to local government and the horizontal pivot outward from the state to business and civil society that have been transforming public policy and community development since the 1970s seem to have only further enhanced the public role of FBOs; Bruce J. Katz and Jeremy Nowak, *The New Localism: How Cities Can Thrive in the Age of Populism* (Washington, D.C.: Brookings Institute Press, 2018). On the other hand, in our late-modern society, the dominance of the metanarrative of secularization is being increasingly challenged; and this, paradoxically, perhaps, seems to bring forth "a new age of religious searching, whose outcome no one can foresee," as Charles Taylor has suggested in *A Secular Age* (Cambridge, Mass.: Harvard University Press, 2007), 535.

13. The initiative was coordinated out of Seattle University.

14. Gary King, Robert Keohane, and Sidney Verba, *Designing Social Inquiry: Scientific Inference in Qualitative Research* (Princeton, N.J.: Princeton University Press, 1994).

15. Glaser and Strauss, *The Discovery of Grounded Theory: Strategies for Qualitative Research* (New Brunswick, N.J.: Transaction, 1967), 2.

16. Ibid., 66.

17. Ibid., 65.

18. Robert Putnam and David Campbell have marshaled evidence suggesting that religion plays a fundamental role in fostering civic virtues. It is positively correlated with volunteering, philanthropy, and being civically active. Religious Americans are more generous neighbors and more conscientious citizens; see *American Grace: How Religion Divides and Unites Us* (New York: Simon & Schuster, 2010). See also, Putnam's treatment of religion and faith communities in *Bowling Alone: The Collapse and Revival of American Community* (New York: Simon & Schuster, 2000).

19. Alexis de Tocqueville, *Democracy in America* [1835 and 1840] (London: University of Chicago Press, 2000).

20. Casanova, "The Religious Situation in the United States 175 Years after Tocqueville," 256.

21. Nancy Ammerman, *Pillars of Faith: American Congregations and Their Partners* (Berkeley: University of California Press, 2005), 2.

22. Theda Skocpol, *Diminished Democracy: From Membership to Management in American Civic Life* (Norman: University of Oklahoma Press, 2003).

23. Patricia O'Connell Killen, "Conclusion—Religious Futures in the None Zone," in *Religion and Public Life in the Pacific Northwest,* eds. Patricia O'Connell Killen and Mark Silk (Walnut Creek, Calif.: AltaMira, 2004), 170–75.

24. Robert Wuthnow, *Saving America: Faith-Based Services and the Future of Civil Society* (Princeton, N.J.: Princeton University Press, 2004).

25. Alexis de Tocqueville, *Democracy in America*.

26. John Dewey, *The Public and Its Problems* (New York: Henry Holt, 1927).

27. Xavier de Souza Briggs, *Democracy as Problem Solving: Civic Capacity in Communities Across the Globe* (Cambridge, Mass.: MIT Press, 2006).

28. Cf. C. Wright Mills, *The Power Elite* (Oxford: Oxford University Press, 1956); and Robert Dahl, *Who Governs?* (New Haven, Conn.: Yale University Press, 1961).

29. Wood, *Faith in Action: Religion, Race, and Democratic Organizing in America* (Chicago: University of Chicago Press, 2002), 4. See also Wood and Fulton, *Shared Future*.

30. See, for instance, Loïc Wacquant, *Punishing the Poor: The Neoliberal Government of Social Insecurity* (Durham, N.C.: Duke University Press, 2009); and David Harvey, "From Managerialism to Entrepreneurialism: The Transformation in Urban Governance," *Geografiska Annaler* 71, no. 1 (1989): 3–17.

31. Against the rational actor framework that narrowly understands social relations in terms of strategic behavior, this approach understands social relations in terms of an iterative process of intersubjective learning that is structured by and structures norms and other cultural forms. What is at play here is one of the fundamental debates in the social sciences—a debate that can be traced back to the different formulations of the contract theory (for example, Hobbes vs. Rousseau), through the homo oeconomicus vs. homo sociologicus dispute ("Das Adam Smith Problem") of the early twentieth century, and up to the theoretical differences in fields like, for example, urban planning, work and organization studies, and international development; see, for instance, Talcott Parsons, *The Structure of Social Action*, vols. 1 and 2 (New York: McGraw-Hill, 1937); Joseph A. Schumpeter, *History of Economic Analysis* (1954; repr. New York: Routledge, 1997); and Jürgen Habermas, *The Theory of Communicative Action*, vols. 1 and 2 (1981; repr. Boston: Beacon Press, 1984 and 1987).

32. Putnam and Campbell, *American Grace*. See also Putnam, *Bowling Alone*.

33. See, for example, Robert N. Bellah, Richard Madsen, William M. Sullivan, Ann Swidler, and Steven M. Tipton, *Habits of the Heart: Individualism and Commitment in American Life* (Berkeley: University of California Press, 1985); and Tipton, *Public Pulpits*.

34. Katz and Nowak, *New Localism*.

35. Briggs, *Democracy as Problem Solving*, ix.

36. Ibid., 38.

37. Charles Sabel, "Beyond Principal-Agent Governance: Experimentalist Organizations, Learning and Accountability," in *De Staat van de Democratie: Democratie voorbij de Staat*, ed. Ewald Engelen and Monika Sie Dhian Ho (Amsterdam: Amsterdam University Press, 2004), 173–95.

38. Jason Corburn, *Street Science: Community Knowledge and Environmental Health Justice* (Cambridge, Mass.: MIT Press, 2005).

39. Briggs, *Democracy as Problem Solving*.

40. Kathleen Eisenhardt, "Building Theories from Case Study Research," in *The Qualitative Researcher's Companion*, ed. Michael Huberman and Matthew B. Miles (Thousand Oaks, Calif.: Sage, 2002), 6–7; and King, Keohane, and Verba, *Designing Social Inquiry*, 43–46.

41. In terms of our data collection method, we triangulated informant interviews, with participant observation of relevant meetings and events, as well as archival research. All interviewees provided informed consent and granted us permission to disclose their identities. Interviews for these case studies were conducted between September and December of 2018. Furthermore, we based our descriptive generalizations on cross-case patterns derived from the analysis of the transcripts and write-ups of our within-case data; Eisenhardt, "Building Theories from Case Study Research."

42. Christine Dubois, "Remembering Archbishop Hunthausen," *Northwest Catholic*, July 26, 2018.

43. Alex Tizon, "Low-Key Leadership and High-Flying Growth—Michael Reichert's Calling," *Seattle Times*, December 16, 1999.

44. According to the Internal Revenue Service (IRS)'s Exempt Organization Business Master File Extract (EO BMF), as of September 2018, CCSWW was the second-highest income-generating FBO in the state of Washington, after World Vision. Toward the close of the twentieth century, Catholic Charities, U.S.A., represented the largest system of private social provision in America. See, for example, Dorothy M. Brown and Elizabeth McKeown, *The Poor Belong to Us: Catholic Charities and American Welfare* (Cambridge, Mass.: Harvard University Press, 2000).

45. Catholic Community Services of Western Washington/Catholic Housing Services, 2017 *Annual Report*, Seattle, July 2018.

46. AM's progenitors within the ecumenical movement in Pierce County in the late nineteenth and early twentieth centuries were the Tacoma Ministerial Alliance, Tacoma Council of Federated Church Women, and the Tacoma Council of Religious Education. These later became the Tacoma-Pierce County Council of Churches and the Ecumenical Urban Ministry of Pierce Council, both of which in turn dissolved when AM emerged in 1969; see "History: A Legacy of United People of Faith," website of Associated Ministries, accessed December 6, 2020, www.associatedministries.org.

47. There are a number of influential nonprofits operating effectively in Pierce County today that were created under this model. Examples include Nourish Food Bank, Hilltop Coalition, and the Pierce County AIDS Foundation.

48. Johnson, Stone & Pagano, P.S., *Associated Ministries of Tacoma/Pierce County, Audited Financial Statements and Supplementary Information*, Fircrest, Wash., September 2017.

49. AM contracts with county and city governments to provide the following homelessness services: the reception and fielding of all incoming inquiries to the countywide coordinated entry system mandated by the U.S. Department of Housing and Urban Development; the provision of diversion (in partnership with CCSWW) and rapid rehousing; a landlord liaison program; and a biannual resource fair.

50. A number of these attendees went on to form an advocacy group tasked with learning more about the City of Tacoma's affordable housing strategy, and in the summer of 2018 they prepared and presented a document to the city council requesting for a specific policy to protect and develop affordable housing for the very poorest. After an initial communitywide communication of this document by AM, six Christian pastors, five of whom were from the mainline tradition, and one reformed Jewish rabbi, officially declared their support; consult Associated Ministries, *Housing Hope: Tacoma Faith Community Policy Priorities for Affordable Housing Action Strategy*, Tacoma, Wash., Summer 2018.

51. The Ministerial Alliance is a group of mostly Protestant pastors who have been meeting since the 1980s to provide community resources such as advocacy, lobbying, and information sharing.

52. In October 2017, the Tacoma city council passed an ordinance making it easier for faith communities to host homeless shelters. The local newspaper questioned the faith community's commitment with the November 7 front page teaser, "Faith Community Needs to Do More to Address Homelessness," referencing the following article: Matt Driscoll, "What Will It Take to Prompt Tacoma's Faith-Based Groups to Help the City Battle Homelessness," *News Tribune*, November 7, 2017.

53. Graduate Tacoma was a communitywide effort that emerged between 2010 and 2014 with the goal of increasing Tacoma's 2010 graduation rate by 50 percent by 2020. With 268 associated community partners, in May of 2018 the goal was reached; see Steve Dunkelberger, "Graduate Tacoma Reaches Key Milestone, Begins Work on Next Phase," *Tacoma Weekly News*, May 3, 2018.

54. There are four Gospel Missions in King, Pierce, and Snohomish counties, all of which are associated with Citygate Network: the Rescue Mission of Tacoma, The Bread of Life Mission (Seattle), Seattle's Union Gospel Mission, and Everett Gospel Mission.

55. Finney, Neill & Company, P.S., *Everett Gospel Mission Inc. Independent Auditors' Report and Financial Statement Year Ended June 30, 2017*, Seattle, February 2018.

56. To cite one example: In 2014, Sylvia Anderson was invited by Mayor Ray Stephenson to cochair the Everett Streets Initiative, a task force of community stakeholders mandated to develop recommendations related to "street-level social issues" in the city's urban center.

57. Cf. Dewey, *The Public and Its Problems*; Max Horkheimer, "Traditional and Critical Theory," in *Critical Theory* (1937; repr. New York: Seabury, 1972), 188–243; Kurt Lewin, "Action Research and Minority Problems," *Journal of Social Issues* 2, no. 4 (1946): 34–46; Charles Lindblom and David Cohen, *Usable Knowledge: Social Science and Social Problem Solving* (New Haven, Conn.: Yale University Press, 1979); and Chris Argyris, Robert Putnam, and Diana McLain Smith, *Action Science: Concepts, Methods, and Skills for Research and Intervention* (San Francisco: Jossey-Bass, 1985).

58. Orlando Fals-Borda, "The Application of Participatory Action-Research in Latin America," *International Sociology* 2, no. 4 (December 1987): 329–47.

59. Meredith Minkler and Nina Wallerstein, eds., *Community-Based Participatory Research for Health: From Process to Outcomes*, 2nd ed. (San Francisco: Jossey-Bass, 2008).

60. Sabel and Jonathan Zeitlin, "Experimentalist Governance," in *Handbook on Governance*, ed. David Levi-Faur (Oxford: Oxford University Press, 2012), 169–85.

61. Étienne Wenger, William Richard McDermott, and William Snyder, *Cultivating Communities of Practice: A Guide to Managing Knowledge* (Boston: Harvard Business School Press, 2002); Corburn, *Street Science*; Sabel, "Beyond Principal-Agent Governance"; and Briggs, *Democracy as Problem Solving.*

62. Two decisions of substantive significance were made early on for logistical reasons. The first decision had to do with the scope of the pilot. Having decided—based on the findings of our study—to give pride of place to organizational models over, for example, religious tradition or denominational distinctions, we considered three possibilities: include either congregations or arms-length faith-based nonprofits; include both types of FBOs; or include both types of FBOs as well as nonsectarian organizations seeking closer collaboration with FBOs. We chose the option that provided the greatest scope, as it seemed most compelling given the exploratory nature of our initiative. The second decision had to do with whether to organize the pilot around subdomains of the homelessness problem. We were skeptical at first because, given our experimentalist approach, we wanted to avoid making any stipulations about the problem domain. However, the need to frame the process along existing intervention pathways as a strategy to focus on project implementation won out in the end. We thus decided to roll out three working groups organized around responses to homelessness where Puget Sound FBOs have played a particularly important role: namely, encampments, tiny houses, and emergency shelter and permanent housing. We agreed, nevertheless, that these three intervention pathways would be taken as a point of departure. Working-group members would be free to develop their projects outside these specific themes if the problem-solving process would take them in such a direction. In the spring of 2018 we disseminated an invitation to apply to one of the three working groups to the approximately 170 Puget Sound organizations we had sampled through our study. In addition to standard information about the organization, the online application requested answers to two clusters of questions. The first cluster inquired, What is the mission of your organization as it relates to homelessness and the housing crisis? What strategies is your organization pursuing to meet its goals? And what is your role in implementing these strategies?, while the second cluster asked, As you contribute to the implementation of these strategies, how would you describe the challenge or "puzzle" around which your organization is trying to innovate? and requested the applicant to please explain the constraints they are working within as well the assets they are relying upon as they seek to problem solve in this area. These questions aimed at evaluating applicants according to two criteria: first, that they could formulate a cogent initiative to address homelessness; and second, that they held a mandate within an organization that would allow them to problem solve around how to implement this specific initiative in light of operational constraints. In other words, we wanted to ensure that potential participants could grapple with civic capacity as a problem of organizational-institutional innovation

with the aim of more effectively addressing homelessness. The selection process included an interview with finalists.

63. The three working groups gathered once a month for two hours at Seattle University from the fall of 2018 to the spring of 2019. Meetings were structured around three activities: (1) a presentation by one of the group members on his or her project and puzzle (thirty minutes); (2) a problem-solving session where group members provided feedback on the presentation, probed its problematic and promising aspects, and provided recommendations for moving forward (one hour); and (3) time for past presenters to update the group on progress that had been made and challenges remaining regarding the implementation of the initiative in question (thirty minutes). This format was repeated until all participating organizations had the chance to present, discuss, and rework their puzzles and related implementation plans. We met with individuals a week or two prior to their respective presentations to support the development of their exposition. The structure of the presentation (and corresponding PowerPoint template) had been disseminated to the working groups at the start of the pilot. Presentations were divided into three parts: Unpacking the Puzzle, Learning from Other Organizations, and Implementation. Presenters began by examining the challenges and constraints they faced in rolling out their project, reflecting specifically on how solving this puzzle would contribute to enhancing the effectiveness of their organization's response to homelessness. They then considered at least two examples of FBOs from the Puget Sound and other municipal areas across the United States that had successfully ("good practice") or unsuccessfully ("lesson learned") grappled with an analogous puzzle. They concluded their presentation by outlining an implementation plan, focusing on project stages and timeline, definitions of success and measurements of impact, resources and funding requirements, issues of sustainability, and monitoring and evaluation. In addition to the monthly working-group gatherings and meetings with future presenters, we also debriefed each participant after every working group, either in person or by telephone. This was an opportunity for us to track both changing understandings of community problem solving by participants and the development of specific initiatives in light of the latest iteration of the process. Our focus during these sessions was on catalyzing the pooling of knowledge and on ensuring the smooth advancement of the problem-solving pilot. We avoided as much as possible setting any specific direction or weighing in on substantive matters, though we did answer questions of clarification and provided recommendations for further reading concerning this or that concept, issue, or organization that had been evoked by the working group. We also encouraged participants within a working group to consider linkages between their respective initiatives as well as facilitated exchanges between participants across working groups with the end of exploring possible partnerships.

64. The social and solidarity economy (SSE) refers to that constellation of economic activity that prioritizes social and environmental objectives, involving producers,

workers, consumers, and citizens, acting strategically and collectively through, for example, cooperatives, mutual associations, philanthropic foundations, research centers, nongovernmental organizations, FBOs, impact investors, public-private partnerships, advocacy and self-help movements, fair trade networks, social enterprises, complementary currencies, community banks, and micro-financing schemes. See, for instance, United Nations Inter-Agency Task Force on Social and Solidarity Economy, *Social and Solidarity Economy and the Challenge of Sustainable Development* (Geneva, Switzerland: June, 2014); Peter Utting, ed., *Social and Solidarity Economy: Beyond the Fringe* (London: Zed, 2015); Carlo Borzaga, Gianluca Salvatori, and Riccardo Bodini, *Social and Solidarity Economy and the Future of Work* (Geneva: International Labour Organization, July 2017), and Antonella Noya and Emma Clarence, eds., *The Social Economy: Building Inclusive Economies* (Paris: Organisation for Economic Co-operation and Development, 2007).

65. Matthew Desmond and Carl Gershenson, "Housing and Employment Insecurity among the Working Poor," *Social Problems* 63 (January 2016): 46–67; and Roland V. Anglin, ed., *Building the Organizations That Build Communities: Strengthening the Capacity of Faith- and Community-Based Development Organizations* (Washington, D.C.: U.S. Department of Housing and Urban Development, 2004).

66. Marquisha Lawrence Scott and Ram Cnaan, "Civil Society and the Welfare State at the Age of New Public Governance," *Nonprofit Policy Forum* 8, no. 4 (2018): 391–410.

67. Joel Swerdlow, "Faith-Based Development: Looking for Land? Start Here," Tax Credit Advisor, National Bellwether Enterprise/Housing and Rehabilitation Association, Washington, D.C. (May 2015).

68. Emily Warren, Melody Waring, and Dan Meyer, "Are U.S. Congregations Patching the Social Safety Net? Trends from 1998 to 2012," *Journal of Sociology & Social Welfare* 46, no. 3 (September 2019): 39–62.

69. Patrick Fowler, Peter Hovmand, Katherine Marcal, and Sanmay Das, "Solving Homelessness from a Complex Systems Perspective: Insights for Prevention Responses," *Annual Review of Public Health* 40 (April 2019): 465–86.

70. Corburn, *Street Science.*

71. Michael Lipsky, *Street-Level Bureaucracy: Dilemmas of the Individual in Public Service*, 30th anniversary expanded ed. (1980; repr. New York: Russell Sage Foundation, 2010).

72. See, for instance, Briggs, *Democracy as Problem Solving.*

73. Chaves, "Debunking Charitable Choice."

74. Swerdlow, "Faith-Based Development."

75. We alluded to the first correlation in an earlier section of this chapter: see Putnam and Campbell, *American Grace: How Religion Divides and Unites Us.* There is an extensive body of research on the positive relationship between social capital and the effectiveness of social policies and social service delivery, the robustness of social safety nets, and the vibrancy of the social dimensions of development, more

generally; see, for instance, Briggs, "Brown Kids in White Suburbs: Housing Mobility and the Many Faces of Social Capital," *Housing Policy Debate* 9, no. 1 (1998): 177–221; and Michael Woolcock and Deepa Narayan, "Social Capital: Implications for Development Theory, Research, and Policy," *World Bank Research Observer* 15, no. 2 (August 2000): 225–49.

76. Michael Lee Owen, "Capacity Building: The Case of Faith-Based Organizations," in Anglin, ed., *Building the Organizations That Build Communities*, 127–64.

Disenfranchising the Unhoused

Urban Redevelopment, the Criminalization of Homelessness, and the Peril of Prosperity Theology in Dallas and Beyond

Michael R. Fisher Jr.

Introduction

The content of this chapter was initially incited by my encounter with Laura Stivers's book *Disrupting Homelessness*. In that provocative text, Stivers examines whether typical Christian responses to the crisis of homelessness empower those who are helped. She seeks to push religious responses to homelessness beyond charity, toward advocacy that eliminates its systemic and structural causes. I was particularly struck by her argument that American society subjects people experiencing homelessness to either assimilation or criminalization efforts, depending on how they respond to their plight.[1] According to Stivers, individuals whom society perceives as victims of misfortune but actively seek help are deemed deserving and are aided in their path toward "responsible citizenship." Conversely, society subjects those viewed as having made bad decisions that led to their homelessness to laws that constrain their freedom. Her point is to underscore two general approaches to the unhoused: (1) assisted assimilation into society via their reformation or (2) their criminalization.[2] Given my background as the former director of advocacy at Miriam's Kitchen—a nonprofit organization whose mission is to end chronic homelessness in the nation's capital—and my interests at the intersection of religion, ethics, and urban studies, I began to think about the connections between religion, the public discourse that spurs policies that criminalize homelessness by framing people experiencing homelessness as "the other," and urban redevelopment.[3] After critical reflection, I realized that while the processes that drive urban redevelopment and the criminalization of homelessness are independent of one another, they converge in U.S. cities that adopt an entrepreneurial approach to economic growth. This convergence results in the increased disenfranchisement and criminalization of people experiencing homelessness. I am particularly interested in and give attention here to how prosperity theology provides a dangerous form of legitimization that reinforces the social disenfranchisement and criminalization of the unhoused.

This chapter is divided into three sections. First, I situate the discourse on homelessness by way of a historical account of the social and political elements that disenfranchise the unhoused. For this task, I find the work of Henry Miller instrumental. His text *On the Fringe: The Dispossessed in America* attends to the social history of the polemic in Western societies about the unhoused and illuminates how their historical archetypes—for instance, the vagabond, vagrant, and beggar—became associated with social disorder. The path toward their stigmatization began in Europe and was subsequently transported to the United States, where it was heightened, prompting ordinances that criminalize homelessness. Drawing from Randall Amster and the "Housing Not Handcuffs" report by the National Law Center on Homelessness and Poverty (NLCHP), I identify the modalities of criminalization in a U.S. context.

The second section examines the intersection between the criminalization of homelessness and urban redevelopment or urban renewal, as it is also known. Beginning in the late twentieth century, cities assumed an entrepreneurial posture as a means to promote urban redevelopment in their spaces. The primary goal of this entrepreneurial posture is to mobilize city space as the quintessential territory for market-oriented economic growth as well as elite consumption practices.[4] Urban redevelopment disenfranchises an already vulnerable urban population through ordinances that criminalize behavior associated with homelessness. I examine Dallas, Texas, as a case study in order to provide a concrete example of the correlation between redevelopment initiatives and criminalization ordinances.

In the final section, I draw from the work of Stephanie Mitchem, Robert M. Franklin, and Keri Day to explore how prosperity theology, as public religious discourse, legitimates the criminalization of homelessness in religious terms. This presents a pressing challenge for Christian faith communities who subscribe to it because prosperity theology potentially inhibits a Christian moral analysis of the social and structural forces that disenfranchise and criminalize the unhoused. I conclude with some thoughts about potential ways forward for Christian faith communities who value the role of religion and theology for addressing urgent social problems in public discourse.

The Historical Context of the Criminalization of Homelessness

In his book *On the Fringe*, Henry Miller traces the historical development of how those in the West perceive homelessness in order to better understand and historically contextualize it in the U.S. According to Miller, the existence of people who have no permanent housing is an ancient phenomenon that has been a prominent feature of Western societies since at least the Middle Ages and perhaps long before.[5] Although the hallmarks attributed to the unhoused—for instance, poverty, laziness, filth, disease, criminality, and the like—place them beyond the pale of Western society today, they were not always subject to such negative stigma or criminalization efforts in the public sphere. In early European history, vagrancy was not viewed as a crime. On this point, Miller states, "During the High Middle Ages, there was a tendency to idealize mendicant poverty; the exemplar, of course, was Saint Francis and his brothers who wandered the realm wrapped in an aura of divine approval."[6] As a consequence of Franciscan valorization of the commitment to withdraw from the world, its riches, and evil worldly temptations, vagrancy was praised as a moral virtue. The unhoused were lauded as moral exemplars, forsaking the corruption of material wealth for lives of sacrificial piety and mendicant holiness. The state of being poor and unhoused during this time was neither a criminal act nor improper. Although these individuals were positioned on the margins of society, their existence was not construed as a social problem.

By the dawn of the fourteenth century, however, social perceptions of vagrancy changed, thereby shifting the connotations of homelessness in the public sphere. This shift was drastically influenced by the collapse of feudalism, which was precipitated by multiple factors. Perhaps the most significant centered on the devastation of Europe caused by the Black Death (also known as the Great Plague). It killed an estimated 30 to 40 percent of Europe's population.[7] The subsequent labor shortage caused by this high level of fatalities transformed labor relations, severing the traditional ties that bound workers to their lord's estate under the feudal system. In England, the emergence of a free and mobile labor force, combined with the development of towns with increasing populations of people who coalesced around manufacturing and distribution centers, stoked fears among the noble class of the potential loss of their privileged position in society.[8]

Driven by these fears, the Statute of Laborers, enacted in the mid-fourteenth century, sought to control the labor force vis-à-vis wages. While the primary objective of the ordinance was to constrain labor mobility and reduce wages in an effort to decrease costs, it had a much more insidious effect. Here is Miller:

More importantly, however, we see the seed of that awful distinction that
was to haunt English Poor Law and American welfare law, for ever after:
the distinction made between the able-bodied and what were later to
be called the worthy poor. This distinction had played no part in the
giving of charity prior to the chaos precipitated by the Black Death. The
Catholic Church, the intuitional center for charity enterprises, bestowed
alms on *all* poor persons; the means test based on a person's need
calculated according to his/her ability and willingness to work was an
invention of incipient capitalism and not a product of ecclesiastical law.[9]

Although the Statute of Laborers failed in its primary objective, it did successfully shift how vagrancy was perceived in the public sphere. "What the statute
did do, however, was to initiate the long legal process that made free labor—and
by implication, idle labor—a condition of some hazard and eventually of op-
probrium. Vagrancy began to be seen as a threat to the social order of things."[10]
During the fourteenth century, that social order was feudalism. Later, with
the development of a market system that revolved around self-interest, the production of commodities, and competition, feudalism would surrender to
capitalism as the dominant social order. In a capitalist society, vagrancy was
no longer valorized as a moral virtue but instead was stigmatized via public
discourse as evidence of personal moral decay. Gone were the days when society perceived poverty and the unhoused in morally favorable terms. Rather,
poverty was construed as the result of one's personal moral failures.

These sentiments were transported to the New World where, according to
Randall Amster, a "Protestant work ethic" and a national narrative of free-
market meritocracy and opportunity in the U.S. reified the association of a
social pathology with the poor, especially the unhoused.[11] American society
came to understand poverty as a consequence stemming from the poor's lack
of hard work and personal responsibility.[12] The poor became characterized by
their moral dereliction and were subsequently demonized in the public sphere
through the use of rhetoric that emphasized mental instability, drug addiction,
disease, violence, and the like. These images, which frame the dominant public perception of the unhoused, stigmatized them and substantiated the idea
that personal social disorder, not institutional structures, is the cause of homelessness.[13] On this point, Amster asserts, "Fast forwarding to the present, it is
apparent that the dominant culture heavily stigmatizes poverty as an 'individual pathology' more than a structural phenomenon, and that the homeless—
because of their inescapably public presence and frequent juxtaposition to
centers of leisure—invariably inspire the most virulent derogation and overt
animus."[14]

Consequently, the union of the idea of an inherent social pathology with the unhoused in the public imaginary and expressed through public rhetoric generates a desire for social distance between people who have housing (for instance, "responsible citizens") and those without (for instance, irresponsible, lazy "freeloaders"). Sociologist J. Talmadge Wright poignantly underscores the effects of a social pathology associated with the unhoused:

> The homeless body in the public imagination represents the body of decay, the degenerate body, a body that is constantly rejected by the public as "sick," "scary," "dirty and smelly," and a host of other pejoratives used to create social distance between housed and unhoused persons. This visual logic of identity, a product of a specific social imaginary that bifurcates bodies into "sick" versus "well," in turn affects the production of social-physical spaces by privileging urban spaces of surveillance, both self-surveillance and control over one's "deviant" body, and the surveillance of those external bodies perceived as too fat, too dirty, too dark, or too sexual.[15]

Wright poignantly identifies the relationship between the social disenfranchisement sedimented through public discourse and the criminalization of the unhoused enacted through law. The desire for social distance by the "virtuous" citizenry from the "degenerates" of society produces efforts of criminalization vis-à-vis the control and removal of their bodies from public sight. The fundamental way this is done is through a process of urban spatial cleansing that entails the policing of (primarily public) urban space and the regulation and enforcement of acceptable forms of public behavior. Cities increasingly use law and law enforcement to cleanse their geographical spaces of people experiencing homelessness. The social processes that brand them as the morally depraved, diseased other establishes their illegality via the implementation of city ordinances that vary widely but constrain the freedom of the unhoused in their everyday lives.

In 2019, the National Law Center on Homelessness and Poverty (NLCHP) published its most recent "Housing not Handcuffs" report based on a survey of 187 U.S. cities that evaluated the number of city ordinances that criminalize the unhoused by prohibiting behavior. The most common bans include: (1) camping in public, (2) sitting or lying down in public, (3) begging in public (panhandling), (4) loitering or loafing in public, (5) sleeping in public, (6) restrictions on living in vehicles, and (7) food sharing.[16] Brief consideration of just the first four is sufficient to understand the nature of the criminalization of homelessness in urban spaces across the nation. Regarding the first, NLCHP reports that 72 percent of the 187 cities surveyed have at least one

law that prohibits camping in public; 37 percent of them have one or more
laws that prohibit camping in public citywide, while 57 percent of them prohibit camping in specific public areas. Although camping definitions vary
across cities, it generally refers to the assembly of any type of temporary structure for habitation. Camping can also include sleeping outside or using resources to shelter from the weather.[17] Bans against sitting or lying down in
public are another example of conduct criminalized by anti-homelessness
ordinances: 55 percent of cities surveyed prohibit sitting or lying down in
public places.[18] This type of ban essentially punishes the unhoused for something that is a biological necessity to maintain life—rest. Bans on begging in
public (also known as panhandling) seek to prohibit the unhoused from "harassing" urban citizens: 83 percent of U.S. cities surveyed have at least one
law restricting begging in public; 38 percent of cities surveyed ban panhandling citywide, while 65 percent ban the practice in particular areas of city
space.[19] Finally, loitering or loafing in public, which can be defined as "remaining idle in essentially one location and [includes] the concepts of spending time idly loafing or walking about aimlessly," is another common ban
that criminalizes people experiencing homelessness: 35 percent of U.S. cities
surveyed in the report ban such activities citywide, while 60 percent of them
ban it in specific public areas.[20]

Violation of these ordinances can lead to arrest and imprisonment, ticketing, or the forcible, potentially violent, removal of the unhoused from public
sight. These ordinances fundamentally criminalize the types of behaviors that
are associated with homelessness. Because the unhoused do not have the lux-
ury of privacy afforded to those with housing, they must conduct what would
otherwise be considered private acts in public. The NLCHP report is unequiv-
ocal in its finding that such ordinances are increasingly being passed in cities
across the nation, the effects of which amount not only to the annihilation of
space, but also the annihilation of an entire group within the city. On this
point, urban geographer Don Mitchell asserts:

> For this is what the new legal regime in American cities is outlawing:
> just those behaviors that poor people, and the homeless in particular,
> must do in the public spaces of the city. And this regime does it by
> legally (if in some ways figuratively) annihilating the only spaces
> homeless people have left. The anti-homeless laws being passed in city
> after city in the United States work in a pernicious way: by redefining
> what is acceptable behavior in public space, by in effect annihilating
> the spaces in which the homeless *must* live, these laws seek simply to
> annihilate homeless people themselves, all in the name of recreating

the city as a playground for a seemingly global capital which is ever ready to do an even better job of the annihilation of space.[21]

Mitchell emphasizes the role of the changing legal structure of public space in U.S. cities and rightly sounds the alarm on how such laws are being implemented within them to expel people experiencing homelessness from the public sphere. By criminalizing behaviors that belong to that particular group of people, cities' anti-homelessness ordinances essentially criminalize the group itself through exclusive targeting. Moreover, there is a correlation between the institution of anti-homelessness ordinances with redevelopment initiatives in U.S. cities. This correlation merits sustained attention.

Society, Redevelopment, and Criminalization: A Case Study of Dallas, Texas

Urban Entrepreneurialism and Redevelopment

Cities play a significant role in the constitution of society. Joseph Grange contends that the city is "the place where human beings express to the fullest degree the perspectives on importance that their culture has bequeathed to them. It is the environmental region within which ideals become enacted, signifiers are elaborated, and categories establish themselves as culturally normative. It is, par excellence, the place where human values come to their most concrete expression."[22] For Grange, the city is the form of "the good" for human civilization. Cities were instrumental geographical spaces that facilitated the transition from feudalism to capitalism in the West, and it is this form of the good that is the quintessential site for consumerist culture and capitalist accumulation. They function as engines of economic growth and are also key centers of economic, political, and social innovation.[23]

In order to drive economic growth in cities, urban elites have increasingly turned to entrepreneurial forms of urban governance and redevelopment projects.[24] Urban entrepreneurialism, which emerged during the 1980s in the wake of a consensus among elites about the positive benefits that await cities that take an entrepreneurial stance to economic growth, emphasizes competitiveness as the core component that frames urban policy formations and urban redevelopment strategies in the U.S.[25] Tim Hall and Phil Hubbard identify a fundamental characteristic of urban entrepreneurialism: the political prioritization of local economic growth. In this sense, one can frame entrepreneurialism as "a distinctive political culture primarily concerned with improving the prosperity of the city and its ability to create jobs and investment."[26] Urban entrepreneurial policies are inherently growth-oriented, the aim of which is to promote the comparative advantage of the city in a competitive environment where other cities similarly seek to attract capital. This approach to economic policy is at the very heart of urban politics. Urban elites view cities as a development machine and govern in ways that channel resources in pursuit of the generation of profit.

As a part of this growth strategy, municipal governments allocate exceptionally high budgets for the promotion and advertisement of the city—what is referred to as "boosterism"—as a favorable environment for business. This market-oriented policy platform is geared toward attracting business from both domestic and international markets as cities rebrand themselves as vibrant and hospitable geographical spaces for corporate and private interests. In order to entice investors, businesses, and residents, marketing teams utilize a series of pamphlets, posters, and other cultural products as a means of communicating a selective image of the city that outside investors and potential residents find attractive. These promotional tools redefine and reimagine the city in ways that erase or conceal negative iconography of urban decline and blight that would effectively block investment opportunities. While the intentional manipulation of city imagery through a process of "imagineering" by urban elites sanitize and distort the identities of cities in accordance with the demand of the global market, as Hall and Hubbard avow, emphasis on city image is a critical component of urban entrepreneurialism. Moreover, the promise of city improvements by aligning local economies with the demands of the global market has valuable social and economic incentives for politicians and policymakers, thus serving as a persuasive argument for the adoption of entrepreneurial forms of governance in U.S. cities.

The aggressive redevelopment of urban space has grave implications for people experiencing homelessness. Because cities function as engines of economic growth, the drive to remove barriers that block or reduce the accumulation of capital becomes critical for administrators and politicians charged with city governance.[27] The public presence of the unhoused in public city space, particularly in gentrifying neighborhoods, poses a threat to intercity competition for capital and the agenda to attract outside investment. Successfully attracting investors to developed and developing city space and the facilitation of capital exchange "depends to a large extent on the packaging and sale of urban place *images*, which have therefore become as important as the measures to keep the downtowns and event spaces clean and free of 'undesirables' and 'dangerous elements' (such as youths, the homeless, beggars, prostitutes, and other potential 'disrupters')."[28] Thus, the institution and aggressive enforcement of anti-homelessness ordinances cleanse city space of the unsightly people who are viewed as beyond the pale of a vibrant urban society where its citizens embody the virtues of hard work and personal responsibility. In entrepreneurial cities, the social and political elements of disenfranchisement of unhoused people coalesce with urbanization and facilitate the increased regulation of their bodies. Dallas, Texas, provides a stunning example.

Redevelopment and Criminalization in Downtown Dallas

The city of Dallas is growing at an exponential rate. U.S. census data indicate that in 2010 the population of Dallas was just under 1.2 million people. In 2018 (the most recent year of available data), that number jumped by 11 percent to over 1.35 million.[29] By 2035, urban planners project that the city's population will rise to approximately 1.6 million. Wages in the city are also increasing. In 2018, the median household income was approximately $52,000, an increase of 3 percent from the previous year.[30] Spurred by these trends, which began after the turn of the millennium, the city implemented a process of urban planning and design to stimulate economic growth and urban redevelopment. Over a twelve-year span, from 2005 to 2017, Dallas adopted more than fifteen citywide plans that emphasized (among other things) neighborhood revitalization, transportation improvements, parks and recreation renewal, and infrastructure.[31] While these documents have much to say about the overall trajectory of Dallas's growth, I focus my attention specifically on the city's downtown area. Urban renewal and redevelopment initiatives often begin within the metropolitan core and spread outward. These downtown areas typically host central business districts, which are instrumental in attracting investment and capital. My focus here on Downtown Dallas will thus sufficiently capture the extent of redevelopment to then identify a correlation with the stringent policing of the unhoused.

In 2011, the city adopted "Downtown Dallas 360: A Path to the Future," a revitalization plan that evolved from previous studies of the downtown area.[32] This plan focused primarily on the seven core downtown districts—together known as the Central Business District—located inside the Freeway Loop (see Figure 1). According to those involved in its conception, which included representatives from city government, private developers, stakeholder groups, and corporations, the plan was initially spurred by "a resurgence in the prominence, relevance, and vibrancy of downtowns and urban environments throughout North America."[33] Dallas envisions itself as the premier urban center in North Texas, and, in particular, its downtown area is framed as "the epicenter of economic, cultural and social activity in the Dallas-Fort Worth Metroplex."[34] Like many cities throughout the U.S., the urban elite of Dallas believe that

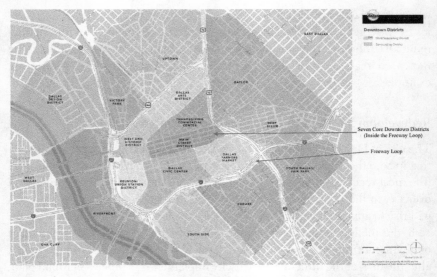

Figure 1. Downtown Dallas Districts Map (2011) (Source: "The Vision for Downtown Dallas," 360 Plan for the City of Dallas [2011], accessed December 6, 2020, www.downtowndallas360 .com)

downtown areas are the primary and most logical spaces to absorb and promote economic growth. Thus, the plan was designed to bolster investment in the urban core by addressing the most pressing urban renewal issues.

The 2011 plan identifies three overarching goals that tend to frame redevelopment initiatives in efforts to fuel a twenty-first-century urban economy. Goal 1 involves the creation of an "exciting urban experience." This goal emerged from the city's belief that Downtown Dallas "should be the most active, vibrant environment and should boast the city's greatest sense of urban life."[35] Critical to this achievement is the role of urban design—that is, building structure, accessibility, and the like. The physical construction of urban space conveys provocative statements about cities' abilities to support the vitality and vibrancy of urban living for residents.

Goal 2 entails the creation of a balanced transportation system and reflects the city's conviction that the future of a successful downtown "rests on its ability to accommodate multiple modes to allow the spontaneity, freedom and accessibility that only an urban environment can provide."[36] According to the plan, the sheer size of Downtown Dallas presents one of its most formidable challenges. A robust transportation system that connects the various parts of the downtown area with relative ease enhances its appeal, further attracting economic activity.

Finally, Goal 3 emphasizes the facilitation of an inclusive environment. The word "inclusive" here primarily—though not exclusively—signifies income diversity. The plan states, "Much of the housing development in the past decade has focused on the upper-income market, driven in many cases by the costs of land and construction. In the future, a wider spectrum of housing affordability will be critical, to provide convenient and achievable housing for entry-level workers, young families, and entrepreneurs whose incomes are dedicated to growing their businesses."[37] The ultimate aim here is the attraction of "the best and the brightest" to the urban core in order to promote growth. Each of these goals is subsequently subdivided by strategies and focus areas for the purpose of implementation.

In 2017, the city of Dallas released an update to its 2011 plan. The revised version expanded the conception of Dallas's downtown area to include more than a dozen neighborhoods within roughly ten additional districts immediately adjacent to the Freeway Loop (see Figure 2). Together these districts and neighborhoods form "the Center City" of Dallas's downtown area. Retitled "The 360 Plan," it reports city growth as of 2017 in the downtown area(s), including ninety new development projects currently underway (seventeen of which are designated as new hotels under construction or recently announced), an increase of 12 percent in new housing units in the Central Business District (between 2010 and 2015), and the establishment of fifty new restaurants since 2011. Over the next five-year period of the plan (2017–22), Dallas intends to continue its trajectory of growth in the Center City by framing redevelopment initiatives through three revised overarching goals: (1) building complete neighborhoods, (2) advancing urban mobility, and (3) promoting great place-making.[38]

The city of Dallas is aggressively on the move to rebuild. Guided by the 360 Plan, the extent of growth and redevelopment in its downtown spaces is undeniable. While promising news for a city in the midst of an urban renaissance, the plan raises an important concern that merits attention. It barely mentions homelessness, despite the fact that homelessness has become an increasing problem in the city in recent years. And what little it does say is problematic:

> The provision of social services, including homeless-related services, has historically centered in and around our nation's urban centers, a phenomenon certainly true in Downtown Dallas and some of the surrounding neighborhoods. Therefore, social service providers must be properly planned and managed in order to abate the chronic concentration of loitering, panhandling, and other quality of life issues related to homelessness. The result, then, will be better neighborhood integration

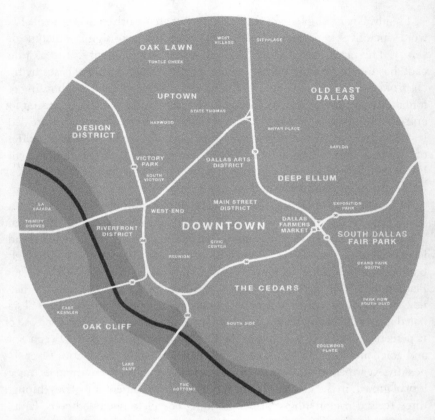

Figure 2. Downtown Dallas Districts Map (2017) (Source: "Vision and Plan Framework," 360 Plan for the City of Dallas [2017], accessed December 6, 2020, www.downtowndallas360.com)

and better service for those experiencing homelessness. Furthermore, equitable dispersion of social services throughout the entire city—in lieu of the current concentration in the City Center—will provide a balanced approach to the city's homeless issues.[39]

The plan suggests that the city of Dallas takes very little ownership of its role in resolving homelessness. According to the 2019 annual point-in-time count of unhoused individuals conducted in January, over 4,500 individuals had no permanent housing in the Dallas–Fort Worth Metroplex. Of that number, nearly 1,500 were unsheltered.[40] This represents a 9 percent increase from the previous year.[41] While Dallas is in the midst of a redevelopment boom, it is also experiencing a rising number of people experiencing homelessness.

The city of Dallas appears to rely on the private sector to address the problems associated with homelessness. As the lead agency for the city's Continuum of Care, the Metro Dallas Homeless Alliance, a nonprofit service organization, spearheads the administration of an effective response system to the homelessness problem. The city of Dallas takes responsibility in addressing homelessness insofar as it relies on the recommendations from the Dallas Commission on Homelessness and the Office of Homeless Solutions to address the problem. Yet the 360 Plan dictates that suggested recommendations from these entities must align with the goals and objectives of residents and property owners in individual neighborhoods.

What I find more striking, however, is that the 2017 version of the plan appears to suggest that the city is concerned with homelessness in redeveloping city space insofar as it seeks to deter the behaviors associated with the unhoused. It stresses the importance of private-sector management of social services in order to assure the abatement of behaviors associated with homelessness. It is not altogether clear of whom the plan is referring when it references "quality of life" concerns. One could reasonably assume this phrase refers to the unhoused. Yet, given the nature, focus, and emphasis of the report on building complete neighborhoods and great place-making for residents, visitors, and businesses alike, one could also legitimately assume that the quality-of-life rhetoric is likely more a reference to the property-owning (and renting) residents than to the unhoused. The sentiments expressed here appear to be representative of Dallas's underlying position concerning the prohibition of undesirable public conduct by the unhoused. Indeed, of the previously mentioned list of ordinances that ban conduct associated with homelessness, the NLCHP's 2016 "Housing Not Handcuffs" report indicates that the city of Dallas has on its books at least five ordinances that prohibit the following: (1) sleeping in public citywide, (2) camping in particular public places, (3) loitering/loafing in particular public places, (4) begging in particular public places, and (5) food sharing citywide.[42]

In fact, the NLCHP included the city of Dallas in its 2016 report's "Hall of Shame," which identifies a small select group of cities that aggressively enforce criminalization laws against the unhoused. Dallas made the 2016 list because of the grotesque number of citations issued to people experiencing homelessness for violation of ordinances that ban sleeping in public. In January of 2016, the *Dallas Observer* reported that between January 1, 2012, and November 15, 2015, Dallas police issued over 11,000 citations for sleeping in public. In 2015, the fine amount per violation was $146.[43] The *Dallas Observer* also indicated that these citations were heavily concentrated in the downtown area. "Among the homeless, it's common knowledge that sleeping on a sidewalk north of

Interstate 30–sometimes even nodding off on a park bench–will net a ticket, or, if the officer's in a good mood, a warning and stern order to move. Step south of the freeway, and the cops don't really care."[44]

It is likely that the heavy concentration of citations issued to people experiencing homelessness in the downtown areas of Dallas is a response to the complaints by residents, businesses, and visitors. In August of 2015, the *Dallas Observer* reported on the festering frustrations with downtown homelessness. At a city council housing committee meeting, an intense exchange between city council members and the CEO of The Bridge Dallas—a homelessness services organization located in Downtown Dallas—underscored the tensions between city leaders and service providers. According to the local news outlet, one council member emphasized the angry emails sent by downtown residents and asserted that the homelessness problem was spreading from the organization's immediate vicinity into the rest of Downtown Dallas, effectively "destroying nascent neighborhoods." Such complaints reflect the growing problem of homelessness in Downtown Dallas, and private companies like Downtown Dallas, Inc., have recently pushed for an increase in the police presence in the Central Business District in efforts to combat "rising nuisance crimes"—that is, public sleeping, panhandling, and public urination.[45]

Reports like these seem to suggest that the city of Dallas's actual response to homelessness does not reflect the language in the one brief paragraph found in its 360 Plan. On the contrary, it appears that enforcement of anti-homelessness ordinances, particularly in Downtown Dallas, is likely driven in large part by the complaints of residents, and their desire for social distance from the unhoused indicates anti-homelessness bias. The city has been exceedingly aggressive in its regulation of the bodies of the unhoused, particularly in newly redeveloped city space. The public discourse about people experiencing homelessness that produces their social disenfranchisement and spurs criminalization efforts is amplified in the context of urban renewal, informed by fears of potential contamination of new, vibrant urban neighborhoods. Having considered the political and economic elements that shape that discourse, I now turn my attention to examine the ways that a seemingly unrelated discourse—prosperity theology—legitimizes criminalization.

The Religious Discourse of Prosperity Theology and the Criminalization of Homelessness

Prosperity theology—also known as the "prosperity gospel" or "prosperity preaching"—exists in many different variations. At its core, however, it is a form of religious discourse that frames material wealth as a consequence of personal piety (obedience and faithfulness to God), where material wealth functions as the primary signifier of one's "blessed" socioeconomic status in society. Prosperity theology espouses, as theologian Stephanie Mitchem avers, that God demonstrates God's favor by bestowing material wealth on believers as a reward for their faithfulness and in fulfillment of God's promises.[46] As Mitchem poignantly demonstrates in her book *Name It and Claim It?*, the extent to which these ideas are expressed, particularly through preaching in U.S. churches by clergy who subscribe to prosperity theology, vary. Nevertheless, the accumulation of material wealth is the righteous moral good that prosperity preachers emphasize. Financial gain is construed as God's "perfect will" for Christian believers, and this idea is reinforced with scripture.[47] Passages like the following three provide fodder for the construction of religious discourse that underscores the materiality of life and valorizes the building of material wealth on religious grounds:

1. But remember the Lord your God, for it is [God] who gives you power to get wealth, so that [God] may confirm [God's] covenant that [God] swore to your ancestors, as [God] is doing today.[48]
2. Bring the full tithe into the storehouse, so that there may be food in my house, and thus put me to the test, says the Lord of hosts; see if I will not open the windows of heaven for you and pour down for you an overflowing blessing.[49]
3. The thief comes only to steal and kill and destroy. I came that they may have life, and have it abundantly.[50]

This interpretation of scripture epitomized in the religious discourse of prosperity preaching has significant implications for society and for Christian faith communities in particular. Religious and nonreligious critics alike have exposed its shortcomings. Social ethicist Robert M. Franklin contends that prosperity theology is a "vulgar form of material worship" that has a corrosive effect on U.S. churches through the promotion of "their own institutional well-being at the expense of serving the vulnerable."[51] Franklin emphatically asserts that prosperity theology subverts the holistic narrative of Jesus in order to reinforce American society's capitalistic attitudes.

Constructive theologian Keri Day argues that prosperity theology enables the rich to religiously justify their wealth by tethering God's favor to financial gain. For Day, prosperity theology ignores the sources and means of profit generation and fails to effectively confront the political-economic structures that disenfranchise poor, vulnerable communities. Consequently, they are not held accountable for the exploitative practices that facilitate the increase in their wealth.[52]

Similarly, urban sociologist Jason Hackworth raises concerns about the legitimizing power of prosperity theology. He argues that it

> provides divine justification for what many are able to justify otherwise only in crass capitalist terms: accumulating wealth. It softens, contradicts, and muddies the notion that accumulation is the disreputable pursuit that socialists and progressive theologians cast it as.[53]

Hackworth maintains that prosperity theology sanctifies private property as an expression of personal piety and reinforces the notion of individual responsibility as the determining factor of one's circumstances.

I find these three criticisms informative. In my reading, they signify the representational impact of prosperity theology on its subscribers. Prosperity theology shapes the Christian believer's interpretation of the world and one's relationship to it, particularly one's knowledge of what constitutes Christian moral fulfillment—for instance, the ultimate end of one's obedience and faithfulness to God. Consider the following words of a prosperity preacher extracted from an actual sermon to a local congregation:

> If you have to shop at Kmart, you are not blessed. If you do not own your own home, you are not blessed. If you can't go out shopping wherever you want, you are not blessed. If you can't wear designer clothes, you are not blessed. And then you need to find out what sins you have committed.[54]

Such rhetoric, while shocking for some, is representative of the religious discourse of prosperity theology and contributes to the production of knowledge that informs an understanding of blessedness for those persuaded by prosperity preaching. As religious discourse, prosperity theology establishes the parameters of Christian moral fulfillment, tethering the idea of blessedness to individual moral behavior. Thus, the absence of material wealth is attributable to one's personal moral failures—that is, one's sins.

In the context of the criminalization of homelessness, the religious discourse of prosperity theology provides the ideational underpinning for the social and political-economic elements that shape the broader public discourse on homelessness and criminalization. Prosperity theology legitimizes this discourse on religious grounds. Its emphasis on personal piety merely repackages the notion of personal responsibility as the determining factor of one's socioeconomic status in society and theologically buttresses the bifurcation of people experiencing homelessness into two distinct groups: the "deserving" and the "undeserving." In the latter case, prosperity theology reinforces the idea of their moral dereliction—that their plight reflects their poor choices—and consequently reifies the rationalizing discourse that asserts that homelessness is the consequence of personal social disorder and moral failure.

Prosperity theology also legitimizes the entrepreneurial drive for capital accumulation in U.S. cities through its divine justification of the attainment of material wealth. If wealth is the signifier of God's divine approval, then the agenda to draw capital into cities through the redevelopment of urban space can be interpreted as a sacred endeavor. Pro-growth strategies designed to attract corporate and private interests and drive capitalist development necessitate the removal of all potential barriers to procure outside investment. Prosperity theology tacitly provides an endorsement of the actions that urban elites take to pursue prosperity in urban space. As such, the religious discourse of prosperity theology provides theological cover for the institution of anti-homelessness ordinances, which fundamentally function as means to remove barriers that prevent the generation of profit. In this regard, prosperity theology at best offers no contestation to the institution of anti-homelessness laws that annihilate the public space of the unhoused. At worse, it provides a dangerous theological endorsement for the type of ethnocidal cleansing of people experiencing homelessness.[55]

The aforementioned consequences primarily operate on the level of language. But I am also interested in the way the religious discourse of prosperity theology also shapes practice—namely, that of moral discernment and analysis among Christian faith communities. As I see it, the danger is that prosperity theology potentially inhibits a Christian moral analysis of social and structural forces that cause conditions of disenfranchisement—for instance, the criminalization of the unhoused. An exclusive emphasis on individual agency undergirded by a theological vision that frames blessedness through the lens of materiality possibly forecloses a structural analysis of homelessness, its causes, and the ways that society "others" and subsequently punishes those seen as beyond the pale of the virtuous citizenry. Religious responses, then, may be prone to fall exclusively in the realm of charity, which far too often characterizes the approach of Christian faith communities that, while valuable, does little to disrupt the social and structural forces that prompt the criminalization of the unhoused or move toward the elimination of homelessness writ large.

The problem I raise here is the peril of prosperity theology to the moral witness of Christian faith communities by circumscribing the scope and depth of their moral inquiry and moral vision. If they are unable to perform a moral analysis of the problem of homelessness that extends beyond the individual level, then the agency of these Christian faith communities will likely be constrained, extending only as far as the parochial knowledge and conventional wisdom that shape their understanding of the issue. This should present cause for concern for any person of faith, but particularly religious activists, religious scholars, clergy, lay leaders, congregations, and the like who value the trans-formative role that religion and theology can play in the public sphere and who want to actively participate in public discourse that tackles our most pressing social problems from a solution-oriented perspective.

Conclusion

The role that religion and theology can, should, or should not play in public discourse is highly contested. Some contend that in the post-Enlightenment era, religion and theology have no place in the public sphere, as they contrib-ute nothing substantive or valuable to public debates over public issues. Others, however, object to such arguments and rather emphasize the utility of religious language, symbols, concepts, and commitments to effectively criticize our pub-lic culture with its associated problems. I sympathize with the latter. In a time and place such as the contemporary U.S., where far too often public discourse is characterized by vitriol, pettiness, bullying, and the like, we could use reli-gion and theology to raise the level of civility and bring attention to our most pressing social problems. Herein lies the promise of public theology.

Religious critic Victor Anderson defines public theology as "the deliberate use and articulation of religious languages, theological principles, beliefs, and doctrines to critique both the relation of American Christianity to our demo-cratic culture and social forces as well as to critique our society in its exercise of power in relation to the demands of Christian faith."[56] For Anderson, the theo-logical capacity to render public life "spiritually meaningful, morally livable, and culturally flourishing" is critical for a sufficient American public theology. I particularly see value in the use of public theology as a counter-religious dis-course that challenges prosperity preaching and the discourse on homelessness in the public sphere and offers an alternative, viable moral vision of society.

Whether inspired by the social gospel, the idea of the Beloved Commu-nity or Kingdom (or "Kin-dom") of God, or something altogether different, a critical part of the task of public theology (or theologies) as counter-religious discourse is to contest and dismantle the religious rationalizations that under-gird the social and political-economic elements that shape the public discourse on homelessness and incite efforts of criminalization. This counter-religious discourse must acknowledge and make explicit the connections between the-ology and religious language and Christian moral agency and problematize and confront controversial theologies, particularly those that tacitly condone selfishness and greed, thereby having an adverse effect on the moral witness of Christian communities. Although the current capitalist social order individualizes social problems so as to deflect from the interlocking structural forces that generate them, our theologies, and by extension our religious communities, must not.

Notes

1. Laura Stivers, *Disrupting Homelessness: Alternative Christian Approaches* (Minneapolis: Fortress, 2011), 56.

2. In this chapter, I use the terms "people experiencing homelessness" and "the unhoused" interchangeably. Both refer to individuals (or families) who have no permanent housing in which to reside. I prefer these terms over the more common locution, "the homeless," for two primary reasons: first, to be more analytically descriptive of a particular population in the U.S. My use of the term "unhoused" is descriptive of a reality of having no permanent housing, while the term "home" is imbued with meaning, which is subjective. And second, to honor the sentiments expressed by many of the unhoused individuals with whom I have spoken who object to the use of the term based on the rationale in my first point.

3. My use of the term "discourse" refers not simply to the use of language in the form of speech or writing. Rather, I emphasize the representational aspects of discourse and its role in knowledge production. In this regard, I find cultural theorist Stuart Hall instructive. He states, "A discourse is a group of statements which provide a language for talking about—i.e., representing—a particular kind of knowledge about a topic. When statements about a topic are made within a particular discourse, the discourse makes it possible to construct the topic in a certain way. It also limits the other ways in which the topic can be construed. A discourse does not consist of one statement, but of several statements working together to form what the French social theorist, Michel Foucault (1926–1984) calls a 'discursive formation.'" Deeply influenced by Foucault, Hall understands discourse as a system of representation that produces knowledge. It is in this regard that I use the term. I am indebted to both Hall and Foucault, who influenced my theoretical understanding of language and discourse; see Stuart Hall, "The West and the Rest," in *Modernity: An Introduction to Modern Societies*, ed. Stuart Hall, David Held, Don Hubert, and Kenneth Thompson (Cambridge, Mass.: Blackwell, 1996), 201. See also Michel Foucault, *The Archaeology of Knowledge and the Discourse of Language* (New York: Vintage, 2010).

4. Neil Brenner and Nik Theodore, eds., *Spaces of Neoliberalism: Urban Restructuring in North America and Western Europe* (Malden, Mass., and Oxford: Blackwell, 2002).

5. Henry Miller, *On the Fringe: The Dispossessed in America* (Lexington, Mass.: Lexington, 1991), xii.

6. Ibid., 2.

7. Ibid., 6.

8. Ibid.

9. Ibid., 8.

10. Ibid., 9.

11. Randall Amster, *Lost in Space: The Criminalization, Globalization, and Urban Ecology of Homelessness* (New York: LFB Scholarly, 2008), 80. Amster's use of the term "Protestant work ethic" is a reference to Max Weber's classic text *The Protestant Work Ethic and the Spirit of Capitalism*. There, Weber identifies the connections between religion and the emergence of capitalism in Western Europe; see Weber, *The Protestant Ethic and the Spirit of Capitalism* (New York: Charles Scribner's Sons, 1958).

12. Laura Stivers provides an insightful overview of some of the dominant American ideologies associated with the unhoused. Her perspective was quite useful in my reflection on homelessness and the elements of social disenfranchisement. See Chapter 3 in Stivers, *Disrupting Homelessness*.

13. It is important to note that these images are predominantly associated with individuals who experience chronic homelessness. The National Alliance to End Homelessness (NAEH) defines chronic homelessness as people who "have experienced homelessness for at least a year—or repeatedly—while struggling with a disabling condition such as a serious mental illness, substance use disorder, or physical disability." This definition reflects the U.S. Department of Housing and Urban Development's definition of the term. According to the NAEH, in January of 2019, there were approximately 96,141 individuals who could be classified as chronically homeless. This represents 24 percent of the total number of people who are experiencing homelessness in the U.S. Thus, those experiencing chronic homelessness represent approximately one-fourth of the total population of unhoused people. Yet the dominant images of homelessness are shaped by encounters with people who are experiencing chronic homelessness. This omits other experiences of homelessness that are often temporary and do not involve a disabling condition or encounters with places not meant for human habitation. For more, see "Chronically Homeless," available on the website of the National Alliance to End Homelessness, accessed February 26, 2020, www.endhomelessness.org.

14. Amster, *Lost in Space*, 80.

15. Talmadge Wright, *Out of Place: Homeless Mobilizations, Subcities, and Contested Landscapes* (Albany, N.Y.: SUNY Press, 1997), 69.

16. Tristia Bauman, Rajan Bal, Karianna Barr, Maria Foscarinis, Brandy Ryan, and Eric Tars, *Housing Not Handcuffs 2019: Ending the Criminalization of Homelessness in U.S. Cities* (Washington, D.C.: The National Law Center on Homelessness & Poverty, December 2019).

17. Ibid., 38.

18. Ibid., 42.

19. Ibid., 44.

20. Ibid., 45.

21. Don Mitchell, "The Annihilation of Space by Law: The Roots and Implications of Anti-Homeless Laws in the United States," *Antipode* 29, no. 3 (1997): 305.

22. Joseph Grange, *The City: An Urban Cosmology* (Albany, N.Y.: SUNY Press, 1999), xv.

23. Bob Jessop, "Liberalism, Neoliberalism, and Urban Governance," in Brenner and Theodore, *Spaces of Neoliberalism*, 119.

24. By "urban elites," I am referring to city administrators, politicians, urban developers, and other political-economic leaders that have great influence and power over how city spaces are fashioned.

25. David Harvey, "From Managerialism to Entrepreneurialism: The Transformation in Urban Governance in Late Capitalism," *Geografiska Annaler: Series B, Human Geography* 71, no. 1 (1989): 3–17. Drawing from Harvey and Jessop, Rachel Weber succinctly summarizes entrepreneurialism as "a combination of competitive, growth-oriented local economic development strategies, intimate public-private collaborations, and boosterism"; see Weber, "Extracting Value from the City," in Brenner and Theodore, *Spaces of Neoliberalism*. Many scholars who study the nature and dynamics of urban change, Harvey, Jessop, and Weber included, contend that "neoliberalism" frames these redevelopment strategies and initiatives in U.S. cities. Neoliberalism is based in the principles espoused by classical political economists of the seventeenth and eighteenth centuries who emphasized individualism, limited government, privatization of industry and property, and open and unregulated markets as the fundamental elements of a thriving political economy. In its revival as a political-economic project in the late twentieth century, neoliberal ideology aggressively frames the restructuring initiatives in U.S. cities (and across the globe). It has, as Harvey avers, "become hegemonic as a mode of discourse."

26. Tim Hall and Phil Hubbard, eds., *The Entrepreneurial City: Geographies of Politics, Regime and Representation* (Chichester, N.Y.: Wiley, 1998), 5.

27. Here I draw from David Harvey's conception of capital as "not a thing but a process in which money is perpetually sent in search of more money"; see Harvey, *The Enigma of Capital and the Crises of Capitalism* (London: Profile, 2010), 40.

28. Helga Leitner, Jamie Peck, and Eric S. Sheppard, eds., *Contesting Neoliberalism: Urban Frontiers* (New York: Guilford, 2007), 94 (italics in original).

29. "United States Census Bureau QuickFacts: Dallas City, Texas," accessed February 26, 2020, www.census.gov.

30. "Dallas, Tex.," Data USA, accessed February 26, 2020, www.datausa.io.

31. City of Dallas, "List of City-Wide Plans," accessed February 26, 2020, www .dallascityhall.com.

32. The traditional understanding of Downtown Dallas includes "the area within the existing freeway 'loop' [also known as Interstates 30, 35, 345, and the Woodall Rodgers Freeway] (also referred to as the Central Business District, or CBD)"; "Downtown Dallas 360: A Pathway to the Future," June 2011, 6, accessed February 26, 2020, www .downtowndallas360.com (brackets mine).

33. Ibid.

34. Ibid.

35. Ibid., 17.

36. Ibid.

37. Ibid., 20.

38. "Complete neighborhoods" refer to neighborhoods "in which a variety of residents' economic, social, and personal needs are met via convenient access to employment, affordable housing, recreation, goods and services, and education."

39. "The 360 Plan (2017)," 2017, 48, accessed February 26, 2020, www .downtowndallas360.com.

40. The Metro Dallas Homeless Alliance, which leads the annual point-in-time homeless count (in January), aggregates its data, which includes statistics from the city of Dallas, Dallas County, and Collin County; see "Dallas and Collin Counties Point in Time Homeless Counts," available on the website of the Metro Dallas Homeless Alliance, accessed February 26, 2020, www.mdhadallas.org.

41. Ibid.

42. Tristia Bauman, Janet Hostetler, Janelle Fernandez, Eric Tars, Michael Santos, Jenifer Brewer, Elizabeth Dennis, Ruth El, and Maria Foscarinis, *Housing Not Handcuffs: Ending the Criminalization of Homelessness in U.S. Cities* (Washington, D.C.: The National Law Center on Homelessness and Poverty, 2016), 68. It is important to note that some of these ordinances, the ban on sleeping in public, for example, have been in effect since the 1990s.

43. Eric Nicholson, "Dallas' Never-ending Crackdown on Sleeping While Homeless," *Dallas Observer*, January 29, 2016, accessed December 6, 2020, www .dallasobserver.com.

44. Ibid.

45. Stephen Young, "Frustration with Downtown Homelessness Simmers," *Dallas Observer*, August 18, 2015, accessed December 6, 2020, www.dallasobserver.com.

46. Stephanie Y. Mitchem, *Name It and Claim It?: Prosperity Preaching in the Black Church* (Cleveland: Pilgrim, 2007), ix.

47. Robert Jackson, "Prosperity Theology and the Faith Movement," *Themelios* 15, no. 1 (October 1989): 17.

48. Deuteronomy 8:18. All passages are quoted from the New Revised Standard Version (NRSV) of the Bible (brackets mine).

49. Malachi 3:10.

50. John 10:10.

51. Robert M. Franklin, *Crisis in the Village: Restoring Hope in African American Communities* (Minneapolis: Fortress, 2007), 119. Franklin makes a distinction between "the gospel of prosperity," which "refers to the cultural ideology of message that suggests that the accumulation of material possessions, wealth, and prosperity are morally neutral goods that are necessary for human happiness," (117) and "the prosperity gospel," which "asserts Christian faith is an investment that inexorably yields material abundance" (118). I maintain that this is a distinction without difference in common parlance. Moreover, both conceptually center on the same fundamental idea.

52. Keri Day, *Unfinished Business: Black Women, the Black Church, and the Struggle to Thrive in America* (Maryknoll, N.Y.: Orbis, 2012), 111.

53. Jason R. Hackworth, *Faith Based: Religious Neoliberalism and the Politics of Welfare in the United States* (Athens: University of Georgia Press, 2012), 45.

54. Quote taken from Mitchem, *Name It and Claim It?*, 38.

55. The use of the term "ethnocidal cleansing" is not mere hyperbole. Amster presents a compelling argument as to why the criminalization of homelessness in the U.S. has reached ethnocidal levels; see Amster, *Lost in Space*.

56. Victor Anderson, "An American Public Theology in the Absence of Giants: Creative Conflict and Democratic Longings," in *Ethics That Matters: African, Caribbean, and African American Sources*, ed. Marcia Y. Riggs and James Samuel Logan (Minneapolis: Fortress, 2011), 197.

Religious Responses to Homelessness in the San Francisco Bay Area

Addressing White Supremacy and Racism

Laura Stivers

Why is 40 percent of the homeless population African American when they only make up 12.5 percent of the U.S. population? Despite this stark statistic, very few analyses of homelessness, including my previous work,[1] examine how racism is connected to homelessness. Furthermore, most religious organizations and congregations do not generally consider structural racism in their approaches to homelessness. While it is individuals who experience homelessness, the phenomenon of homelessness is a social problem related to poverty and factors that contribute to poverty, such as low-wage work, lack of affordable housing, high medical costs, and more. In order for congregations to adequately address homelessness, they need to be educated about these structural causes of homelessness, including the significant role that structural racism has played and continues to play in increasing the chance that people of color will experience homelessness.

Since the beginning of our nation, our institutions and systems have been built on white supremacy. That is, our institutions and polices have been set up to maintain and defend a system of wealth, power, and privilege for whites. White supremacy was obvious and overt during colonization up until the Civil Rights Movement. While more covert and harder to identify today, institutional decision-makers are still primarily white (and mostly male) in our society. Without an analysis of white supremacy and racial injustice, the efforts of religious congregations to address homelessness will not touch the deep root causes of the problem.

There is a tendency to define homelessness as an individual problem rooted in presumed character flaws of homeless people and to avoid the structural causes of homelessness. To focus attention on the moral fitness of the homeless person is to run the risk of blaming the victims of an inadequate and unjust housing market for their homelessness. Implicit racism makes this even more the case for people of color. Strategies to address homelessness that ignore race and the impact of racial discrimination will likely not identify the policies that need to be changed to prevent homelessness for people of color.

While I will not examine all the policies that have caused, and continue to cause, racial disparity in relation to housing, I will focus on policies related to two areas relevant to homelessness and race: segregated neighborhoods and the prison industrial complex. In the first half of the essay I will use examples from the San Francisco Bay Area to examine specific policies that have caused racial disparity in relation to housing. Given that blacks have the highest rate of homelessness, this essay will focus explicitly on public policies that have contributed to homelessness among African Americans. In the second half of the essay, I will argue for an ethics of societal transformation rather than individual responsibility, drawing on values of solidarity and interdependence as well as God's movement for freedom of *all* humans. I will conclude by highlighting the ways in which several Bay Area faith-based congregations have developed these values in relation to racial justice and homelessness.

How Segregation Impoverished Black Families

Snapshot of Segregation in the San Francisco Bay Area

Currently the San Francisco Bay Area is undergoing a massive process of gentrification based in part on the growth of tech businesses in Silicon Valley. While high-tech jobs generally have high pay and good benefits, a 2014 U.S. Equal Employment Opportunity Commission (EEOC) study found that the industry does not match the racial diversity of the Bay Area.[2] Couple that with the statistics on national median wealth for different families—$130,800 for non-Hispanic white families, $9,590 for black families, and $17,530 for Latinx families[3]—and we get a picture of who can no longer afford to live in many of the thriving Bay Area communities. Not only do these wealth indicators reflect who can afford to buy homes in the Bay Area, but they are the direct consequence of years of public policies.

Fifty-eight percent of San Francisco Bay Area residents are people of color,[4] and while there are multiracial neighborhoods, segregation is still evident.[5] Policies that I explore in this essay have clustered African Americans in several areas: Richmond, West and South Oakland, Hunters Point in San Francisco, and Marin City. Latinx are more dispersed but are more likely to live in inner-ring suburbs like Vallejo or Hayward and in South Oakland. Marin County,

San Francisco, Berkeley, East Oakland, and the areas over the hills of the East Bay are predominantly white. The more white an area, the less likely it will have affordable housing. Race rather than median income is the demographic factor associated with how many affordable housing units a city has.[6]

In the last ten to twenty years full gentrification of San Francisco and Oakland has further exacerbated affordability, pushing many families out to the inner-ring suburbs. Oakland, while currently one of the most ethnically diverse U.S. cities, has nevertheless lost nearly 25 percent of its black population since 2000 because of gentrification.[7] The black population of San Francisco is half of what it was in the 1970s (5.8 percent), and the Latinx population in the Mission District of San Francisco has decreased from 60 to 48 percent since 2000.[8]

There are clear benefits to living in stable and thriving neighborhoods. There is less unemployment, the schools are better funded, the crime rate is lower, there is access to quality food, and there is more green space and less environmental pollution. Structural exclusion of people of color from middle- to high-income neighborhoods has negative implications. In the San Francisco Bay Area, unemployment is concentrated in neighborhoods of color, with more than one in four of the unemployed living in neighborhoods where over 80 percent of residents are people of color.[9] Per-pupil spending gaps in the public schools affect the life trajectories of youth. For example, in 2014–15, Palo Alto Unified school district, with a higher white and Asian student population, spent $16,067 per student, and 82 percent of their graduates were eligible to apply to four-year colleges compared to the higher black and Latinx population of Oakland Unified school district, with $11,854 per student spent and 57 percent of their graduates eligible to apply to four-year colleges.[10]

The top twenty-five safest suburbs in the San Francisco Bay Area based on crime rate statistics are all majority white.[11] "Food deserts"—low-income areas where a large number of residents have low access to a large grocery store—are also concentrated in communities of color.[12] Last of all, the brunt of environmental pollution—heavy industry, oil refineries, highways—are situated near or in communities of color. The oil refineries in Richmond's communities of color, just a bridge away from the open space preserves in predominantly white Marin, illustrate this inequity.

Policies That Segregated Neighborhoods and Caused Racial Inequality

While gentrification is currently causing more homelessness in the Bay Area (across all races but especially for people of color), historically there have been many policies that have purposely segregated neighborhoods, resulting in the disparity of wealth between whites and people of color. Two recently published books examine these policies: *Toxic Inequality: How America's Wealth Destroys Mobility, Deepens the Racial Divide, and Threatens Our Future*, by Thomas M. Shapiro; and *The Color of Law: A Forgotten History of How Our Government Segregated America*, by Richard Rothstein. Shapiro notes the connection of wealth acquisition to home ownership and family inheritance. He conducted interviews with black and white families between 1998 and 1999 and then again between 2010 and 2102. He writes:

> Place of residence was important to how much wealth a family managed to build and thus impacted mobility. Desirable, resource-rich neighborhoods allowed families to build housing wealth, which by far accounts for the largest wealth reservoir for middle- and lower-middle-class families. Two-thirds of net wealth held by the middle 60 percent of families is home equity. For families able to access home ownerships in neighborhoods with higher-priced homes and stable values, building wealth in this way was a real possibility. . . . Race played a large role in which neighborhoods had stable and climbing versus volatile and declining housing values.[13]

Of the ninety-seven families who gained wealth in Shapiro's study, institutional rather than individual behaviors were the foundation for their wealth accumulation—namely, owning homes in stable neighborhoods, having good-paying jobs with benefits, and receiving financial assistance from family networks.

Rothstein covers the many governmental policies that created racially segregated neighborhoods and how one's neighborhood of residence impacts intergenerational patterns of social, economic, and educational mobility. As Shapiro puts it, "Growing up in a low-income, racially segregated neighborhood reduces a child's ability to build financial security, gain an education, and accumulate assets over his or her lifetime."[14] Rothstein focuses on governmental policies that kept African Americans from owning homes in middle-class neighborhoods, debunking the common belief (even espoused by Chief Justice John Roberts) that segregation was caused by private individual choices and prejudices alone.

Public Housing

Our image today of public housing is of high-rise projects in poor inner cities, predominantly housing people of color. Rothstein points out that most public housing today is smaller apartments, townhouses, or homes. Public housing was first created for working-class white families and was not heavily subsidized. During the First World War, white defense workers and their families were given public housing. From the 1930s to early 1950s there was a housing shortage, and so President Franklin D. Roosevelt created the first public housing for civilians. He opened it to African Americans, but segregated buildings by race. The construction of this New Deal housing was a project of the Public Works Administration (PWA).

Before PWA housing, many neighborhoods were integrated because workers walked to work at nearby factories. The PWA projects imposed rigid segregation on integrated communities, and of course the white projects were in nice areas with green space and community centers, while the black projects were put in low-income neighborhoods near industries and railroad tracks. Legal segregation continued until the Civil Rights Movement, with stark results seen today. For example, Hunters Point and the Western Addition (originally an integrated neighborhood before segregated public housing) in San Francisco were public housing projects created for African Americans during the Second World War (WWII). After the war, African Americans remained in these neighborhoods because they were barred—through restrictive housing covenants and individual racism—from living anywhere else in the city.[15]

While public housing was once for middle-class families when housing was short, after WWII the housing shortage lessened, and new regulations made public housing primarily for the very poor. Opportunities for whites to get home loans and move to the suburbs meant that primarily poor people of color remained in public housing. Loss of middle-class rents and lack of sufficient subsidies by the government meant that public housing buildings deteriorated, furthering the stigma that low-income housing has today.

Zoning Policies

In the early twentieth century, when African Americans were leaving the South for other parts of the country, several cities adopted ordinances that kept blacks (and other minorities) from buying homes in predominantly white neighborhoods. This continued for years, despite a 1917 Supreme Court decision (*Buchanan v. Warley*) ruling that racial zoning ordinances infringed on the right of property owners to sell to whom they want. Many cities flagrantly violated the decision, arguing that their rules were an exception. After the Civil Rights Movement, when it became harder for zoning to be explicitly based on race, cities started zoning neighborhoods based on technically non-race-related factors, such as only allowing single-family homes in suburban areas (that, of course, African Americans had trouble getting loans to buy) or zoning areas by neighborhoods of color for commercial use, allowing toxic industrial development and other nefarious uses such as nightclubs and houses of prostitution.

These zoning rules further degraded the neighborhoods of color and the health of residents. Rothstein notes that minorities live near incinerators at a rate 89 percent higher than the national median.[16] Later the zoning designations kept African Americans from qualifying for insured mortgages because banks claimed that the commercial development was a risk to their property.[17] Zoning worked historically and currently to keep people of color out of white neighborhoods and put unwanted land uses in minority neighborhoods. For example, today in Marin County with its 80 percent white population, zoning is primarily designated as "residential" and "open space," while across the bridge in Richmond, with a 70 percent minority population, "commercial" zoning is prevalent.

Redlining

Beginning in 1917 the federal government promoted an "Own-Your-Own-Home" campaign to get white families to own homes so that they would be invested in the capitalist system and against communism. White low-income and middle-income homeownership increased substantially after 1933 when the Home Owners' Loan Corporation (HOLC) offered low-interest amortized mortgages with payment up to 15 years (and later to 25 years). To ensure segregation, the HOLC mapped out neighborhoods, circling the riskiest in red and the safest in green (that is, redlining). Neighborhoods with residents of color were lined red even if the residents were middle-class.[18]

The government then created the Federal Housing Administration (FHA) in 1934 to insure bank mortgages and made racial segregation a requirement of the mortgage insurance program. That is, no homes in "risky" neighborhoods qualified for mortgage insurance, and the FHA discouraged banks from making loans in any urban neighborhoods. They would also not insure mortgages for whites to move into integrated neighborhoods. The biggest effect the FHA had on segregation was to finance entire suburban developments, many of which had restrictive covenants that only allowed white families to buy homes.[19] This financing of subdivisions with restrictive covenants lasted until 1962, when President Kennedy signed an executive order that prohibited federal funds being used for racial discrimination in housing.[20] Denied mortgages to purchase a home and not being allowed to live in most places meant that African Americans ended up paying high rents for crowded conditions. Some managed to buy homes through contract arrangements, but monthly payments

were often inflated in these arrangements, and many contracts ended in eviction. Furthermore, buying a home through contract meant that African Americans had no mobility until their homes were paid in full.[21]

Blockbusting and Highway Development

There were many other policies and practices that kept neighborhoods segregated and minority neighborhoods poor. If some African Americans moved
into a white neighborhood, real estate agents, through ads and other tactics,
worked to panic white homeowners to put their houses up for sale, a practice
called "blockbusting." The agents then bought the homes at lowered prices
and turned around and sold them at higher prices to African Americans des-
perate for housing. Paying a high price for housing left few funds to keep their
properties up.[22] When developers wanted to shift African Americans away from
downtown areas they wanted to revitalize, they designated an area a "slum" or
"blighted" area. The construction of the federal interstate highway system
between 1940 and 1960 was a powerful tool of slum clearance. Many African
American neighborhoods were destroyed to make way for highways that white
commuters could use to get to work, with no relocation compensation given
to those who were displaced.[23]

Mortgage Discrimination

From the mid-1930s until the 1970s whites were able to access low-interest home
loans to move into the suburbs, a time when home prices were relatively cheap.
Meanwhile, African Americans and other minorities lived in neighborhoods
with substandard schools and few good jobs. Even if they had decent wages,
the expenses in their neighborhoods were higher than in the suburbs. When
Civil Rights legislation passed there was hope that things would change, but
inflation increased housing prices, giving whites increased equity in their
homes and keeping home ownership out of reach for many people of color. In
2010, African American and Latinx families made up three-quarters of the families living in urban neighborhoods with concentrated poverty. Nationally,
blacks are eight times and Latinx five times more likely than whites to live in
high-poverty neighborhoods.[24]

In the late 1990s it became easier for people of color to get home loans; however, banks started practicing a form of "reverse redlining" when they targeted
minority communities for exploitative subprime loans to purchase homes, leading to the 2008 financial collapse. Despite this widespread practice, there was
little state or federal regulatory response. Rothstein notes that 41 percent of all

subprime loan borrowers in 2000 and 61 percent in 2006 would have qualified for conventional loans with lower rates. African Americans were three times more likely than white borrowers to have subprime loans.[25] The Recession, according to Shapiro, was the "largest loss of minority wealth in U.S. history" (over 50 percent for African Americans and 66 percent for Latinx).[26] Since the housing crisis, private real estate companies and financial speculators have bought homes at depressed foreclosure prices, then rented them out or offered rent-to-own schemes.

Affordable Housing

Today there is a lack of affordable housing in many cities. The Housing and Urban Development (HUD) budget has never revived since Reagan slashed it in the 1980s by more than three-quarters—from 83 billion to 18 billion. The Western Regional Advocacy Project says that in 2008, homeowners' tax breaks cost the federal treasury $144 billion, with 75 percent of the benefits going to households making more than $100,000. In contrast, all federal low-income housing assistance totals 36 billion.[27] Section 8 housing assistance (that covers 60 percent of rent up to a maximum cap) has helped many families afford housing, but most cities have long waiting lists (some of them officially closed), and Section 8 tends to bolster segregation because the rents in affluent communities are too high and landlords in those neighborhoods often refuse to take Section 8 vouchers. Private developers can receive tax subsidies (for instance, Low-Income Housing Tax Credit) if they dedicate a certain percentage of their development for low-income housing, but the housing is often not for the poorest of the poor and can go to market rate after ten years.[28] Many affluent communities have had a "not-in-my-backyard" (NIMBY) perspective toward affordable housing and have successfully blocked such developments.

For lack of space I have only covered some of the intentional policies that gave African Americans and other minorities less opportunity, and hence less ability to create wealth. Apart from wealth building, people of color also experience the negative effects of living in segregated low-income communities, such as poor schools, more violence and police surveillance, lack of green space and exposure to environmental contaminants, few jobs, and little access to quality food, banks, and other amenities. In addition to policies intended to keep people of color segregated in poor neighborhoods, I will examine in the next section how the increase of mass incarceration in the 1980s, especially with the War on Drugs, also negatively affected African American and Latinx communities. The "pipeline" to prison often starts in the schools, where low-

Table 1

Race/Ethnicity	Percent of US population	Percent of U.S. incarcerated population	National incarceration rate (per 100,000)
White (non-Hispanic)	64	39	450
Hispanic	16	19	831
Black	13	40	2,306

income black and Latinx students are disproportionately suspended, expelled, or even arrested for minor offenses.

Mass Incarceration

Snapshot of Incarceration in the Bay Area

Mass incarceration is affecting many individuals and families in our nation, but African American and Latinx communities have been hit the hardest. According to a 2017 report by the Prison Policy Initiative:

> The American criminal justice system holds more than 2.3 million people in 1,719 state prisons, 102 federal prisons, 901 juvenile correctional facilities, 3,163 local jails, and 76 Indian Country jails as well as in military prisons, immigration detention facilities, civil commitment centers, and prisons in the U.S. territories.[29]

There are an estimated four and a half million more adults who are out of prison but under correctional supervision.[30] This is a massive increase from the 200,000 people who were incarcerated in 1972 in the U.S.[31] These national statistics do not show the stark racial and ethnic disparities of imprisonment. Blacks are incarcerated five times more than whites, and Latinx are nearly twice as likely to be imprisoned as whites. Table 1 shows the disproportionate rate of imprisonment.[32]

In California, the incarceration rate for blacks is even worse—3,036 per 100,000—and for American Indian/Alaska Native the rate is 996 per 100,000.[33] According to social scientists Bryan Sykes and Michelle Maroto, "Among cohorts born in the late 1970s, 68% of African American men with less than a high school education served time in state or federal prison by the height of the prison boom in 2010."[34]

The statistics of incarceration in Alameda County (for instance, San Francisco East Bay) illustrate the reality people of color are facing. Afomeia Tesfai and Kim Gilhuly of Human Impact Partners examine the difficulties formerly incarcerated people have securing housing. They write,

In Alameda County, there are almost 4,800 people returning from state prison, 3,200 people in county jail on any given day in 2014, and an estimated 375,000 people in Alameda County have a criminal record.[35]

They estimate that over half of this reentry population is at risk of "residential instability," especially considering that gentrification has made Oakland either the fourth- or sixth-most-expensive housing market in the country. Between 2000 and 2010, 34,000 African Americans left Oakland, and the number of low-income blacks living in Bay Area suburbs increased 9 percent.[36]

Other researchers document the gender imbalance among African Americans in Alameda County and Contra Costa County (north of Alameda County). They write, "In the Bay Area, about 12,500—or 12%—of primarily working-age black men (ages 25 to 54) are, in a sense, 'missing' from daily life."[37] For example, Alameda County in 2008 was 12 percent African American, yet 55 percent of the inmates in the county's jail were black.[38] Not only do the men themselves face difficulties when they get out of prison, their families suffer when they are in prison. Considering there are more than 2.7 million children in the United States who have an incarcerated parent, the effect of imprisoned fathers is devastating to families and communities.[39] Women also bear the brunt of the financial and emotional costs when so many men of color are imprisoned. The number of women being incarcerated is also increasing, however. There was a 700 percent surge between 1980 and 2019, with African American women being imprisoned over 1.7 times the rate of white women in 2014.[40]

Policies That Disproportionately Put People of Color in Prison

The criminal justice system and homelessness are connected. Tesfai and Gilhuly estimate that between 25 and 50 percent of people who are homeless have a history of incarceration.[41] Thus, it is not such a big surprise that 40 percent of the U.S. homeless population is black when 40 percent of that population is incarcerated. The number of people who are homeless steadily increased beginning in the 1980s. While a number of factors caused this increase in homelessness (for instance, declining wages, inflation of rents/home prices, loss of blue-collar jobs, steep cuts to social programs), incarceration and homelessness are risk factors for each other. Some homeless populations, especially individuals with mental illness, veterans, and youth, are at risk of incarceration.[42] And people with past incarceration face more barriers to being housed, from not being able to access federal housing assistance to challenges of securing employment and/or housing because of a criminal record.[43]

Just as governmental policies created segregated neighborhoods, explicit government policies also increased the number of people incarcerated in our nation. Policies associated with the War on Drugs, such as stop-and-frisk laws, forfeiture laws, and tough-on-crime policies, like the Three Strikes Law in California, have had a devastating effect on communities of color. Increased militarism of the police, more power for prosecutors to get poor people to plead guilty, and a greater number of monetary charges at different stages of arrest and imprisonment have also taken their toll on families and communities of color. While the policies themselves are written to be "race neutral," the use of racial profiling across the country has meant that African Americans and Latinx have been especially targeted. When these policies are coupled with a lack of investment in poor and minority neighborhoods (often one and the same), the metaphor of "school to prison pipeline" is apt. Youth of color are exposed to zero tolerance policies and the use of police in schools, socializing them from a young age to prison-like conditions rather than educational environments that seek to prepare young people for life as active citizens. African American high school dropouts are the most vulnerable to imprisonment. Their incarceration rate has increased from 10 percent in 1980 to 37 percent by 2008.[44]

War on Drugs

According to historian Elizabeth Hinton, a war on crime began in 1965 under the Johnson administration. While Johnson is known for his War on Poverty, it is less known that at the same time he was administering welfare programs, he was also bolstering police training and focusing on young black men inspired by civil rights advocates, who were advocating for black self-determination and community control. Rather than addressing the lack of jobs in poor neighborhoods of color, the rhetoric and policy focus was centered on juvenile delinquency, putting black youth under surveillance and leading the way for the more intensive policing of urban space by future administrations.[45]

In her book *The New Jim Crow: Mass Incarceration in the Age of Colorblindness*, Michelle Alexander gives a detailed account of the ways in which mass incarceration is a major form of institutional racism in our society today, consigning men of color to a permanent underclass and disenfranchising and impoverishing families and communities of color.[46] She argues that President Ronald Reagan's announcement of the War on Drugs in 1982 is when the imprisonment of people of color rapidly increased.[47] Tandem with the announcement was a mass media campaign to convince people there was a crack cocaine crisis in poor black neighborhoods, justifying the policing and imprisonment of people of color. Alexander argues that the impetus for the War on Drugs was never drugs but instead a public concern over race. In the 1980s, the larger issue in communities of color was economic collapse, with blue-collar factory jobs disappearing, not a drug crisis. Rather than addressing the structural factors that caused poverty and joblessness in these communities, the government instead incarcerated black and brown men who were danger-ous according to media depictions. She writes, "In less than thirty years, the U.S. penal population exploded from around 300,000 to more than 2 million, with drug convictions accounting for the majority of the increase."[48] Accord-ing to the National Association for the Advancement of Colored People (NAACP), African Americans and whites use drugs at similar rates, yet Afri-can Americans are arrested on drug charges six times that of whites.[49]

Since the 1980s many resources have been shifted from welfare and public housing toward the penal budget, under both Republican and Democratic presidents. Reagan offered massive cash grants to local law enforcement to em-brace the War on Drugs. Several policies led to a more militarized police force. The 1981 Military Cooperation with Law Enforcement Act gave local police forces access to military bases intelligence, research, and weapons. A 1984 amendment to an earlier forfeiture law then allowed law enforcement of-ficials to seize and forfeit any property connected to people suspected of drug use or sales, with the federal law enforcement able to keep all proceeds, and state and local police agencies able to retain up to 80 percent. Thus, law enforcement was incentivized by profit to step up their campaign on drugs. Alexander notes that these laws allow those with large assets to buy their free-dom, while small-time dealers ended up in prison. Furthermore, most for-feiture cases do not involve criminal charges yet are not contested because most people cannot afford a lawyer.[50]

"Crime Prevention" Strategies

Other policies also put more people in prison. Stop-and-frisk laws give police substantial leeway to stop, question, and frisk people under the pretext of "rea-sonable" suspicion. African American and Latinx males have routinely been deemed suspicious and dangerous in our country, and the media campaign to associate communities of color with drug problems meant that stop-and-frisk laws equated to racial profiling. Eighty-three percent of stop-and-frisk cases from 2004 to 2012 in New York City were of black or Latinx people, de-spite the fact that they accounted for only half of the population.[51] Get-tough-on-crime laws, like the "three strikes" laws in California that sentence anyone convicted of a third offense to life in prison, have not only put more low-level

offenders in prison, but also have given enormous power to prosecutors. Prosecutors routinely scare people with the risk of long prison sentences by adding
a number of charges that would not likely win in court simply to get them to
plead guilty to lesser offenses.

Shaping Social Inequality

There have been multiple negative results of imprisoning so many men of
color. Sociologists Bruce Western and Becky Pettit write about the social inequality produced by mass incarceration. They argue that it is invisible, cumulative, and intergenerational.[52] It is invisible to mainstream society because
it is segregated and concentrated along race and class lines. It is cumulative
because serving time in jail or prison diminishes social and economic opportunities. Western, in his book *Punishment and Inequality in America*, says that
having a prison sentence reduces annual earning by a third and confines ex-
prisoners to jobs with high turnover and little opportunity for advancement.[53]
Imprisonment also takes a member out of a poor working family's network,
leaving many single moms trying to make ends meet. Add on top of the lost
income the additional expenses of imprisonment (for instance, prison visits,
money sent to prisoners, and many newly instituted fees for things like pre-
trial detention, public defender applications, and jail booking fees), many prisoners and their families end up in what Alexander calls "debtors' prison."[54]

Social inequality produced by mass incarceration, similar to the effects of
segregated neighborhoods, is intergenerational. Multiple studies show that
parental incarceration destabilizes families and greatly affects children. Children
with an incarcerated parent are three to four times more likely to develop juvenile delinquency and two and a half times more likely to develop a serious
mental disorder.[55] Individuals living in communities with high imprisonment
rates not only struggle financially but also deal with deep cynicism about institutions and systems within the U.S. Furthermore, there is an unspoken
shame and internalized oppression, despite the fact that institutional racism
has played such a large role in creating these results.[56]

While incarceration negatively affects the financial and emotional stability of minority families and communities, possibly increasing their chance of
homelessness, ex-prisoners definitely struggle to find housing. Housing discrimination against ex-prisoners is legal. As Alexander says, "Rather than racially restrictive covenants, we have restrictive lease agreements, barring the
new 'undesirables.'"[57] Ex-prisoners have trouble getting any housing assistance,
whether Section 8 or public housing. The Anti-Drug Abuse Act of 1988 allowed
public housing agencies to evict tenants engaged in any criminal activity and

later any tenant or member of the tenant's family believed to be using illegal drugs or abusing alcohol. By the 1990s the Department of Housing and Urban Development (HUD) was screening tenants for criminal records.[58] The Ella Baker Center for Human Rights claims that 79 percent of people incarcerated were ineligible or denied public housing.[59]

An Ethics of Individual Responsibility versus Societal Transformation

Why is it important for churches and religious organizations to focus on race in relation to homelessness? Without a focus on the way systemic racism has been implicit in policies that have caused such a high percentage of people of color, especially African Americans, to be homeless, we will continue to focus on changing people instead of changing structures, with no real effect on the problem of homelessness. While the focus in this essay is on public policy and structural analysis, individual race prejudice also supports the existence of systemic forms of racism. For example, proposals to build affordable housing in neighborhoods that are not low-income or policy changes that might integrate white neighborhoods are vehemently resisted by middle- and upper-income white people. White churches will need to address systemic and individual racism simultaneously.

Since the white residents of these neighborhoods are often segregated from people who are affected by mass incarceration and homelessness, they are more likely to blame the victims than they are to identify the systemic causes of homelessness. Our culture's anti-black media depiction of African Americans as criminals, gangsters, and welfare moms fuels race prejudice and further justifies our not seeing or caring about the plight of those who are marginalized from society through prison and/or homelessness. Segregated neighborhoods allow structural racism to be invisible to whites. Most white parishioners do not understand how the policies I have outlined have affected wealth creation, nor do they realize how detrimental mass incarceration is to whole communities. Congregations of color are likely to be more aware of the systemic roots of homelessness but can nevertheless propose solutions that focus on changing individuals rather than structures. In general, most congregations respond to homelessness through charitable measures, like soup kitchens, food banks, clothing drives, or possibly even hosting a tent camp or offering parking spaces to people living in their cars. Most do not organize to change unjust structures, let alone have an analysis of racism and white supremacy.

I am not advocating a lack of accountability for people who make bad decisions and harm others and/or themselves, but I am arguing that there are systemic reasons that communities of color are disproportionately suffering from incarceration and homelessness. In this essay I've outlined a few ways in which our institutions and systems have been built on white supremacy. We cannot continue to advocate individual responsibility to those who are marginalized and exploited if we do not address white supremacy and transform our structures and neighborhoods so that people can succeed and live flourishing lives. In addition, continuing to address homelessness through charity without transforming policies and structures simply keeps the status quo of power, privilege, and oppression in place. Christian ethicist Rebecca Todd Peters, in her book *Solidarity Ethics: Transformation in a Globalized World*, writes about how white people can be in solidarity with people of color. She argues that solidarity requires genuine accountability and concrete answerability to oppressed people, not sympathetic and temporary gestures.[60]

The question for religious leaders in privileged, primarily white congregations is how they will help their parishioners see that white supremacy and systemic racism are factors in homelessness. Peters says that the first step for moving into an ethics of solidarity is for people to come to terms with their own privilege, to recognize and understand that policies and structures in our society have benefited some at the expense of others.[61] As Christian theologian Kelly Brown Douglas points out, our country's racial history has been determined by white America's aim to protect the "wages of whiteness."[62] While it does not help to blame white people for policies of the past, they do need to understand that these past policies affect mobility and freedom today and that many current policies contribute to racial injustice. Philosopher Iris Marion Young argues that while we can only be guilty for things we have done, we are all subject to collective responsibility for actions and policies that cause suffering for others, especially if we are members of a group that benefits.[63] Solidarity entails an *obligation* to transform unjust policies and structures. White congregants who benefit from policies and structures that support the white supremacist status quo have a collective responsibility not to remain silent in the face of injustice.

In her book *Stand Your Ground: Black Bodies and the Justice of God*, Douglas advocates for moral memory—that is, taking seriously the past that continues to shape America's racial history. She says:

> To right the past is to acknowledge the ways in which our systems,
> structures, and ways of being in society are a continuation of the
> myths, the narratives, the ideologies of the past and then to transform
> these present realities.[64]

Douglas argues that a moral memory uncovers relationships between past and present policies, such as the relationship between "the slavocracy and the

Prison Industrial Complex"[65] or segregated neighborhoods and the War on Crime.

Moving from moral memory to solidarity will require privileged white parishioners to step out of their segregated communities and find ways to work in mutual relationship with communities of color to mobilize policy change. Claiming solidarity as a foundation for economic policy, Peters argues, is based in two theological principles: the sacredness of life and the interdependence of the human community and the natural world. And Christian ethicist David Hollenbach writes, "Solidarity leads members of a community to recognize their well-being is shared."[66] Indeed, solidarity has its foundation in a universal common good where the health and flourishing of the Earth and all of its inhabitants are interconnected. Jesus modeled a universal common good in his inclusive ministry and mutual fellowship with people who were routinely oppressed or marginalized by the dominant society. In Luke 7:36–50, Jesus was dining at a Pharisee's house when a woman who was known in the city for her sinfulness entered with a gift and shed tears at Jesus's feet. The Pharisee Simon was appalled that a prophet like Jesus would let a sinner touch him, but Jesus treated the woman with full respect, honored her dignity and faith, and accepted her into the home.

In a solidarity economy, the burden for success would not rest primarily on the backs of individuals but on economic and social policies that create the foundations for human well-being and sustainability: policies that support the sacredness of each human being and encourage interdependence over competition in a capitalist system of winners and losers. Paul in his ministry promoted such a solidarity economy in the early Christian communities where members shared belongings and connected love of God with love of neighbor as the core of a common good.

One primarily white congregation that takes seriously the principle of solidarity with marginalized communities is First Unitarian Church of Oakland. The ministers started with the national Unitarian Universalist church's excellent curriculum on white supremacy, structural racism, and white privilege.[67] Then they did a church study on mass incarceration. At a Social Justice and Empowerment weekend, they decided that education needed to lead to action. To make sure they were working in solidarity *with* communities of color, they partnered with the Ella Baker Center for Human Rights. Following in the footsteps of civil rights activist Ella Baker, the center organizes "with Black, Brown, and low-income people to shift resources away from prisons and punishment and towards opportunities that make our communities safe, healthy, and strong."[68]

Members of First Unitarian Church of Oakland worked on a campaign related to California's Public Safety Realignment Initiative of 2011 to reduce the numbers of people incarcerated at the state level by shifting prisoners with low-level offenses to county jails. This law shifted money from the state to counties. The Ella Baker Center, along with people of faith, organized to make sure that half of the money went toward prison reentry efforts rather than all of it going to the sheriff's office, especially since the Alameda County sheriff is a strong advocate of militarized police. Putting money toward prison reentry is a transformative way to prevent homelessness for African Americans and Latinx.

Implementing economic and social policies that support human well-being and sustainability is related to the "freedom of God" that Douglas develops theologically in her book. The first aspect of freedom, according to Douglas, is that to be created in the image of God means that humans are created to be free. She notes that in an African understanding, all reality is sacred.[69] These theological claims have been profoundly important for African Americans who have and do suffer various forms of bondage. The theological truth of human sacredness and freedom is a crucial counter-message to the cultural and systemic racism of our society. The second aspect of freedom, says Douglas, is "God's movement in the world on behalf of freedom." She writes,

> In short, that God chose the Israelites is first an indication that God
> chooses to be in the world. Second it indicates God's preferential
> option for freedom. What it does not indicate is God's choice for any
> particular people above all other people. The exodus story tells us that
> God's choice of the Israelites was not about blood, but about freedom.
> The story says that God looked down and saw that they were in
> bondage, not that they were Israelites.[70]

Douglas also outlines how Jesus is the embodied reality of the freedom of God. Jesus intentionally ministered to the outcasts of his day. Not only was he in relationship with people who were marginalized and crucified, but he was also in solidarity with them in his commitment to fostering and nurturing life.[71]

The movement of God for freedom in the world and Jesus's example of solidarity with the marginalized and exploited are foundational for critiquing unjust policies that compromise the mobility and freedom of whole groups of people, like those outlined in this essay. They also serve to empower people of color to "claim the freedom of God that is theirs, knowing that God is fighting with them."[72] African American churches in Oakland have done just this by joining forces with the Dellums Institute for Social Justice to organize against gentrification and the displacement of families of color in Berkeley, Oakland, and Hayward. Our Beloved Community Action Network, which comprised nonprofits and churches, was formed to address specifically the racialization of the problem of homelessness.[73]

Our Beloved Community Action Network has had several notable wins in relation to immediate strategies they have undertaken to disrupt displacement. Through three budget campaigns they have gotten $65 million of public funds to be directed toward an Anti-Displacement Safety Net that would help pay for legal protection for renters, emergency rental assistance, and other services for residents at risk of displacement or homelessness. They also secured anti-displacement terms in the city of Oakland's $100 million Housing Bond. They worked with the Richmond Safe Return Project to craft and pass the Richmond Fair Chance Housing policy that removes housing barriers for formerly incarcerated residents. Last of all, they assisted the East Oakland Black Cultural Zone Collaborative in developing a collective ownership model business plan for the Black Culture Zone Hub.[74] All of these strategies are important for preventing homelessness. Although these policies can help low-income people of all races, Our Beloved Community Action Network is strategically focused on preventing eviction and homelessness for residents in communities of color.

Beginning in spring 2018 their organizing efforts were focused on a Restitution Movement that aims to hold responsible parties who have caused segregation, gentrification, displacement, and homelessness (for instance, financial institutions, outside speculators funded by venture capitalists, and the tech economy).[75] A central premise of the Restitution Movement is accountability from people and organizations in power who have caused injustice. Restitution is about societal transformation—that is, it requires addressing and changing the policies that continue to marginalize communities of color.

Conclusion

Moving from an emphasis on individual responsibility to an ethics of societal transformation is not easy for churches and religious organizations, and most have not shifted paradigms. As I have shown in this essay, multiple policies have been put in place to create segregated neighborhoods and mass incarceration, many of which people are unaware. Educating ourselves is a first step. Churches and religious organizations can be an educational partner for racial justice by teaching parishioners that incarceration did not increase because of heightened crime and that people did not simply choose to live in segregated neighborhoods, but that intentional governmental policies created our current injustices. The good news is that no matter how complex and overwhelming, policies can be changed. Thus, the second step is organizing to make change happen. Identifying policies that are in fact not race-neutral but keep the status quo of white supremacy in place will be key. Working in coalitions with other congregations and nonprofit organizations like the Ella Baker Center and the Dellums Institute for Social Justice is necessary to have sufficient power to hold government and private corporations accountable.

The movement of God for freedom in the world and Jesus's example of solidarity with the marginalized and exploited are important normative foundations for pastors to emphasize in their ministry. Too often, however, white supremacy and race are dropped from both analysis and action in lieu of a more vague call to address poverty. White parishioners are especially uncomfortable when religious leaders challenge white supremacy. We will not be able to end homelessness without explicitly transforming our policies and structures that keep white supremacy intact and continue to impoverish and imprison communities of color. Race analysis of homelessness is necessary if we are actually serious about creating communities where all may flourish and have a home.

Notes

1. See Laura Stivers, *Disrupting Homelessness: Alternative Christian Approaches* (Minneapolis: Fortress, 2011).

2. Compared to overall private industry, the high-tech sector employed a larger share of whites (63.5 percent to 68.5 percent), Asian Americans (5.8 percent to 14 percent) and men (52 percent to 64 percent), and a smaller share of African Americans (14.4 percent to 7.4 percent), Hispanics (13.9 percent to 8 percent), and women (48 percent to 36 percent); see U.S. Equal Employment Opportunity Commission (EEOC), *Diversity in High Tech* (Washington, D.C.: May 2016).

3. Kimberly Amadeo, "Racial Wealth Gap in the United States: Is There a Way to Close It and Fill in the Divide?" *The Balance*, accessed on June 25, 2019, www.thebalance.com.

4. In 2015, Bay Area demographics were as follows: 42 percent white, 24 percent Asian, 21 percent Latinos, and 8 percent black; see PolicyLink and PERE, *An Equity Profile of the San Francisco Bay Area Region* (Oakland, Cal.: PolicyLink and the University of Southern California [USC] Program for Environmental and Regional Equity [PERE], 2015), 16.

5. See Kalima Rose and Margaretta Lin, *A Roadmap Toward Equity: Housing Solutions for Oakland, California* (Oakland, Calif.: PolicyLink and City of Oakland, 2015).

6. Kevin Truong, "Study Finds Whiter Bay Area Cities Are Shirking Their Affordable Housing Goals," *San Francisco Business Times*, August 25, 2017, accessed November 22, 2020, www.bizjournals.com.

7. "Oakland, California Population 2020," World Population Review, accessed November 22, 2020, www.worldpopulationreview.com.

8. Peter Moskowitz, *How to Kill a City: Gentrification, Inequality, and the Fight for the Neighborhood* (New York: Nation, 2017), 126.

9. Rose and Lin, *Roadmap Toward Equity*, 34.

10. Susan Ferriss, "Get Up, Stand Up: California's Search for Educational Equity," The Center for Public Integrity, Washington, D.C., February 6, 2017, accessed November 23, 2020, www.publicintegrity.org.

11. "2020 Safe Suburbs in the San Francisco Bay Area," Niche, accessed November 23, 2020, www.niche.com.

12. Rose and Lin, *Roadmap Toward Equity*, 83.

13. Thomas M. Shapiro, *Toxic Inequality: How America's Wealth Destroys Mobility, Deepens the Racial Divide, and Threatens Our Future* (New York: Basic Books, 2017), 45–46.

14. Ibid., 46.

15. Richard Rothstein, *The Color of Law: A Forgotten History of How Our Government Segregated America* (New York: W. W. Norton, 2017), 17–37.

16. Ibid., 55.

17. Ibid., 44–50.

18. Ibid., 59–64.

19. Ibid., 65–79.

20. Ibid., 88.

21. Ibid., 97.

22. Ibid., 95–96.

23. Ibid., 127–31.

24. Shapiro, *Toxic Inequality*, 75.

25. Rothstein, *Color of Law*, 109–11.

26. Shapiro, *Toxic Inequality*, 40.

27. "History of Slashing HUD Budget," Fact Sheet of the Western Regional Advocacy Project (WRAP), San Francisco, Calif., accessed November 23, 2020, www.weap.org.

28. At least 20 percent or more of the residential units in a development are restricted to individuals whose income is 50 percent or less than the area median gross income, and at least 40 percent or more by individuals whose income is 60 percent or less than the area median gross income.

29. Peter Wagner and Bernadette Rabuy, "Mass Incarceration: The Whole Pie 2017," Prison Policy Initiative (March 14, 2017), accessed November 23, 2020, www .prisonpolicy.org.

30. Bryan L. Sykes and Michelle Maroto, "A Wealth of Inequalities: Mass Incarceration, Employment, and Racial Disparities in U.S. Household Wealth, 1996 to 2011," *The Russell Sage Foundation Journal of the Social Sciences* 2, no. 6 (October 2016): 130.

31. Todd R. Clear, "The Effects of High Imprisonment Rates on Communities," *Crime and Justice* 37, no. 1 (2008): 97.

32. Leah Sakala, "Breaking Down Mass Incarceration in the 2010 Census: State-by-State Incarceration Rates by Race/Ethnicity," available on the website of the Prison Policy Initiative (May 28, 2014), accessed November 23, 2020, www .prisonpolicy.org.

33. Ibid.

34. Sykes and Maroto, "Wealth of Inequalities," 130–31.

35. Afomeia Tesfai and Kim Gilhuly, *The Long Road Home: Decreasing Barriers to Public Housing for People with Criminal Records* (Oakland, Calif.: Human Impact Partners, May 2016), 9.

36. Ibid., 10.

37. Charu Kukreja and Matthew Green, "MAP: Why Black Women Outnumber Black Men in the Bay Area and Beyond," *KQED News* (July 16, 2016), accessed November 23, 2020, www.kqed.org.

38. Tesfai and Gilhuly, *Long Road Home*, 12.

39. Katie Kramer and Sharon McDonnell, *Children, Parents, and Incarceration: Descriptive Overview of Data from Alameda and San Francisco County Jails* (San Leandro, Calif.: Alameda County Children of Incarcerated Parents Partnership/San Francisco Children of Incarcerated Parents Partnership/Zellerbach Family Foundation: January 2016), 5.

40. The Sentencing Project, "Incarcerated Women and Girls," Factsheet, Washington, D.C. (November 2020).

41. Tesfai and Gilhuly, "Long Road Home,"19.

42. "Incarceration and Homelessness: A Revolving Door of Risk," *In Focus: A Quarterly Research Review of the National Health Care for the Homeless Council* 2, no. 2 (November 2013).

43. Ibid.

44. Bruce Western and Becky Pettit, "Incarceration and Social Inequality, *Daedalus* 139, no. 3 (Summer 2010): 10.

45. Elizabeth Hinton, *From the War on Poverty to the War on Crime* (Cambridge, Mass., and London: Harvard University Press, 2016), 13–50.

46. Alexander, *The New Jim Crow: Mass Incarceration in the Age of Colorblindness* (New York: New Press, 2010).

47. Hinton argues that the war on crime actually began in 1965 with the Lyndon Johnson administration, and while the Reagan administration is credited with the domestic policy shift of confinement and urban surveillance, its policies were not a sharp departure, but simply an intensification of the war on crime that Johnson implemented; see Hinton, *From the War on Poverty to the War on Crime.*

48. Alexander, *The New Jim Crow*, 6.

49. National Association for the Advancement of Colored People (NAACP), "Criminal Justice Fact Sheet," accessed November 23, 2020, www.naacp.org.

50. Alexander, *The New Jim Crow*, 35–114.

51. Editorial Board, "Racial Discrimination in Stop-and-Frisk," *New York Times*, August 12, 2013, accessed November 23, 2020, www.nytimes.com.

52. Western and Pettit, "Incarceration and Social Inequality," 12.

53. Western, *Punishment and Inequality in America* (New York: Russell Sage, 2006), 128.

54. Alexander, *The New Jim Crow*, 154–55.

55. Clear, "The Effects of High Imprisonment Rates on Communities," 110.

56. Alexander, *The New Jim Crow*, 161.

57. Ibid., 144.

58. Ibid., 144–45.

59. Tesfai and Gilhuly, "Long Road Home," 4.

60. Rebecca Todd Peters, *Solidarity Ethics: Transformation in a Globalized World* (Minneapolis: Fortress, 2014), 64.

61. Ibid., 69.

62. Kelly Brown Douglas, *Stand Your Ground: Black Bodies and the Justice of God* (Maryknoll, N.Y.: Orbis, 2015), 205.

63. Iris Marion Young, *Responsibility for Justice* (Oxford: Oxford University Press, 2013), 75–94.

64. Douglas, *Stand Your Ground*, 222.

65. Ibid.

66. David Hollenbach, S.J., "The Glory of God and the Global Common Good: Solidarity in a Turbulent World," *CTSA Proceedings* 72 (2017): 56.

67. See Unitarian Universalist Association, "Curricula & Trainings on Anti-Racism, Anti-Oppression, and Multiculturalism," accessed November 23, 2020, www.uua.org.

68. See "About the Ella Baker Center," Ella Baker Center for Human Rights website, accessed November 23, 2020, www.ellabakercenter.org.

69. Douglas, *Stand Your Ground*, 150.

70. Ibid., 159.

71. Ibid., 181.

72. Ibid., 165.

73. See "Our Beloved Community Action Network," The Dellums Institute for Social Justice, accessed November 23, 2020, www.dellumsinstitute.org.

74. Ibid.

75. Interview with Margaretta Lin, executive director and cofounder of The Dellums Institute for Social Justice (December 4, 2017).

Homelessness and Health in Seattle

Challenges and Opportunities of Faith-Based Services

Lauren Valk Lawson

A connection exists between health and homelessness. Poor health can trigger an event, such as job instability or bankruptcy from medical costs, that leads to homelessness. An acute infection or injury while homeless often leads to chronic health problems because healing is difficult without an adequate place to recuperate. Additionally, lack of stable storage creates challenges for compliance with medications or wound dressings.[1] These and many other circumstances increase the prevalence of poor health among people experiencing homelessness. An understanding of this connection between health and housing can provide insight for faith-based organizations (FBOs) into the experience of the unhoused and the services that these organizations can provide.

The purpose of this chapter is fourfold: (1) discuss the role of FBOs in the provision of services; (2) describe the relationship between health and homelessness; (3) identify conceptual models for incorporating health care into services for unhoused people; and (4) provide a case study of a successful faith-based program working at the intersection of health and homelessness.

Provision of Faith-Based Services

FBOs—defined in this chapter as providers of social services that are either religiously motivated or affiliated—play a significant role in the provision of services to unhoused people.[2] It is estimated that FBOs provide approximately 60 percent of all overnight shelter and save millions of dollars a year through donated services.[3]

From the beginning of recorded history in what would become the United States, FBOs provided services to unhoused people. During early colonial days, local parishes assumed responsibility for the impoverished in their district by providing tangible aid and support. Though secular efforts emerged, such as vagrancy laws and jail cells for "tramps," these services criminalized the problem.[4] FBOs were unique in their attempt to include a spiritual aspect to their care for the unhoused, which was reflected in the provision of both tangible aid (such as housing) and religious support.[5] Though these services were founded in faith, unfortunately prevailing moral attitudes were also reflected. An example was the belief that homelessness revealed a moral defect.[6]

In the years leading up to and during the Great Depression, there was an unprecedented increase in the number of unhoused people in the United States. The most visible were transient men, often depicted as "riding the rails."[7] To address the issue, the Federal Transient Service (FTS) was passed in 1933. As part of the New Deal Era, one aspect of the FTS got communities directly involved to improve local services. The funding only lasted for two years, but it demonstrated the first effort of federal support to local services for the homeless.[8]

The Charitable Choice provision of the 1996 Welfare Reform Act was another more recent effort by the federal government to increase services for the unhoused by engaging community efforts. Charitable Choice provided FBOs the opportunity to "compete for federal grants and contracts related to welfare reform without diminishing their basic religious character."[9] In particular, the grants supported smaller community-based services that still have close ties to local congregations, often sharing physical space. The grants were also intended to help faith-based service organizations develop capacity.[10]

First Charitable Choice, then the creation of the White House Faith-Based and Community Initiative in 2001, established FBOs as providers of federally funded welfare services. For the first time, FBOs could deliver government-sanctioned services while maintaining their religious expression.[11] In a primer to assist local officials to engage with FBOs, Stephen Goldsmith and colleagues identified a number of "unique strengths and attributes" of these organizations. They found that FBOs:

1. are generally trusted by the community;
2. create and provide leadership;
3. have access to human (volunteers) and financial (donations) capital;
4. are anchors within their community and culture;
5. are more willing to provide a holistic approach ("mind, body, and soul"); and
6. are driven by a "higher calling."[12]

There are some identified challenges for FBOs toward accessing funding, such as a need to formalize the services they provide. Lack of program policies and procedures and outcome evaluations is an issue. FBOs will also need to demonstrate capacity to manage services. It is essential that an FBO has identified a management structure and a financial system.[13]

Social Determinants of Heatlh

For the purposes of this chapter, health is defined as "the state of complete physical, mental and social well-being and not merely the absence of disease or infirmity."[14] This definition of health includes the influence of social determinants on the health of individuals, families, and communities. Social determinants are factors in a society or environment that affect health outcomes—factors such as discrimination, level of education, and adequate housing.[15] As an example, the availability of employment with health care benefits directly affects a person's health. It is a social determinant that eludes many unhoused people, exacerbating chronic health conditions and challenging access to care.

The aftermath of Hurricane Katrina in the city of New Orleans in 2005 demonstrates the effect of social determinants on housing and health. Though the hurricane indiscriminately descended upon New Orleans, one month later, the people who remained homeless were more likely to be African American and have chronic health problems.[16] Many lived in racially segregated areas of dense poverty prior to the disaster. Following the hurricane, these same areas experienced the worst flooding because of poor infrastructure and inadequate levees.[17] Where people live, their economic status, and their racial heritage are just a few of the social determinants that affect health and can put a person at risk for homelessness.

Social-Ecological Model

The process of becoming homeless is complex. Though a single event or social determinant of health may precipitate the experience, often a confluence of multiple factors results in homelessness. Common social determinants have been identified that may lead to housing instability, such as mental illness and lack of access to safe housing, though no one cause explains the scope of the problem. The social-ecological model is useful to understand the complexity of interconnected factors that may result in loss of housing.[18]

The social-ecological model provides a structure to observe complex relationships between factors of health in which the person is viewed within the larger social context.[19] To do this, the model is conceptualized as four concentric rings, each representing a level of influence on a person's well-being.

The levels are labeled "Individual," "Interpersonal Relationships," "Community," and "Society."[20] Individual factors may include poor physical and mental health, chronic illness, substance abuse, and lack of education. Interpersonal relationships consist of the quality of an individual's personal relationships and the availability of close contacts for tangible aid and support. The community represents the availability of supportive factors, such as overnight shelters, as well as public attitudes toward the unhoused. And the societal level represents factors such as availability of affordable housing and policies on health and human resources.[21]

To provide an example, a person may be at risk for housing instability because of individual social determinants such as a low-paying job and substance abuse. The person may be able to cope until a triggering event occurs, such as loss of housing following a divorce (interpersonal relationship factor). If the person lived in a rural community, there may be few resources available for temporary housing and addiction services (community factor). Finally, if there were addiction services available, the person may not be able to access immediate in-patient services because of lack of affordable health insurance (societal factor). In this example the interaction of the individual, interpersonal, community, and societal factors makes homelessness possible. Use of the social-ecological model not only helps to identify potential risk factors, it can determine protective factors, as well.[22] Protective factors include easily accessible mental health services, availability of low-cost housing, supportive community attitudes, and a social safety network for families.

Access and Utilization of Health Care Services

There are multiple factors that influence the use of health care services by unhoused people. As an example, without proper documentation, such as a driver's license, it can be difficult to obtain appointments at some clinics. These requirements impede access to care because maintenance of personal documents is a challenge when homeless. Other factors include lack of insurance, challenges with transportation, and fear of poor treatment because of staff attitudes toward homelessness.[23]

Access

"Access" refers to entry into the health care system and includes three important components: coverage, services, and timeliness.[24] Coverage is the availability of health care insurance and the ease in obtaining services so people can receive care when needed. Without insurance, unhoused people avoid seeking care for fear of being turned away or incurring debt. Services refers to the delivery of quality health care that provides illness management as well as preventive care. These are the components of "primary care," and access to a primary care provider is an important social determinant that improves the health of populations.[25] When people have access to a consistent source of primary care, it has been found that they have better health outcomes at a lower cost to themselves and society.[26] Finally, timeliness implies that health care services are available when needed. An example of timeliness is the availability of an appointment without a long wait. Among unhoused people, when regular health care appointments were easy to access, even those with chronic mental illness and/or a history of drug abuse were not deterred from seeking care.[27]

Utilization

"Utilization" refers to the factors that incline a person to either seek or avoid health services. Three categories of factors influence utilization: predisposing factors, enabling factors, and the perception of the need for care.[28] Predisposing factors encompass attitudes toward illness, help-seeking behaviors, and past experiences with the health care system. As an example, an abscessed wound that is the result of illicit drug use may prevent a person from getting available treatment because of his feelings of guilt and worthiness. Enabling factors are the personal means by which services are accessed or obstacles encountered.[29] How people choose to spend their time is an enabling factor. For unhoused people, meeting their immediate needs, such as obtaining food and shelter, often outweigh the perceived benefits of preventive and primary health care.[30] For instance, a two-month prospective cohort study of 250 older homeless adults from Boston, Massachusetts, found that those individuals who obtained housing experienced improved depressive symptoms and reduced acute care utilization—that is, visited emergency departments (ED) less frequently—compared with those who remained homeless.[31]

"Need," the final factor of utilization, is evident in the overuse of emergency medical services by unhoused people. Indeed, as I have just intimated, because of unmet health needs and issues regarding access and utilization of basic health care, people experiencing homelessness frequently wait until symptoms are perceived as life-threatening before seeking care and resort to the use of an ED for emergent and nonemergent care. A study of ED usage published in 2010 revealed a rate of ED visits among an unhoused population to be 72 per 100 per year, which compares to 40 visits per 100 people in the housed population.[32] The unhoused people also tend to be acutely ill with preventable chronic conditions, such as hypertension and diabetes. Prioritizing survival needs such as food and shelter over health may indicate that threshold of urgency is necessary before seeking medical attention.[33]

Simplifying entry into primary care clinics may address the issue. As an example, Neighborcare Health in the Seattle area opened a clinic specifically to meet the basic medical needs of unhoused people. The clinic provides a wide array of services, such as comprehensive medical care, mental health counseling, and drug and alcohol services, all provided in a single location, using methods that are essential to caring for high-risk patients, such as relationship-based and trauma-informed care, with the aim of overcoming the deep mistrust or fear that is often rooted in trauma and the multiple barriers to care faced by homeless persons.[34]

Health and Homelessness

The individual risk factor of being without stable housing has detrimental effects on a person's health. Sometimes poor health, such as mental illness, precipitates the event of losing housing. Once homeless, chronic health conditions worsen. There may be no safe place to store medications or a lack of healthy foods that exacerbate a health condition. Recovery from illness and injury becomes difficult. Homelessness makes everything worse.

Chronic Illness

Common chronic health conditions identified among the unhoused include hypertension, diabetes, cardiovascular diseases, skin conditions, cancer, and infectious diseases such as HIV/AIDS and Hepatitis C.[35] The mortality rate from these chronic health conditions is three to four times higher among the unhoused than the housed population, with an average age of death between forty-two and fifty-two years. This statistic is significantly lower than the life expectancy in the United States of 78.7 years for the total population.[36] Even when compared to housed people of a low socioeconomic status with the same chronic health problem, unhoused people die more frequently at a younger age.[37] The key social determinant factor is the lack of stable housing. Trimorbidity, or the combination of one or more chronic medical conditions with a mental illness and substance abuse, also influences the younger mortality rate.[38] Trimorbidity is associated with a higher risk for early death than substance abuse or mental illness alone.

The conditions of being chronically homeless can lead to other commonly seen health problems. "Chronically homeless" refers to people with a disabling condition who are either continuously homeless for one year or more or have four episodes of homelessness in a three-year period.[39] Due to vagrancy ordinances and lack of affordable housing, prolonged homelessness can lead to a transient lifestyle with a lack of access to safe places for personal hygiene. Hygiene practices can also be limited because of significant mental illness and substance abuse.[40] Commonly encountered health problems include chronic skin diseases, such as methicillin-resistant *Staphylococcus aureus* (MRSA), and dental caries. Lack of personal hygiene resources and abilities can also lead to poor foot care and a myriad of complications from *tinea pedis* (athlete's foot) to immersion foot, also known as trench foot, which is a result of prolonged exposure to cold, wet socks and shoes.[41]

Mental Illness

About 64 percent of the homeless individuals surveyed during Seattle/King County's 2019 point-in-time count reported a psychiatric or emotional condition.[42] And according to the National Alliance on Mental Illness (NAMI), approximately 26 percent of homeless adults staying in shelters have a serious mental illness.[43] Common diagnoses of mental illness include schizophrenia, schizoaffective disorder, bipolar disorder, and major depression. These serious mental health conditions result in difficulty forming and maintaining relationships and the potential to react irrationally in social situations. Poor mental health can also affect physical health because of poor self-care, inadequate hygiene, and neglect of health problems, such as not taking medication for hypertension.[44] It is estimated that nearly half of all people identified as chronically mentally ill and unhoused also self-medicate using illicit drugs and alcohol. As mentioned earlier, this trimorbidity of mental illness, drug use, and chronic health conditions puts people at higher risk for early death.

Prior to the early 1960s, people with significant mental illness were often admitted to in-patient psychiatric hospitals, either state-run or charity faculties sometimes referred to as "insane asylums."[45] People with chronically severe mental illnesses were basically warehoused away from the community. Little was known at that time about effective treatments, and patients received custodial care. With the advent of new pharmacological interventions in the 1950s, such as the antipsychotic drug chlorpromazine, coupled with advancements in psychiatry for treating mental illnesses, attitudes began to shift away from confining people in facilities to incorporating their care into communities. Part of the motivation was based in funding. The premise was that patients transferred from state-funded facilities could receive better care in their neighborhoods through less expensive federally funded programs. As an example, elderly patients with dementia would be better served in nursing homes funded through federal programs such as Medicare.

This process came to be known as "deinstitutionalization," or the public policies created to move residents of psychiatric hospitals back into their communities to receive mental health care services.[46] Deinstitutionalization occurred primarily as the result of federal efforts to improve mental health services by funding community mental health centers (CMHCs). These policies include the 1963 CMHC Construction Act signed by President John F. Kennedy that authorized federal grants for the building of these centers. Once granted, these centers provided comprehensive mental health and addiction services to help people function at their best within the community where they resided.[47]

Deinstitutionalization, which began as a means to improve the quality of life for people experiencing mental illness, revealed a lack of consideration for the neediest people, those with significant mental illness. As an example, policies did not provide sufficient resources to address where people would live and the support they would need to remain safely in housing. This neglect has been credited with the increased visibility of people experiencing symptoms of severe mental illness while unhoused.[48]

Supportive housing is a needed evidence-based model that has demonstrated success for people with severe mental illness and addictions. Supportive housing refers to affordable housing that provides additional services, such as case managers and mental health counselors, to assure a person is successful in living independently.[49] In a qualitative study, previously unhoused residents living in supportive housing reported experiencing major improvements, especially improved physical and mental well-being, in their quality of life, and a sense of increased involvement in their community.[50] The ability for CMHCs to provide sufficient housing resources is challenging, particularly in cities where the availability of low-income housing has been displaced through gentrification as well as through cutbacks of housing subsidies, such as the federal government's Housing Choice Voucher Program (Section 8). Seventy-five percent of the respondents of the 2019 Seattle/King County point-in-time count survey indicated that rental assistance and more affordable housing would help them to obtain permanent housing and thus were key to ending their homelessness.[51] Indeed, the need for permanent supportive housing is greater than the resources currently available.

One example of a successful method of supportive housing is the Housing First model. Housing First refers to a systems approach where unhoused people are quickly moved into permanent housing and supported to maintain housing, along with opportunities to improve their quality of life.[52] Supportive services such as case management and mental health or addiction care are available, though services are not a requirement for housing. There are no requirements for sobriety or commitment to a rehabilitation program. One study showed that after a year in a Housing First type program, 90 percent of the participants remained housed.[53] Another study in Seattle reported that common risk factors for recidivism, such as mental illness, substance abuse, and psychiatric symptoms, did not result in a return to homelessness for a majority of the residents of a single-site or project-based Housing First program.[54]

Substance Abuse

Substance abuse has been identified as the single-largest cause of housing insecurity, both as a pathway to and a consequence of homelessness.[55] It is difficult to get a true picture of the number of people who use substances while homeless. Of respondents to the 2019 Seattle/King County point-in-time count survey, 32 percent reported drug or alcohol abuse. The share doubled to 64 percent for individuals experiencing chronic homelessness.[56] During an assessment of unhoused people in a neighborhood in north Seattle, moreover, 67 percent reported daily use of alcohol for at least a month.[57] Variation in responses may reflect reluctance to self-report substance use because of fears of stigma and an implication of criminal activities. In this context, another pathway to homelessness is self-medication with drugs and alcohol by mentally ill people who do so to manage their psychiatric symptoms.[58]

Substance abuse among unhoused people is a complex problem to address. Commonly used substances include alcohol, heroin, and opioids (such as prescriptive opioid medications for pain and the street availability of fentanyl), cocaine, methamphetamine, and marijuana. For many, addiction problems lead to homelessness as a result of loss of employment, difficulties with personal relationships, and a focus on drug-seeking habits.[59] Others may begin to use substances as a means of coping with the hardships of having no safe place to sleep. It has also been reported that among unhoused people there is a social aspect to sharing substances that can create a sense of comradery and belonging.[60]

Unfortunately, addictive behaviors are a barrier to getting out of homelessness. Meeting basic needs, like finding food and shelter, are overwhelmed with the immediate need to procure and use a drug. It is difficult to focus on long-term goals, such as housing and treatment, and complete the follow-up requirements to enter substance-abuse programs. Low-barrier programs such as Housing First provide an option by eliminating the requirement of sobriety for shelter.

Veterans

In 2019, the reported rate of homelessness among adults eighteen years and older who identified as veterans was slightly higher in Seattle/King County (7 percent) than in the United States (8 percent).[61] A majority of all unhoused veterans identified as male and white, which reflects the demographics of the U.S. armed forces. The majority of these unhoused veterans experience chronic homelessness.[62]

Poverty and a history of mental illness and/or substance abuse are common risk factors for unhoused veterans. One study compared two groups of veterans who received health care through veteran services; one group comprised chronically unhoused veterans, the other veterans unhoused for the first time.[63] The chronically unhoused veterans, like the general chronically unhoused population, were more likely to report substance abuse and have serious mental illnesses such as schizophrenia or bipolar disorder. They were also more likely to have a chronic health problem such as diabetes or hypertension. The initially unhoused veterans had other mental health diagnoses, such as traumatic brain disorder, and histories of heart disease and joint pain. Traumatic brain injuries are associated with veterans who were deployed during Operation Enduring Freedom and Operation Iraqi Freedom, beginning in 2001 and existing through the present day.[64] Long-term effects of brain injury include memory impairment, difficulty regulating emotions, challenges with communication, aggressive behaviors, and acting out.[65] The difference between the chronically unhoused veterans and the first-time unhoused may reflect the era in which they served in the military as well as the existing potential risk factors for homelessness that existed prior to enlistment.[66] Understanding the complexity of veteran experiences can help to identify the provision of health care services.

Women and Families

During the January 2019 national point-in-time count, 29.2 percent of people experiencing homelessness identified as female.[67] The rate was higher in Seattle/King County at 40 percent.[68] Another study found that women made up one-fourth of all chronically unhoused people.[69]

Unhoused women on average are more likely to be younger than homeless men, though they experience many of the same conditions, including mental illness, substance abuse, and chronic health problems such as hypertension. Women are more likely to be unemployed and on government assistance. Another significant difference is that women are more likely to have experienced childhood sexual abuse, the foster care system, and an abusive partner. Also, the percentage of women veterans among the chronically unhoused is greater than the percentage of women veterans within the general population.[70] Health issues for unhoused women reflect the toll a lack of stable housing has on health, including an increased prevalence of chronic illnesses such as chronic obstructive pulmonary disease, substance abuse, and mental illness. In addition, women are more likely to experience interpersonal violence, especially from male partners.[71]

One means of survival for unhoused women is to form a bond with a male partner. Along with protection, this bond can provide economic survival that may include tangible items like shelter and drugs. In exchange, some women engage in survival sex, which refers to the exchange of sex to obtain basic needs, such as food and a sense of safety.[72] Not only do these relationships put women at risk for interpersonal violence, there is also the risk of sexually transmitted diseases and pregnancy. The rate of unintended pregnancies among unhoused women is higher than among all other women in the United States.[73] Unfortunately, it is difficult for women to obtain reproductive health care for many of the same reasons expressed earlier: priority of needs like food and shelter, lack of transportation, difficulty with making and meeting scheduled appointments, and fear of stigmatization.[74] The Public Health Seattle–King County's (PHSKC) Medical Mobile Van program is an example of how women's health needs can be met. The van provides health care, including women's health, by showing up at scheduled times at services such as free meal programs and encampments for the unhoused. An appointment is not required to obtain health care. The van includes other services such as assistance connecting to housing resources.[75] Meeting people where they are, both physically and emotionally, is key to providing entry into health care.

A combination of other factors can also lead to family homelessness—factors such as decreasing government supports at a time of extreme poverty, current housing rates, and the challenges of single-parent households, especially for women with low-paying jobs.[76] Though women constitute 39 percent of all unhoused people in the United States, they represent 90 percent of the head of households for unhoused families with children. The typical unhoused family is a single mother in her late twenties with two children six years old or younger.[77] Of these families, domestic violence often played a major role in their journey to homelessness.[78]

Nationally, approximately a third of all people who were homeless during January of 2019 were in families with children. During the Seattle count, 22 percent of all respondents reported being in a family, which represented 763 families. Of these families, 97 percent were sheltered.[79] What these counts are unable to represent are the number of families that are doubled up. "Doubled up" refers to families who need to stay with extended family members or friends when they are unable to continue in their own housing. The number of households with more than one family has been on the rise since 2003.[80]

The effect that homelessness has on children is profound. Children experience trauma including exposure to violence, a constant high level of stress, the lack of a sense of safety, and both physical and emotional losses.[81] Some of the emotional conditions that children experience include anxiety, aggressive behaviors, and social withdrawal. They may also demonstrate social and emotional developmental delays and perform poorly in school.[82] Unaddressed childhood trauma and adverse experiences have been associated with long-term health impacts that can continue into adulthood.[83]

It is often difficult for children, while unhoused, to receive proper nutrition. The experience of food insecurities can result in hoarding or overeating, which may result in obesity. Lack of adequate nutrition can also cause dental caries and delays in growth and development. Other health conditions experienced by homeless children at a higher rate than housed children include asthma, attention deficit disorders, ear infections, and preventable diseases of childhood, such as chicken pox.[84] Routine well-child care is often neglected when the parent's focus is on obtaining shelter and food. Another challenge is that some parents may be reluctant to take their children to health clinics for fear of involvement with child protective services.[85]

Several school programs now include support services for unhoused children and their families. These programs often assist with coordination of services and provide advocacy in navigating systems. Engagement with the entire family assists with the establishment of stability for the children.[86] As an example, Head Start programs, which aim to promote the school readiness of preschool-aged children from low-income families, disproportionately prioritize unhoused families. Attendance in classrooms provides the children with a stable environment along with age-appropriate activities and learning. The home visiting program supports the family through strengthening parenting skills activities and assistance in navigating community resources.[87]

Youth

The number of unaccompanied youth and children in the United States has slowly increased over the past ten years.[88] On a single night in 2019, about 35,000 people were experiencing homelessness as unaccompanied youth under twenty-five years old, which represented approximately 6 percent of the total unhoused population.[89] In Seattle/King County during the same count, 1,089 youth under twenty-five years represented 10 percent of the total unhoused population, the majority between the ages of eighteen and twenty-five years. The local share is nearly double the national share.[90] Once unhoused, youth are more likely to be unsheltered than adults.[91]

Prior to becoming unhoused, youth often come from households where they experienced a profound trauma, such as domestic violence, substance abuse, or personal exposure to physical or sexual abuse. Many youths were in foster care, and the event of their aging out of the system precipitated homelessness.[92] Though living on the streets is hazardous, 64 percent of youth were unsheltered in Seattle during the 2019 point-in-time count.[93] The high rate may reflect the distrust and fear of exploitation that accompanies staying in adult overnight shelters. Another challenge for some youth is that most adult shelters require people to sleep in either a women's or men's room, a practice that limits options.

Exposure to violence and distrust of adults are particularly true for youth who identify as lesbian, gay, bisexual, or transgender (LGBT).[94] LGBT youth represent 34 percent of the unaccompanied youth in the 2019 Seattle/King County point-in-time count, which is double the rate of all respondents.[95] Nationwide it is estimated that people who identify as LGBT make up 20 to 49 percent of unhoused youth. The event of "coming out" as LGBT to family and guardians can be a precipitating event leading to homelessness for youth and is an associated risk for homelessness among younger youth.[96]

Due to the significant exposure to traumatic events, both prior to and after becoming unhoused, all youth are at high risk of depression, suicide attempts, and other chronic mental illnesses. Other health issues can be the result of risk-taking activities such as substance abuse and survival sex. High rates of HIV and sexually transmitted infections among unhoused youth are two examples. Asthma, diabetes, and communicable diseases, such as tuberculosis and Hepatitis B, have also been reported.[97]

ROOTS is an example of services geared specifically for unhoused young adults. It is located in the University District, an area of Seattle with the highest concentration of people under the age of twenty-five. Most of the staff are also young adults, which helps to develop trust and create supportive relationships. ROOTS provides low-barrier, emergency overnight shelter for youth aged eighteen to twenty-five years.[98] Other services provided include a hygiene center with showers, clothing, meals, and assistance navigating community resources, such as health care referrals.

Models of Health Care for the Homeless

In an effort to "provide urgently needed assistance to protect and improve the lives and safety of the homeless," the federal government passed the

McKinney-Vento Homeless Assistance Act in 1987.[99] The McKinney-Vento Act included provisions for the creation of the Health Care for the Homeless (HCH) program to support projects nationwide that address access and use of health care at a local level.

HCH projects represent a wide variety of program models and are characterized by a community-based response to local needs. Characteristics of these programs comprise engaging with unhoused people through the provision of comprehensive outreach, including use of an interdisciplinary approach and working in partnership with other HCH agencies in the community.[100] The National Health Care for the Homeless Council provides resources, technical assistance and training, and advocacy for programs providing health to the homeless.[101] HCH grantees in the Puget Sound area include Public Health–Seattle & King County's Health Care for the Homeless Network, Metropolitan Development Council, and Sea Mar Community Health Centers.

HCH grantees create a safety net of services for unhoused people and families through a variety of program models. Three examples of program models that incorporate aspects of the HCH characteristics and demonstrate strategies to effectively improve access and use of health care services are street outreach, community clinics, and medical respite.[102]

Street Outreach

The key characteristics of a street outreach program include mobile services and provision of health care where people are located. Service locations may include soup kitchens, shelters, or any encampment where unhoused people are found.[103] A common strategy is to build rapport with individuals who may be resistant to seeking health care and connect them with services through case management activities such as advocacy and linkages.[104]

Key to street outreach is the ability to meet people where they are, both in relationship and space. Street outreach can be useful to connect with the chronically unsheltered severely mentally ill who are distrustful of service agencies. However, engagement takes time and requires awareness of approaches to address people's fears. The challenge of intense street outreach is that any measure of success, such as getting someone into housing, requires time, and results may not appear cost-effective.[105]

Community Clinics

Another approach is the integration of health care services into existing services such as overnight shelters or current health services. The intention of both strategies is the creation of fixed sites to address barriers to access.[106] Partnerships with existing services also help to increase the availability of health care for the unhoused. One example is nurse-managed drop-in clinics held during an evening meal. Activities include foot care, monitoring blood pressure, and referrals to health care services. The intention of the nurse-managed clinic is to engage people where they are and provide health promotion and health-protection interventions.[107]

Existing community health clinics also play a role through operational or structural changes such as drop-in hours in the evening that do not require an appointment. As an illustration, the Federally Qualified Health Centers (FQHCs) have been an essential component in the health care safety net since their designation in 1991. To be eligible for FQHC funding, community health centers must meet criteria that include the provision of services to medically underserved populations, such as the unhoused, and comprehensive care through enabling services that address issues of health care access.[108] Examples of enabling services include assistance with transportation and allowing walk-in appointments. Having multiple services co-located is also beneficial. Health care clinics with mental health and addiction services in the same building are associated with improved usage of all services.[109] As mentioned earlier, NeighborCare Health's Ballard Homeless Clinic is an example of a program that provides these types of low-barrier services.

Medical Respite

The medical respite program, sometimes referred to as a recuperative care program, is a model of health care that emerged to address post-hospital readmission rates among unhoused people. The Respite Care Provider's Network (RCPN) provides advocacy and support for efforts nationwide to meet the health and recuperative needs of people post-hospitalization.[110] Medical respite is the "acute and post-acute medical care for unhoused patients who are too ill or frail to recover from physical illness or injury while living in shelter or streets, but who are not sick enough to be in a hospital."[111] Edward Thomas House in Seattle provides people with a stable place to recuperate and includes nursing care and mental health services to support recovery. Other case management services are provided, such as assistance with finding housing and connection to ongoing primary health care.[112] The Illumination Foundation in Stanton, California, in their recuperative program, demonstrated a 50 percent reduction in hospital readmission and transitioned 33 percent of their clients into stable housing.[113] The single most prevalent obstacle to getting people housed following recovery is the lack of safe, affordable housing.

Models of Care for Health Services

A model of care provides a broad foundation in which human services can be envisioned. Generally, models of care are evidence-based and arise out of best practices. Once identified, these models provide the foundation for the development of health care programs and practices.[114] A number of current models of care exist for the provision of services to unhoused people, most notably trauma-informed care and harm reduction.

Trauma-Informed Care

Trauma-informed care (TIC) reflects the knowledge that traumatic events have adverse effects on a person's physical and mental well-being.[115] Trauma may refer to personal or familial violence, abuse, neglect, and loss. It may also refer to community or societal factors such as natural disasters and school shootings. Initial insight into the lifelong impact trauma has on health resulted from a Kaiser Permanente study done in the mid-1990s in collaboration with the Centers for Disease Control and Prevention (CDC). The study identified a strong relationship between adverse childhood experiences (ACEs) and poor health outcomes in adults.[116]

ACEs are grounded in the understanding that a person's neurophysiological system regulates the brain and body during stress. When children experience unpredictable and stressful events, their nervous systems are overwhelmed.[117] Attempting to cope, they may respond to a distressing experience, such as child abuse or domestic violence, in maladaptive ways. These include feeling overwhelmed or powerless and may experience anger, overeating, and poor school performance.[118] Early and ongoing traumatic events in childhood have been found to have significant lifelong effect.[119] People with experiences of trauma may react to current situations in a physical or emotional way based on their past maladaptive strategies. These responses often appear out of context with the present.[120]

Unaddressed emotionally harmful experiences from the past have significant effects on adult health, as well. ACEs have been associated with poor physical and mental health (for instance, obesity, diabetes, and depression), behaviors (addictions such as, for instance, drug, alcohol, and tobacco), and life potentials (loss of jobs and lack of academic achievements, for example).[121] Early death has also been linked to ACEs.[122] The Substance Abuse and Mental Health Services Administration (SAMHSA) reports that ACE events are common among people experiencing poor mental health or substance abuse disorders.[123]

TIC is an approach to services that influences recovery and is grounded in the understanding that past trauma, such as ACE events, affects health and well-being. TIC is a strengths-based model as opposed to a deficit-orientation. Health services that incorporate TIC approaches assist people to identify their own strengths and develop healthier coping strategies. TIC is focused on the future and utilizes skills building to further develop resiliency.[124]

Approaches recommended by SAMHSA for a TIC perspective include the recognition of signs and symptoms of trauma not only in the people using services, but in their family members and service providers, as well.[125] They also encourage organizations to include a trauma-informed framework with systems changes, such as adapting policies and practices that create a safe environment and avoiding the retraumatization of clients and staff. As an example, an organization can involve their clients in the identification and development of services.[126] The intended result is organizations committed to the creation of therapeutic environments that support healing and do no further harm.[127]

To implement a trauma-informed approach, SAMHSA recommends six key principles. These principles are: (1) safety, so people feel physically and psychologically secure; (2) trustworthiness and transparency, achieved through organizational accountability with the goal of creating trust among people receiving services and staff; (3) peer support and mutual self-help, which is vital to develop trust and empowerment; (4) collaboration and mutuality, recognizing that healing happens in partnerships; (5) empowerment, voice, and choice, distinguishing peoples' resilience and ability to heal and recover from a trauma; and (6) cultural, historical, and gender issues, addressing moving past biases and offering services that honor everyone.[128]

Resilience is an outcome and a protective factor of the experience of trauma. It is the "process of adapting well in the face of adversity."[129] An important skill for surviving homelessness, resilience can be learned. Common qualities among resilient people include a positive social supportive system, constructive coping skills, and spiritual connections.[130] Laurie Leitch recommends that providing people experiencing homeless with positive physical skills, such as muscle relaxation and deep breathing, will help them learn calming skills during stressful moments.[131] Spirituality is another approach that has been used to develop resilient skills.[132]

Harm Reduction

Harm reduction is another model of care that grew out of services for drug and alcohol abuse. It is a public health strategy that focuses on reducing and eliminating the morbidity and mortality of risky practices, such as substance abuse and sexual behaviors.[133] The principles of harm reduction are: (1) an acceptance of people regardless of where they are in their journey; (2) acknowledgment that everyone deserves to be treated with dignity, whether they are engaging in risky behavior or not; (3) recognition that people are responsible for their own actions; (4) assurance that people have a voice in their recovery; (5) a focus on the reduction of the potential harmfulness of a behavior, not on the behavior itself; and (6) outcomes that are determined in partnerships, such as between the client and the provider.[134]

Implementing a program with TIC and harm reduction as models of care can be challenging. It often requires a shift in understanding about how to approach people. Acceptance of a person's stigmatized activity necessitates careful discernment to see beyond the negative coping methods of trauma-inflicted people.

Incorporating Health into Faith-Based Services: A Case Study

Early fall in 2008, a group of undergraduate nursing students from Seattle University College of Nursing (SUCON) "discovered" a drop-in center for the unhoused, called God's Li'l Acre (GLA), while completing an environmental assessment for their community health clinical course about seven miles northeast of downtown Seattle in Lake City. The chance encounter began an enduring partnership between the Seattle Mennonite Church (SMC) community ministries and SUCON. Key to the partnership has been a commitment to social justice in action.

The SMC's community ministry for the unhoused began with the development of personal relationships with people who found shelter in the church's breezeway. Sensitive to these people's plight, members of the congregation sought to engage them in fellowship. Creating companionship began with shared meals and conversation—actions that led to the development of trust and partnership. A key principle in the process was a focus on self-determination, relationships that acknowledged people's competence to identify their own needs and potential solutions.[135] Because of these efforts, the unhoused people developed a sense of belonging with the church.[136]

Through conversation, areas of service became apparent, and the Stop, Drop and Roll (SDR) program was created. A significant challenge for unhoused people, especially those who are street dwelling, is finding a safe place to store personal belongings. SDR provided the space for people to leave their belongings while they headed out during the day for jobs and other pursuits, such as medical appointments. Originally held in the foyer of the church, SDR was opened once a week in the morning for drop-off and again in the evening for pick-up. The SDR, along with weekly community meals, provided additional opportunities for companionship and community planning. SDR grew, and the program moved on July 1, 2008, to a nearby house owned by the SMC. Given the name "God's Li'l Acre" by community members, the drop-in center continues to provide a safe storage area, laundry, and kitchen facilities and a bathroom with a shower. GLA staff provide hospitality and companionship, spiritual care, and assistance navigating housing and social services. The program is now open five days a week, staffed by the community ministry and volunteers. In 2015, GLA moved into its current location on the first floor of the Lake City Valor Apartments, subsidized housing for previously unhoused veterans.[137]

In June 2007, SMC added to its commitment to the homeless with the addition of community ministers Melanie and Jonathan Neufeld. Jonathan Neufeld serves neighborhood unhoused with advocacy and resources as well as the management of GLA. He estimates that GLA serves approximately 180 people a year. Though most of these encounters are one-time visits, there is a core group of people who regularly use GLA, many who grew up in the area and consider Lake City to be their home. Most of the GLA community are older white men who are chronically unhoused. Since the opening of GLA, an estimated 200 people have been housed as a result of persistent efforts and advocacy.[138]

The intention of the GLA ministry is to break the cycle of homelessness by looking beyond a person's immediate needs. Transactional interactions, such as giving away stuff, continues a dependency on charity and does not empower a person toward recovery. Working with someone to get into housing requires building intentional relationships.[139]

Community minister Melanie Neufeld, who is also a social worker, was hired because of her experience in community organizing. Through her ministry, she has continued the SMC process of developing community partnerships, a vital step to eliminating homelessness. As an example, she became the director of the Lake City Task Force on Homelessness (LCTH), a community coalition that meets monthly to address neighborhood concerns about the unhoused and provide opportunity for dialogue regarding activities and resources. The LCTH currently coordinates a winter nighttime shelter held in various churches in the area. Melanie also represents the SMC on other civic coalitions.[140] To add to the richness of community engagement, the SMC's community ministry has drawn people from many faiths to volunteer. In fellowship with the Mennonites and the GLA community are Unitarians, Christian Scientists, Muslims, Catholics, Jews, Sufi, Latter Day Saints, and Bahá'í.[141]

The community ministry also became a natural partner for the Seattle University College of Nursing's community health faculty and students. Community engagement for SUCON began with sitting around the dining room table at GLA talking with people, both customers and staff, in addition to listening to people's health concerns and referring them to appropriate resources. Topics focused on health promotion and disease prevention, referrals to health care resources, and advocacy, such as assistance with medical insurance. Graduate students also provided staff trainings on health and safety issues; identified safe needle disposal strategies; and developed health-related policies, such as are needed for overnight shelter.

Offers to take a blood pressure are another service provided. Though in itself taking a blood pressure is not a reliable assessment tool, the action provides a means of direct physical contact and personal attention, two social interactions often missing in an unhoused person's life. Providing foot care is another offered health service. People who are unhoused often have poor foot care because of lack of resources such as clean socks or adequate shoes or the ability to bathe. Good foot care takes time and includes conversation, healthy physical touch, and the provision of clean socks. Foot washing has been connected to the ministry of Christ, appropriate for students at a Jesuit university.

In 2012, a community assessment was completed in Lake City as part of a community-based participatory research (CBPR) project to identify the health concerns of unhoused people. The project involved community members who were unhoused as research assistants. A major concern identified by the assessment was the circumstance of someone being discharged from a hospital without a safe place to stay, sometimes returning to street dwelling. A grant from the Senegal Foundation made it possible to create a medical respite, a safe place for someone to recuperate. The medical respite JustHealth opened May 22, 2014, as a pilot project. During the project, twenty-three people were provided a room in a motel along with case management services that assisted with follow-up medical appointments and connections to other services, such as housing resources. Most referrals to JustHealth came from a local hospital with abscess or wound care, the most common reason for the admission.[142]

JustHealth was staffed by a public health nurse case manager, an outreach worker, and Melanie Neufeld, who served as the program manager. JustHealth also relied upon numerous volunteers from the SMC and Lake City community. SUCON undergraduate nursing students provided program support through visits to respite clients and menu development. The first public health nurse case manager hired was a graduate of SUCON's master's program who already had a relationship with community members through her clinical experience as a student.

The medical respite program closed on August 14, 2015, with the completion of the grant. Though the program was successful in meeting recuperative needs, the challenge moving forward will be to identify stable funding. The goal of the JustHealth board of directors, which has developed into the Lake City Partners to End Homelessness, is to explore means for sustainable funding such as hospital subsidies and Medicare/Medicaid reimbursements as two possible sources.

This description presents the efforts of an FBO to incorporate health services into their community outreach program through an academic partnership. The successful partnership continues as we seek additional funding and build on existing community resources.

Notes

1. Consult, for example, "Understanding Homelessness" and "Frequently Asked Questions," on the website of the National Health Care for the Homeless Council (NHCHC), accessed November 26, 2020, www.nhchc.org. See also NHCHC, "Homelessness & Health: What's the Connection?," Fact Sheet (February 2019).

2. Stephen Goldsmith, William B. Eimicke, and Chris Pineda, "Faith-Based Organizations versus Their Secular Counterparts: A Primer for Local Officials," Harvard University Ash Institute for Democratic Governance and Innovation (Spring 2006).

3. Byron Johnson, William Wubbenhorst, and Alfreda Alvarez, *Assessing the Faith-Based Response to Homelessness in America: Findings from Eleven Cities* (Waco, Tex.: Baylor University Institute for Studies of Religion, 2017), 5–143.

4. Kenneth L. Kusmer, *Down and Out, On the Road: The Homeless in American History* (New York: Oxford University Press, 2002).

5. Goldsmith, Eimicke, and Pineda, "Faith-Based Organizations versus Their Secular Counterparts."

6. Jason Adam Wasserman and Jeffrey Michael Clair, *At Home on the Street: People, Poverty and a Hidden Culture of Homelessness* (Boulder, Colo.: Lynne Rienner, 2010).

7. Kusmer, *Down and Out, On the Road*, 194.

8. Richard M. Clerkin and Kristen A. Grønbjerg, "The Capacities and Challenges of Faith-Based Human Service Organizations," *Public Administration Review* 67, no. 1 (January 2007): 115–26.

9. Kevin Kearns, Chisung Park, and Linda Yankoski, "Comparing Faith-Based and Secular Community Service Corporations in Pittsburgh and Allegheny County, Pennsylvania," *Nonprofit and Voluntary Sector Quarterly* 34, no. 2 (June 2005): 207.

10. Clerkin and Grønbjerg, "Capacities and Challenges of Faith-Based Human Service Organizations."

11. Ram A. Cnaan and Stephanie C. Boddie, "Charitable Choice and Faith-Based Welfare: A Call for Social Work," *Poverty and Welfare Reform* 47, no. 3 (July 2002):

224–35; and Rebecca Sager, "Faith-Based Social Services: Saving the Body or the Soul? A Research Note," *Journal for the Scientific Study of Religion* 50, no. 1 (March 2011): 201–10.

12. Goldsmith, Eimicke, and Pineda, "Faith-Based Organizations versus Their Secular Counterparts," 4.

13. Clerkin and Grønbjerg, "Capacities and Challenges of Faith-Based Human Service Organizations."

14. "Constitution of the World Health Organization," in *Basic Documents: Forty-Ninth Edition*, including amendments adopted up to May 31, 2019 (Geneva: World Health Organization, 2020), 1. This charter was adopted by the International Health Conference in July of 1946 and it entered into force in April of 1948.

15. Consult, for example, "Social Determinants of Health," on the website of the U.S. Department of Health and Human Services Office of Disease Prevention and Health Promotion, accessed November 26, 2020, www.healthypeople.gov. See also Commission on Social Determinants of Health, *Closing the Gap in a Generation: Health Equity Through Action on the Social Determinants of Health*, Final Report (Geneva: World Health Organization, 2008).

16. Bret Kloos, Kate Flory, Benjamin L. Hankin, Catherine A. Cheely, and Michelle Segal, "Investigating the Roles of Neighborhood Environments and Housing-Based Social Support in the Relocation of Persons made Homeless by Hurricane Katrina," *Journal of Prevention & Intervention in the Community* 37, no. 2 (2009): 143–54.

17. Chester Hartman and Gregory D. Squires, "Pre-Katrina, Post-Katrina," in *There Is No Such Thing as a Natural Disaster: Race, Class, and Hurricane Katrina*," ed. Chester Hartman and Gregory D. Squires (New York: Routledge, 2006), 1–12.

18. Lawrence W. Green and Marshall W. Kreuter, *Health Program Planning: An Educational and Ecological Approach* (Boston: McGraw-Hill, 2005); Roger M. Nooe and David A. Patterson, "The Ecology of Homelessness," *Journal of Human Behavior in the Social Environment* 20, no. 2 (March 2010): 105–52.

19. Shelley D. Golden and Jo Anne L. Earp, "Social Ecological Approaches to Individuals and Their Contexts: Twenty Years of *Health Education & Behavior* Health Promotion Interventions," *Health Education & Behavior* 39, no. 3 (2012): 364–72.

20. See Division of Violence Prevention of the National Center for Injury Prevention and Control, "The Sociological Ecological Model: A Framework for Prevention," on the website of the Centers for Disease Control and Prevention (CDC), accessed November 26, 2020, www.cdc.gov. Consult also Etienne G. Krug, Linda L. Dahlberg, James A. Mercy, Anthony B. Zwi, and Rafael Lozano, eds., *World Report on Violence and Health* (Geneva: World Health Organization, 2002).

21. Green and Kreuter, *Health Program Planning*.

22. Kloos et al., "Investigating the Roles of Neighborhood Environments and Housing-Based Social Support in the Relocation of Persons made Homeless by Hurricane Katrina."

23. Stephen W. Hwang, Catharine Chambers, Shirley Chiu, Marko Katic, Alex Kiss, Donald A. Redelmeier, and Wendy Levinson, "A Comprehensive Assessment

of Health Care Utilization Among Homeless Adults under a System of Universal Health Insurance," *American Journal of Public Health* 103, Suppl. 2 (2013): 294–301.

24. Consult "Access to Health Services," on the website of the U.S. Department of Health and Human Services Office of Disease Prevention and Health Promotion, accessed November 26, 2020, www.healthypeople.gov.

25. Ibid.

26. L. Gelberg, R. M. Andersen, and B. D. Leake, "The Behavioral Model for Vulnerable Populations: Application to Medical Care Use and Outcomes for Homeless People," *Health Services Research* 34, no. 6 (2000): 1273–302.

27. Ibid.

28. Amy B. Bernstein, Esther Hing, Abigail J. Moss, K. F. Allen, Arlene B. Siller, and Ronald B. Tiggle, *Health Care in America: Trends in Utilization* (Hyattsville, Md.: National Center for Health Statistics, 2003).

29. Green and Kreuter, *Health Program Planning*.

30. Kate Law and William John, "Homelessness as a Culture: How Transcultural Nursing Theory Can Assist Caring for the Homeless," *Nurse Education in Practice* 12, no. 6 (May 2012): 371–74.

31. Rebecca T. Brown, Yinghui Miao, Susan L. Mitchell, Monica Bharel, Mitkumar Patel, Kevin L. Ard, Laura J. Grande, Deborah Blazey-Martin, Daniella Floru, and Michael A. Steinman, "Health Outcomes of Obtaining Housing Among Older Homeless Adults," *American Journal of Public Health* 105, no. 7 (2015): 1482–88.

32. Bon S. Ku, Kevin C. Scott, Stefan G. Kertesz, and Stephen R. Pitts, "Factors Associated with Use of Urban Emergency Departments by the U.S. Homeless Population," *Public Health Reports* 125, no. 3 (May–June 2010): 398–405.

33. James J. O'Connell, *Premature Mortality in Homeless Populations: A Literature Review* (Nashville, Tenn.: National Health Care for the Homeless Council, 2005).

34. See "Neighborcare Health at Ballard," on the webpage of Neighborcare Health, accessed November 26, 2020, www.neighborcare.org.

35. O'Connell, *Premature Mortality in Homeless Populations*.

36. Ibid.; consult also Jiaquan Xu, Sherry L. Murphy, Kenneth D. Kochanek, and Elizabeth Arias, "Mortality in the United States, 2018," NCHS Data Brief no. 355 (Hyattsville, Md.: National Center for Health Statistics, January 2020).

37. Cheryl Zlotnick and Suzanne Zerger, "Survey Findings on Characteristics and Health Status of Clients Treated by the Federally Funded (US) Health Care for the Homeless Programs," *Health and Social Care in the Community* 17, no. 1 (2009): 18–26.

38. O'Connell, *Premature Mortality in Homeless Populations*.

39. United States Department of Housing and Urban Development, "The 2019 Annual Homeless Assessment Report," by Meghan Henry, Rian Watt, Anna Mahathey, Jullian Ouellette, and Aubrey Sitler, Abt Associates (Washington, D.C.: January 2020), 2.

40. Jessica H. Leibler, Daniel D. Nguyen, Casey León, Jessie M. Gaeta, and Debora Perez, "Personal Hygiene Practices among Urban Homeless Persons in Boston, MA," *International Journal of Environmental Research and Public Health* 14, no. 8 (August 2017): 928.

41. Dean Carpenter, "On the Front Lines: A Case of Trench Foot in a Homeless Woman," *Homeless Health Care Case Report: Sharing Practice-Based Experience* 3, no. 2 (June 2007).

42. Applied Survey Research, *Count Us In: Seattle/King County Point-In-Time Count of Persons Experiencing Homelessness* (Seattle, Wash.: All Home, 2019), 11.

43. National Alliance on Mental Illness (NAMI), "Mental Health Facts in America" (Arlington, Va.: n.d).

44. National Coalition for the Homeless (NCH), "Mental Illness and Homelessness" (Washington, D.C.: June 2017).

45. Consult, for instance, Leona L. Bachrach, "A Conceptual Approach to Deinstitutionalization," *Hospital & Community Psychiatry* 29, no. 9 (1978): 573–78; and H. Richard Lamb, "Deinstitutionalization and the Homeless Mentally ill," *Hospital & Community Psychiatry* 35, no. 9 (1984), 899–907.

46. David Mechanic and David A. Rochefort, "A Policy of Inclusion for the Mentally Ill," *Health Affairs* 11, no. 1 (Spring 1992): 128–50.

47. Ibid.

48. Ibid.

49. See "Supportive Housing," on the website of the United States Interagency Council on Homelessness (USICH), accessed November 27, 2020, www.usich.gov.

50. Gregory Nelson, Juanne Clarke, Angela Febbraro, and Maria Hatzipantelis, "A Narrative Approach to the Evaluation of Supportive Housing: Stories of Homeless People Who Have Experienced Serious Mental Illness," *Psychiatric Rehabilitation Journal* 29, no. 2 (February 2005): 98–104.

51. Applied Survey Research, *Count Us In*.

52. Richard Cho, "Four Clarifications about Housing First," *News*, June 6, 2014, website of the United States Interagency Council on Homelessness, accessed November 27, 2020, www.usich.gov.

53. Molly Brown, Leonard A. Jason, Daniel K. Malone, Debra Srebnik, and Laurie Sylla, "Housing First as an Effective Model for Community Stabilization among Vulnerable Individuals with Chronic and Nonchronic Homelessness Histories," *Journal of Community Psychology* 44, no. 3 (April 2016): 384–90.

54. Susan E. Collins, Daniel K. Malone, and Seema L. Clifasefi, "Housing Retention in Single-Site Housing First for Chronically Homeless Individuals with Severe Alcohol Problems," *American Journal of Public Health* 103, no. Suppl. 2 (December 2013): 269–74.

55. Consult "Substance Abuse and Homelessness" (July 2009), on the website of the National Coalition for the Homeless, accessed November 27, 2020, www .nationalhomeless.org.

56. Applied Survey Research, *Count Us In*.

57. Lauren V. Lawson, "A Community Assessment of Lake City to Inform a Community-Based Participatory Research Project Addressing Medical Respite Care for a Homeless Population," unpublished manuscript (Seattle: University of Washington, 2013).

58. National Coalition for the Homeless, "Substance Abuse and Homelessness."

59. Ibid.

60. Megan Ravenhill, *The Culture of Homelessness* (Burlington, Vt.: Ashgate, 2008).

61. United States Department of Housing and Urban Development, "The 2019 Annual Homeless Assessment Report"; Applied Survey Research, *Count Us In*.

62. United States Department of Housing and Urban Development, "The 2019 Annual Homeless Assessment Report."

63. Suzannah Creech, Erin Johnson, Matthew Borgia, Claire Bourgault, Stephen Redihan, and Thomas P. O'Toole, "Identifying Mental and Physical Health Correlates of Homelessness among First-Time and Chronically Homeless Veterans," *Journal of Community Psychology* 43, no. 5 (July 2015): 619–27.

64. Terri Tanielian and Lisa H. Jaycox, eds., *Invisible Wounds of War: Psychological and Cognitive Injuries, Their Consequences, and Services to Assist Recovery* (Santa Monica, Calif.: RAND Corporation, 2008).

65. Ibid.

66. Jack Tsai, Bruce Link, Robert A Rosenheck, and Robert H Pietrzak, "Homelessness among a Nationally Representative Sample of US Veterans: Prevalence, Service Utilization, and Correlates," *Social Psychiatry and Psychiatric Epidemiology* 51, no. 6 (June 2015): 907–16.

67. United States Department of Housing and Urban Development, "The 2019 Annual Homeless Assessment Report."

68. Applied Survey Research, *Count Us In*.

69. Ellen Lockhard Edens, Alvin S. Mares, and Robert A. Rosenbeck, "Chronically Homeless Women Report High Rates of Substance Use Problems Equivalent to Chronically Homeless Men," *Women's Health Issues* 21, no. 5 (September–October 2011): 383–89.

70. Gillian Silver and Rea Pañares, *The Health of Homeless Women: Information for State Maternal and Child Health Programs* (Baltimore, Md.: Johns Hopkins University School of Public Health, 2000).

71. Committee on Health Care for Underserved Women, "Health Care for Homeless Women," Committee Opinion no. 576 (Washington, D.C.: American College of Obstetricians and Gynecologists Women's Health Care Physicians, October 2013).

72. Shanna K. Kattari and Stephanie Begun, "On the Margins of Marginalized: Transgender Homelessness and Survival Sex," *Affilia* 32, no. 1 (2017): 92–103.

73. Committee on Health Care for Underserved Women, "Health Care for Homeless Women."

74. Lillian Gelberg, Carole H. Browner, Elena Lejano, and Lisa Arangua, "Access to Women's Health Care: A Qualitative Study of Barriers Perceived by Homeless Women," *Women & Health* 40, no. 2 (2004): 87–100.

75. See "Mobile Medical Care for People Living Homeless," under the section on Public Health for Seattle and King County, available on the King County website, accessed November 27, 2020, www.kingcounty.gov.

76. National Center on Family Homelessness, "The Characteristics and Needs of Families Experiencing Homelessness" (Needham, Mass.: December 2011).

77. Ellen L. Bassuk, Camela J. DeCandia, Corey Anne Beach, and Fred Berman, *America's Youngest Outcasts: A Report Card on Child Homelessness* (Waltham, Mass.: American Institute for Research National Center on Family Homelessness, November 2014); and Applied Survey Research, *Count Us In*.

78. United States Interagency Council on Homelessness (USICH), *Opening Doors: Federal Strategic Plan to Prevent and End Homelessness* (Washington, D.C.: USICH, June 2015).

79. Applied Survey Research, *Count Us In*.

80. United States Department of Housing and Urban Development, "The 2019 Annual Homeless Assessment Report."

81. USICH, *Opening Doors*; J. Yoon, Administration for Children and Families, *Early Childhood Homelessness in The United States: 50-State Profile* (Washington, D.C.: United States Department of Health & Human Services, January 2016).

82. See "Expanding Early Care and Education for Children Experiencing Homelessness," Office of Early Childhood Development, Administration for Children and Families, U.S. Department of Health and Human Services, accessed November 27, 2020, www.acf.hhs.gov.

83. Laurie Leitch, "Action Steps Using ACEs and Trauma Informed Care: A Resilience Model," *Health and Justice* 5, no. 5 (2017): 1–10.

84. Silver and Pañares, *Health of Homeless Women*.

85. Committee on Health Care for Underserved Women, "Health Care for Homeless Women."

86. Institute for Children, Poverty, and Homelessness (ICPH), *The Seattle Atlas of Student Homelessness* (New York, N.Y.: November 2017).

87. Office of the Assistant Secretary for Planning and Evaluation (ASPE), "Head Start Children and Families Experiencing Homelessness: Trends, Characteristics, and Program Services," ASPE Research Brief (Washington, D.C.: U.S. Department of Health and Human Services Office of Human Services Policy, September 2017).

88. Child Trends Data Bank, *Homeless Children and Youth: Indicators on Children and Youth* (Bethesda, Md.: Child Trends, October 2015).

89. United States Department of Housing and Urban Development, "The 2019 Annual Homeless Assessment Report."

90. Applied Survey Research, *Count Us In*.

91. USICH, *Opening Doors*.

92. Juli Hishida, *Engaging Youth Experiencing Homelessness: Core Practices and Services* (Nashville, Tenn.: National Health Care for the Homeless Council, January 2016).

93. Applied Survey Research, *Count Us In*.

94. USICH, *Opening Doors*.

95. Applied Survey Research, *Count Us In*.

96. USICH, *Opening Doors*.

97. James M. Van Leeuwen, Christian Hopfer, Sabrina Hooks, Roxanne White, Jerene Petersen, and John Pirkopf, "A Snapshot of Substance Abuse among Homeless and Runaway Youth in Denver, Colorado," *Journal of Community Health* 29, no. 3 (June 2004): 217–29.

98. Consult "Services," on the Roots website, accessed November 27, 2020, www .rootsinfo.org.

99. Marsha McMurray-Avila, *Organizing Health Services for Homeless People: A Practical Guide*, 2nd ed. (Nashville, Tenn.: National Health Care for the Homeless Council, 2001).

100. National Health Care for the Homeless Council, "Service Adaptations for Special Populations," (Nashville, Tenn.: February 2005).

101. Consult "Statement of Principles and Mission," on the website of the National Health Care for the Homeless Council, accessed November 27, 2020, www .nhchc.org.

102. McMurray-Avila, *Organizing Health Services for Homeless People*.

103. Evan C. Howe, David S. Buck, and Jim Withers, "Delivering Health Care on the Streets: Challenges and Opportunities for Quality Management," *Quality Management in Health Care* 18, no. 4 (October–December 2009): 239–46.

104. McMurray-Avila, *Organizing Health Services for Homeless People*.

105. Richard C. Christensen, "Psychiatric Street Outreach to Homeless People: Fostering Relationship, Reconnection, and Recovery," *Journal of Health Care for the Poor and Underserved* 20, no. 4 (2009): 1036–40.

106. McMurray-Avila, *Organizing Health Services for Homeless People*.

107. Christine L. Savage, Christopher J. Lindsell, Gordon L. Gillespie, Anita Dempsey, Roberta J. Lee, and Adele Corbin, "Health Care Needs of Homeless Adults at a Nurse-Managed Clinic," *Journal of Community Health Nursing* 23, no. 4 (2006): 225–34.

108. Dan Hawkins and DaShawn Groves, "The Future Role of Community Health Centers in a Changing Health Care Landscape," *Journal of Ambulatory Care Management* 34, no. 1 (2011): 90–99.

109. Rebecca Wells, Rajeshwari S. Punekar, and Joseph Vasey, "Why Do Some Health Centers Provide More Enabling Services Than Others?," *Journal of Health Care for the Poor and Underserved* 20, no. 2 (2009): 507–23.

110. See "What Is Medical Respite Care, and How Can I Learn More?," on the website of the National Health Care for the Homeless Council, accessed November 27, 2020.

111. Sarah Ciambrone and Sabrina Edgington, *Medical Respite Services for Homeless People: Practical Planning* (Nashville, Tenn.: National Health Care for the Homeless Council, June 2009), 1.

112. Consult "Seattle-King County Medical Respite: Edward Thomas House at Jefferson Terrace," under the section on Public Health for Seattle and King County, available on the King County website, accessed November 27, 2020, www .kingcounty.gov.

113. Illumination Foundation, "Importance of Recuperative Care," Infographic pamphlet (Irvine, Calif.: 2016).

114. Agency for Clinical Innovation, *Understanding the Process to Develop a Model of Care: An ACI Framework* (Chatswood, New South Wales, Australia: May 2013).

115. Leitch, "Action Steps Using ACEs and Trauma Informed Care."

116. Vincent J. Felitti, Robert F. Anda, Dale Nordenberg, David F. Williamson, Alison M. Spitz, Valerie Edwards, Mary P. Koss, and James S. Marks, "Relationship of Childhood Abuse and Household Dysfunction to Many of the Leading Causes of Death in Adults: The Adverse Childhood Experience (ACE) Study," *American Journal of Preventive Medicine* 14, no. 4 (May 1998): 245–58.

117. Ibid.

118. Carmela J. DeCandia, Kathleen Guarino, and Rose Clervil, *Trauma-Informed Care and Trauma-Specific Services: A Comprehensive Approach to Trauma Intervention* (Washington, D.C.: American Institutes for Research, October 2014).

119. Felitti et al., "Relationship of Childhood Abuse and Household Dysfunction to Many of the Leading Causes of Death in Adults."

120. Ibid.

121. Ibid.

122. Substance Abuse and Mental Health Services Administration (SAMHSA), *Trauma-Informed Care in Behavioral Health Services*, Treatment Improvement Protocol (TIP), Series 57 (Rockville, Md.: U.S. Department of Health and Human Services SAMHSA, July 2014).

123. Trauma and Justice Strategic Initiative, *SAMHSA's Concept of Trauma and Guidance for a Trauma-Informed Approach* (Rockville, Md.: U.S. Department of Health and Human Services SAMHSA, 2014).

124. Elizabeth K. Hopper, Ellen L. Bassuk, and Jeffrey Olivet, "Shelter from the Storm: Trauma-Informed Care in Homelessness Services Settings," *Open Health Services and Policy Journal* 3 (2010): 80–100.

125. Trauma and Justice Strategic Initiative, *SAMHSA's Concept of Trauma and Guidance for a Trauma-Informed Approach*.

126. Brenda Proffitt, "Delivering Trauma-Informed Services," *Healing Hands* 14, no. 6 (Nashville, Tenn.: National Health Care for the Homeless Council, December 2010).

127. DeCandia, Guarino, and Clervil, *Trauma-Informed Care and Trauma-Specific Services*.

128. Substance Abuse and Mental Health Services Administration, "Guiding Principles of Trauma-Informed Care," *SAMHSA News* 22, no. 2 (2014).

129. American Psychological Association, *The Road to Resilience* (Washington, D.C.: n.d.).

130. Sayani Paul, Simon Corneau, Tanya Boozary, and Vicky Stergiopoulos, "Coping and Resilience among Ethnoracial Individuals Experiencing Homelessness and Mental Illness," *International Journal of Social Psychiatry* 64, no. 2 (March 2018): 189–97.

131. Leitch, "Action Steps Using Aces and Trauma Informed Care."

132. Health Care for the Homeless Clinicians' Network, "Delivering Trauma-Informed Care," *Healing Hands* 14, no. 6 (Nashville, Tenn.: National Health Care for the Homeless Council, 2010).

133. National Harm Reduction Coalition, *Principles of Harm Reduction* (New York: 2020).

134. National Health Care for the Homeless Council, "Harm Reduction: Preparing People for Change," Fact Sheet (Nashville, Tenn.: April 2010).

135. Manon A. M. Krabbenborg, Sandra N. Boersma, William M. van der Veld, Wilma A. M. Vollebergh, and Judith R. L. M. Wolf, "Self-Determination in Relation to Quality of Life in Homeless Young Adults: Direct and Indirect Effects through Psychological Distress and Social Support," *Journal of Positive Psychology* 12, no. 2 (2017): 130–40.

136. Jonathan Neufeld, personal communication, March 5, 2018.

137. Ibid.

138. Ibid.

139. Ibid.

140. Melanie Neufeld, personal communication, February 27, 2018.

141. Jonathan Neufeld, personal communication, March 5, 2018.

142. Lake City Partners Ending Homelessness, "JustHealth Recuperative Care Program: Pilot Project Report," unpublished document (2016).

PART II

*Religious Worldviews and the
Common Good Reimagined*

Homelessness and Coast Salish Spiritual Traditions

Cultural Resources for Programmatic Responses in British Columbia

Bruce Granville Miller

Introduction

The Coast Salish peoples' cultural/spiritual practices have elements that are adaptable to addressing the contemporary problems of homelessness among Indigenous peoples of North America. In fact, the use of spiritually based individual and institutional efforts to assist the unhoused has already begun, but can be amplified. This appears paradoxical, because historical Coast Salish society had no homelessness, short of the very few people who suffered banishment from their communities. Even banishment was commonly short-term, with people returning to their home communities after a period of affiliating with another community. Yet, it is the very absence of homelessness that creates the grounds on which Coast Salish cultural practices have relevance today. One might ask, why did they not have homelessness historically? How did they conceive of home and the relations of people to territory such that people were housed? These ideas have a special relevance because today the rate of homelessness of Indigenous people far exceeds that of the mainstream population. In Vancouver, Canada, for example, 31 percent of the homeless are Indigenous despite comprising only 3 percent of the regional population.[1]

I will show here how concepts of "claiming," "covering," kinship, and other specific spiritual practices contribute to a culture that features a sense of belonging that can be extended beyond blood and affinal kin to a larger Indigenous world. Further, several Coast Salish spiritual leaders have already begun to operationalize these concepts in facing the many social and personal problems, specific both to their communities and to society at large, that contribute to homelessness. There are many possibilities for extending their work.

What I will not attempt is to examine the many explanations as to why Indigenous people are unhoused, although I reference work done by a Coast Salish community in providing its own distinct insights; nor will I address the expanding literature on homelessness in Indigenous communities. I leave these efforts to others.

The Swinomish Tribal Mental Health Project published *A Gathering of Wisdoms* that described the problems facing contemporary Coast Salish people from a Coast Salish perspective.[2] They describe a "triad of major disturbances" of depression, alcohol, and stress-related acting out as a result of the grief associated with the losses coming after contact, and experiences of everyday racism, in what is commonly referred to as intergenerational trauma.[3] The triad, they write, reflects something akin to post-traumatic stress syndrome. In youth, this can culminate in a pervasive sense of personal doom in which individuals struggle to connect with the mainstream society and their own "doomed" culture.[4] These are characteristics of the alienation experienced by many of the unhoused, which other authorities have also pointed out, sometimes under the rubric of "colonization."[5] The Swinomish authors note that Indigenous traditions provide ways to cope with issues of cultural identity and perceived cultural loss.

A note of explanation—the Coast Salish are the members of a language family and cultural grouping whose members continue to occupy portions of Washington State, in the United States, and British Columbia, in Canada. More specifically, concentrations of Coast Salish live along the Fraser River and southeastern Vancouver Island and the adjacent mainland in British Columbia, Puget Sound in Washington, and in other communities in Oregon, central British Columbia, and the Washington coast. These communities are still located in urban settler centers, including Seattle, Vancouver, and Tacoma. There are some fifty Coast Salish bands in Canada and more than 21,000 enrolled members.[6] The Coast Salish peoples comprise a number of tribes, including named tribes in the United States with recognized relations with the U.S. government and bands in Canada with a similar relationship with the Canadian government. There are, in addition, several groups that remain unacknowledged by the respective governments.

All of these Coast Salish communities have been hit hard by the colonial era, beginning even before the arrival of Captain Vancouver's ships in what is now Vancouver, British Columbia, waters in 1792. Smallpox, arriving overland, had already reduced the size of the population before the arrival of white people, and epidemics continued to roll through the region for another century. In addition, non-Indigenous settlement centered on the Coast Salish region, with the establishment of New Westminster, Seattle, Port Townsend, and other communities by the middle of the nineteenth century. Unlike some regions subject to British colonization, the British and Americans quickly moved from off-shore fur trading to establishing their own communities in order to live permanently in Coast Salish lands and to use the waterways. Weakened by disease, the Coast Salish peoples were rapidly displaced from the majority of their villages, restricted from accessing their historic locations for hunting, fishing, and gathering, placed on reserves/reservations, and restricted from their historic spiritual practices and in their movements.[7]

The colonizers, the British, Americans, and after 1867, the Canadians, set out to disrupt Indigenous ways of living. Most notably, the prohibition on potlatching activities in the 1880s in both the U.S. and Canada had the intention of disrupting ritual life and aiding the assimilation and eventual amalgamation of the Coast Salish and other Indigenous peoples. Some of the historic cultural and spiritual practices went underground; in other cases they became dormant. But by the 1970s, a spiritual revival had begun and the fundamental practices reestablished and invigorated.[8]

In practical terms, it is difficult to separate out spiritual and cultural practices of the Coast Salish, since they are so closely intertwined. As noted, "Spirituality pervades every aspect of life in ways difficult to grasp for most non-Indian Americans."[9] It is a fundamental reality of everyday life. Scholars working with communities ordinarily do not specialize in something like the religious studies of the Coast Salish. These scholars' interests, of necessity, are broader. However, a few have published detailed accounts of contemporary spiritual life. A caution, however: some features of Coast Salish spiritual practice are secret, are not ordinarily discussed with outsiders or even other community members, and are potentially dangerous if exposed. In this discussion of spiritual practices as they relate to homelessness I will not trouble this boundary.

Methods

It is customary in Coast Salish society to establish one's kin connections to those that one encounters. For academics working with communities the equivalent is to engage reflexively and to indicate what our involvement might be. In my case, I came to work with Coast Salish communities and individuals in the 1970s, when I first became interested in the problems facing nonrecognized tribes of Puget Sound. Later, as a Ph.D. student, I worked with the Upper Skagit Indian Tribe in the State of Washington to represent them in federal court concerning their treaty claim to shellfishing rights. My dissertation concerned one important form of post-contact change—namely, the gender system and tribal political life. Later still, as a member of the Department of Anthropology at the University of British Columbia, and at the request of the Stó:lô Nation, I organized a residential ethnographic field school and lived during summers through the 1990s in the longhouse of a hereditary chief and spiritual leader, Frank Malloway (Siyémches) of Yeqwyeqwí:ws First Nation, one of the Stó:lô communities. Living in the longhouse, the site of spirit dancing in the winter, gave me a chance to understand firsthand the role of leaders such as Siyémches in their dealings with the disadvantaged, unhoused, or spiritually disturbed people in their own communities, and on several occasions unhoused people resided in the longhouse along with me.

In recent years, I have participated in the city of Vancouver annual homeless count and have spoken with a number of unhoused Indigenous people in carrying out that work. I have had the opportunity to think about the circumstances of Indigenous peoples, including the unhoused, in public spaces and to explain this to the British Columbia Human Rights Tribunal in written and oral expert testimony. Over the last forty years I have had the opportunity to watch Indian doctors at work, to attend potlatches, funerals, and other sacred events, and to talk with the many Coast Salish ritual practitioners about what they are doing. I've learned about publically funded projects undertaken by Coast Salish leaders to address social problems. Equally important are the daily conversations about the circumstances of unhoused people with my wife, Laraine Michalson. She is a public health nurse and adjunct professor in the School of Nursing at the University of British Columbia and has worked for the last twenty years with street-entrenched pre- and perinatal woman, 70 percent of whom are Indigenous, in the Sheway project located in the Downtown Eastside of Vancouver. Ms. Michalson previously worked as a public health nurse for the Lummi Nation, one of the Coast Salish communities.

All of this has led me to my view that there are significant implications of Coast Salish spiritual life and practices for the problems of homelessness. My research includes conversations with a small group of Coast Salish spiritual leaders in which I asked them, in individual meetings, how they saw the connection between Coast Salish culture, and in particular the winter ceremonial complex, and the homeless and the unhoused. But first, I provide a look at the spiritual traditions of these Coast Salish communities, because the ideas I present next underlie the perspectives of the spiritual leaders themselves.

Coast Salish Spiritual Traditions

Historic Coast Salish spiritual life has been divided into distinct domains in the anthropological literature, including the High God tradition, magic, the winter ceremonial (sometimes called spirit dancing), and the Shaker Church.[10] The latter is a post-contact religious practice that incorporates Christian and historic Coast Salish perspectives. My interests here are with the winter cere- monial, or longhouse, practices. These longhouse buildings are sometimes re- ferred to as smokehouses and metonymically stand in for the associated spiritual beliefs and practices. It is not my intent to give a detailed description, nor is it necessary to do so for the work at hand. A brief outline of Coast Salish spiritual practices follows in order to set the stage for understanding the spiri- tual nature and role of winter dancing in the contemporary world, particularly because historic precedent is heavily drawn on in the present.[11] I also draw on what I have learned with spiritual leaders. Here I have primarily used English translations of Coast Salish words and concepts, except where Coast Salish terms are used in everyday life. My point here is not that historic practices con- tinue unabated or that all of the Coast Salish peoples follow longhouse prac- tices. They don't; many are Catholic or Pentecostal or belong to other Christian denominations. Many participate in more than one tradition, and funerals commonly have components from different religious and spiritual traditions.

Cosmology is not necessarily consistent between communities or even be- tween the extended corporate family groups that compose the primary units of the contemporary Coast Salish world.[12] There is no requirement that it be so, and teachings and traditions vary. Some components of the spiritual world, such as magic, for example, are held privately within families. But there are concepts and practices that are widely shared. A starting point can be the mythic times, a period that was peopled by both humans and animals who could mutually communicate, and also by dangerous beings. The myth age came to end when the Transformer (or in some versions brother and sister Transformers) moved generally from east to west through the world, transform- ing these beings and even humans into rocks and animals and making the world safe for present-day human beings. Transformer then disappeared into the west, the land where the sun sets. In some instances, powerful human chiefs dueled with Transformer. Female versions of the Transformer myths are somewhat different than male versions and emphasize more of Transformer's concern for human welfare.[13] The Transformer(s) is not a High God but, rather, a powerful spiritual being or beings. Even after the transformation of the earth and the creation of safety for humans, many powerful spiritual beings remain, and a principal activity of humans is to gain the spiritual knowledge and strength to deal respectfully with these beings on one's own behalf and on be- half of the family. This remains true today.

Groups have their own versions of their founding. In some instances, the tradition holds that a founder dropped from the sky at the location that became

the site of the winter village or summer camps occupied by that group. Transformer gave special local knowledge to these founders, establishing a powerful bond with the local environment. Of particular note is that members of
Coast Salish groups regard their connection to the animals as one of kinship,
as their myths tell of human descent from salmon, sturgeon, or deer, or vice
versa, and of marriage into the salmon people, for example. These myths
are paired with the idea that these relationships ensure that the salmon
people, in their form as fish, will return to their run for human benefit. Mutual respect and aid underlie these myths.

Salmon, in particular, are thought to live in their own villages and return to
the rivers, where they spawn only if their relationship with humans remains
respectful. A special ceremony, the First Salmon Ceremony, helps maintain
this relationship, and the first salmon of the season, the salmon chief who offers
himself to humans, is ritually distributed to the community and the bones carefully preserved and restored to the water. Humans and salmon, then, participate
in a mutual reincarnation, with the descendants of the humans harvesting the
descendants of the salmon over many generations. There is an analogous
First Berry Ceremony.

Although humans are thought of as the weakest of the sentient beings
(which includes beings other than those recognized in the Western tradition,
such as rocks or landscapes), humans are nonetheless spiritually complex. A
living human has components only visible to those with appropriate spiritual
training. These components are the life, the person, and the shadow. In addition, spiritual beings who become attached to humans become a part of that
human. The first component, the person, can become detached, lured away
by dangerous beings, or depart, as in dreams. Without the return of the person, illness and death are the result, and the return of the person remains the
work of shamans known locally as Indian doctors. After death, another component becomes the ghost, which remains near living humans and might become reborn as a descendent. In Coast Salish cosmology, there is a not fully
articulated notion of reincarnation. This concept is best seen in the domain
of ancestral names, which are bestowed to those who appear to family elders
to have characteristics of deceased family members. These names are given
in ritual events and acknowledged by those in attendance from beyond the
immediate group.

Some of the Coast Salish groups speak of a land of the dead to which ghosts
go, while others do not; nevertheless, ancestral ghosts are a hazard, especially
after death, when they may attempt to bring a human life, or soul, with them.
These ancestral spirits, on the other hand, are thought to look after their descendants in various ways and to be objects of interest and veneration, but not

worship. In brief, they remain important to the living people. One significant manifestation of the relationship between the living and the dead is the annual ritual burnings many families hold that are attended by their ancestral ghosts, who may communicate to the ritualist and who also consume the spiritual essence of food that is burned in a fire on their behalf. The ghosts benefit from this reciprocal relationship with the living.

A distinction is drawn between the ordinary world and the sacred, which may be understood as forbidden, dangerous, and powerful. Among those that fall into this domain of sacred are pubescent girls, menstruating women, those whose relatives have recently died, and those things that are highly abnormal. All of the entities that are sacred must be treated with special care. This concept reveals that Coast Salish mythology and cosmology are not so much concerned with teleological struggles between good and evil, but rather with maintaining respectful relations between entities that have the capacity to do good or bad in human terms. Indian doctors, for example, can use their power to cure but also to spiritually attack. Communities have mythic stories of the harm perpetrated by salmon beings on youths who mistreat them in the course of their run up the river. Many Coast Salish people remain wary of spiritual danger and actively consult those who can provide spiritual help, a significant point in the argument I will develop here regarding homelessness.

Historically, Coast Salish people sought out spirit helpers who would help guide them through both mundane and spiritual tasks. All adults at one time, including some slaves, would have had such a helper. Today, many people have such spirit helpers, although some Coast Salish people do not participate in this spiritual tradition, and even avoid it. Starting early in life, people began to train for the spiritual purity necessary to attract a spirit helper. Historically, relatives woke up children, starting at perhaps seven years old, to bathe in cold water and later to seek and return with sticks placed in mountainous areas. They learned to control their appetite for food and intake of water. Eventually, this led to a period of vision questing, in which they sought out spirit helpers in an encounter in which the human lost consciousness and encountered the spirit being who bestowed on them knowledge or skills. Today some families practice these forms of spiritual training, although encroachment on the Coast Salish territories has limited those spaces where interaction with spiritual beings and where spiritual training can take place. Most people today gain their relationship with spirit beings through spiritual activities in the longhouse during the winter season.

The spiritual beings take the forms of animals, trees, and natural phenomenon such as lightning. High-status families are thought to have the ability to train their children to obtain important spirit helpers, and those of lesser families must be content to seek lesser powers. Some of these powers were historically of direct use in economic activities. One might have the power to hunt with great success or to dive underwater to repair damaged fishing weirs. Those noted for outstanding weaving or woodworking and various other sorts of activities might have powers specific to those activities. These spiritual entities are also manifest in songs and dance particular to each individual and learned by the initiate, known as a "baby," during the winter ceremonials.

A very significant feature of this spiritual complex is that the powers acquired through vision questing are private because direct knowledge of someone's powers can open them to spiritual assault or result in the loss of the power. Others may intuit what someone "has" by virtue of the abilities demonstrated. However, family members who help the initiate gain control of the relationship with the spirit being have some insight into what these powers are and the songs appropriate to the power. Some spirit beings are inherited within a family group.

During the winter, when the energy of the sun is lowest, a number of community members in Coast Salish communities assemble in longhouses under the patronage and control of senior spiritual leaders. These babies gain a spiritual helper and, gradually, knowledge regarding their relationship with their helper. There are many prohibitions during this liminal period, and the babies are sacred and hence potentially dangerous to outsiders. The babies face restrictions in food and water intake. They enter doors backward and cover their eyes with fringe to avoid accidentally giving spiritual harm. They are ordinarily confined to the longhouse together with the other initiates. After a period of learning and training, a cycle of longhouse events throughout the Coast Salish world is begun, and community members travel to various longhouses weekly. The babies engage their spirit helper and dance/sing, with each performance expected to be done perfectly. They are helped by their family members in attendance. They wear a special costume solely for this purpose and paint their faces in black or red paint or a combination, indicating the category of spiritual helper they have acquired. The particular song/dance also is an indication. A distinction is drawn between spirit helpers who bring shamanic powers and those who do not. But, significantly for regional integration, no Indian doctor is thought to have a complete range of abilities, and historically communities sought spiritual assistance from outside their own family or community. It remains a feature of spiritual life today, particularly in the long process of the restoration of the historic practices in communities without their own practitioners.

There are a variety of spiritual practices that are outside the purposes here. One practice, however, is of special interest in that the underlying concept has been generalized to new events of direct interest to the problems of the un-housed, as I explain later. For the moment, I point to *cleansing ceremonies*. Kin groups still maintain the rights to perform cleansing rituals that confer high status to the dancers. One is the *sxwayxwey* mask and associated rituals that require the participation of both male dancers and female singers, who inherit the prerogative. These masked dancers are hired for memorials for de-ceased relatives and many other events. Cleansing ceremonies in general are used to wipe away a disgrace and to enhance occasions such as the giving of ancestral names. Related cleansing ceremonies have historically helped to find lost objects, determine culpability in the event of crime, and spiritually cleanse both the people present and the longhouse. Contemporary cleansing ceremo-nies have incorporated the unhoused to help them make the journey from alienation back to community living.

In all of the important Coast Salish spiritual events, people are *assembled* both to conduct the ritual events and to orate the local host's understanding of genealogy and ancestry and support and maintain sociability and the social order more generally. Orators state emphatically, although often humorously, how their ancestors acted honorably and how that should be the state of af-fairs in the present in a life well lived. But there is another group present—namely, all of the people from outside the group hosting the event. These people are thought of as witnesses who, by virtue of their presence, acknowl-edge the veracity of the event and who take news of the event back to the family members not present and to their community. In addition, they are expected to support the work undertaken and to testify to the work in the future, should the need arise.

Those who act as witnesses are thanked by being fed and being given food to eat on their return trip home. Historically, some gatherings lasted several days, and while the events are now temporally truncated, they frequently last all day and well into the night. A subset of the witnesses, those regarded as significant to the particular work being conducted and of high status, are called upon to speak at the event. After speaking, quarters are placed in their hands by the members of the host family to acknowledge their contribution. Later, I point to neo-traditional events that are built on these concepts and that pro-vide help in resolving homelessness.

What is most important regarding Coast Salish spiritual beliefs and prac-tices that I have just outlined is that the unhoused, brought into community in ways I describe later, themselves assemble for winter ceremonial events and hear the speaker talk about a life well lived and witness the practices of the dancers and drummers and the coming of spiritual beings. These are power-ful forces in overcoming the alienation the unhoused commonly experience, and spiritual leaders explicitly use these experiences in working with the unhoused.

Ties That Bind

Because my argument about the utility of Coast Salish spiritual and cultural concepts for the issue of the unhoused relies on the ways in which people identify and act on behalf of each other, even the unhoused, my attention now points to the forms of aggregation. These provide a model of integration and care.[14] So far, I have pointed to families, communities, and the winter ceremonial world as having integrative abilities. In addition, I have noted the role of Indian doctors in integrating communities. Perhaps most important are the large events, sometimes called potlatches, that draw people together from beyond one's own kin group. The ratification of ancestral names or chiefly titles, for example, depends on the role of these outsiders. Those people who have become spirit dancers and joined the society of longhouse ceremonials are not necessarily kin, or members of the same tribe/band, or of the same community (reservation/reserve or town). Although Coast Salish people are deeply connected to their place of birth and to their family, the society has found ways to avoid permanent fissioning and conflict. In addition, because historical Coast Salish society was bilateral and marriage partners, at least for the upper class, could not be among known relatives, there is a cultural bias toward a broad spectrum of affiliated people. It is a kind of social contradiction, but one that enables new forms of connection today.

Cover Somebody, Claim Somebody

One smokehouse leader, Willie Charlie (Chaqqwet), noted that "everything we have, your birthright, comes from who you are, what you belong to." He observed that the status of respected persons, *Siem*, is attained by making wise decisions over many years and acting in the best interests of other people in one's social world, rather than self-aggrandizement. The title *Siem* is not a formal status and is not self-conferred. Others hold the *Siem* to these difficult standards, and cultural practices exist to express dissatisfaction, including ceremonies to remove ancestral names. Many Coast Salish people speak of greediness as an offense against society that is punished spiritually. This concept supports practices of sharing and mutual support.

These statements connect spiritual beliefs to very specific local social practice. Elite people, the spiritual, familial, and political leaders, become so and are recognized as such because they embody the idea of connection and sharing; understanding the connections between people, families, institutions, and the spiritual domain (as I have pointed out) enables one to identify and promote the mutual good. The smokehouse leader's observations can be understood as both cultural and spiritual ideals, never fully obtained, but as constant aspirations.

When people meet, they commonly try to establish connections through conventional kinship going back many generations and through another form of kinship established by mutual participation in winter spirit dancing. Those who enter as babies the same season are regarded as brothers and sisters for life, and all dancers belong to a ritual congregation as family. Willie Charlie points out that Siyémches "has a huge family of blood and Smokehouse." These connections create mutual responsibilities and obligations. Further, trust relationships and the openness for dialogue are established through such connections. Several Stó:lô people, including an elder and her grandson, gather blankets, clothes, and food that they distribute to homeless people, a practice that is a manifestation of their spiritual training of connection and mutuality.

The concepts of connection and belonging are extended in contemporary Coast Salish practice in several ways. A Squiala First Nation family, for instance, hosts a welcome ceremony for babies in the community that incorporates Coast Salish spiritual practices. A senior woman is covered (that is, a blanket is placed over her shoulder), and a procession, with singing, to welcome newcomers is held in the tribal hall. The idea of a welcome ceremony has diffused beyond the halls and longhouses of Coast Salish communities themselves. The Sheway pregnancy outreach program in the Downtown Eastside of Vancouver, which services a largely Indigenous clientele as I have noted, acknowledges that the program is situated in what remains unceded Coast Salish territory and hence gives precedence to Coast Salish spiritual practice among the practices of the various Indigenous peoples who reside in the region. Sheway has consulted elders regarding appropriate protocol and borrows directly from Coast Salish concepts in establishing its own welcome ceremony for babies born to their clients. The ceremony engages Coast Salish ideas of rituals as an encounter between the host and guests who validate the "work" (the Coast Salish term for the ritual to establish a social claim, to a chiefly title, or a marriage, for example). Babies (in this case, infants, not initiates into winter dancing) are welcomed and established and claimed as members of society, of the family of Sheway clients and staff, and their spiritual presence acknowledged. (Coast Salish concepts of infanthood include the idea of a close connection to the spiritual dimension unmitigated by adults.) The hosts call witnesses who are covered and who speak about the underlying spiritual values and who are thanked with the gift of quarters given by staff. It is an integrative ceremony and aims at creating a sense of belonging. Cleansing and welcoming ceremonies open people, including the unhoused, to transformation and to overcoming alienation.

In both of these welcoming ceremonies, one performed in a Coast Salish band hall and the other in an urban center, the welcoming affirms the spiritual presence of those newcomers and their mothers and fathers and underlines the location of the babies' home. *Home* is a central concept, and the spiritual advisor noted the practice of some Stó:lô families to bury the placenta behind the house or village. This is done by the husband with the help of the mother's brothers. The belly button is saved and the child, when seven or eight years old, goes to the place where the placenta is buried and buries the belly button (or umbilical stump). This is "so they never forget where their home is." Both welcoming ceremonies rely on the idea of "covering" with a blanket, creating a spiritually pure space to work, and creating the grounds to "claim." These practices hold direct grounds for the return of unhoused people to their home community later in life, who themselves must be reclaimed and restored. These ideas are supported in the mythology.

Mythologies of the Unhoused

There are Coast Salish mythologies and "stories which are true" (*sxwoxwiyam*) concerning people without homes, told here by Naxaxalhts'i. One is the "Aggasiz Boy" story regarding Tom Tomiyeukw, whose name means "flipping things over." His antisocial behavior, including stealing men's wives, and his tremendous spiritual powers enabled him to terrify his own community. In one version, the villagers dismantle their longhouses at night and move across the river, leaving Tom homeless and in a form of banishment. In another version, he travels to a neighboring community where he slays a powerful serpent whose stench made it impossible to approach. In this other community, he is a hero, but he remains an outcast to his own people and lives in a cave.

Another is the story of an abandoned boy, Tewit. In this story, the protagonist repeatedly begs for food from other families, and his shamed father takes him to the mountains, under the false pretense of teaching him, for the purpose of deserting Tewit. While Tewit is in the mountains, the family takes apart their longhouse and moves away. The grandmother alone feels sorry for him and leaves fire for him in a clamshell. Tewit realizes he is abandoned, and his dog discovers the fire, enabling both to survive. In time, Tewit, whose name means "professional hunter," teaches himself to hunt and becomes a great hunter. The Creator, *Chichen Siem*, gives him a bluejay skin cape so he can fish underwater. After these successes, Tewit asks Crow to fly down to his grandmother to give her the word to move back and share his wealth of food with her. Later, everyone moves to benefit from Tewit's spiritual powers, including, eventually, even his mother and father. Tewit becomes the *Siem* for the whole community and eventually is turned into stone inadvertently by the Transformer.

The Tewit story brings out the idea that all people, even those who act shamefully, have their own gift, their own role, and something to give back to their society, a point emphasized by the Swinomish.[15] The Agassiz Boy story points to the significance of the proper use of spiritual power and of the necessity for respecting other people and their spiritual presence. Coast Salish spiritual concepts hold that each individual is unique in his or her capacity, as are even Tewit and Tom Tomiyeukw. Both stories point to the extreme nature of banishment and reveal homelessness as unnatural and spiritually dangerous but potentially powerful for the individual and the community.

While individuals historically have sought spirit helpers in isolation, they must return to their homes with their new gifts. In addition, many stories tell of Coast Salish people, often culture heroes, who leave their homes intentionally, enter spiritual domains, and return with important gifts. These people encounter spiritual dangers, enlist the help of spiritual beings, and return. One set of these stories concerns people who clamber into the sky when it is too low, too near the earth, sometimes climbing up arrows shot into each other. They enter into the communities of spiritual beings, marry, and eventually return to earth with important gifts. In other stories, cultural heroes go underwater, living for long periods with the spiritual beings there, and are given gifts in return for assistance to the underwater beings, in one instance removing illness. These heroes, too, return.[16]

This concept of departure, the encounter with danger, and return is also taken up in in the work of Indian doctors, who travel to the spiritual world to diagnose illness, to remove dangerous objects from people's bodies, or to replace dislodged souls. They, too, return, after their work. It is possible within a Coast Salish perspective that homelessness, too, could be thought of as a spiritual journey imparting new gifts, powers, or insights. With the exception of the Aggasiz Boy, those who depart violate spiritual or cultural norms, are thought of as long lost (one day underwater, for example, is a year at home), yet are eventually recognized and acknowledged when they return. It is the cultural theme of *transformation* that underlies much of Coast Salish thought. Even origin myths affirm this; people fall from the sky to establish new communities; people become salmon or the other way around. In the contemporary world, men who have misspent their early years sometimes become transformed into valuable political leaders. This idea of transformation applies to

the unhoused, as well. They, too, can return to a home. But it is not forgiveness, but rather a fundamental property of humans that underlies the thought
that people, like other beings such as salmon, which transform from those living in a village to a species which can be eaten, can change in fundamental
ways.

Stó:lô cultural advisor Naxaxalhts'i (Sonny McHalsie) observed that the late
Elizabeth Hurley told him that "if you are Stó:lô, at puberty you get a spirit
power. The [puberty] ceremony is to find out what it is. Everyone has one. If
you don't do a puberty ceremony to find out your spirit power, then you do
winter ceremonial." Further, everyone has *shweli*, or life force, which connects
individuals to the larger world. The stories emphasize the Coast Salish spiritual notion that individuals must belong to communities and have a purpose
and that the communities rely on these spiritually connected members. Even
the unhoused have *shweli* and a purpose.

Contemporary Actions Regarding the Unhoused

Actions in relation to the homeless take place at the individual level, following from cultural and spiritual teachings, as in the example of the family
distributing food and clothing to unhoused people. Action is also motivated
by the more specific requirements of spiritual and political leadership. Finally, actions arise programmatically as an expression of spiritual values and
practices.

Spiritual Practices of Leaders

Next, I consider actions resulting from this second category, more specific spiritual requirements of leaders. Siyémches, leader of the Richard Malloway
Memorial longhouse, recounted many examples of care he and his longhouse
have provided to the unhoused of various sorts. He observed that, growing up,
he knew of no homeless people and that people in his First Nations community often offered people places to stay, particularly those traveling through to
another destination. Consequently, there is a prior practice of housing the temporarily unhoused. As an adult longhouse leader, he has provided shelter to
men discharged from prison who have asked to stay with him. Another instance
concerns loggers who are laid off in the winter, some of whom were distant
relatives, who had no house on their own reserve. A mentally ill Indigenous
man stayed for three years, and a white man stayed for four months in a period of unemployment. Other examples are of an unhoused man with two
months left in his jail term who was released to work in the community. Si-

yémches brought this man to the fish processing camps to help elders there. Yet another man, who resided in the longhouse during the period in which I spent summers with Siyémches, stayed for several years, finding the longhouse a place to learn about medicines and spiritual teachings. Others have stayed on after becoming initiated into the winter ceremonial in the Malloway longhouse.

Recently, during a period of devastating fires in the interior of British Columbia in 2017 that forced the evacuation of entire towns and regions, Siyémches invited seventy unhoused evacuees to live in his large longhouse. This invitation was turned down because the provincial emergency system could not accommodate the request; nonetheless, the seventy evacuees attended a dinner at the longhouse.

These examples illustrate the sort of work Siyémches and other longhouse leaders undertake. A variety of temporarily unhoused people have found shelter at the longhouse. Leaders are not financially compensated for this work but see it as coming from spiritual teachings and obligations of high-status, well-trained people—*Siem*—to take care of others. They have grown up in a culture where this is a regular pattern. Further, there is a spiritual notion that aid for these undertakings will arrive, often from unexpected sources. Leaders such as Siyémches are characteristic of leaders of small-scale societies who are expected by their own communities to use their wealth for the common good and who, as a consequence, are often without funds.

Institutional Longhouse Programmatic Responses

Longhouse leaders have developed several institutional programs of benefit to the unhoused, drawing on their spiritual training and guidance and on their sense of obligation to the community beyond the larger winter ceremonial congregation. A longhouse leader at Sts'ailes First Nation in British Columbia introduced earlier, Willie Charlie, emphasized the idea that Coast Salish humans are social beings, not meant to live alone. Coast Salish people have historically emphasized the strength of their extended family and connections to distant relatives. "People will find out who you are, how you are related." These people, he says, can be *claimed* and *covered*. This concept is generalized today in services his nation has created. Elders, who occupy a significant role in Coast Salish society, may provide spiritual and material assistance to younger people who are not kin.[17]

In 2010, Vancouver hosted the Winter Olympics, and Sts'ailes sought funding under the mandate to prepare the city for inviting the world to the city for the games. The three-year Talmuth program, promoted by the province, was

aimed at a region of Vancouver called the Downtown Eastside and characterized by the presence of the unhoused, by open drug use, and by poverty and
social problems generally. This is the region in which the Sheway project is
located. Financial support, although insufficient, was provided by Vancouver
Coastal Health, a publicly funded network of primary care clinics, hospitals,
community health centers and long-term care homes. Unhoused youth living
on the street in the Downtown Eastside were brought to the rural reserve, some
ninety miles from Vancouver and tucked among the rivers and mountains,
where spiritual teaching was shared, as Chief Charlie says, "our way," in a treatment program. Those non-Coast Salish youth from other Indigenous nations
were expected to later go home to their own elders for spiritual help. In effect,
the treatment program provided shelter, spiritual guidance, and a form of referral back to the home community. This program follows directly from spiritual teachings and is deeply embedded in cultural practices. The participants
witnessed and participated in the spiritual practices of the winter ceremonial
that I described earlier.

Another program initiated by Sts'ailes is in conjunction with Correction Services Canada and is held in a minimum-security facility. This program was
promoted by then lieutenant governor Stephen Point, a Stó:lô man and judge,
but also a *Yuwel Siem* (grand chief) and spiritual worker. Chief Point referred
the idea to Siyémches, who, in turn, referred to Sts'ailes. In this program, a
longhouse has been created in the correctional institution, which previously
used a boot-camp model of treatment for the inmates. The institution, with
the encouragement of Sts'ailes, has shifted to a Coast Salish healing village
model, the Kwikwexwelhp Healing Village. The approach has, according to
Willie Charlie, produced low recidivism among former inmates. The underlying concept is that the inhabitants are made to feel part of the local Indigenous community. To achieve this, as new inmates are brought to the facility,
a monthly welcome ceremony is held and the inmate and the staff are *wrapped*
with blankets. Significantly, all are incorporated into the same ceremony and
receive spiritual teachings of the Sts'ailes people. When the inmates depart, a
farewell ceremony is held. A major aim of the program is to create a sense of
belonging. This program directly addresses the sense of alienation felt by many
young Indigenous people, from the mainstream society, and even from their
own community as documented in the Swinomish research.

A third program developed by the Sts'ailes is the Tulalim ("The House")
project, funded by the provincial Children and Families ministry and managed
by the First Nation. Willie Charlie explained this project by noting that historically and into his own lifetime, families were at the center of life and decision-
making. In his experience, everyone in his family went to Grandmother's house,

and a sense of belonging and security emanated from this practice. Too often today, he says, this is missing from the experience of youth. Further, the child welfare systems of the present day separate children from their family when they need support. The removal of children from Indigenous homes remains a national tragedy in both the U.S. and Canada. Instead, the Sts'ailes program keeps the whole family together in a house. The program is aptly named for The House, which here refers culturally to the dwelling place and the corporate group that organizes shelter, food, and personal security. These factors, missing from the contemporary world in many instances, are linked to the problems of alienation and homeless pointed out by the Swinomish.[18]

The Sts'ailes have sought clients from, again, the center of homelessness in the lower mainland of British Columbia, the Downtown Eastside. A story jointly narrated by Mr. Charlie and Ms. Michalson concerns "Andy" (a pseudonym), a man whose children were removed by social workers during a period in which he became street-entrenched and a drug user along with his pregnant and vulnerable female partner. Andy remembered the healing house program described earlier and got in touch with his wife's mother and explained to social workers and the child welfare manager that he wished help of this sort. He was enrolled in the Tulalim program, and he and his wife and children spent two years in semi-independent housing provided by the program on the Sts'ailes reserve. This gave them the opportunity to finish high school, receive treatment for addiction, and, most significantly, to participate in the spiritual practices of the community. The key to the program was that Andy felt like part of a family and a community. He later became an advocate for the program, leading tours for dignitaries.

A project aimed at keeping families together has the side benefit of keeping people off the street and in housing and in preparation for work and housing afterward. Jimmie Charlie's grandfather taught him that our lives should be lived communally and ideally within a strong family. The concept for the project, Willie Charlie explained, goes back to the longhouse teachings: "People will find out who you are, how you are related, cover you with a blanket and money to cover the costs of what you are doing." Grandmother, he said, knows everyone, always knew who was missing, who was out practicing [sport]. Aunties knew too, and they always asked about Chief Charlie's brothers. Among Coast Salish people, historically, he pointed out, people gave children to their relatives if they were without or with few children.

This was part of a larger practice of "claiming" children as favorites or even as children. (Historic Coast Salish culture equated first cousins and siblings.) Mr. Charlie's father, he noted, "claimed" lots of relatives, to whom one had a duty of care for the rest of one's life. Claiming someone as a relative contained a duty to correct and teach younger people and to be corrected and taught by those senior. This conceptual scheme, in effect, is translated into the Tulalim project, whose success led to the creation of Tulalim II.

The Swinomish tribe, located in Puget Sound, Washington, has also created programming that addresses issues linked to homelessness. The authors of their text write, "Often traditional healers resolve mental and emotional problems, such that these situations never come to the attention of conventional mental health providers."[19] However, these traditional healers rarely receive financial support or professional respect.[20] (Here they use the term "healers" for what I have called Indian doctors or spiritual leaders.) They note that some tribes have used funds to create tribally based mental health programs. While they do not specify the issue of homelessness, the mental health issues they discuss are directly linked. Among the funds used by these U.S.-based tribes are grants under the Indian Child Welfare legislation. In addition, Indian Health Service grants have been used to provide culturally appropriate help. Efforts are made to fund traditional healers (which include people such as Siyémches and Willie Charlie mentioned earlier).

Conclusion

Coast Salish spiritual values, concepts, and practices permeate the lives of its citizens, even those who do not attend the longhouse or directly espouse these values. Consequently, they provide a basis for developing programs that can reach the unhoused, commonly adrift in cities and outside reserve/reservation life, or even urban Indigenous communities. The spiritual/political leaders see their spiritual practices and spiritual world as redemptive, literally transformative, and thereby able to help the unhoused overcome the alienation the Swinomish talk about.

Some of these values and practices are specifically Coast Salish, and others have a broader basis. The concepts include the ideas of "home," "recognizing," "wrapping," "welcoming," and "claiming." Mythologies support the concept of return from periods of being unhoused and reflect the idea that important gifts derive from the experiences outside of the home. The story of an abandoned boy, Tewit, who, together with his dog but otherwise alone, gains spiritual help to become an outstanding hunter and is reintegrated into his community as a leader, is one such story. These stories are not merely from the past; they directly inform the actions of people today who regard them as sources of knowledge that can help them make wise decisions.

Coast Salish ideas of *shweli* provide the notion that all members of society have value, even unseen qualities that benefit the larger community. All these concepts have their bases in historical practice, and in some cases historic practice is generalized into new forms, such as the welcome ceremonies. All of these concepts directly mitigate the problems of the post-contact shock the Swinomish so ably address and that lead to alienation, trauma, and, sometimes, homelessness.

The existing programs I have described undertaken by the Sts'ailes in Canada and the Swinomish in the United States are not unique among Coast Salish. In some cases, these programs are directly aimed at reducing homelessness, and in others, useful outcomes are created through other foci but that nevertheless are responsive to the problems of the unhoused. A major issue, though, is recognizing the value of institutionalized programs and providing adequate funding. The Swinomish have long since pointed to the ways in which Indian Health Service and other federal funds might be used, as have the Sts'ailes. Much more work can be done with this, and connections between these programs and homelessness can be more fully articulated.

A different, more elusive problem is creating support for the work of the *Siem*, longhouse leaders, and Indian doctors, who support unhoused people in many ways to reestablish themselves in community. The spiritual gifts of these leaders lend themselves directly to what we in contemporary times refer to as the problem of homelessness. This could be enhanced: exemptions for reserve/reservation lands could be sought to local zoning ordinances to allow people such as Siyémches to carry out such actions as temporarily housing the seventy people driven from their homes by fire and temporarily unhoused.

A further question concerns the generalizability of Coast Salish practices to the larger Indigenous world. While all Indigenous communities have their own, highly specific spiritual practices, there are a number of relevant concepts and practices in common. Concepts of "wholism," "respect," and "balance," while important, can be treated as banalities. Instead I point to ideas held in common, including the central idea of transformation; the importance of leaders similar to *Siem* in some cases; the existence of a spiritual, animated world (which means many sorts of spiritual entities, all with their own identities and properties); myths of removal or departure/encounter/return with gifts; and, most significantly, a sense of kinship with the spiritual world that goes beyond kinship (to affinally and consanguineously related humans), as sometimes expressed in the phrase "all my relations," that is a basis for acting on behalf of others. Finally, all communities' members suffer from the contact-induced problems of alienation from their own society and the larger society that is a primary driver of homelessness and that is directly addressed by engagement in the spiritual world of the longhouse or other local spiritual traditions.

Undoubtedly there are cultural values and practices in all Indigenous communities of North America that support the aid and recognition of the intrinsic worth of the unhoused and that can be amplified and supported financially,
both as individual action and within formal policies and programs. There are
people in these Nations, too, just as there are among the Coast Salish, who
were raised to care for others and to see the unhoused as valuable and as members of families and communities.

Notes

1. Metro Vancouver, *Addressing Homelessness in the Metro Vancouver Region*
(February 24, 2017), 5.

2. Swinomish Tribal Mental Health Project, *A Gathering of Wisdoms* (LaConner,
Wash.: Swinomish Tribal Community, 1991).

3. Ibid., 52.

4. Ibid., 54.

5. See Julia Christensen, *No Home in a Homeland: Indigenous Peoples and
Homelessness in the Canadian North* (Vancouver, B.C.: University of British
Columbia Press, 2017), 166; and Jaylene Anderson and Damien Collins, "Prevalence
and Causes of Urban Homelessness among Indigenous Peoples: A Three-Country
Scoping Review," *Housing Studies* 29, no. 7 (2014): 959–76. Christensen advances
the related idea of spiritual homelessness or anomie. Similarly, Paul Memmott,
"Differing Relations to Tradition amongst Australian Indigenous Homeless People,"
Traditional Dwellings and Settlements Review 26, no. 2 (Spring 2015): 58–72,
describes Australian Indigenes who have lost their traditions and are spiritually and
chronically homeless.

6. Bruce Granville Miller, "Salish," in *Aboriginal Peoples of Canada*, ed. Paul
Robert Magosci (Toronto: University of Toronto Press, 2002), 238.

7. Good treatments of these issues are in Cole Harris, *The Resettlement of British
Columbia: Essays on Colonialism and Geographical Change* (Vancouver, B.C.:
University of British Columbia Press, 1997); and George Guilmet, Robert Boyd, David
Whited, and Nile Thompson, "The Legacy of Introduced Disease: The Southern
Coast Salish," *American Indian Culture and Research Journal* 15, no. 4 (1991): 1–32.

8. John Edward Michael Kew, *Coast Salish Ceremonial Life: Status and Identity
in a Modern Village* (Ph.D diss., University of Washington, 1970); Pamela Amoss,
Coast Salish Spirit Dancing: The Survival of an Ancestral Religion (Seattle:
University of Washington Press, 1978).

9. Swinomish Tribal Mental Health Project, *A Gathering of Wisdoms*, 126.

10. Amoss, *Coast Salish Spirit Dancing*.

11. Important accounts of Coast Salish spiritual life appear in June M. Collins,
Valley of the Spirits: Upper Skagit Indians of Western Washington (Seattle:
University of Washington Press, 1974); Sally Snyder, *Skagit Society and Its*

Existential Basis: An Ethnofolkloristic Reconstruction (Ph.D. diss., University of Washington, Seattle, 1964); Jay Miller, *Lushootseed Culture and the Shamanic Odyssey: An Anchored Radiance* (Lincoln and London: University of Nebraska Press, 1999); Amoss, *Coast Salish Spirit Dancing*; and Wayne Suttles and Barbara Lane, "Southern Coast Salish," in *Handbook of North American Indians*, vol. 7, *Northwest Coast*, ed. Wayne Suttles (Washington, D.C.: Smithsonian Institution Press, 1990), 485–502.

12. Bruce G. Miller, "The Legacy of Introduced Disease: The Southern Coast Salish," *American Indian Culture and Research Journal* 15 (Lincoln: University of Nebraska Press, 2007).

13. Crisca Bierwert, *Brushed by Cedar, Living by the River: Coast Salish Figures of Power* (Tucson: University of Arizona Press, 1999).

14. J. E. Michael Kew and Bruce G. Miller, "Locating Aboriginal Governments in the Political Landscape," in *Seeking Sustainability in the Lower Fraser Basin: Issues and Choices*, ed. Michael Healey (Vancouver, B.C.: Institute for Resources and the Environment/Westwater Research, 2000), 47–63.

15. Swinomish Tribal Mental Health Project, *A Gathering of Wisdoms*, 149.

16. Sonny McHalsie, "We Have to Take Care of Everything that Belongs to Us," in *Be of Good Mind: Essays on the Coast Salish*, ed. Bruce G. Miller (Vancouver, B.C.: University of British Columbia Press, 2007), 82–130.

17. Swinomish Tribal Mental Health Project, *A Gathering of Wisdoms*, 155.

18. Ibid., 145.

19. Ibid., 87.

20. Ibid.

In These United States, Homelessness Is Who You Are

Examining a Socially Constructed Category through the Lens of an Interfaith Encounter in Downtown Boston

Nancy A. Khalil

"A homeless" is a phrase I have heard often enough. It is grammatically incorrect and easily reveals the Arabic original language of those who use it. Comments like, "Be careful next to that guy, he is *a homeless*." Or, "He is on drugs and now *a homeless*." Or, as a threat, often following a youth's rebellion or age-fitting rambunctiousness, "Do you want to grow up and be *a homeless?*" To go beyond the syntax of the phrase and reflect on its semantics reveals a layer of comprehension, imagination, and understanding of the formation of the idea of homelessness and those who classify it as such in the United States. In fact, there is no Arabic equivalent of the word "homeless." The use of it as a noun in translation has telling implications and revelations.

For a native English speaker who says or hears the word "homeless," it is typically as an adjective or an adverb. Phrases such as "a homeless man," "to be homeless," "the problem with homelessness" are all familiar and are considered grammatically proper to native English speakers. How then does a residential status, an often legal status at that, become understood as an identity in a uniquely American fashion? Consequently, how do those perceived as occupying that status become stigmatized in a similar fashion to others contending with racial, religious, ethnic, or gender-based identity politics? Exploring an unexpected relationship between an Episcopal Church in downtown Boston and an Arab-immigrant, Muslim-owned café next door, we glimpse in this chapter how homelessness emerges as an identity-based analytical category that is nationally particularized. While we bureaucratically treat homelessness as a condition, we have, in parallel, socially constructed it as a category that is distinctly imagined in the United States.

U.S. Homelessness

There is a uniquely American conception and comprehension of the term "homeless" as it is used in everyday discourse. The phrase "a homeless," while it may not correctly capture the grammatical translation, the societal conception the term implies, and an understanding of a population that occupies it, very well describes the identity politics associated with the American conception of homelessness that "nounifying" the term reveals. Homelessness, under its many different appellations, has been present in the U.S. since the eighteenth century. From the destitute and wanderers to vagabonds, hobos, and beggars, the population grew by the end of the century as the country's cities did. Some were so labeled because they lacked a shelter, others because their shelter was deemed insufficient, or because it was temporary, and some simply because of perceived belonging to one of those categories. The challenge of defining homelessness and anyone that term may be applied to is not a new one.

In the 1970s, with a purported sudden onslaught of American homelessness following the end of the Vietnam War and a shift in policies that resulted in the closing of several mental health facilities and psychiatric wards, scholars argued that homelessness was a result of mental health issues.[1] A decade later, anthropologists conducted fieldwork with homeless populations to discover that there were in fact homeless people whose mental health was well intact. In turn, several argued that the cause of homelessness was instead a housing crisis resulting from unemployment, decline in government subsidies, and rapid changes in the economy affecting the housing market. They also pointed to the shutting down of skid row housing in the seventies and eighties that transformed homelessness into a matter of public concern because people began encountering homeless populations living on the streets.[2] More recently, anthropological work has shifted away from the cause of homelessness, looking instead at how it is understood or perceived, the lives of those who identify as such, and analyzing the breadth of responses to addressing it.[3] This now creates an opening for scholars to use a glocal lens and ask, What does it mean to be homeless? How do we understand home? And what about our U.S. culture informs the conception of that idea in this nation and contributes to the policies and challenges that surface as a result of homelessness?

Bureaucratically, there are those with access to housing whom we consider homeless and those without access whom we do not. The framing of "homelessness" as a crisis also takes on an American ethos when around the world there are people residing in conditions and structures that would here deem

them "homeless" but elsewhere classify them as housed.[4] The existing disso-
nance between homelessness and the idea of being in housing emerges in the
U.S. context with a nationalized salience. In fact, the concept of homelessness as an identity also emerges in a distinctly "American" form. Events such
as feeding "the homeless" or health screenings for "the homeless" fuel the concept of homelessness as an identity and not simply a status of being in between housing. The identity politics that emerge around a status, like those
around a religion or a race, target minority populations and perpetuate their
marginalization. The fact that "the homeless" are a concern or that "bums"
are a threat becomes a stigmatization of a status, and it creates an identity
around the stigmatized status. Those who fall under or can be placed under
this identity can find themselves locked in it, not necessarily owing to policy,
resources, or health—although all of these are critical factors in any individual's access to general welfare—but instead because of the accompanying stigma
and marginalization the perception of experiencing housing vulnerability now
carries.

A Muslim Lens

Every year, early in the morning, on the fourth Thursday in November, a community of nearly 200 people gather in the lower level of the Cathedral Church
of St. Paul on Tremont Street in Boston around trays of mashed potatoes, corn,
salad, stuffing, bread, gravy, and no less than fifty turkeys, all prepared by Black
Seed Café and Grill next door. Black Seed and St. Paul's relationship is going
on twenty-plus years. It is an interfaith relationship grounded in activism, theology, worship, and friendship—and a rather atypical one at that, the Christians represented by a very large and staffed house of worship, one of hundreds
across the country tied to the American Episcopal Church, the Muslims by
an Egyptian-American who immigrated to the U.S. in his early twenties and
happens to own the café next door to the church. The former is a staffed institution with both human and physical resources affiliated with a national
organization and governing body all established for the purpose of building
spiritual community, the latter a for-profit business under the authority of its
sole proprietor. Their relationship extends beyond Thanksgiving.

The church is host to the weekly congregational prayer Muslims observe
on early Friday afternoons welcoming several hundred Muslims through its
doors for each of the two services offered to accommodate the increasing attendees in downtown Boston on Fridays at lunch time and unable to make
their way during the workday to a mosque. In fact, when the church completed
a major renovation during the 2015–17 time period, they included Muslims'

use in their structural changes, updating the space used for the Friday prayers and adding particular elements, like ablution stations,[5] so Muslims can more comfortably wash up before prayers as they need. The church also provides space for Ramadan iftars organized, catered, and hosted by Black Seed's owner.[6] Whenever he needs a large space for his religious activity, he turns to the church. When they want to hold events or programs that benefit from the presence of food, they turn to Black Seed.

Their shared Thanksgiving Day event is a special one each year. Receiving a lot of media attention and regularly covered by the *Boston Globe*, it has grown to be an event that now brings in volunteers from area mosques and serves hundreds of people that holiday morning.[7] "I love it," Black Seed's owner shared.

> The woman who used to do it [organize the Thanksgiving Day meal] left and they were going to cancel it. I wanted to do something for them because they have been great neighbors. I told them, as long as I'm alive, I will take care of the Thanksgiving meal. You don't have to worry about it. I love it, really. People from different religions. Everyone is the same that day. A homeless, not a homeless, doesn't matter . . . it's like Hajj!

The owner of Black Seed excitedly proclaimed these words, his tone happy, like someone who located a forgotten memory he had been in search of for some time. The *Hajj* is an annual pilgrimage that takes place in Makkah, Saudi Arabia, every year in the last month of the Islamic calendar. It brings together annually two to three million Muslims from around the world, all performing the same rituals, congregated in the same spaces, wearing attire that is very similar to one another. As Malcolm X describes it in his Letter from Mecca,

> You may be shocked by these words coming from me. But on this pilgrimage, what I have seen, and experienced, has forced me to rearrange much of my thought-patterns previously held, and to toss aside some of my previous conclusions. This was not too difficult for me. Despite my firm convictions, I have always been a man who tries to face facts, and to accept the reality of life as new experience and new knowledge unfolds it. I have always kept an open mind, which is necessary to the flexibility that must go hand in hand with every form of intelligent search for truth. . . . During the past eleven days here in the Muslim world, I have eaten from the same plate, drunk from the same glass, and slept on the same rug—while praying to the same God—with fellow Muslims, whose eyes were the bluest of blue, whose hair was the blondest of blond, and whose skin was the whitest of

white. And in the words and in the deeds of the white Muslims, I felt
the same sincerity that I felt among the black African Muslims of
Nigeria, Sudan and Ghana.[8]

Wanting to distill why he found that Thanksgiving gathering to be so special,
I pressed, "What do you mean everyone is the same? Do people look differently otherwise?" "No," he quickly responded. "They treat them good." I was
slightly confused. "What do you mean they treat them good?" A relative comment, I wondered if "they" were perhaps mistreated during other times or
events. "Everyone talks to everyone the same, eats the same food, sits together
the same, you don't feel there's difference. You don't know who's a homeless
and who's not. It's good. Really beautiful."

His comments struck me and reaffirmed that he grasped that homeless
did not necessitate a particular image or caricaturing of people living that
situation. His use of "a homeless" conversely signals an understanding of
those who have vulnerable, or no, housing as an identity-based population.
"Homeless" here is a noun, not an adjective. At the same time, his comments
here stood in contrast to other thoughts he expressed on who "the homeless"
are and his belief that homelessness was primarily caused by addiction. We
had several conversations about this topic. How were people living on the
streets impacted by the effects of an addiction occluded on that special day?
Either the event targeted a different population, or the "appearance" of
homelessness took on many forms, or both. For Black Seed's owner, homelessness directly correlated with street life, but, as we will later see, it was not
strictly street life that categorized an individual as "a homeless." I asked him
if he knew of any Muslims who were homeless. "It's new," he said. "We didn't
have any before. But now I see some, Moroccan, Algerian, Lebanese, Suda-
nese. They're all men." I mentioned to him that there were shelters. "Yea," he
said. "Some women live there, not the men. The men are dealing with the
drugs. It puts them on the street, no one wants drugs in their house. The
shelter is a home."

Trying to understand his perception of what it meant to be homeless was
not easy, and one could hardly fault him for it. As discussed earlier, in our U.S.
history, the term has been hard to bound. He continued:

> A lot of them have an addiction, but it's more than that. We failed
> them. The government failed them. Even if they have someone who
> loves them, they don't know how to go home anymore. They've
> become someone it's hard to have in your home, or they are too
> embarrassed to be seen like this and they don't know how to change it,
> and the government doesn't help them good.

St. Paul's began in the nineties as a feeding ministry and evolved into a ministry that empowers those it serves to co-lead and organize and serve each other. They have nearly two dozen projects, a significant shift from their founding days as a soup kitchen. As with many congregations aiming to aid the underprivileged, it is clear from the progression of St. Paul's services that their understanding of homelessness has become more nuanced as those they serve have risen in number over the years.[9] Homelessness and hunger often go hand in hand in the eyes of those disconnected from people classified or labeled as "homeless"; in fact, numbers on hunger and the homeless are regularly conflated.

Many of the services offered by Muslim relief organizations around the U.S. target food-related events and programs. Popular ones include soup kitchens, can drives, the packing and distributing of lunch bags, and large meal events. Today, at St. Paul, the distinction between homelessness and hunger is fairly clear. They can be correlated but need not be. Despite the vast numbers of people who have housing but cannot find enough food, or nourishing food, to sustain themselves and their families, it is also not uncommon for individuals to be unhoused, yet have access to food and nourishment. Some would argue, food is not the issue. "The homeless need our help. They need shelter. They need people to help them take their medicine on time. Food isn't the problem," said the owner of the Black Seed Café and Grill in downtown Boston. "What about the homeless who aren't living in the street?" I asked him. "What kind of help do they need?" He was silent for a moment. "They're not the majority," he insisted. He then mused:

> Almost all of the homeless are the ones on drugs. It's hard to be in the street. To manage that life, they turn to drugs. Being on drugs makes people not want to be around them, so they will kick them out, even if it's a friend. This is what our taxes need to fix. Helping them get off the drugs. Then they will feel like a person; behave like a person. There was this one man, he used to come around here all the time. When he took his medicine, he was fine; completely normal; a nice guy. When he didn't, he behaved like an animal, wild. I haven't seen him in a while actually, I don't know what happened to him, if he died or got better. He tore up the café one time and we had to stop him. It [his behavior] didn't make sense at first. That's when I learned about his medicine.

His perspective is, of course, biased. As the owner of a successful café, food is not his challenge in serving. If food could prevent one from becoming "a homeless," he would likely feed them all. For him, to be "a homeless" was to

belong to a particular community. His conception of who fits in that term, notably, did not initially include the individuals at his mosque living in a shelter.
He assessed:

> I know we have some women in the shelter with their kids, they are
> not the homeless," he told me. "The homeless have a problem, that's
> why nobody wants them in their house. They also get embarrassed by
> their problem, so they stay on the street. Addiction or problem in their
> head of something. It's not easy to fix it."

For him, "the homeless" are the people society and its structures failed. "I
want to help them," he, further, shared with me in a conversation,

> But I have to do it from a distance. I can't have them around my store.
> It's not good for my business. Without my business, I can't help
> anyone. If I give them food directly, it'll make a big problem for me. It
> has to be from a distance.

"Is the church your vehicle then to help them?" I asked him. "Yessss, may God
always enlighten you, exactly, it allows the distance," he responded. It struck
me how he defined "distance." The church and the café abutted one another,
side by side, on one of the busiest streets in downtown Boston.

Homelessness and Poverty

Scholars and activists around the country theorize as to what causes homelessness. Naturally, many believe that to resolve the "crisis of homelessness"
or, at times, the "problem of homelessness," locating the source of the issue is
a necessary step. Fewer of us, however, question the idea of homelessness itself and how we as an American society have come to define and understand
what that means. For Black Seed's owner, his understanding of homelessness
became identity-based. A type of people that could not house themselves and
others did not want to house out of fear, revolt, or frustration—not lack of capacity. Some agencies in Massachusetts that serve those experiencing homelessness, however, espouse a different perspective. They frame homelessness
primarily as an effect of poverty.

The Massachusetts Coalition for the Homeless (MCH) indicates that the
"number of people experiencing homelessness and housing instability" is "very
high."[10] They provide some data, including over 18,471 people accounted for
in the state as homeless.[11] Massachusetts has an Emergency Assistance (EA)
shelter program for families. According to the coalition's website, as of
March 2018, there were forty-six families in this program that reside in motels.

The coalition is clear to note that this "number does not count those families who are doubled up, living in unsafe conditions, or sleeping in their cars."[12]

Throughout the webpage, they point to poverty as a primary reason of homelessness. "Not surprisingly, poverty has a direct correlation to a family or individual losing their housing." The implication here that if we address the policies and laws that result in poverty, homelessness will decrease. Correlation, however, does not necessarily mean causality. Nor is the category of homelessness universally defined. For some it is the lack of permanent housing; for others, it is understood as a lifestyle resulting from poor choices or illnesses; and yet for others, it can be an indication of lack of safety, not resources. The category of "homelessness" that can encompass such a range of situations to create and capture a type of person emerges distinctly in the United States.

Sociologist Matthew Desmond conducted a multi-year study, including a full year of fieldwork in Milwaukee, Wisconsin, following tenants and landlords to understand eviction.[13] He demonstrates and argues that unlike the common conception that poverty leads to eviction, instead, it is eviction that often leads to poverty. In the methods and process of capturing data by MCH, there is a lack of clarity as to whether in Massachusetts the correlation mentioned earlier between homelessness and poverty is necessarily causal, and, if so, what the causal direction is. In other words, is housing insecurity the explanatory variable? Or rather is it poverty, as Desmond seems to imply?

On the Official Blog of the Website of the Commonwealth of Massachusetts, we see a more nuanced description. It states that "there are many reasons why people become homeless . . . that can make it difficult, if not impossible, for people to pay rent or make mortgage payments."[14] The reasons here include poverty, but they also include a number of situations that can result in lack of access to resources to maintain housing, such as divorce, violence, or illness. The blog's language is sensitive enough to capture not only causes that can lead to lack of resources, but also causes that can lead to lack of access to resources. In both cases, the coalition and the state's Official Blog, homelessness is not posited as an identity, but as a housing status. In his 2015 ethnography of a Western Massachusetts shelter, Vincent Lyon-Callo argues that much of the neoliberal economy, with its emphasis on individual competitiveness and a capitalist market dominance, imbued both the rise and response to homelessness and served as one of its main determinants.[15]

These systemic and structural critiques underlie the comments coming from Black Seed's owner. The man who could not get ahold of the medicine he needed because it was unaffordable without a government subsidy, the user who was regularly arrested and released yet not offered treatment to fight his addiction, and the alcoholic who cannot manage to become sober are each examples of broader failures—they are "a homeless" not because they are poor; nor because they have an addiction or suffer from mental illness; but because they can be and are marginalized as victims of structural discrimination. Like Lyon-Callo, for Black Seed's owner, homelessness is a systemic epidemic, and to be homeless is to be someone whom the government discriminates against and fails.

Homelessness in Your Other Home?

"What about in Egypt," I asked him. "Are there homeless people there?" "It's not the same," he said. Black Seed's owner has lived in the United States for over thirty years. Before that he spent his first two decades growing up in a relatively small, part rural, part urban town on the Egyptian Delta. Since immigrating, he regularly travels to Egypt spending time in his hometown, the two major cities, Cairo and Alexandria, and vacationing on various shores. He reflected:

> The government in Egypt can't help its people the same as the government here. Part of it is corruption and part of it is they don't have the same wealth. The people there are really poor. They live in places no one in this country can live, and they're still not homeless. The community takes care of each other. Gives each other food and clothes. You're not forgotten.

He was referring to the differences in poverty and the categorical distinctions between the U.S. and Egypt when it comes to homelessness and, inexplicitly, when it comes to relationships and community. "You're not addicted and alone on the street like they are here," he went on. "So," I interjected, wanting to clarify his perspective, "there aren't drugs and addicts in Egypt?" "No, no, no, of course there are. We have it of course," he said. And he continued:

> There's hashish, and heroin, and other things, but the rich people have access to the drugs there. If you're poor, you can't get drugs. There's some homeless there but it's not a lot. It's very hard to be a homeless in Egypt. There are streets a lot of people use as a home who aren't a homeless.

His comments are anecdotal, and it is not clear if they are a popular portrayal of Egyptian society or a singular glimpse. I share them here less as a reflection of Egypt and instead as a contrast that helps crystallize how he formulated his structural critiques of the U.S. For him, Egypt did not have homeless, not because it was devoid of people living in the streets, but because, according to him, society there did not leave individuals forgotten and in despair.

This was a sentiment that was echoed multiple times during the 2011 uprisings in Egypt when the masses occupied Tahrir square. They constructed a city in the square full of all needed services. If you were sick, there was a tent for that. If you needed electricity, they set that up. They set up childcare and places of worship for Muslims and Christians. They provided food, water, managed waste, and kept the millions of protestors safe for weeks in a row. Egyptians consistently attributed the success of the Tahrir occupation to the decades of training they had under a Mubarak regime they argued failed them. "We knew how to make Tahrir work because we've been taking care of ourselves for decades," was the sentiment many Egyptians echoed.[16] This sentiment effectively illustrates the description of homelessness that Black Seed's owner was trying to express and how the concept of "a homeless" in the United States emerges and develops into a socially constructed category neither easily defined nor bounded, nor, given the national epidemic currently confronting the nation, dispensable.

Abureaucratic Service

There remains one additional critical element that distinguishes this unique and popular relationship between one singular church and a local urban café. The community service observed from Black Seed's charity is nearly abureaucratic. Unlike institutionalized and registered nonprofits that need to abide by regulations for nonprofit status, need to have a vision and mission to incorporate, need to fundraise to support their work, and need to track and hold themselves accountable to their supporters to have continued fundraising success, Black Seed is limited to the desire of one man, motivated by his conviction and understanding of his Muslim faith, to help a neighboring community. His support was notable and appreciated enough by the community that the café became the namesake for the Black Seed Writers Group, a literary workshop for homeless women and men, and the authors of most articles published in the *Pilgrim*, a magazine distributed to the church congregants and several hundred other subscribers. Mr. James Parker, a columnist from the *Atlantic* who has been featured in the *Boston Globe*, the *Boston College Magazine*, and *Spare Change News*, along with several online blogs, founded the Black Seed Writers Group and helps St. Paul publish the magazine, now quarterly (in prior times it was ten issues per year).

Mr. Parker oversees a weekly class and teaches the mechanics of writing to those who attend. When I asked Black Seed's owner to tell me more about the Writers Group, he kept trying to place it but was clearly unfamiliar with it. "Maybe they meet in your café?" I asked him, assuming that's how the name came to be, and confused, given his earlier comments about helping from "a distance." "No," he said, "there are no writers in my café. You sure it's the Black Seed Writers Group?" "Yes," I assured him, "there are a lot of articles about it." "I don't know . . . ," he trailed. And, despite being one man, receiving no donations, seeking no promotion, his work serving homeless populations in the city of Boston inspired others. Perhaps it moved Mr. James Parker, or perhaps Mr. Parker's student authors published in the *Pilgrim*, or perhaps it was the church staff that may have suggested calling the weekly gathering the "Black Seed Writers Group." Much like the role of the Egyptian citizenry in Tahrir, Black Seed Cafe's owner embodied what it meant to be in community and modeled what is arguably the only tried solution to the problem of "the homeless."

Notes

Many thanks to Manuel Mejido for his patient stewardship over almost two years. A special note of gratitude also goes to my scholar colleagues in this volume for their feedback during our two workshops, with notable thanks to Jim Spickard who graciously sent me astute and detailed notes with much direction and guidance on a body of scholarship that became critical to analyzing my data and framing this piece.

1. Christopher Jencks, *The Homeless* (Cambridge, Mass.: Harvard University Press, 1995).

2. Irene Glasser and Rae Bridgeman, *Braving the Street: The Anthropology of Homelessness* (New York: Berghahn, 1999).

3. Ibid.

4. Ibid.

5. Ablution in a Muslim context is a ritual washing completed before prayer that includes wetting the arms, face, head, and feet. It takes on various detailed forms depending on the observer's jurisprudential understanding. The motivation behind designing custom stations is often to both physically ease the process to wet the feet and to reduce the excessive splashing that results from ablution conducted in a hand sink.

6. Ramadan is the ninth month in the Islamic calendar. During this month many Muslims participate in the Ramadan obligatory fast, which includes refraining from all food and drink from dawn to dusk. The *iftar* is the breaking of the fast meal, which takes place at sunset.

7. Andy Rosen, "Thanksgiving: A Holiday for Healing," *Boston Globe*, November 24, 2016, accessed November 24, 2020, www.bostonglobe.com.

8. Malcolm X, *The Autobiography of Malcolm X*, reprint ed. (New York: Ballantine, 2015).

9. Consult, for example, "History: Our Cathedral Today" and "Strategic Plan of the Cathedral," available on St. Paul's website, accessed November 24, 2020, www .stpaulboston.org.

10. "Basic Facts on Homelessness in Massachusetts and Across the Country," available on the website of the Massachusetts Coalition for the Homeless (MCH), accessed November 24, 2020, www.mahomeless.org.

11. United States Department of Housing and Urban Development, "The 2019 Annual Homeless Assessment Report," by Meghan Henry, Rian Watt, Anna Mahathey, Jullian Ouellette, and Aubrey Sitler, Abt Associates (Washington, D.C.: January 2020).

12. MCH, "Basic Facts on Homelessness in Massachusetts and Across the Country," accessed November 24, 2020, www.mahomeless.org.

13. Matthew Desmond, *Evicted: Poverty and Profit in the American City*, reprint ed. (New York: Broadway, 2017).

14. "Housing Resources for Massachusetts Homeless," The Official Blog of the Website of the Commonwealth of Massachusetts, accessed November 24, 2020, blog .mass.gov.

15. Vincent Lyon-Callo, *Inequality, Poverty, and Neoliberal Governance: Activist Ethnography in the Homeless Sheltering Industry*, 2nd ed. (Toronto: University of Toronto Press, Higher Education Division, 2015).

16. H. A. Hellyer, *A Revolution Undone: Egypt's Road Beyond Revolt*, 1st ed. (Oxford: Oxford University Press, 2016).

Religion and Civic Activism Reconsidered

Situating Faith-Based Responses to Homelessness

John A. Coleman, S.J.

I was asked to contribute a chapter to this book because of earlier work I did on faith-based organizations (FBOs), social service, and citizen activism.[1] My work looking at six FBOs stemmed from earlier work I had done on the Christian as citizen and on the relation between discipleship and citizenship.[2] In later work I expanded the look at the six FBOs to include a study that focused on the Jesuit Refugee Service, Pax Christi, and Green Sisters hosting ecological farms. I also took a look at Catholic Charities U.S.A. in its work on welfare reform.[3] While none of these earlier studies focused on FBOs and homelessness, my findings may shed light on such groups as they tackle helping the homeless. I will end this chapter with some reflections about the correlations between my earlier work and faith-based groups addressing the homeless.

Discipleship and Citizenship

I want to share my conclusions about the relation of discipleship and citizenship by espousing three defensible theses about the relation of discipleship and citizenship.

Discipleship and Citizenship Exist in a Kind of Permanent Tension

In his book *The Machiavellian Moment*, John G. A. Pocock comments that the saints almost always wear their mantle of citizenship lightly. No earthly home mirrors the New Jerusalem.[4] Michael Walzer captures this tension between saints and citizens when he claims for citizenship, almost in relief, that "the standards are not all that high; we are required to be brethren and citizens, not saints and heroes."[5] From the perspective of the Christian moral ideal of discipleship, the alternative morality of citizenship often seems less than fully moral. Many Christians fear it might mean a loss, corruption, leveling or co-optation of the distinctly moral voice of discipleship. If in a given pluralistic society, citizenship is a more inclusive and universal category than discipleship, discipleship, at times, protects against the almost inescapable political temptation toward narrow patriotism or uncritical nationalism, inasmuch as discipleship, in principle if not always in empirical fact, includes a more global horizon than the nation-state.

A brief word of explanation and caution here. "Discipleship" is a Christian-based word. In my usage it is a shorthand word to refer to the governing ethos, the principal cultural, spiritual, and behavioral expectations that Christian groups bring to their interactions with their society and government. Obviously, "discipleship" is not an apt word to deal with Jewish, Buddhist, or Muslim organizations. Instead of the shorthand word, we need to state it for them as the "governing ethos, the principal cultural, spiritual and behavioral expectations which [Jewish, Buddhist, or Muslim, etc.] groups bring to their interventions with their society and government."

Since my own research centered on Christian groups, I will continue to use the term "discipleship," but when dealing with non-Christian groups, we need to use other terms. Moreover, we need to remember that Catholics, Orthodox, mainline Protestants, and Evangelicals may have somewhat differing notions and norms of discipleship.

Discipleship (however much one may argue about its precise contours) surely includes a substantive vision of human life, society, and the human good. Notoriously, modern democracies are agnostic about the good. Democratic citizenship, it is usually argued, must be relatively blind to all substantive arguments concerning social goods. Fair procedure, equal access, societal peace, and consensus, the art of the possible, take precedence over substantive visions. As Walzer puts it, "The state does not nourish souls." He hastens to add, "Nor does it kill them."[6] Most modern democracies espouse some variant of Elizabeth I's fine phrase, "The government may not build windows into men's souls." So, there is a kind of permanent distinction between any community of disciples and a genuinely political and democratic commonwealth of citizens.

Walzer puts the point succinctly:

Democracy is a way of allocating power and legitimating its use. . . . Every extrinsic reason is ruled out. What counts is argument among the citizens. Democracy puts a premium on speech, persuasion, rhetorical skill. Ideally, the citizen who makes the most persuasive argument—that is, the argument that actually persuades the largest number of citizens—gets his or her way. It is not only the inclusiveness, however, that makes for democratic government. Equally important is what we might call the rule of reasons. Citizens come into the forum with nothing but their arguments. All other political goods have to be deposited outside: weapons and wallets, titles and degrees.[7]

And many would add, "creeds or ethics of discipleship." The game of citizenship constrains, to some extent, the saint's language system. Whatever their background revelational foundation, disciples, many argue, can make their case as citizens only in a discourse of secular warrant and public reason. As the Christian ethicist Robin Lovin once put it, "Theological affirmations make poor premises for public moral arguments because they are held by a limited group of the faithful" in an arena that is more universal than the world of the saints.[8] So, it is simply impossible to construe citizenship in a religiously pluralistic world only on the categories of discipleship. Or, for that matter, to construe discipleship in the pallid terms of a citizenship ideal alone. Later, I will discuss situations where it is legitimate to use discipleship language in public, if for no other reason than to show a disciple's true meanings in acting.

Moreover, as Paul Ricoeur so clearly saw, we confront two pedagogies: the pedagogy of power and the pedagogy of nonviolent discipleship. This, one notes, is not so different from Max Weber's famous dichotomy between the ethics of absolute ends found, he said, in "The Sermon on the Mount," and an ethics of pragmatic responsibility, *Wert* versus *Zweck* rationality.

Let me just cite a few quotes from Ricoeur's early political essays:

> It is not responsible (and it is even impossible) to deduce a politics
> from a theology. This is so because every political involvement grows
> out of a truly secular set of information, a situational arena which
> proffers a limited field of possible actions and available means, and a
> more or less risk-taking option, a gamble, among these possibilities.[9]

Elsewhere Ricoeur argues that, inasmuch as any state relies on (often enough grows out of, initially) violence or coercion, "The state is a great mystery. The state represents an unresolved contradiction, lying always midway between rationality and coercion." Thus, Ricoeur goes on to state, "There is no such thing as a Christian politics, only the politics of Christians who are also citizens."[10]

Just to list a few of the salient issues involved in thinking about citizenship (which is essentially a membership category involving rights, responsibilities, loyalties, and special duties toward co-citizens that may be weightier than to noncitizens, we can ask, Does citizenship derive ultimately from membership in a nation-state, or is it more closely linked to membership in a national community with distinct boundaries, history, ethos, and, perhaps, a common language? Following Jacques Maritain in *Man and the State*, I prefer the second of these construals, since it makes us see the state as the servant coordinator of society.[11] Is citizenship unitary or multicultural? (One thinks of Charles Taylor's construal of citizenship.)[12] How do you adjudicate between competing secular concepts of citizenship, especially consensual (based on civic republicanism and a notion of the common good and necessary shared citizen virtues) versus liberal, pluralist theories of citizenship? While I strongly endorse the first concept from civic republicanism, empirically it is more difficult to sustain or win the day for it in deeply pluralist societies, so, in the end, purely procedural and not substantive notions of the good (either in utilitarian or deontological construals) prevail.

Generally Disciples Must Take Their Common Citizenship Seriously as a Moral Obligation

The choices range from whether, with Augustine, you harbor rather narrow hopes for the morality of citizenship and the ability to find very many comings together between discipleship and citizenship (yet even Augustine argued some forms of "rough justice" here below were more humanly fitting, even if they lacked any salvific consequences) to, with more modern thinkers, you assume that somehow, as Edward Schillebeeckx argues in his Christ book, "Humanity is the arena where the struggle against good and evil actually takes place and, therefore, represents a potent revelation of God as grace and judgment," such that you contend you cannot separate human flourishing and liberation and salvation without, however, totally identifying them.[13] In either way of construing the City of God and the City of Man, disciples must take common citizenship seriously.

To be sure, I would add that discipleship augments citizenship, and disciples may, indeed perhaps must, be sometimes different kinds of citizens. As Denis W. Brogan once put in his book *Citizenship Today*, "A Christian citizen has more duties than and different from those that the state defines and demands."[14] They share the common duties but as disciples may have more duties (for example, to charity beyond justice; to self-sacrifice beyond common citizenship duties).

Again, I find the thought of Ricoeur helpful in articulating the Christian's duties as citizen. On the one hand, recognizing the arena of politics as a field of contradiction between rationality and justice and power and coercion, the

Christian, Ricoeur argues, must "simultaneously work to improve the political institutions in the sense of the achievement of greater rationality and to remain wary of the abuse of power that is ingredient in every state system."[15]

In several places in his political writings, Ricoeur lifts up three distinct themes of what a disciple can add to citizenship: a promise of an alternative possibility (utopian imagination); counter-cultural judgments; and vocation as the task of constructing a new social order. Ricoeur speaks of a kind of "salvation through imaginative power and a revolution in the images that guide our life."[16] Against the dangers of power, he poses the Christian nonviolent counterpoise; against the temptation to greed or the alienation of commodity fetishism in possession and property, he suggests Franciscan movements of simplicity and/or the Calvinist sense of careful stewardship of earthly goods that really belong to all; against culturally restricted values, he proposes catholicity, keeping alive a human project that envisions a global unity transcending national boundaries.

It is not that the disciple has any preordained pat answers (or is the only one who can embody alternative imagination, countercultural judgments, or the vocation to construct a new and better social order). But Ricoeur does argue that a special task for the Christian in politics or culture is "so to act that in society the issues of the use and meaning of power, the pleasure principle and human autonomy as a value can be brought at least, once again, into serious public discussion."[17]

Moreover, citizenship also adds distinctive qualities to discipleship. It widens the reach of religious solidarity to include all other citizens in its range, thereby reminding religious people that God's grace and truth reign outside church borders. It provides a taxing reality test, an experiential proving ground for claims for a this-worldly liberative, regenerative potential in grace and redemption.

Discipleship and Citizenship Can Mutually Enrich Each Other

This is especially the case when we inspect the evidence of how discipleship creates social capital—those bonds of reciprocity and trust—and its wide democratic input and influence.[18] In order to test the democratic potential of discipleship, I and six research assistants over a several-year period looked at the data concerning discipleship's democratic potential and production of social capital. We looked at six FBOs engaged in social services and citizenship activism.

1. Habitat for Humanity. Founded by an evangelical person but drawing widely from the whole range of religious and secular America, Habitat builds low-cost housing as a nonprofit organ-

ization. The housing is mainly for low-income people, not for the homeless. Habitat is the seventeenth-largest home builder in America.[19]

2. PICO. The name, an acronym for the Pacific Institute for Community Organizing, is now a misnomer, because PICO has affiliates all over the country and in Honduras and Africa. It is the second-largest (after the Industrial Areas Foundation) church-based community organizing group in the United States. Founded by a Jesuit, John Baumann, PICO helps give ordinary Americans a voice by mobilizing and equipping them with citizen skills; it brings together the moral vision of the churches with participant democracy to revitalize urban neighborhoods and demand better police protection, improved schools, and economic development.[20]

3. Bread for the World. This is a large hunger-lobby group that also engages in education and research on hunger issues. Founded by a Lutheran pastor, Art Simon, Bread draws strongly from a mainline Protestant and Catholic base.

4. Pax Christi, U.S.A. Pax is a Catholic peace education and activist organization that tries to affect both the Catholic Church and our government. It is open to membership by non-Catholics. Pax Christi was chosen, among other reasons, in order to include in our study a more radical version of citizenship-activism, since a number of Pax's members engage in civil disobedience.

5. Focus on the Family. This evangelical ministry, based in Colorado Springs, was founded by the well-known family radio pundit and best-selling author Dr. James Dobson. Focus engages in public policy and is affiliated with public interest groups at the state and national level that lobby for family-related legislation and policy—for instance, taxation, vouchers, home schooling, protection of heterosexual marriage, and divorce legislation. Focus and its affiliates also galvanize local church members into greater political involvement through its grassroots Community Impact Forum. While a number of Focus affiliates have loose alliances with the Christian Right, Focus spokespersons distance themselves somewhat from the hard Christian Right and foster a more moderate image.

6. The African Methodist Episcopal Church. We sampled four large megachurches of the A.M.E., the oldest historic black church in America. For example, Bethel, the site we studied in Baltimore, manages the high school equivalency program for that city. The congregation in Los Angeles we focused on—First African Methodist Episcopal, familiarly known as FAME, spearheaded the community

development renaissance after the communal uprisings at the time of the Rodney King trial and has spawned dozens of nonprofit spin-offs. We were determined to include a sample from the black churches, since few other American churches do as good a job as the black churches do in wedding discipleship to citizenship.

Let us now look at the evidence and data that discipleship and church membership contain strong pushes for citizenship activism and create strong pools of social capital.

Evidence That Religion Disproportionately Generates Social Capital

The churches regularly and straightforwardly act as communication networks that foster civic volunteerism. Robert Wuthnow puts it this way:

> Religious organizations tell people of opportunities to serve, both within and beyond the congregation itself and provide personal contacts, committees, phone numbers, meeting space, transportation or whatever it may take to help turn good intention into action.[21]

The sociological evidence linking religion to social capital is overwhelming. Two-thirds of those active in social movements in America (even more secular-sounding ones such as the Sierra Club) claim that they draw on religious motivation for their involvement. Two-thirds of all small groups in America are directly connected with or meet in space provided by churches and synagogues.[22]

As Wuthnow has put it, in his national study of student volunteers in America, "Churches and synagogues remain the primary places where instruction is given about the spiritual dimension of caring."[23] Americans give seven times as much to churches as to political campaigns and several times as much as they give to secular charities.[24] They also seem to think that the churches and synagogues are better able to deal with "problems facing our city or local community."[25] Fifty-seven percent of respondents, in one Gallup survey, deemed churches to be more apt than other social institutions to deal with such problems. Less than a third thought local businesses, government, or political parties were effective vehicles for "compassionate and just solutions to the problems of our local communities."[26]

People are more likely to give money and time, even to secular efforts, if they are church members.[27] They are also significantly more likely to vote if they are church members.[28] In his study of volunteers in America, Wuthnow demonstrates that religiously motivated volunteers are more likely to employ a communitarian language to describe their involvements and appeal to some sense of the common good, rather than rely on merely individualistic language to explain their behavior.[29] Another study shows that even having neighbors who attend church is a critical factor in predicting whether youths in the neighborhood will have jobs, use drugs, or engage in criminal activity. The social capital of churches, it seems, spills over, beyond their members, into whole neighborhoods.[30]

The Democratic Potential in Religion

In their massive study of political and civic volunteerism in America, Sidney Verba and colleagues argue that religion significantly increases the democratic potential of the United States.[31] Churches are superior to their two main competitors—the workplace and nonpolitical civic organizations, such as the Rotary Club, in providing civic virtues and social capital and in bringing transferable civic skills to the more disenfranchised.[32] The workplace and nonpolitical civic organizations tend to reward those who already have human capital and are middle class. Those who already have get even more opportunities. Verba and his colleagues conclude their study with these remarks: "Only religious institutions provide a counterbalance to this cumulative resource process. They play an unusual role in the American participatory system by providing opportunities for the development of civic skills to those who would be otherwise resource poor."[33]

Indeed, a blue-collar worker in America is more apt to gain opportunities to develop and practice civic skills in church than in a union, "not because American unions are particularly deficient as skill builders but because so few American blue-collar workers are union members and so many are church members."[34] The study by Verba and colleagues exhibits the special strength of black churches in generating and investing social capital in their neighborhoods. They also show that even nonblack churches provide our society with a more participatory, more egalitarian, and more communitarian ethos than it would have without them.[35] Even a secularist might, plausibly, desire a more public role for churches in our civic society, precisely because of what the secular spin-off churches provide: greater volunteering; greater contributions to public civic organizations and charities; and greater voting behavior.

Robin Gill has exhaustively shown that this secular ethical and civic impact of churchgoing is not exclusive to the United States. In British social surveys and in the European Value Systems Study Group surveys (conducted in the 1990s), churchgoing predicts a socially significant greater concern for the vulnerable and needy; lower rates of racism and higher rates of openness to international concerns; a higher sense of purpose in life; a greater attention to the environment; a stronger tendency to value moral order; a greater concern for and sense of being able to make a positive contribution to world problems; and a tendency to volunteer (even in secular groups).[36] Controlling for church-going, regular weekly churchgoers, in Gill's sample, drawn from data from more than twelve countries, are two to three times more likely to be engaged in volunteerism as are the sporadic (several times a year) church attenders and ten times as likely as those who never go to church.[37] Belonging to actual con-gregations, Gill shows, does breed a distinct constellation of attitudes, civic habits, and presuppositions conducive to active citizenship involvement.[38] The language that was prevalent in the Charitable Choice movement of calling for a greater role of "faith-based" groups in the delivery of social services—language found across the political spectrum, especially after President George W. Bush opened up money from the Department of Housing and Ur-ban Development (HUD) for such faith-based groups—was an implicit recog-nition of this "secular" or "civic" spin-off from churches in our society.[39]

We should not be surprised that churches, especially local congregations, are major sites for the generation of social capital. Few other organizations think of themselves so explicitly as communities. Few so insistently raise up norms of reciprocity—"neighbor love and care." It is almost part of the expected ethos of a church that it will have wider outreach to the needy. Indeed, the American public tends to identify "service to the needy" and "helping" more generally as religious values.[40]

Are There Limits to the Social Capital Generated by Churches in Society?

It is important to remember that Robert Putnam, in his classic "Bowling Alone" essay, contends that social capital is clearly not "a unidimensional concept."[41] Social capital focuses primarily on norms and networks of organized reciprocity, trust, and civic solidarity ("bonding" social capital) that are capable of spinning off ("bridging" social capital)—for education, urban poverty, unemployment, control of crime and drugs, health—new solidarities and potentialities. Not all bonding social capital, however, becomes bridging social capital.

Some religious units pay scant attention to the social capital they generate or do not know how to turn it into politically or civically relevant social move-ments, service, and volunteerism. Much of the social capital of some congrega-tions remains frozen within the local unit or is even isolated into separate pockets of friendship cliques within the congregation and, therefore, does not spill over into the larger society. Daniel Olsen has suggested that friendship networks within congregations can implode, thus impeding any outward reach either in evangelism or civic service.[42] John Wilson and Thomas Janoski show that many conservative evangelical Protestants who are active in their churches are actually less likely to get involved in secular volunteerism.[43] They turn their energies inward into their own congregation rather than outward to the community at large. Without certain inner theological and cultural work within the churches, the social capital they generate lies dormant and lacks any civic impact.

Some congregations define themselves essentially as sanctuary havens from a heartless world. Not every congregation sees itself as having a civic public mission. In particular, as Robert Wuthnow claims, the local congregation may find that public debates about economics and civic matters inside the very heart of the church "can easily become polarized, bringing an aura of antagonism that runs against the grain of religious teachings and fellowship and reconciliation."[44] There exists—as Gallup data repeatedly show—a widespread and strong dislike in America of religious leaders playing too direct a role in politics.[45] Finally, there is some empirical evidence that congregations show reluctance to becoming involved in civic outreach that they do not themselves sponsor. They want to keep outreach programs "close to home" with close ties to their own congregation.[46] This limits the expansionary potential of any social capital they might generate. In Putnam's terms, they do not turn their "bonding capital" into a "bridging capital," which embraces diversity of race, gender, and social class.[47]

Much of the research on religion and social capital focuses, relatively uniquely, on the congregation as the relevant unit of analysis. It closely ties religious social capital to formal church membership and measures of church attendance. Yet congregations frequently find themselves too small and limited to address even local and community problems such as homelessness, ecological deterioration of a neighborhood, and police protection.[48] At best their civic outreach tends toward immediate payoffs:

> Churches do not provide massive monetary relief, health care or housing to the poor. Churches avoid the doctrine of entitlements that undergirds public assistance programs. But churches meet short-term emergency needs among their own members, contribute to the needs of other people who may be working to keep their own churches alive, and provide volunteer assistance that may be lacking from other agencies.[49]

Nancy Ammerman, in her important book *Congregation and Community*, suggests that the social capital generated by congregations gives them a comparative civic leg up because:

1. They are presumptively legitimate. "Groups recognized as congregations receive, by definition, a measure of acceptance, and the social
   identifies enshrined in those congregations are therefore recognized."[50]
2. Congregations (and, by inference, at least some para-church
   groups) are presumed in American society to be driven by a moral
   imperative, not merely naked self-interest. Given the pervasive
   American cynicism about the "putatively moral" rhetoric of politicians,
   corporations, and other secular public agencies, congregations retain
   the weight of cultural expectation that their behavior will not just
   mirror self-interest, but some altruism and concern for the public good.[51]
3. Generally, congregations "have the most pervasive infrastructure for
   meeting community needs along with the expectation that their
   provision of such services is to be trusted."[52]

Para-Church Organizations and Civic Activism

Clearly, we should not limit our study of religion and social capital only to local congregations. To be sure, the overwhelming majority of congregations
do sponsor some civic outreach program.[53] But even at local levels, much of
the food bank, soup kitchen, homeless shelter programs, and low-cost housing initiatives derive not directly from congregations but from special-purpose
para-church or para-denominational organizations, independently incorporated and autonomous from congregations or even denominations. These
para-church special-purpose groups closely tap into local congregations to obtain
monetary support and committed volunteers. Larger para-church organizations
such as Habitat for Humanity and Bread for the World and para-denominational
organizations such as the Salvation Army, Volunteers of America, and Catholic
Charities U.S.A. have become important units for religiously based outreach
in social service and civic education.

Even many congregational social service programs would not be terribly
effective without a linkage to such para-church or para-denominational organizations. For example, in my parish, Saint Ignatius, we have a Sandwich Sat-
urday program through which parishioners make batches of sandwiches to be
delivered to homeless shelters. But only its linkage to the San Francisco Interfaith Council lets it determine where the sandwiches go. Similarly, my parish
has an advocacy committee focusing on human trafficking. But its actions
would be less effective without its taking part in a para-church organization,
the San Francisco Collaborative Against Human Trafficking, which trains volunteers and links them to similar volunteers from other congregations and
synagogues. A final example, as Saint Ignatius parish seeks housing for a refu-

gee woman from Mexico seeking asylum, they are dependent on a connection with another para-church organization, Hamilton Housing.

Few studies of para-church groups—their constituencies and relation to congregations—exist at national or regional and local levels.[54] Special-purpose religious units may be especially adept at turning the intense, bonding social capital of local congregations into a larger bridging capital. As Mary Cole-Burns, a West Coast affiliate director of Habitat for Humanity, put it to our research team in an interview, "I always tell people the housing is merely the vehicle. The real work of Habitat is our notion of community and what it means to be together. It expands my notion of who my neighbors are."

Special-purpose religious groups do expand the social capital they garner originally from congregations. At Habitat building sites, the typical congregational volunteer will rub shoulders with the sweat-equity, lower-income homeowner and other volunteers of different religions and race. Church members are unlikely to meet and mingle in such a social mix in their own home congregations (or, for that matter, in any other "secular" social setting)! Similarly, church-based community organizing groups bunch together clumps of social capital found in congregations into larger aggregate units that bridge race, social class, and geographical territory to further civic purposes, such as finding better police protection in neighborhoods, reducing school classroom size, and enabling a charter school movement.

Precisely because of the widespread taboo against introducing controversial political issues into the local congregation—even when they have some clear moral or religious overtones—para-church groups serve the local congregations by providing outlets for a social and public faith without dividing the congregation as such. As one Bread for the World informant told our research team, "I see in my own church that talking about the arms race raises a lot of hackles and divides people." But many of her fellow congregants could easily work together on hunger issues around the world through Bread for the World.

The congregation and the para-denominational organizations need each other to generate a public church in America, because most local congregations do not know how to use the social capital they generate. Sam Reed, a major executive in the PICO network, put it this way to us:

> I would suggest that community organizing in the churches in which I am hired helps them learn how to make their institutions effective. I don't think that what the community organizing staff provides the church is beyond the self-interest of the church institution itself. I don't think local congregations know how to make values real. I think they want to, but they don't know how.

Norm Rodert, a pastor in Kansas City, Kansas, echoes Reed. He says that community organizing, with its focus on building relationships and nurturing the skills of leadership, actually taught him for the first time how to be an effective pastor. The spill-over is not just to society but within the church itself.

Congregations and para-denominational organizations relate in a symbiosis. The latter, we found in our research, are not, in themselves, good units for generating discipleship, because they are specifically focused, involving limited liability commitments. "I don't look to Habitat to fulfill my basic religious needs; that's what the church is for" and "I always expect that we should bring our religious beliefs with us to Habitat rather than vice versa" were typical comments in our interviews. Discipleship—that is, taking seriously religious norms and messages—mainly takes place in families or congregations. Para-church organizations draw on that discipleship energy generated in the churches to link it to citizenship. Over and over again, the respondents in our study of the six para-church groups said they got involved in civic volunteerism mainly because of their religious motivation, which had been nurtured for them in congregations. Yet the same people who told us their sense of discipleship moved them to civic action waxed enthusiastic about how it was the denominational group rather than a parish that taught them how to put their faith into concrete action.

Martin Marty (perhaps the dean of all observers of the American religious scene), in his book on public religion, *Politics, Religion and the Common Good*, could argue to the growing social importance of the proliferating special-purpose para-church organizations: characteristically, these groups know that: (1) there are energies in the public that denominational agencies cannot summon; (2) special interest groups can move more rapidly than congregations or denominations can; (3) if they are successful at fundraising and gathering political constituencies, they have to be reckoned with; (4) they will draw media attention while more staid and laid-back religious organizations cannot; and (5) they can promote causes that further polarize society. Whereas churches are burdened down with agendas or causes other than the civic or political, the religious special-interest groups, while trading on religious impulses formed for other than political reasons, can focus on the issues at hand.[55]

Such interest groups are drawn together by people who set examples, take risks, are rhetorically skilled, and can evoke loyalties. They do not have to worry about "the other half of the congregation or denomination"; their congregation or denomination is ad hoc, made up of the like-minded. And they have another advantage over congregations or denominations; whereas the traditional institutions must address so much of life, including worship, education, works of mercy, and civic engagements, voluntary associations can be adaptive, brisk, and alert to special signals of public interest or expressions of need.[56]

How Legitimate Are Public Appeals to Religious Language or Religious Motivation in the Civic Engagement of FBOs?

One objection to public religion claims that equal respect for common citizenship demands that religious believers couch their public cases for policy in secular or public reason. Nonbelievers should not be expected to accept or even understand claims to public policy whose sole or primary warrant is religious (that is, couched in appeals to the Bible or religious language and motivation). Such things as important as human rights or common citizenship rights and duties are simply too essential and crucial to rest on private and non-universally accessible (to a nonbeliever) accounts, warrants, and appeals.[57]

My response to this objection is both empirical and theoretical. The empirical piece comes from my research team's interviews with over 300 respondents in the six para-church organizations engaged in civic activism. Over and over again, our respondents told us they got involved in civic voluntarism mainly because of religious motivation. The respondents very closely linked, even often conflated, their sense of discipleship and their citizenship. In their interview accounts, they claimed discipleship drove their citizenship energy. Tom Burke, a respondent from our sample of Pax Christi, U.S.A. (the Christian peace activist group) put it this way: "I am not a citizen exclusive of who I am as a member of my faith community." Sally Jepson echoed this sentiment: "I tend to think of myself living my life as a disciple and that being how I am also a citizen." Bread for the World (the Christian lobby group against hunger), we heard, "asks people to do their discipleship by being citizens." Randy Heckman, from Focus on the Family (the evangelical lobby group), makes the same kind of links: "The best disciples should be the best citizens because they are not living for themselves. There is a clear link between discipleship and citizenship in my mind."

Some of the respondents in our interviews were rather adept at translating their faith-driven positions into seemingly "secular" accounts without the "Christianese," as they put it. But one Pax Christi informant made a case for a broader democratic inclusion in speaking about the claims of some secularists to exclude any mention of religious language from our common citizenship deliberations:

I can talk to them about the same values and the end-product in a language that they would hopefully find more acceptable. And I would try to do that, and in the process I would also probably invite them to reflect on what it is about faith that nettles them so. And I would argue that whether one wishes to exclude all faith language in a secular setting or not, that faith language is indeed a central reality in the lives of many people and that it is better to face and deal with that dimension of reality than it is to try to hide it away, or ignore it, or try to suppress it. I would oppose this gag rule because it wars against my conception of who I am as a human person with God-given dignity and the right to speak and the right to share my vision. Not to force it on others, but to share it with others and at least to put it out there for consideration. While I could say I can speak in a secular way and be an advocate for reform and that kind of thing, it would be a sorrow to do that, because I would not be celebrating the depth and richness from which my conviction grows and which is nourished by my faith every day.

My own theoretical position on allowing appeals to religious morality in public discussions about law and public policy is informed by the assumption, as Martin Marty puts it, that in a deliberative democracy, "a republic would be better off if everyone could bring into the open whatever truly motivates them and impels the citizens to decide and act."[58] Stephen Carter would tend to agree. He thinks that John Rawls and Bruce Ackerman's gag rule on religious language in public and the need to always translate all accounts into a secular language is "both undemocratic and unrealistic."[59] He thinks that Rawls and Ackerman's theories of public discourse "describe debates from which deeply religious people are simply absent."[60] Therefore, he argues "when the religionist speaks on a proposition, the religionist's purest voice will be the voice that convinced him in the first place."[61] In a deliberative democracy, participants should be able openly to share their deepest and most real reasons for policy and action. As Carter puts it:

> What is needed is not a requirement that the religiously devout choose a form of dialogue that liberalism accepts, but that liberalism develop a politics that accepts whatever form of dialogue a member in public offers. . . . What is needed, then, is a willingness to listen, not because the speaker has the right voice but because the speaker has the right to speak. Moreover, the willingness to listen must hold out the possibility that the speaker is saying something worth listening to.[62]

How Do the Foregoing Data and Argument Direct Us as We Look at FBOs and the Issue of Homelessness?

Homelessness is a complicated issue to address, since it stems from a deficit in affordable housing units; the massive depletion of single rental rooms in our cities; loss of jobs; inadequate welfare stipends that aren't large enough to cover not only housing but food and other necessities; substance abuse among the homeless; domestic violence; incarceration; and mental and physical health issues. Also a key feature of the homeless: lack of relationships.[63] The homeless include men, women with children, and veterans. Some homeless are only episodically so. Others are chronically homeless. The chronically homeless use up some 90 percent of the resources for dealing with homelessness.[64]

Again, FBOs dealing with homelessness are eligible for government funds from HUD provided they take part in a city or county's Continuum of Care unit. Also, they cannot force clients to religious services (they can, however, make them available) or restrict clients or even their service providers to their own religion. The advantage of belonging to a Continuum of Care unit for the organization dealing with the homeless is that an FBO can relate to other FBOs or secular ones in dealing with homelessness in the city or county. But some FBOs do not want to accept government money or the restrictions placed on them by HUD about demanding clients attend religious services or restricting service providers to those of their own religion. In a number of cities an FBO is the Continuum of Care unit, organizing the various groups involved with providing facilities for the homeless. Catholic Charities provides that service for Baltimore and Salvation Army for Washington, D.C. Volunteers of America does it for Baton Rouge.

What is not surprising, given the data we have already seen, is the abundance of FBOs involved in treating the homeless. An important study made of eleven cities in the United States and their programs for homelessness (Atlanta, Baltimore, Denver, Houston, Indianapolis, Jacksonville, Omaha, Phoenix, Portland, San Diego, and Seattle) conducted by Baylor University's Institute for Studies of Religion showed that FBOs provided 58 percent of emergency shelter beds in those eleven cities versus 42 percent by non-FBOs. In some cities the proportion was higher: In Omaha 90 percent of emergency shelter beds were provided by FBOs, while in Baltimore and Indianapolis this share was 74 percent and 77 percent, respectively. In Baton Rouge, while FBOs only represent 43 percent of the organizations dealing with homelessness, it was estimated that they provided 80 percent of the services for the homeless.[65] But since the HUD data does not include congregations that do not accept HUD funds or the stipulation about not requiring religious services or that all of its providers be of their religion, the actual percentage of FBOs' provision for the homeless is certainly higher than that found in HUD data.[66]

The key findings of the Baylor study are the following:

1. What government agencies and public policymakers see as the cause of homelessness—namely, the lack of housing—many FBOs see as a symptom of a deeper problem. As one FBO service provider put it, "People don't become homeless when they run out of money, at least not right away. They become homeless when they run out of relationships."

2. FBO homeless ministries are in the forefront of program innovation and organizational transformation for improving positive outcomes for the homeless individuals and families served.

3. Housing First policies (from HUD) and Continuum of Care units do not always effectively engage with FBOs, especially congregation-based efforts that do not seek federal funding.

4. There are other FBOs serving homeless men and women—especially those struggling with addictions—that are operating under the radar and are not included in HUD's homeless count.

5. The program outcomes for successful participants from FBO residential recovery and job readiness programs in the eleven cities studied generate an estimated $119 million in taxpayer savings during the three years following the exit of clients from the FBO's housing program. They do not need the help that would be otherwise necessary if they remained homeless.[67]

Poll data show Americans think religious groups are best able to feed the homeless (52 percent versus 21 percent who think nonreligious groups and another 21 percent who think government agencies are). Asked about whether they favor allowing government funding for FBOs engaging in social service, 68 percent say such people providing the services would be more caring and compassionate. Seventy-four percent support the restriction that says that religious organizations that receive government funds to provide services should not be able to hire only people who share their religious beliefs.[68] But the evidence indicates that in FBOs working on homelessness, as we saw of the other kinds of FBO's earlier: (1) members of the FBOs take their common citizenship as a moral obligation and (2) FBOs' religious ethos and citizenship ideals can mutually enrich each other.

FBOs working on homelessness vary widely from one another. Some are purely congregation-based. Others involve separately incorporated denominational units—for example, Catholic Charities, the Salvation Army, and Volunteers of America. Still others are interfaith organizations (for instance, Minneapolis's Metropolitan Interfaith Council on Affordable Housing). We can ask, as I did in my own earlier study of FBOs, whether congregations, as such, are as effective as the separately incorporated denominational units and the interfaith ones in dealing with homelessness. One faith-based provider noted that:

> The preponderance of congregations have not yet found the proper equation for significant community impact. Although many run soup kitchens or youth programs successfully, expanding into building housing or economic development is a huge leap that most congregations do not have the capacity to accomplish.[69]

Many FBOs working on homelessness, particularly smaller ones, relying more extensively on volunteers than their secular counterparts, may lack the professional staff skilled in organizational and financial management necessary for expansion. Local communities often show more trust in FBOs working on homelessness than their secular counterparts, typically if they have had longstanding histories and involvement in the local community. In distressed neighborhoods, in particular, FBOs have earned "moral capital" through FBO leaders who spearhead wider community development efforts and through FBO members. FBOs have gained the trust of distressed communities for staying when other local institutions have left. As a result, FBOs have become important community anchors over the years.[70]

FBOs working on homelessness do have unique strengths and resources, some of which overlap with secular organizations, while others do not. Among the strengths of FBOs are: (1) they are generally trusted by their communities, particularly in distressed areas; (2) they create and provide community leadership; (3) they can access human and financial capital in the form of volunteers and donations; (4) they are community and cultural anchors in areas where they have long been located; (5) they are typically holistic in nature; and (6) they are driven by a higher calling. Some of the more secular organizations may share these strengths, but differences exist in the following areas between FBOs and their secular counterparts: revenue sources, organizational capacity, programs and services, effectiveness, and community perceptions.[71]

FBOs also exhibit a continuum of religiosity, ranging from faith-saturated (or pervasively sectarian) to FBOs that seem more "secularly" oriented. The more faith-saturated the organization is, the more likely it is to approach service holistically. Faith-saturated organizations hold that religion is central to their mission and the services they provide. Some homelessness FBOs may "seem" as secular as secular organizations, and their only connection to religion may be through their board members. There is also a middle ground held by some FBOs dealing with homelessness, inasmuch as they recruit many volunteers and receive donations from churches that keep alive a religious motivation in the FBO.[72] Moreover, as in some other kinds of FBOs, FBOs addressing homelessness can share their inspiration and motivation with people of religious backgrounds different than theirs or those who are not religious (for example, as happens in Catholic Charities and some faith-based universities who have faculty and students who are not of that faith). It demands an effective institutional sharing of the main ethos of the FBO.

Some argue that social services for the homeless are more effective, at least for most people, if they contain a faith component. They claim that FBOs will change the values and behaviors of the disadvantaged while meeting their physical needs. Others argue that the effectiveness of FBOs in public service delivery is not any greater than that of their secular counterparts.[73]

Saint Ignatius, San Francisco, my parish, also supports financially a Mexican woman with five children who is seeking to be granted asylum because of physical abuse by her husband. We raised money to see she was able to rent an apartment and not be homeless. Moreover, the parish actually provides a room for several homeless people to sleep in the basement of the church. Given the amount of homelessness in San Francisco and the high cost of rentals, a parish cannot ignore the issue of homelessness in its social outreach programs.

Another important example of a faith-based group working on issues of homelessness is the Ignatian Spirituality Project with main offices in Chicago. Its story began in 1998 when friends of Ed Shurma, a long-time community organizer, and Bill Creed, S.J., a renowned spiritual director, came together in the hopes of creating an initiative to help build community, hope, and transformation among those experiencing homelessness. Creed and Shurma found that the spiritual life was a source of hope for the homeless amid deep discouragement more generally. They developed a retreat that drew upon the 500-year-old tradition of the Spiritual Exercises of St. Ignatius and upon the contemporary language of the twelve-step recovery movement. Word of the retreats spread, and a national network was born. In 2006 they incorporated as a 501(c)3 organization and in 2008 hired their first full-time staff.

The network has grown to around twenty-six cities across the United States and Canada (including Chicago, Cincinnati, Boston, Denver, St. Louis, Detroit, Seattle, and Toronto) and includes over 800 volunteers, serving over 2,000 retreatants a year through over 200 retreats.

The Ignatian Spirituality Project offers men and women who are homeless and in recovery from addiction (note this important addendum to their homelessness status) the opportunity to change their lives. It assumes that Ignatian spirituality and retreats are effective and important resources in laying a foundation of hope that can lead to further and long-lasting transformation. The fivefold approach of the project is as follows:

1. They offer retreats inspired by Ignatian Spirituality to those who are homeless and seeking recovery.
2. They form teams with men and women who are homeless, in order to conduct Ignatian retreats, offer witness, and provide spiritual companionship. (Note this latter speaks to the data that a key thing about the homeless is they lack relationships. The retreats offer them a chance to foster relationships.)
3. They reach to new cities to build and form retreat teams for their programs. (I know and spoke to one such person in Seattle who does these retreats there. He told me about their format and effectiveness.)
4. They seek to further their established national network or dedicated volunteers to respond to the spiritual needs of those who are homeless.
5. They collaborate with communities and agencies working to end the injustice of homelessness.[74]

A final issue deals with the effect of government money on FBOs working on homelessness. Some studies claim accepting public money mutes the religious character of an FBO. In contrast, FBOs that do not accept such funding are more likely to:

(a) base the design of a major program on religious values; (b) use religious teachings in staff training; (c) use religious teaching to encourage staff to make changes in their behavior; and (d) urge clients to make a personal religious commitment in their lives.[75]

On the other hand, it is argued that FBOs that accept government money begin to look and act similarly to their secular counterparts. Other studies have shown that while most, if not all, FBOs that take public money may be "subject" to some "secularizing pressures," they do not necessarily become more secular. So, we need further research to find out why some FBOs that accept government money may become more secular, while other FBOs who accept government money "lean toward retaining religious uniqueness."[76] An FBO working on homelessness can lean toward retaining its religious uniqueness if it works at cultivating its institutional ethos and its religious vision.

I leave to the other essays in this book to give us a more far-reaching and deeper view of the FBOs engaged in combating homelessness. It is clear to me that it is a far-ranging subject, calling for many important distinctions and further research.

Notes

1. John A. Coleman, "Under the Cross and the Flag: Reflections on Discipleship and Citizenship in America," *America* 174, no. 16 (May 11, 1996), 6–14; Coleman, "Religion and Public Life: Some American Cases," *Religion* 28 (1998): 155–69; Coleman, "Public Religion and Religion in Public," *Wake Forest Law Review* 36, no. 2 (Summer 2001): 297–304.

2. Coleman, "The Christian as Citizen," *Commonweal*, September 9, 1983, 457–62; Coleman, "The Two Pedagogies: Discipleship and Citizenship," in *Education for Citizenship and Discipleship*, ed. Mary Boys (New York: Pilgrim, 1989), 35–75; Coleman, "De-Privatizing Religion and Re-Vitalizing Citizenship," in *Religion and Contemporary Liberalism*, ed. Paul Weithman (Notre Dame, Ind.: University of Notre Dame Press, 1997), 264–90; and Coleman, "Discipleship and Citizen Revisited," *Journal of Catholic Social Thought* 6, no. 2 (Summer 2009): 337–51.

3. Coleman, "Social Movements and Catholic Social Thought: A Sociological Perspective," *Journal of Catholic Social Thought* 10, no. 2 (2013): 259–80; Coleman, "American Catholicism: Catholic Charities U.S.A. and Welfare Reform," in *Religion Returns to the Public Sphere: Faith and Policy in America*, ed. Hugh Heclo and Wilfred McClay (Baltimore: Johns Hopkins University Press, 2003), 229–67.

4. J. G. A. Pocock, *The Machiavellian Moment: Florence Political Thought and the Atlantic Tradition* (Princeton, N.J.: Princeton University Press, 1975).

5. Michael Walzer, *The Spheres of Justice: A Defense of Pluralism and Equality* (New York: Basic Books, 1983), 278.

6. Ibid., 246.

7. Ibid., 304.

8. Robin Lovin, *Christian Faith and Public Choices* (Minneapolis: Fortress, 1984), 3.

9. Paul Ricoeur, *Politiek en Geloof: Essays van Paul Ricoeur*, ed. Ad Peperza (Utrecht: Ambo, 1968), 82. [My translation from the Dutch.]

10. Ibid., 87.

11. Jacques Maritain, *Man and the State* (Chicago: University of Chicago Press, 1951).

12. Charles Taylor, ed., *Multiculturalism: Examining the Politics of Recognition* (Princeton, N.J.: Princeton University Press, 1994).

13. Edward Schillebeeckx, *Gerechtigheid en Liefde: Genade en Bevrijding* (Amsterdam: H. Belissen, Nelissen Bleomendaal 1977), 539. [Translation from the Dutch mine.]

14. D. W. Brogan, *Citizenship Today* (Chapel Hill: University of North Carolina Press, 1963), 123.

15. Ricoeur, *Politiek en Geloof*, 86n12.

16. Ibid., 198.

17. Ibid., 103.

18. See, for instance, Robert Putnam, "Bowling Alone: America's Declining Social Capital," *Journal of Democracy* 6, no. 1 (1995): 75–68; and Putnam, *Bowling Alone: The Collapse and Revival of American Community* (New York: Simon & Schuster, 2000).

19. See Jerome Baggett, *Habitat for Humanity: Building Private Homes, Building Public Religion* (Philadelphia: Temple University Press, 2000), for the results of our team's study of Habitat.

20. See Richard Wood, *Faith in Action: Religion, Race and Democratic Organizing in America* (Chicago: University of Chicago Press, 2002), for the results of our team's study of PICO.

21. Robert Wuthnow, *God and Mammon in America* (New York: Free Press, 1994), 242–43.

22. Hilary Cunningham, *God and Caesar at the Rio Grande: Sanctuary and the Politics of Religion* (Minneapolis: University of Minnesota Press, 1995), 97.

23. Wuthnow, *Learning to Care: Elementary Kindness in an Age of Indifference* (New York: Oxford University Press, 1995), 9.

24. Sidney Verba, Kay Lehman Schlozman, and Henry E. Brady, *Voice and Equality: Civic Volunteerism in American Politics* (Cambridge, Mass.: Harvard University Press, 1995), 78.

25. Wuthnow, *The Crisis in the Churches: Spiritual Malaise, Fiscal Woe* (New York: Oxford University Press, 1997), 189.

26. George Gallup Polls, *Public Opinion*, 1990, 67–68 (polls dealing with religion and social problems).

27. Wuthnow, *Learning to Care*, 87–88.

28. Kenneth Wald, "Church Involvement and Political Behavior," in *Rediscovering the Religious Factor in Politics*, ed. David Leege and Lyman A. Kellstedt (Armonk, N.Y.: M. E. Sharpe, 1993), 129.

29. Wuthnow, *Acts of Compassion: Caring for Others and Helping Ourselves* (Princeton, N.J.: Princeton University Press, 1991), 325n21.

30. Anne C. Case and Lawrence F. Katz, "The Company You Keep: The Effects of Family and Neighborhood on Disadvantaged Youth," National Bureau of Economic Research (NBER) Working Paper 3705 (May 1991), 22.

31. Verba et al., *Voice and Equality*, 18.

32. Ibid., 17–18.

33. Ibid., 18.

34. Ibid., 520.

35. Ibid., 328–30.

36. Robin Gill, *Churchgoing and Christian Ethics* (New York: Cambridge University Press, 1999); see 101–2, 105–10, 125–28, 170, 173, 188–89, 197.

37. Gill, *Churchgoing and Christian Ethics*, 105–7, 172–73.

38. Ibid., 105–10.

39. See Nancy Tatom Ammerman, *Congregation and Community* (New Brunswick, N.J.: Rutgers University Press, 1996), 361. Consult also Robert Wuthnow, *Saving America: Faith-Based Services and the Future of Civil Society* (Princeton, N.J.: Princeton University Press, 2004).

40. Ibid., 366–67. See also Ammerman, *Pillars of Faith: American Congregations and Their Partners* (Berkeley: University of California Press, 2005).

41. Putnam, "Bowling Alone: America's Declining Social Capital," 76. See also Putnam, *Bowling Alone*; and Robert Putnam and David Campbell, *American Grace: How Religion Divides and Unites Us* (New York: Simon & Schuster, 2010).

42. Daniel Olsen, "Church Friendships: Boon or Barrier to Church Growth?," *Journal for the Scientific Study of Religion* 28, no. 4 (1989): 432, 445.

43. John Wilson and Thomas Janoski, "The Contribution of Religion to Volunteer Work," *Sociology of Religion* 56 (1995): 137, 149.

44. Wuthnow, *God and Mammon in America*, 263.

45. See Brad Knickerbocker, "Why the Line Is Fading between Politics and Piety. Both Sides Invoke Faith for Strategic Gain. Is It Too Much?," *Christian Science Monitor*, September 1, 2000, 12.

46. Wuthnow, *The Crisis in the Churches*, 192.

47. Putnam, "Bowling Alone," 22–23.

48. Wuthnow, *The Crisis in the Churches*, 187–96, indicating the financial inadequacies of many churches to aid in growing community problems. See also, Wuthnow, *Saving America*.

49. Ibid., 192–93.

50. Ammerman, *Congregation and Community*, 363.

51. Ibid., 367–68.

52. Ibid., 367.

53. See Ram A. Cnaan, with Robert J. Wineburg, and Stephanie C. Boddie, *The Newer Deal: Social Work and Religion in Partnership* (New York: Columbia University Press, 1999), 28.

54. One treatment of para-church groups can be found in Wesley K. Willmer and J. David Schmidt, with Martyn Smith, *The Prospering Parachurch: Enlarging the Boundaries of God's Kingdom* (San Francisco: Jossey-Bass), 1999.

55. Martin Marty, *Politics, Religion and the Common Good* (San Francisco: Jossey-Bass, 2000), 140–41.

56. Ibid.

57. This is the argument of John Rawls and Bruce Ackerman; see Ackerman, *Social Justice in the Liberal State* (New Haven, Conn.: Yale University Press, 1980); and John Rawls, *Political Liberalism* (New York: Columbia University Press, 1996).

58. Marty, *Politics, Religion and the Common Good*, 47.

59. Stephen Carter, *God's Name in Vain: The Rights and Wrongs of Religion in Politics* (New York: Basic Books, 2000), 155.

60. Ibid., 161.

61. Ibid., 153.

62. Carter, *The Culture of Disbelief: How American Law and Politics Trivialize Religious Devotion* (New York: Anchor, 1994), 230–31.

63. See Matthew Desmond, *Evicted: Poverty and Profit in the American City* (New York: Crown, 2016).

64. Willie Green Jr., "An Analysis of Faith-Based Homeless Service Providers in Baton Rouge, Louisiana and Their Role in Helping Homeless People" (master's diss., University of New Orleans, 2006), 9.

65. Ibid., 44.

66. Byron Johnson, William Wubbenhorst, and Alfreda Alvarez, *Assessing the Faith-Based Response to Homelessness in America: Findings from Eleven Cities* (Waco, Tex.: Baylor University Institute for Studies of Religion, 2017), 5–143.

67. Ibid., 7.

68. Pew Forum on Religion and Public Life, *Church-State Concerns Persist: Faith-Based Programs Still Popular, Less Visible* (Washington, D.C.: Pew Research Center, November 16, 2009), 8.

69. Darren Walker, "Not by Faith Alone," *Shelterforce: The Original Voice of Community Development* 115 (January/February 2001), accessed November 25, 2020, www.shelterforce.org.

70. Stephen Goldsmith, William B. Eimicke, and Chris Pineda, "Faith-Based Organizations versus Their Secular Counterparts: A Primer for Local Officials," Harvard University Ash Institute for Democratic Governance and Innovation (Spring 2006): 6.

71. Ibid., 4–5.

72. See Malcolm L. Goggin and Deborah A. Orth, "How Faith-Based and Secular Organizations Tackle Housing for the Homeless," Nelson A. Rockefeller Institute of Government (October 2002)—focusing on FBOs and secular organizations in Grand Rapids, Michigan.

73. For an argument that FBOs are more effective than their secular counterparts, see Peter Dobkin Hall, "Historical Perspectives on Non-Profit Organizations in the United States," in *The Jossey-Bass Handbook of Nonprofit Leadership and Management*, ed. R. D. Herman and Associates (San Francisco: Jossey-Bass, 2005), 24. For a different view, cf. John L. Saxon, "Faith-Based Social Services: What Are They? Are They Legal? What's Happening in North Carolina?," *Popular Government* 70, no. 1 (Fall 2004): 5–6; and Helen Rose Ebaugh, Paula F. Pipes, Janet Saltzman Chafetz, and Martha Daniels, "Where's the Religion? Distinguishing Faith-Based from Secular Social Service Agencies," *Journal for the Scientific Study of Religion* 42, no. 3 (2003): 412–14.

74. For further information about this initiative, consult www.ispretreats.org.

75. Kevin Kearns, Chisung Park, and Linda Yankowski, "Comparing Faith-Based and Secular Community Service Corporations in Pittsburgh and Allegheny County, Pennsylvania," *Nonprofit and Voluntary Sector Quarterly* 34, no. 2 (June 2005): 216.

76. James R. Vanderwoerd, "How Faith-Based Social Service Organizations Manage the Secular Pressures Associated with Government Funding," *Nonprofit Management & Leadership* 4, no. 3 (Spring 2004): 242.

On the Passionality of Exile in Medieval Kabbalah

An Invitation to Historicize Contemporary Religious and Public Discourses on Homelessness

Jeremy Phillip Brown

IN MEMORIAM
EDNA AIZENBERG (1945–2018)

Medieval Kabbalah as a Resource for Social Thought

What can be gained by turning to medieval religion in order to sharpen our focus on contemporary social phenomena? In the ongoing debates regarding the vocation of religious studies, some have argued that social engagement comes at the cost of scholarly rigor and, moreover, that such engagement risks closing off the very margin of critical distance that makes analysis possible in the first place. Others have maintained that religion scholarship can (and should) have an emancipatory character, without compromising its epistemological foundations.[1] I offer the present study as an example of how—when done with due respect for the emic integrity of the discourse in question—socially engaged religion scholarship can, beyond the satisfaction of scholarly standards, even bolster the rigor of the work at hand. By reading medieval kabbalistic texts as resources for social thought, I show how they reveal themselves in ways that have not heretofore been represented in the scholarship. But in correlating medieval kabbalistic constructions of exile and contemporary public discourses of homelessness, my goal is not to elide their characteristic differences. Instead, I aim to coordinate the intersections and divergences of these two discursive fields in a manner that occasions a novel assessment of both past and contemporary horizons. Thus, the present study moves within a hermeneutical circle, wherein the critique of present social conditions potentiates a historically grounded analysis, and reciprocally, a lucid interpretation of religious history contributes to the refinement of present-day advocacy.

By facilitating a nuanced understanding of how one particular historically situated religious discourse of homelessness has been constructed, I invite con-

temporary advocates of social change to submit the historical, cultural, theological, and ethical presuppositions of their own discourses to a comparable
degree and mode of criticism. In this connection, it is crucial to observe the
extent to which ancient theological constructions of exile retain their capacity to structure the contemporary human experience of homelessness and how
religious conceptions of charity continue to inform even post-confessional approaches to advocacy. Whether or not such social engagement is promoted as
the explicit mandate of faith-based organizations or liturgical communities,
the structures and figures of such activism bespeak a cultural inheritance of a
specifically religious character, one that demands a measure of scrutiny comparable to the degree of direct community intervention. In relation to social
advocacy, religious studies have a unique role to play. They are tasked with
the daunting responsibility of elucidating the religious genealogy of contemporary civic discourse. The imperative of historicizing the consciousness
of advocacy involves also its pluralization, a reckoning with non-Christian
religions.

The modern study of Judaism—whether conceived as a subfield of the
broader domain of religious studies or a provincializing response to that
domain[2]—has wrestled with the cognate themes of exile, migration, displacement, and diaspora from its inception. And more than just the stuff of the-
matic analysis, these themes have conditioned the field's own history in an
acute manner. Some have debated whether scholarly discourse has constructed
the very category of "diaspora" in a paradigmatically Jewish manner, even as
scholars work to calibrate this category to non-Jewish communities and cultures.[3] While it lies beyond the scope of this study to represent the broad
range of perspectives on exile vis-à-vis Jews and Judaism, it is instructive to
delineate two pervasive historiographic tendencies that will lead readers
astray in their efforts to understand the distinctive nexus of ambivalences and
ambiguities that characterize the medieval kabbalistic discourse of exile. On
one extreme is the (1) so-called "lachrymose" or negative conception of diaspora as a condition leading to the attenuation of a distinctive sense of Jewish
identity; and (2) at the other end of the spectrum, the celebration of diaspora
as nurturing a Jewish sense of cultural hybridity and cosmopolitanism.[4]

The present study demonstrates how the discourse of homelessness in medieval kabbalah unsettles both historiographic paradigms. What comes into
view is a *passional* construction of the exile, emphasizing the atoning character of God's own displacement alongside the dispersion of Israel. Within this
discourse, the Jews are cast in a number of seemingly contradictory roles: as
vulnerable homeless subjects; as children within an unstable divine family; as
victims of Christian tyranny; as guilty perpetrators of God's homelessness; as

vicarious beneficiaries of God's expiatory suffering; even as sacramentally empowered ethical actors. This passional construction of exile draws medieval Jews into a discursive engagement with their Christian neighbors in ways that are characteristically antagonistic, but also nominally sympathetic, as well as hermeneutically creative. Antagonistic, because polemical. Sympathetic, insofar as the discourse depicts Christians as beloved by God because they instigate Israel's redemptive suffering. And hermeneutically creative, because, as I will show, the discourse of exile in medieval kabbalah should be read as an inversion of the Christological passion. In examining source material, I work through the Hebrew writings of the thirteenth-century sage R. Ezra ben Solomon of Gerona and selections from subsequent Iberian kabbalists writing in his tradition. These documents disseminate a mystical discourse of homelessness, fashioned in both theosophic and historiosophic terms, which, I will argue, yields a novel articulation of social ethics.

R. Ezra ben Solomon of Gerona

While there is no figure whose teachings singly encompass the manifold range of medieval rabbinic esoteric traditions, several factors recommend R. Ezra's writings as the focus for a study of the kabbalistic discourse of exile. Little biographical information has been preserved about this enigmatic figure, apart from what hints may be gleaned from the few treatises and letters that scholars ascribe to him and his associates.[5] Among his extant writings, his commentary on the Song of Songs (Perush Shir ha-Shirim), probably composed shortly after 1240, is the most studied.[6] The text's relative authority may be because of its misattribution to Naḥmanides (1194–1270). From what has been reconstructed of the early history of kabbalistic literature, R. Ezra's composition appears to be the first to explicate the classical exilic theologies of the biblical and rabbinic corpora in the terms of a kabbalistic theosophy and historiosophy. Thus, much of the exilic discourse espoused by subsequent Castilian kabbalists organized itself according to the general structures of R. Ezra's teachings.[7] While it has become conventional for historians of kabbalah to focus on Sefer ha-Bahir and the teachings attributed to R. Isaac the Blind as the starting points for classical kabbalistic doctrine, recent historical criticism of the early literary traditions cautions a more conservative approach.[8]

Theosophy: Exile and the Dynamics of Divine Family Life

Georges Vajda qualified R. Ezra's understanding of exile as a historical phenomenon intimately bound up with the conjugal patterns of the tenfold Godhead.

According to this paradigm, the individuated powers of the androgynous divinity are differentiated into male and female poles.[9] In particular, the historical situation of exile corresponds to the ontic modality of separation between these contrasexual facets of divinity: *tiferet* (the male glory) and *shekhinah* (the female presence) respectively.[10]

> The feminine, which kabbalistic speculation attributes to *shekhinah* with an audacity that does not cease to astonish those who consider Judaism solely as a monotheism pure of all mythology, confers to *shekhinah* the quality of wife in relation to the masculine aspect of the divinity, *tiferet* for the Kabbalists, and that of mother of the chosen nation, whose exile and sufferings she shares, just as she, in turn, owes the renewed freedom and prosperity of her children to the boon of being reunited again to her husband, from whom the sins of her children had separated her.[11]

Just as the sanctioned performance of the traditional Mosaic commandments by Israel arouses the intercourse of the contrasexual poles of divinity[12] (whose relation to Israel may be compared to the "world parents" of Erich Neumann's analytical psychology),[13] Israel's sinful neglect or violation of the commandments results in their isolation from the father, *tiferet*, and the concomitant displacement of the maternal *shekhinah* together with her children from the father's protective domain.[14]

What is the situation for the male pole of divinity, *tiferet*, when his bride is exposed to exile? Vajda suggests that the function of this power

> does not depend directly on earthly events, but takes place entirely in the divine world: if there is a departure for him, it is towards the higher regions of the divine, which his wife—who is exiled because of the sins of her children—will only be able to reach once the final redemption has been accomplished.[15]

Vajda further characterizes the removal of *tiferet*, his abandonment of wife and children, as indicative of "the rupture provoked within the divine world by the sin of Israel"; accordingly, "this means that the last *sefirah*, destined to share the misfortunes of her children, is somehow abandoned to herself, while her spouse will join the upper sefirot."[16] R. Ezra's comment to Song 6:2 illustrates this modality well.

> *My beloved has gone down to his garden, to the beds of spices, to browse in the gardens, And to pick lilies* (Song 6:2). . . . All this takes place during the period of exile, a time bereft of festival offerings, thanksgiving

offerings and the [daily] meal offerings. The spiritual entities ascend and are drawn to the place from which they suckle. This is the meaning of *because of the corruption, the righteous one is gathered up* (Is 57:1). Therefore, [human] efforts are necessary to stimulate emanation and to draw forth the blessing to the fathers, so that the children too are imbued with the divine substance.[17]

Functionally speaking, the disintegration of the divine family is an asymmetrical scenario. The displacement of exile impacts mother and children in a manner wholly disproportionate to its effect upon the father.[18] Though separated from his wife and children, the father retains access to the source of his endowment from the upper powers.[19]

This way of representing the exile combines both biblical and rabbinic theological narratives within the specifically kabbalistic framework of divine family life. In the first case, it assimilates the biblical premise that the multiple exiles of Israel are punishments from God for Israel's transgressions. Ante-Nicene theologians, on the one hand, attributed such guilt to Israel's alleged crucifixion of Jesus of Nazareth.[20] The rabbis,[21] on the other hand, generally claimed that Israel's sin was "gratuitous hatred" (*sinat ḥinam*).[22] To be clear, this biblical premise legitimates the inculpation of the homeless subject. In fact, it blames the victim. In the second case, the kabbalistic discourse of exile incorporates the rabbinic notion that *shekhinah*, the divine presence that formerly dwelled in the Jerusalem Temple, now travails with Israel in its dispersions.[23]

The older rabbinic idea that the divine presence accompanies Israel in its exile is a celebrated trope, which had already furnished Jews in antiquity with an account of God's homelessness. In other words, the ancient sages already possessed a venerable theology avowing the predicament of divine displacement.[24] However, R. Ezra's writings recast the ancient theology of homelessness in terms of the theosophic structures and dynamics of divine family life. According to his model, the good or bad behavior of the children leverages the parents' intimacy or alienation, respectively, and determines the divine family's cohesion or instability. It is within the drama of divine family instability that R. Ezra characterizes the successive displacements of the Jewish people and especially the subjection of this people to the most recent episode in Israel's exile—namely, the humiliation of rule by Christians.[25] Thus, R. Ezra's theosophic representation of exile is at once a recounting of Israel's sacred history. In other words, it is a historiosophy[26]—an epochal way of accounting for the passage of time calibrated to the mechanics of kabbalistic metaphysics.

Nonetheless, the espousal of such a historiosophic orientation does not eclipse the creative agency of human subjects as authors of their own historical destinies.[27] To the contrary, R. Ezra's paradigm promotes *radical responsibility* on the part of the human agents—the "children" at the center of the theosophic drama.[28] It has become conventional for scholars to regard such responsibility in terms of "theurgy."[29] Within this framework, the provision of shelter and stability is contingent upon Israel's legal compunction.[30] The children must conduct themselves according to the commandments if they expect to benefit from the father's sheltering resources.[31] In a manner that is functionally similar to how contemporary ideologies of homelessness are enmeshed in civic conceptions of criminality, the discursive distinction between licit and illicit behavior determines the concrete material threshold between home and displacement. R. Ezra likewise makes the allocation of resources (both material and divine) contingent upon the maintenance of marital unity, whereas the disintegration of nuclear family and loss of shelter go hand in hand. That situation is, in turn, predicated upon the naturalization, even divinization of a set of heteroerotic domestic norms and a correspondingly patriarchal distribution of economic agency. Thus, the paternal figure, *tiferet*, is invested with the role of patron and benefactor, while *shekhinah*, the maternal figure, embodies the very principle of dependency.[32]

R. Ezra reads the erotic longing of the Shulamite woman for her beloved in the Song of Songs as expressing this dependence of *shekhinah* upon *tiferet*.[33] In exile with Israel, she bemoans her exposure and her children's resort to slave labor in Egypt.

> She complains and thunders forth about her being in exile, traveling darkened with the angelic forces apportioned to the world's nations. She says, *I am dark* (Song 1:5): Swarthy from exile. If I am not lovely, *like the pavilions of Solomon* (Song 1:5): The name of the Holy One, blessed be He [that is, *tiferet*, the husband from whom she has become estranged]. . . . *Do not stare at me* (Song 1:6): Do not despise me because I am swarthy, *because the sun has gazed upon me*, because I am situated amongst my children who are enslaved, at hard labor, performing all of their work in the field.[34]

This representation of *shekhinah* as embarrassed of her sun-darkened complexion typifies medieval characterizations of the conjecturally poor, who, in their on-again-off-again state of poverty, intend to refrain from "exposing the face"—that is, from "shame-facedly" begging alms.[35] Her complexion reveals the fact that homelessness has compelled her to expose her face, but her sense of shame bespeaks her high origins, as it were, and reveals that she is not ultimately resigned to such a fate. Her poverty, displacement, enslavement, and offending appearance allude to the fact that she has been sequestered from the world of divine masculinity, which, by contrast, embodies resources, shelter, freedom, and beauty. She is darkened as a slave to the ranks of angels who supervise ontologically inferior nations, and who obstruct the illuminating influx of divine substance, which is her patrimony.

Historiosophy: An Exile among the Edomites

In the previously cited passage, R. Ezra invokes the ancient angelological motif that angelic princes determine the individual fates of the world's nations over whom they are appointed.[36] Medieval kabbalistic cosmology assimilated this motif, but envisioned the angelic or spiritual domain as mediating between the world of the *sefirot* and the material world.[37] *Shekhinah*'s dispossession is aggravated by the belligerent assault of the national archons, into whose domain she has descended. This is the theosophic situation corresponding to Israel's subordination to the rule of foreign nations, a condition that the eschatological repatriation of the *shekhinah* will overcome. R. Ezra's comments on Song 1:6 describe the offenses against her.

> *Quarreled with me* (Song 1:6): They raged against me and banished me from my place, as our sages say:[38] "No nation falls until its angelic prince is first cast down." As it says: *On that day, the Lord will punish the host of heaven on high and the kings of the earth on the earth* (Is 24:21); and: *How are you fallen from heaven, O shining one, son of dawn! How are you felled to earth, O vanquisher of nations!* (Is 14:12); and says further: *For My sword shall be seen in the sky; Lo, it shall come down upon Edom* (Is 34:5)."[39]

While Israel's exile corresponds to the *shekhinah*'s captivity by hostile archons generally, R. Ezra singles out the particular nation of Edom, by which he indicates the Roman Empire and, more emphatically, Christendom.[40] It is the rule of this particular nation that, R. Ezra imagines, will precede the final redemption.[41] I will return to this problem later.

Again, in her personification as the Song's Shulamite woman, *shekhinah* laments her subjugation to the nations, who demand her service in a manner that impedes her maternal supervision of her people Israel, her own vineyard.

> *They made me guard the vineyards [my own vineyard, I did not guard]* (Song 1:6): I am belabored in fulfilling the needs of the nations and ensuring their preservation. I have no leisure to watch over My people, for they are not in their land and I accompany them in their exile. The nation is designated a *vineyard*, for just as a vineyard requires labor,

pruning, and watering, so too does a people. Everything existing within the world is in need of the primary forces for their growth and blossoming.[42]

The care that she would provide for her children—the labor, pruning, and watering of her vineyard—comes by means of what she has secured from the resources of her estranged benefactor, who, in turn, mediates her access to the world-sustaining "primary forces"—that is, the upper *sefirot*. However, the hardships to which they are exposed deprive *shekhinah* and her children of access to such resources.

To be sure, there are two mutually reinforcing tiers of historical causation that produce this hyperdimensional situation of exile, a situation that impacts human, angelic, and divine realities alike. These are (1) the sins of Israel and (2) the rule of Edom (meaning the hegemony of Christendom). On the one hand, one may assume that the latter factor is subordinated to the former in R. Ezra's etiology, just as a proximate cause is secondary to an ultimate cause. But insofar as the vicissitudes of exile bring about a loss of Torah knowledge (especially knowledge pertaining to the rationales of the commandments, and the secrets of kabbalistic speculation),[43] Christian hegemony perpetuates Israel's propensity for transgression. In that case, ranking these causal factors is not tenable. In other words, R. Ezra attributes the situation of Israel's homelessness to structural factors, on the one hand, and to the responsibility of homeless subjects, on the other, in such a way that both factors exacerbate a vicious cycle. And to complicate the picture further, I will show how, in R. Ezra's view, subjugation to foreign domination has an expiatory, even redemptive function that promises to foreshorten Israel's exilic sentence. Thus, while a chief cause of their homelessness, Christian hegemony dialectically expedites Israel's homecoming.

Recent scholarship on thirteenth-century kabbalah and the vicissitudes of medieval Iberian Jewish-Christian relations has represented the kabbalists' characteristically polemical engagement with their confessional competitors in contrasting terms. It will suffice here to point out two divergent approaches. In the first instance, Elliot Wolfson has stressed the boldly ethnocentric, self-divinizing, even xenophobic nature of this polemical discourse. "To state the matter starkly," he affirms, "the demonization of non-Jewish nations in kabbalistic texts has much to do with rabbinic xenophobia."[44] By contrast, Ellen Haskell has painted a more empowering portrait of the kabbalists' anti-Christian polemic, emphasizing how the composition of the *Zohar*, in that case, embodied the self-possessed opposition of a dissident subculture against the oppressive machinations of Christian domination. She has asserted that, when viewed against the historical background of developments in medieval Christian art, the zoharic literature comes into view as a "hidden transcript" of political resistance to Christian hegemony.[45] She has claimed that the creation of "worlds within worlds of words" provided the Zohar's authors with an introverted means of resisting the triumphalist assertions of the dominant religious culture. With respect to R. Ezra's construction of the national myth of Israel's exile, it is profitable to acknowledge the ethnocentric character of the early kabbalistic discourse while recovering something of the critical and emancipatory intention of the patently xenophobic representations of the Christian other.

In his commentary, R. Ezra utilizes the images of various biblical creatures to typify the historiosophical scheme of Israel's ethno-angelic oppressors. He glosses God's "covenant of the pieces" (berit bein ha-betarim) with Abraham, in which Israel's patriarch offers various animal species to consecrate God's promise to Israel of a future territory.[46] These animal species, taken together with the beasts depicted in Daniel 7,[47] provide R. Ezra with a historiosophic typology for Israel's successive captors: Assyrian, Babylonian, Greek, and Roman. With respect to the current exile, that of Edom, Israel initially came under Roman authority when Rome superseded the Hellenistic empire as the foreign rulers of the land. After twenty-six years of peaceable occupation, however, Rome turned on Israel, destroying its Jerusalem Temple.

> The turtledove represents the wicked one, the fourth awful and mighty beast seen by Daniel. He desired to comprehend its true meaning, as it is written: I approached one of the attendants and asked him the true meaning of all of this (Daniel 7:16). It is said concerning this beast: it will devour the whole earth, tread it down and crush it. R. Yoḥanan said:[48] "It is requisite that Rome's nature spread throughout the entire world."[49]

When read in light of another old rabbinic prediction,[50] R. Ezra speculates that R. Yoḥanan's dictum means that the Messiah, "the son of David will not come until the dominion of the kingdom of Rome spreads over the entire world for nine months, just as the other three kingdoms spread over the entire world."[51] Accordingly, the messianic redemption, corresponding to the restoration of Israel's dominion, will come only after the divinely apportioned punishment of exile has first reached its fullest and most severe extent. More than that, R. Ezra stipulates that Christendom must first expand its dominion to encompass the entire globe and consolidate its sovereignty for nine months before the messianic homecoming will transpire.[52]

> It is said in Daniel (7:25) concerning the fourth beast: He will speak words against the Most High, that is, he will say words that cannot

conceivably be said: "these are *my* words." *And he will harass the holy ones of the Most High*: [This refers to the harassment of] Israel. This is the meaning of *in the presence of the vengeful foe* (Ps 44:17). *He will think of changing times and laws* (7:25): in their interpretation and to change the law. *And they will be delivered into his hands for a time, times and half a time* (ibid.): that is to say that redemption will not come to Israel until *a time, times and half a time*. As it is said: *the beast was killed . . . its body was destroyed and it was consigned to the flames* (ibid., v. 11).[53]

This fourth and most belligerent beast, Christendom's pernicious advocate, will disseminate impossible lies, claiming, "These are *my* words." This prediction is indicative of the Jewish grievance that Christians have effectively displaced Israel by misappropriating the prophecies of Hebrew scripture. Similarly, the archon's "changing times and laws" refers to Christian calendrical and jurisprudential innovations based upon misguided exegesis. These are clear condemnations of Christian supersessionism in the language of one of kabbalah's foremost architects. After this unjust and fraudulent ideology predominates for an apportioned measure of time, the angelic representative of Christian sovereignty will be assassinated and consigned to flames, following Daniel's prophecy.[54]

It is evident that this account of Israel's redemption—a narrative in which human agents, angelic antagonists, and the lower gradations of divinity interact—is emphatically *not* a vision of interreligious *convivencia*. To the contrary, R. Ezra cannot imagine a just resolution to history that does not involve either the subjugation, expulsion, or demolition of the current regime. Put positively, Israel's justification entails a comprehensive dismantling of the historical factors that have effectively exposed this people, and its God, to the precarious condition of homelessness. Nonetheless, this ethnocentric narrative of Israel's vindication reproduces, albeit within an inverted frame of reference, the very hegemonic rhetoric that had so alienated Israel.[55]

For Isaac Loved Esau: Exile as Penitential Narrative and Inverted Passion

Return, Return, O Shulemite! Return, return that we might gaze upon you (Song 7:1): The *shekhinah* says: "If Israel returns in penance, then we will gaze upon you, we will see you in joy and honor."[56]

We all broke into tears at the great joy [we experienced] when we heard of the suffering of the *shekhinah* because of our sins, her voice like [that of] an ill woman in her pleas to us.[57]

Although it is clear from his writings that R. Ezra imagined the redemption near at hand, he likewise promoted a paradigm in which the horizon of eschatological expectation intersected with a mystical framework of religious life in the present. Both the eschatological and mystical frameworks agree on the primary goal of reconciling, whether permanently or provisionally, the male and female poles of divinity. As the previous extract attests, this reconciliation transpires through Israel's repentance and its performance of the commandments during the remainder of its dispersion. However, before expanding upon R. Ezra's normative mysticism, it is necessary to acknowledge what positive, expiatory value the kabbalist assigned to the Jews' present situation of homelessness.

Israel's sacred history is a penitential narrative that has the positive function of removing sin.[58] This notion is operative in an especially piquant statement from a letter ascribed to R. Ezra arguing that the biblical commandment to settle the Land of Israel is not presently incumbent upon Jews. His contention is informed by the rationale that if homelessness is a divinely apportioned punishment for Israel's sins, then the sentence of exile should be served in full in order to accomplish its expiatory purpose.

> At this time, [the people of] Israel are already exempted from the obligation [of settling] the Land of Israel. For it is an *altar of atonement* (*mizbeah kaparah*) for them when they suffer exile for the love of the blessed Holy One, and undergo affliction and subjugation. As it is said: *for Thy sake are we killed all the day* [*we are accounted as sheep for the slaughter*] (Ps 44:23).[59]

Because the biblical verse that R. Ezra cites as his prooftext is the *locus classicus* for rabbinic martyrology, readers of this document face an interpretive problem. Does the letter submit that actual martyrdom at the hands of Christians, such as slaughter at the hands of crusaders, is the sanctioned method of expiation? As I read it, the letter suggests that subjugation to Christian rule generally, which *sometimes* occasioned loss of Jewish life, is the penitential sentence Israel must serve.[60] And at a parallel level of signification, the statement refers to a theosophic scenario of divine self-sacrifice. That is, it indicates the *passional* dispersion of the *shekhinah*, troped here as an altar, the sefirotic site of Israel's redemptive suffering in exile.[61]

Of interest is a comparable statement attributed to R. Ezra's disciple Nahmanides (1194–1270). The Hebrew account of his 1263 disputation in Barcelona with Christian interlocutors refers to the self-sacrificial nature of Jewish worship under Christian dominion:

When I serve my Creator under your jurisdiction, in exile, torment
and subjection, exposed constantly to universal contempt, I merit great
reward; for I offer of my own flesh a sacrifice to God.[62]

The martyrological character of this statement seems to be rather figurative,
a reference to the ascetic discipline required to persevere in traditional forms
of Jewish worship against historical odds. Without discounting the proximity
of R. Ezra and Naḥmanides on this score, it is important to distinguish between the former, who wielded the imperative to suffer exile in order to sus-
pend the biblical commandment to settle the Holy Land, whereas the latter
ruled the commandment eternally binding,[63] and even immigrated to Palestine from Catalonia in his old age.[64]

Likewise, R. Joseph ben Abraham Gikatilla (mid-thirteenth century to early
fourteenth), a Castilian kabbalist who contributed substantially to the development of R. Ezra's kabbalah, expressed the expiatory and ultimately redemptive function of Israel's homelessness. He couched his views in an exegesis of
the scriptural phrase "For Isaac loved Esau" (Gn 25:28). Read through a medieval rabbinic lens, this phrase actually typifies the patriarch's affection [!] for
Christendom. More provocative yet, however, is the kabbalistic reading, which
regards Isaac as the divine attribute of fear and judgment, thus: God, the very
patron of Israel, harbors an affection for Christendom.[65]

Could it possibly be that Isaac, our father, from whom *shekhinah*
never parted for a moment, could love someone as completely wicked
as Esau? How is it possible? Rather, this verse speaks of a great
essential meaning of the Torah. Know that Isaac . . . could envision
the future and he saw that the children of Jacob would sin and enrage
the Lord, may He be blessed, and the judgment of Gehinnom would
be their inheritance. When Isaac saw that Israel was in the exile of
Esau, he was glad, and he said: "Exile atones for sin."[66] And he said:
"Yes, I really love the tribulations of Esau, so that they should pay
Israel's debt and their harsh judgment shall be finished in the exile of
this world," hence, the verse, *For Isaac loved Esau because he had the
game trapped in his mouth.* What does it mean, *the game trapped in
his mouth?* He saw that the children of Jacob would be trapped by the
judgments of Gehinnom. He saw this and was saddened. When he
saw the exile of Edom, however, and he saw the game of Gehinnom
trapped in the mouth of Esau, He was happy and said: "Exile atones
for sin." . . . For God, Blessed be He, has merited Israel through the
exile of Esau.[67]

Thus, painful as it may be, Israel's homelessness redeems this people from the greater agony that will be enjoined upon Christians in Gehinnom, by releasing them from any further accountability for their sins.[68] Exile, following the ancient rabbinic teaching, is purgatory, though this text alludes to the hidden correspondence between Isaac the Patriarch and the divine gradation of fear (*pahad yishaq*), whose affection for Esau—that is, his perplexing *xenophilia* and expressed love of exile—actually benefits the Jews.[69] As the text expresses it, "Even though the attribute of Isaac is fear, its intention is to bring merit to Israel."[70]

Perhaps the most counterintuitive aspect of these positive appraisals of exile for contemporary audiences is that they are not based upon a correspondingly affirmative assessment of non-Jewish peoples and cultures. In fact, just the opposite is the case. Because expediting punishment for sin is a priority, these penitential narratives are based upon an inverse correlation between Israel's appraisal of its oppressors, on the one hand, and its assessment of the diasporic condition, on the other. The greater the antagonism, the more redemptive the exile. In the kabbalists' expiatory account of the *shekhinah*'s passional exile with Israel, Christendom is cast in the demonic, but wholly expedient role of persecutor. To offer an observation, which, to the best of my knowledge, has been overlooked by previous scholars,[71] this is an exact inversion of the Christological representation of Jews as the diabolical, yet necessary instigators of Christ's atoning passion.[72]

Kabbalah and Social Ethics: Capacity as Function of Vulnerability

As I have detailed throughout, the discourse of homelessness in the writings of R. Ezra abounds with complexity and ambivalence. It espouses an ethnocentric theosophy of divine homelessness that seeks teleological justification for the displacement of homeless subjects in its very critique of prevailing social structures. Additionally, by attributing exile to the sins of Israel, even magnifying Israel's guilt as the cause of God's own suffering, R. Ezra expands the biblical victim-blaming narrative to the hyperbolic dimensions of a divine family drama. This discourse, moreover, naturalizes a patriarchal set of gendered biases regarding the control and allocation of resources by inflating it to the level of divine economy.[73]

And yet the burden borne by Israel for causing its own and God's suffering is not imagined in an ultimately debilitating manner. The exile, rather, arouses a feeling of ethical, even sacramental urgency for the improvement of this state of affairs. Though hyperbolically construed, Israel's radical responsibility for its own condition gains concrete traction in R. Ezra's understanding of social ethics. According to his novel rationalization of the traditional command-ments,[74] one of many spheres of human action incentivized by the theosophic discourse of exile is precisely that of social ethics—or *gemilut ḥesed*. This class of commandments, in observance of which human agents "walk in God's ways," includes almsgiving and care for those in precarious social and eco-nomic situations.[75] When the construction of agency in this exilic discourse is properly assessed, it becomes clear that social ethics is not directed at a ben-eficiary whose condition is radically other than that of the benefactor. Rather, care for the socially vulnerable is intrinsic to the kabbalistic construction of the homeless subject, whose responsibility is constellated within a network of sympathetically dispossessed subjects—human *and* divine.[76] While it reifies and even divinizes certain socioeconomic binaries, this sacramental discourse of social ethics also presumes an intersubjective ontology that erodes over-wrought distinctions between benefactor and beneficiary roles.[77]

Although it promotes a heroic notion of sacramental (or "theurgical") agency, the kabbalistic social ethic may nonetheless be compared to the phil-osophical anthropology of Paul Ricoeur, which "does not presuppose individ-uals as being purely autonomous and rational agents, naturally capable of providing themselves with the means of their own existence."[78] At the very least, ethical agency is conditioned by the historical, if not historiosophical, structural constraints of Christian hegemony. R. Ezra represents both God and Israel, the primary subjects of this national paradigm, as "intersubjectively con-stituted fragile beings of needs and feelings, capable of *social suffering*."[79] Put in terms informed by the work of both Ricoeur and Julia Kristeva,[80] R. Ezra's discourse posits a network of both human and divine agency wherein capabil-ity is a function of vulnerability and vulnerability is likewise a function of ca-pability. To be sure, in braving this construction of social ethics, the discourse exposes itself to the criticism of usurping the sanctified status of the most vulnerable strata of the population and, furthermore, failing, in its expansive understanding of displacement, to make critical distinctions between sweep-ing historiosophic generalizations and the concrete particulars of human life on the verge. And yet, seen from another vantage, the exiled kabbalist as so-cial agent is—so long as he identifies together with God as a homeless subject—never alienated from the vulnerable for- and with Whom he acts.

Notes

I thank Manuel Mejido, Margaret Breen, and Hannah Hunthausen for graciously hosting me at Seattle University in 2017 and 2018. I am also grateful to Michael Centore and Patrick Koch for commenting on early drafts of this essay.

1. For an overview of this debate, see Michelle Gonzalez, *A Critical Introduction to Religion in the Americas: Bridging the Liberation Theology and Religious Studies Divide* (New York: New York University Press, 2014), 1–24.

2. See Susannah Heschel, "Revolt of the Colonized: Abraham Geiger's *Wissenschaft des Judentums* as a Challenge to Christian Hegemony in the Academy," *New German Critique* 77 (1999): 61–85; and Jeremy P. Brown, "Jewish Historical Testimony at the Table of Christian Hospitality," in *A Sukkah in the Shadow of Saint Ignatius*, ed. Jeremy P. Brown (San Francisco: University of San Francisco Press, 2020).

3. See Jonathan Boyarin and Daniel Boyarin, *Powers of Diaspora* (Minneapolis: University of Minnesota Press, 2002), 1–34; and Robin Cohen, *Global Diasporas: An Introduction*, 2nd ed. (London: Routledge, 2008), 21–38.

4. For a critical overview of the historiographic problem, see David Engel, *Historians of the Jews and the Holocaust* (Stanford, Calif.: Stanford University Press, 2010), especially 29–133.

5. On R. Ezra, see Gershom Scholem, *Origins of the Kabbalah* (Princeton, N.J.: Princeton University Press, 1987), 365–496; Azriel ben Menaḥem of Gerona, *The Commentary to the Talmudic Aggadot*, ed. Isaiah Tishby (Jerusalem: Magnes, 1983), esp. editor's introduction [Hebrew]; ben Menaḥem, *Studies in the Kabbalah and Its Branches* (Jerusalem: Magnes, 1982), 1:3–35 [Hebrew]; Ephraim Gottlieb, *The Kabbalah in the Writings of R. Baḥya ben Asher ibn Ḥalawa* (Jerusalem: Kiryat Sepher, 1970), 38–73 [Hebrew]; Gottlieb, "The Significance of the Story of Creation in the Interpretations of the Early Cabbalists," *Tarbiz* 37 (1967/68): 294–317 [Hebrew]; Georges Vajda, *Le Commentaire d'Ezra de Gérone sur le Cantique des Cantiques* (Paris: Aubier-Montaigne, 1969); Moshe Idel, "Some Remarks on Ritual and Mysticism in Geronese Kabbalah," *Journal of Jewish Thought and Philosophy* 3 (1993): 111–30; Haviva Pedaya, *Name and Sanctuary in the Teachings of Isaac the Blind* (Jerusalem: Magnes, 2001), 254–61; Yakov M. Travis, "Kabbalistic Foundations of Jewish Spiritual Practice: Rabbi Ezra of Gerona—On the Kabbalistic Meaning of the Mitzvot" (Ph.D. diss., Brandeis University, 2002).

6. On early kabbalistic exegesis of the Song, see Arthur Green, *The Heart of the Matter: Studies in Jewish Mysticism and Theology* (Philadelphia: Jewish Publication Society, 2015), 101–15.

7. On the topic of exile in the zoharic literature, see Isaiah Tishby, *Wisdom of the Zohar*, trans. David Goldstein (Oxford: Littman Library of Jewish Civilization, 1989), 1:382–85; Elliot Wolfson, *Luminal Darkness: Imaginal Gleanings from Zoharic Literature* (Oxford: Oneworld, 2007), 1–28, 144–227; and Wolfson, *Venturing Beyond: Law and Morality in Kabbalistic Mysticism* (New York: Oxford, 2006), s.v. "exile"; in Safedian kabbalah, see Bracha Sack, "Exile and Redemption in R. Shlomo ha-Levi Alkabetz's *Berit ha-Levi*," *Eshel Beer Sheva* 2 (1980): 265–86 [Hebrew]; Lawrence Fine, *Physician of the Soul, Healer of the Cosmos: Isaac Luria and His Kabbalistic Fellowship* (Stanford, Calif.: Stanford University Press, 2003), 41–77; and Miguel Beltrán, "El exilio de Dios en la cábala de Safed, según Scholem," *Cuadernos salamantinos de filosofía* 35 (2008): 85–96. For more recent studies of the related

kabbalistic discourse on the transmigration of souls, see Moshe Idel, "Commentaries on the Secret of Impregnation in the Kabbalah of Catalonia in the Thirteenth Century, and Their Importance for Understanding the Early Kabbalah and Its Development," *Da'at* 72 (2012): 5–49 [Hebrew] and its sequel in *Da'at* 73 (2012): 5–44 [Hebrew]. On the development of this area of speculation by later kabbalists, see Assaf Tamari, "Sparks of Adam: Principles of the Lurianic Doctrine of Gilgul and Its Anthropology" (Master's thesis, Tel Aviv University, 2009) [Hebrew].

8. This is not to conclude that R. Ezra was the first proponent of a kabbalistic doctrine of exile per se, but that his extant writings appear to be the earliest that *explicitly* document such a doctrine. For a compelling critique of scholarship on pre-Geronese kabbalah, see Avishai Bar-Asher, "Illusion versus Reality in the Study of Early Kabbalah: The Commentary on Sefer Yeṣirah Attributed to Isaac the Blind and Its History in Kabbalah and Scholarship," *Tarbiz* 86 (2019): 269–384 [Hebrew]. Indeed, earlier scholars have attributed kabbalistic lore concerning *shekhinah*'s exile to figures prior to R. Ezra; Scholem hazarded its attribution to *Sefer ha-Bahir*, which supported his argument that a gnostic mythology analogous to the ancient Valentinian lore of the fallen Sophia had influenced the Bahir; see Scholem, *Origins of the Kabbalah*, 90–92. Another early attribution is that of Haviva Pedaya, who maintained that R. Abraham ben David of Posquières promoted this lore already in Provence; see Pedaya, "Los comienzos de la cábala en Provenza: El Nombre divino y el Templo en la enseñanza de R. Isaac el Ciego," in *Ensayos sobre cábala y misticismo judío*, ed. Yom Tov Assis, Moshé Idel, and Leonardo Senkman (Buenos Aires: Lilmod, Centro Internacional para la Enseñanza Universitaria de la Cultura Judía, 2006), 102–10.

9. Space limitations do not permit a full bibliography of this facet of kabbalistic speculation, but most apropos to this study is Wolfson, "Woman—The Feminine As Other in Theosophic Kabbalah: Some Philosophical Observations on the Divine Androgyne," in *The Other in Jewish Thought and History: Constructions of Jewish Culture and Identity*, ed. Lawrence Silberstein and Robert Cohn (New York: New York University Press, 1994), 166–204. For an overview of the scholarship thereon, see Hava Tirosh-Samuelson, "Gender in Jewish Mysticism," in *Jewish Mysticism and Kabbalah: New Insights and Scholarship*, ed. Frederick Greenspan (New York: New York University Press, 2011), 191–230.

10. For the hypothesis that R. Ezra was one of the first kabbalists to divulge this doctrine in a manner that was theretofore disclosed only allusively in the *Sefer ha-Yihud* of Provençal sage R. Asher ben David, nephew of R. Isaac the Blind, see Jonathan Dauber, "Esotericism and Divine Unity in R. Asher ben David," *Jewish Studies Quarterly* 21 (2014): 225–26.

11. Vajda, *Le Commentaire d'Ezra*, 320. My trans.

12. For an overview of the scholarship on gender and sexuality in early kabbalah, see Daniel Abrams, *Kabbalistic Manuscripts and Textual Theory: Methodologies of Textual Scholarship and Editorial Practice in the Study of Jewish Mysticism* (Jerusalem: Magnes, 2010), 144–69. On gender in Castilian kabbalah, see Jeremy P.

Brown and Avishai Bar-Asher, "The Enduring Female: Differentiating Moses de León's Early Androgynology," *Jewish Studies Quarterly* 27 (2020): 1–33.

13. Erich Neumann, *The Origins and History of Consciousness* (Princeton, N.J.: Princeton University Press, 1954), 5–130.

14. On Adam's prototypical sin, its impact upon the lower gradations of divinity, his transition from angelic to mortal being, and his banishment from Eden, see the text attributed to R. Ezra, translated in Scholem, *On the Mystical Shape of the Godhead: Basic Concepts in the Kabbalah* (New York: Shocken, 1991), 65–68.

15. Vajda, *Le Commentaire d'Ezra*, 326–27. On the restoration of the feminine to the upper strata of the Godhead in the ultimate redemption and the question of her assimilation into the masculine, see Wolfson, "Bifurcating the Androgyne and Engendering Sin: A Zoharic Reading of Gen. 1–3," in *Hidden Truths from Eden: Esoteric Readings of Genesis 1–3*, ed. Catherine Vander Stichele and Susanne Scholz (Atlanta: Society for Biblical Literature, 2014), 83–115, esp. 105–10.

16. Vajda, *Le Commentaire d'Ezra*, 327–28.

17. Ezra ben Solomon of Gerona. *Perush Shir ha-Shirim*, in *Kitve Ramban*, ed. Charles Ber Chavel, 2 (Jerusalem: Mossad ha-Rav Kook, 2006), 504; adapted from Travis, "Kabbalistic Foundations," 102; cf. Seth Lance Brody, "Human Hands Dwell in Heavenly Heights: Worship and Mystical Experience in Thirteenth Century Kabbalah" (Ph.D. Diss. University of Pennsylvania, 1991), 106. On the premise that this passage demonstrates R. Ezra's adaptation of the neo-Platonic dynamic of *reversio*, see Idel, *Kabbalah and Eros* (New Haven, Conn.: Yale University Press, 2005), 183.

18. See Brown, "The Body of the Shekhinah at the Threshold of Domestic Violence," *AJS Perspectives* (Fall 2019): 54–55.

19. On this theosophic configuration of the divine family (*tiferet*-father; *shekhinah*-mother; Israel-child), see Abrams, "Divine Jealousy—Kabbalistic Traditions of Triangulation," *Kabbalah* 35 (2016): 7–54; Leore Sachs-Shmueli, "'I Arouse the Shekhinah': A Psychoanalytic Study of Anxiety and Desire of the Kabbalah in Relation to the Object of Taboo," *Kabbalah* 35 (2016): 227–66 [Hebrew].

20. See, for example, Justin Martyr, *Dialogue with Trypho* 16.4; and Tertullian, *Adversus Judaeos* 13.24–28. For the medieval canard that Jews perpetrated the ritual murder of Christian children with the intention of reversing the exilic punishment for deicide, see Thomas of Monmouth, *The Life and Miracles of St. William of Norwich* (Cambridge: Cambridge University Press, 1896), 93–94.

21. See, for example, BT *Yoma* 9b. For R. Ezra, on the other hand, any transgression whatsoever brings about a weakening of the sheltering unity of the divine structure (*binyan 'elohi*). On the theosophic language of "divine structure" as indicative of the toraitic commandments in their entirety, see Travis, "Kabbalistic Foundations," esp. the conclusion of R. Ezra's treatise on the commandments, 285–86.

22. For the suggestion that this rabbinic conception of diaspora as punishment is a response to the new Christian theology of exile, see Israel Jacob Yuval, "The Myth of the Exile from the Land: Jewish Time and Christian Time," *Alpayim* 29 (2005): 9–25 [Hebrew].

23. See Ephraim Urbach, *The Sages: The World and Wisdom of the Rabbis of the Talmud*, trans. Israel Abrahams (Cambridge, Mass.: Harvard University Press, 1979), 42–43, 54–55.

24. For rabbinic theologies of exile, see Arnold Eisen, *Galut: Modern Jewish Reflection on Homelessness and Homecoming* (Bloomington: Indiana University Press, 1986); Chaim Milikowsky, "Notions of Exile, Subjugation and Return in Rabbinic Literature," in *Exile: Old Testament, Jewish and Christian Conceptions*, ed. James Scott (Leiden: Brill, 1997), 265–96; and Devorah Shoenfeld, "'You Will Seek from There': The Cycle of Exile and Return in Classical Jewish Theology," in *Theology of Migration in the Abrahamic Religions*, ed. Elaine Padilla and Peter Phan (New York: Palgrave Macmillan, 2014), 27–45. And see especially Wolfson, "Divine Suffering and the Hermeneutics of Reading: Philosophical Reflections on Lurianic Mythology," in *Suffering Religion*, ed. Wolfson and Robert Gibbs (New York and London: Routledge, 2002), 101–7.

25. See Vajda, *Le Commentaire d'Ezra*, 325: "The sin of a part of Israel was the cause of the historical situation of exile . . . ; exile is also experienced, already in the old aggadah, by *shekhinah*; the kabbalah, which sees in this entity the mother of the chosen nation and which applies to her the biblical epithet of 'Guardian of Israel,' makes the *shekhinah*'s exile a privileged subject of speculations."

26. On nineteenth- and twentieth-century messianic and political applications of the historiosophies promoted by modern kabbalists, see Jonathan Garb, "Rabbi Kook and His Sources: From Kabbalistic Historiosophy to National Mysticism," in *Studies in Modern Religions, Religious Movements and the Babi-Bahai Faiths*, ed. Moshe Sharon (Leiden: Brill, 2004), 77–96. However, unlike the modern historiosophies discussed by Garb, which purportedly accelerated the migration of Jews to Palestine, R. Ezra's understanding of history, as I will show, favored a penitential narrative emphasizing the redemptive function of dwelling among the nations, albeit one based upon decidedly xenophobic premises.

27. Thus, the kabbalistic model demonstrates that traditional Jewish historiosophy need not eclipse historical agency of Jewish subjects; this is a premise that runs counter to the prevailing ethos of contemporary historians described in Engel, "Historians of the Jews and the Holocaust," 34.

28. A well-known zoharic exegesis of God's expulsion of Adam and Eve from the Garden (Gn 3:24) takes this kabbalistic understanding of radical responsibility to a further extreme, when it "flips the script" to assert that, through his sin, it is Adam who puts God out of Eden—or more specifically, he expels the feminine aspect of God, *shekhinah*; see Anonymous (Pseudo-Simeon bar Yoḥai), *Sefer ha-Zohar*, ed. Reuven Margaliot, 4th ed. (Jerusalem: Mossad ha-Rav Kook, 1964), 3 vols.

29. Idel, *Kabbalah: New Perspectives* (New Haven, Conn.: Yale University Press, 1988), 173–99. However, Idel's oft-cited discussion *does not* present the matter in terms of ethical responsibility.

30. On rabbinic theologies of shelter related specifically to the Feast of Tabernacles rites and symbolism, see Jeffrey Rubenstein, "The Symbolism of the Sukkah," *Judaism* 43, no. 4 (1994): 371–87, esp. 382–84, discussing zoharic motifs.

THE COMMON GOOD REIMAGINED

31. In his comment to Song 1:4, R. Ezra stresses that reciting the *Qedushah* portion of the liturgy has the sheltering effect of "drawing forth and emanating the energies of the fathers to the other *sefirot*, their children. With respect to this matter and in accord with the interpretation which I have provided here, our Sages have stated in the Midrash to Canticles (*Song of Songs Rabbah*, 8:13:1): *The King has brought me into his chambers*: 'These are the chambers of the Garden of Eden.'" R. Ezra also characterizes the transmission of substance to the feminine as a patriarchal vocation in his comments to Song 3:6 (Brody, "Human Hands Dwell in Heavenly Heights," 67), and Song 6:2 (Brody, "Human Hands Dwell in Heavenly Heights," 106). This characterization is founded upon the esoteric correspondence of the "the fathers"—that is, the biblical patriarchs Abraham, Isaac, and Jacob, with the sefirot *ḥesed*, *gevurah* and *tiferet*.

32. I discussed this particular facet of R. Ezra's kabbalah at the January 2018 Symposium for the Study of Kabbalistic Literature: The Kabbalah in Gerona, Mandel Scholion Center, Jerusalem, in an essay I am now developing, called "Espousal of the Impoverished Bride in Early Franciscan Hagiography and the Kabbalah of Gerona."

33. As shown in the previously cited presentation, the kabbalistic exegesis of this particular motif bears several compelling parallels to the early Franciscan romance of St. Francis of Assisi and Lady Poverty, especially the account presented in *Sacrum Commercium beati Francisci cum Domina Paupertate*, a text composed at approximately the same time as R. Ezra's work. For an English translation, see *Francis of Assisi: Early Documents*, ed. Regis Armstrong, J. A. Wayne Hellmann, and William Short (Hyde Park, N.Y.: New City Press, 1999), 1:529–54.

34. Chavel, *Kitve Ramban*, 2:486; Brody, "Human Hands Dwell in Heavenly Heights," 43–44.

35. See Mark Cohen, "Maimonides and Charity in the Light of the Geniza Documents," in *Die Trias des Maimonides: Jüdische, Arabische und Antike Wissenskultur*, ed. Georges Tamer (Berlin: de Gruyter, 2005), 72–74.

36. See Ioan Culianu, "The Angels of the Nations and the Origins of Gnostic Dualism," in *Studies in Gnosticism and Hellenistic Religions*, ed. Roel B. van den Broek and M. J. Vermaseren (Leiden: Brill, 1981), 78–91.

37. On kabbalistic discussions of the archons appointed over the nations, see Johann Maier, "Politische aspekte der Sefirotlehre des Josef ben Abraham Gikatilla," in *Aspetti della storiografia ebraica*, ed. Fausto Parente (Rome: Carucci editore, 1987), 213–26; Roland Goetschel, "Le Motif des *Sarim* dans les Ecrits de Joseph Giqatilia," *Michael* 11 (1989): 9–31; and Wolfson, *Venturing Beyond*, 111–21. On related three-world cosmological speculation among the Iberian kabbalists, see Scholem, "An Investigation of the Kabbalah of R. Isaac ben Jacob ha-Kohen, II: Evolution of the Doctrine of the Worlds in the Early Kabbalah," *Tarbiz* 2, no. 4 (1931): 415–42, and its sequel in *Tarbiz* 3, no. 1 (1931): 33–66; and Brown, "Of Sound and Vision: Medieval Kabbalistic Rituologies of the Ram's Horn," in *Qol Tamid: The Shofar in Ritual, History and Culture*, ed. Joel Gereboff and Jonathan Friedman, (Claremont, Calif.: Claremont School of Theology Press, 2017), 98–99.

38. *Mekhilta de-Rabbi Ishmael, Masekhta de-Shirata* 2 (referring to the Israelites' utterance of praise at the sight of the national archon of Egypt (*"sarah shel malkhut"*) as the angel plummets from heaven into the Red Sea; cf. *Song of Songs Rabbah*, 8:13:1; and *Tanḥumah, Beshalaḥ*, 13:2.

39. Chavel, *Kitve Ramban*, 2:486; Brody, "Human Hands Dwell in Heavenly Heights," 44.

40. On the development of this typological motif, see Israel Jacob Yuval, *Two Nations in Your Womb: Perceptions of Jews and Christians in Late Antiquity and the Middle Ages*, trans. Barbara Harshav and Jonathan Chipman (Berkeley: University of California Press, 2006), 1–30; on the evolution of the motif in medieval kabbalah, see Oded Yisraeli, *Temple Portals: Studies in the Aggadah and Midrash in the Zohar*, trans. Liat Keren (Berlin: De Gruyter, 2016), 134–56.

41. Without going as far as the kabbalists of Castile, who did not shrink from identifying Edom (that is, Christendom) with the satanic figure of Samael, his citation of the *Mekhilta*'s angelological gloss on *Helel ben Shahar* in this connection—bearing in mind that Is 14:12 is the *locus classicus* for Luciferian expulsion lore in Christian exegesis—may suggest that R. Ezra already harbored a comparable view, though articulated in more muted tones. On Is 14:12 in medieval Christian exegesis, see Karl Ludwig Schmidt, "Lucifer als gefallene Engelmacht," *Theologische Zeitschrift* 7 (1951): 161–79. In the spirit of elucidating religious narratives of displacement, it is noteworthy that here R. Ezra locates the ultimate resolution of Israel's exile with the expulsion of Edom. In other words, rather than an interreligious *convivencia*, the kabbalist imagined the emancipation of Israel in terms of Christendom's banishment. Of course, Christians had similarly demonized the Jews since antiquity; for an overview, see Roberto Bonfil, "The Devil and the Jews in the Christian Consciousness of the Middle Ages," in *Antisemitism Through the Ages*, ed. Shmuel Almog (New York: Pergamon, 1988), 91–98. On the demonization of Edom as Samael in thirteenth-century Castilian kabbalah, see Wolfson, *Luminal Darkness*, 185–227; and Wolfson, *Venturing Beyond*, 93n307, 104–5, 126–27, 142–46; in fifteenth-century Castilian kabbalah, see Abraham Gross, "Satan and Christianity: The Demonization of Christianity in the Writings of Abraham Saba," *Zion* 58 (1993): 91–105 [Hebrew].

42. Chavel, *Kitve Ramban*, 2:486; Brody, "Human Hands Dwell in Heavenly Heights," 44.

43. Chavel, *Kitve Ramban*, 2:479; Brody, "Human Hands Dwell in Heavenly Heights," 22.

44. Wolfson, *Venturing Beyond*, 40. In subsequent studies Wolfson has depicted the polemical culture of medieval kabbalah as simultaneously xenophobic *and* xenophilic, expressing overt repulsion while concealing covert attraction in relation to the confessional other. See, for example, Wolfson, "Textual Flesh, Incarnation, and the Imaginal Body: Abraham Abulafia's Polemic with Christianity," in *Studies in Medieval Jewish Intellectual and Social History: Festschrift in Honor of Robert Chazan*, ed. David Engel, Lawrence Schiffman, and Wolfson (Leiden: Brill, 2012),

189–226. Also see Robert Sagerman, *The Serpent Kills or the Serpent Gives Life: The Kabbalist Abraham Abulafia's Response to Christianity* (Leiden: Brill, 2011).

45. Ellen Haskell, *Mystical Resistance: Uncovering the Zohar's Conversations with Christianity* (New York: Oxford University Press, 2016).

46. Chavel, *Kitve Ramban*, 2:500; Brody "Human Hands Dwell in Heavenly Heights," 96.

47. On the book of Daniel as an exegetical battleground for medieval Jewish and Christian apocalyptic speculation, see Ram Ben-Shalom, *Medieval Jews and the Christian Past: Jewish Historical Consciousness in Spain and Southern France* (Portland, Ore.: Littman Library of Jewish Civilization, 2016), 14–15, 16–19, 35, 39, 51, 68, 78–79, 80, 96–98, 135, 174; on the four kingdoms in medieval rabbinic exegesis of Daniel, see Wout Jacques van Bekkum, "Four Kingdoms Will Rule: Echoes of Apocalypticism and Political Reality in Late Antiquity and Medieval Judaism," in *Endzeiten: Eschatologie in den monotheistischen Weltreligionen*, ed. Wolfram Brandes and Felicitas Schmieder (Berlin: De Gruyter, 2008), 101–18; and Michael Wechsler, "Four Empires—Medieval Judaism," *Encyclopedia of the Bible and Its Reception* (Berlin: De Gruyter, 2014), 6:521–24; on apocalyptic speculation in medieval kabbalah, see Idel, "'The Time of the End:' Apocalypticism and Its Spiritualization in Abraham Abulafia's Eschatology," in *Apocalyptic Time*, ed. *Albert Baumgarten* (Leiden: Brill, 2000), 155–86; and Idel, "On Apocalypticism in Judaism," in *Progress, Apocalypse, and Completion of History and Life after Death of the Human Person in the World Religions*, ed. Peter Koslowski (Dordrecht: Springer, 2002), 40–74.

48. BT *Avodah Zarah*, 2b.

49. Chavel, *Kitve Ramban*, 2:501; Brody, "Human Hands Dwell in Heavenly Heights," 97.

50. BT *Yoma*, 10a.

51. Chavel, *Kitve Ramban*, 2:501; Brody, "Human Hands Dwell in Heavenly Heights," 99.

52. In light of this prediction, it is conceivable that R. Ezra regarded crusading and *reconquista* campaigns as indicative of just such a Christian bid for world domination. Be that as it may, he likely imagined that once Christian rule had become comprehensive and absolute, the Messiah would deliver the sovereignty it had consolidated into the hands of Israel.

53. Chavel, *Kitve Ramban*, 2:502; Brody, "Human Hands Dwell in Heavenly Heights," 101.

54. On the polemical representation of Jesus as the Pascal sacrifice in the Zohar, see Jonatan Benarroch and Israel Jacob Yuval, "From an Egyptian Abomination to a Christian Rite: A Zoharic Homily on the Paschal Lamb," *Zion* 84, no. 4 (2019): 523–46.

55. Although referred to Jewish texts, my reading is informed by a hermeneutical imperative that theologian Musa Dube has applied to the New Testament—namely, a mode of reading of religious texts that, for all their emancipatory rhetoric, interrogates their historical propensity for "imperial sponsorship"; see Dube, *Postcolonial*

THE PASSIONALITY OF EXILE IN MEDIEVAL KABBALAH

Feminist Reading of the Bible (St. Louis: Chalice, 2000), 18 and 33. In the case of medieval Jewish anti-Christian polemic, readers face a dynamic more complex than that of the oppressed assimilating and inverting the oppressor's imperial rhetoric. This is because Christian authors articulated their discourses of hegemony as exegeses on the Hebrew Bible. Accordingly, polemicists like R. Ezra did not merely invert the rhetoric of the oppressor, but also sought to repatriate "indigenous" discourses of Israelite sovereignty, which had been exploited for the purposes of Christian empire.

56. Chavel, *Kitve Ramban*, 2:513; Brody, "Human Hands Dwell in Heavenly Heights," 133.

57. From the sixteenth-century epistle of Solomon Alqabets, printed in the initial pages of Joseph Karo, *Maggid Mesharim* (Jerusalem: Orah, 1960), 18; translation adapted from Louis Jacobs, *The Schocken Book of Jewish Mystical Testimonies* (New York: Schocken, 1996), 126. On the exaltation of expiation caused by the suffering of the divine mother, see Brown, "Body of the Shekhinah."

58. On the penitential discourse of medieval Jewish mysticism, see Brown, "Distilling Depths from Darkness: Forgiveness and Repentance in Medieval Iberian Jewish Mysticism" (Ph.D. diss., New York University, 2015).

59. Scholem, *Studies in Kabbalah* (Tel Aviv: Am Oved, 1998), 1:34 [Hebrew]; note that this statement is only attested in one of the two manuscript witnesses Scholem consulted in editing this text. Translation adapted from Aviezer Ravitzky, *Messianism, Zionism, and Jewish Religious Radicalism*, trans. Michael Swirsky and Jonathan Chipman (Chicago: University of Chicago Press, 1996), 218; on the views of other Geronese kabbalists regarding the obligation to settle the land, or exemption therefrom, see ibid., 218–20; see Idel, "The Land of Israel in Medieval Kabbalah," in *The Land of Israel: Jewish Perspectives*, ed. Lawrence Hoffman (Notre Dame, Ind.: University of Notre Dame, 1986) 170–87; Pedaya, "Land of Spirit and Land of Reality: R. Ezra, R. Azriel and Nahmanides," in *The Land of Israel in Medieval Jewish Thought*, ed. Moshe Halamish and Aviezer Ravitzky (Jerusalem: Ben Zvi Institute), 233–89 [Hebrew]; Oded Yisraeli, "Jerusalem in Nahmanides's Religious Thought: The Evolution of the 'Prayer over the Ruins of Jerusalem,'" *AJS Review* 41, no. 2 (2017): 409–53. On this verse (Ps 44:23) as prooftext for Jewish martyrology, see Boyarin, *Dying for God: Martyrdom and the Making of Christianity and Judaism* (Stanford, Calif.: Stanford University Press, 1999), 109–10; cf. Rom 8:36. Concerning R. Ezra's view that gentile persecution of the Jews in exile functions as an expiatory altar for Israel, one should note the inversion of that theme in *Perush Shir ha-Shirim* (Brody, "Human Hands Dwell in Heavenly Heights," 62–63; Chavel, *Kitve Ramban*, 2:492; Pedaya, *Name and Sanctuary*, 205). Accordingly, when the Jerusalem Temple stood, and Israel was established in their land, the gentiles who dwelled in the land alongside Israel received expiation through the cult of Temple sacrifice, and, correspondingly, through the optimal intercourse of divine powers. In sum, when Israel is in exile, they receive atonement through subjugation to the nations, whereas, when redemption restores Israel's sovereignty, the nations will atone through Israel.

60. This reading need not override the interpretive possibility that the statement also refers to an exilic mode of ascetic piety represented in figurative terms of martyrdom.

61. The theosophic correspondence of the sacrificial altar to *shekhinah* is a commonplace of kabbalistic symbolism. For example, see Brody, "Human Hands Dwell in Heavenly Heights," 579–600.

62. Trans. from Yitzhak Baer, *History of the Jews of Christian Spain*, trans. Louis Schoffman (Philadelphia: Jewish Publication Society, 1961), 1:247–48; in the Hebrew account of the disputation, self-sacrifice is a central theme of Naḥmanides's reading of the "suffering servant" prophecy (Is 53). Though careful to dissociate biblical references to this virtue from Christological narratives, the text nonetheless regards preparedness for self-sacrifice as a praiseworthy attribute proper to the Messiah of Israel. On this issue, see Robert Chazan, *Barcelona and Beyond: The Disputation of 1263 and Its Aftermath* (Berkeley: University of California Press, 1990), 163–66; and Yisraeli, "Jerusalem in Naḥmanides's Religious Thought."

63. See Naḥmanides's addendum to Maimonides, *Sefer ha-Miṣvot*, Positive Commandment no. 4.

64. Still, a return to Palestine need not contradict the religious imperative to suffer the subjugation of exile, at a time when sovereignty over the land is exercised by foreign rulers. See the opinion of the sixteenth- and seventeenth-century emigrant kabbalist Isaiah Horowitz, discussed in Aviezer Ravitzky, *Messianism, Zionism, and Jewish Religious Radicalism*, trans. Michael Swirsky and Jonathan Chipman (Chicago: University of Chicago Press, 1996), 227.

65. For a comparable exegesis from an earlier composition, see Joseph ben Abraham Gikatilla, *Sha'arei Ṣedeq* (Krakow: 1881), 25b.

66. BT *Berakhot* 56a; *Sanhedrin* 37b; Maimonides, *Mishneh Torah, Hilkhot Teshuvah*, 2:4; Judah Halevi, *Kuzari*, V:23; cf. Gikatilla, *Ginnat Egoz* (Zolkiew: 1773) 63a–b; compare also Marc Saperstein, *Decoding the Rabbis: A Thirteenth-Century Commentary on the Aggada* (Cambridge, Mass.: Harvard University Press, 1980), 71.

67. Joseph ben Abraham Gikatilla, *Sha'arei Orah*, ed. Joseph Ben Shlomo (Jerusalem: Mosad Bialik, 1996), 1:227–28; adapted from Gikatilla, *Gates of Light: Sha'are Orah*, trans. Avi Weinstein (Walnut Creek, Calif.: Altamira, 1994), 201–2. On the theopolitical implications of this passage, see Johann Maier, "Politische aspekte," 222–23.

68. For the idea that Abraham deemed Israel's exile more merciful than their punishment in Gehinom, see Genesis Rabbah 44:21; Pesiqta de-Rav Kahana 5:2; Exodus Rabbah 51:7; Midrash to Psalms 52:8; and especially Zohar II:83b, III:173b (Rav Metivta) and III:299a.

69. For the idea that Isaac's love of Esau refers to the nourishment of Esau from the attribute of judgment, see R. Menahem Recanati, *Perush al ha-Torah*, ed. Amnon Gross (Tel Aviv: Gross, 2003); that it refers to the related opinion that Esau's nourishment derives from his angelic counterpart, see Bahya ben Asher ben Hlava, *Be'ur al ha-Torah*, ed. Charles Ber Chavel (Jerusalem: Mosad ha-Rav Kuk, 1966–68),

Be'ur al ha-Torah. On this verse, also compare Zohar I:137b and 139a; and Moses de León, *Responsa*, in Tishby, *Studies in Kabbalah and Its Branches: Researches and Sources* (Jerusalem: Magnes, 1982) 1:47.

70. Gikatilla, *Sha'arei Orah*, 228; Gikatilla, *Gates of Light*, 202.

71. See Wolfson's interpretation of the early modern kabbalistic doctrine of ṣimṣum in light of Christological paradigms of divine suffering; Wolfson, "Divine Suffering and the Hermeneutics of Reading." For a fuller bibliography of scholarship on Christianity and medieval Iberian kabbalah, see Benarroch, "'Son of an Israelite Woman and an Egyptian Man'; Jesus as the Blasphemer (Lv 24:10–23): An Anti-Gospel Polemic in the Zohar," *Harvard Theological Review* 110, no. 1 (2017): 101n3.

72. On the passion and Jewish-Christian relations, see Jeremy Cohen, *Christ-Killers: The Jews and the Passion from the Bible to the Big Screen* (New York: Oxford University Press, 2007); Cohen, "On Pesach and Pascha: Jews, Christians, and the Passion," in *Engaging the Passion: Perspectives on the Death of Jesus*, ed. Oliver Larry Yarbrough (Minneapolis: Fortress, 2015), 335–58; see also Benarroch and Yuval, "From an Egyptian Abomination to a Christian Rite"; and Brown, "Body of the Shekhinah."

73. On this gendering of economic functions, see Brown and Bar-Asher, "Enduring Female."

74. I refer to the textual unit comprised within R. Ezra's *Perush Shir ha-Shirim*, in the form of a treatise on the 613 commandments; *Kitvei ha-Ramban*, II:521–48; see Adolph Jellinek, *Quntres Taryag* (Vienna: 1878), §124; and Travis, "Kabbalistic Foundations."

75. Chavel, *Kitve Ramban*, 2:546–47; Travis, "Kabbalistic Foundations," 254. The *gemilut hesed* category, which I designate "social ethics," includes the following commandments: "[To leave for the poor]—the gleanings,—the forgotten produce, and—the corners [of the field], and—the forgotten sheaf. To leave the unripened of the grapevine, and—the fallen of the grape harvest,—the monetary severance gift provided for one's [freed] Israelite female slave, and one's Israelite male slave, and—To betroth one's Israelite female slave [who reaches maturity], and if one does not wish to betroth her,—To [monetarily] redeem her,—To provide alms for the poor,—To grant loans to the poor,—To give a tithe to the poor on the third year,—To return the [poor's] deposit,—To pay the wage of the hired laborer in a timely manner, and—To allow for [him] to eat while on the job,—To help another unload himself, and—his animal, and—To help load up the animal, and—To return a lost object. This includes the prohibition—To not evade [the lost object]." For a disambiguation of *gemilut hasadim* as a specific category of rabbinic social ethics, see Tzvi Novick, "Charity and Reciprocity: Structures of Benevolence in Tannaitic Literature," *Harvard Theological Review* 105, no. 1 (2012): 33–52.

76. On a less sympathetic note, it is possible to argue that the kabbalistic model superimposes the mediating narrative of divine homelessness, with its related imperative to shelter divinity, onto the more concrete ethical need—namely, the immediate reckoning with social pathologies and the concomitant requirement to

act directly on behalf of those impacted. On the one hand, this may be viewed as a buffering mechanism. But within R. Ezra's ontology, where the delineation of primary and secondary fields of ethical agency may not be feasible, acting on behalf of the *shekhinah* is an ultimately incentivizing as well as compassionate model.

77. In this way, the discourse is analogous to the earlier rabbinic principle of obligating the poor in almsgiving, an ethic that similarly undermines the calcification of economic functions; BT *Gittin* 7a–b; cf. *Sefer ha-Hinnukh* (Jerusalem: Mosad HaRav Kook, 1990), §449 (576).

78. Gonçalo Marcelo, "Making Sense of the Social: Hermeneutics and Social Philosophy," *Études Ricœuriennes* 3, no. 1 (2012): 69.

79. Ibid.

80. Julia Kristeva, "Liberty, Equality, Fraternity . . . Vulnerability," in *Hatred and Forgiveness*, trans. Jeanine Herman (New York: Columbia University Press, 2010); Paul Ricoeur, "Autonomy and Vulnerability," in *Reflections on the Just*, trans. David Pellauer (Chicago: University of Chicago Press, 2007), 72–90. For secondary discussions, see Elizabeth Purcell, "Narrative Ethics and Vulnerability: Kristeva and Ricoeur on Interdependence," *Journal of French and Francophone Philosophy* 21, no. 1 (2013): 43–59; and Nathalie Maillard, *La vulnérabilité: Une nouvelle catégorie morale?* (Geneva: Labor et Fides, 2011). On Kristeva's Christological understanding of the "therapeutics of exile," a framework that is alternately apropos and troubling in view of my presentation, see her *Strangers to Ourselves*, trans. Leon Roudiez (New York: Columbia University Press, 1991), 77–93, esp. 82. Particularly relevant is Leora Batnitzky's assessment of the "feminine" as a problematic figure for human vulnerability in the writings of Martin Buber, Franz Rosenzweig, and Emmanuel Levinas: "The account of the human as dependent and vulnerable is philosophically and politically valuable[, h]owever . . . perhaps ironically, the notion of 'the feminine' attached to Jewish existentialist and feminist views of the human as dependent and vulnerable undermines the critical value of this construction of the human, for historical, philosophical, and political reasons"; Batnitzky, "Dependency and Vulnerability: Jewish and Feminist Existentialist Constructions of the Human," in *Women and Gender in Jewish Philosophy*, ed. Hava Tirosh-Samuelson (Bloomington: Indiana University, 2004), 128. To the great extent that medieval kabbalah identifies Jewish vulnerability with the travails and dependency of the divine female, Batnitsky's critique applies there, too—especially insofar as Buber, Rosenzweig, and Levinas, to come full circle, were generally conversant with the kabbalistic theology of *shekhinah's* exile. For a neo-Thomist approach to vulnerability, see Alasdair MacIntyre, *Dependent Rational Animals: Why Human Beings Need the Virtues* (Chicago: Open Court, 1999).

PART III
Theological Insights for Homeless Ministries

Wounds of Love

Spiritual Care and Homelessness in the Streets of Seattle

Paul Houston Blankenship

For Fear of Wounding Her (or: Introduction)

River is calling me from a psychiatric hospital. Last week, her husband died of an overdose. She held him in her arms as he stopped breathing; she watched as his face turned blue. When the paramedics got to their unsanctioned encampment, where they were living homeless, she was pulling the purple hair from his scalp and weeping violently. The gravity of the situation, she said, broke her into tiny pieces.[1]

I pick up the phone.

Neither of us know quite what to say. I gaze out the murky window of the public bus I am riding on to downtown Seattle. "River, what do you need?" "Just your company," she says.

She, though we say goodbye, is holding on to our conversation. "I love you," she says. For fear of wounding her, of taking any of the air she is gasping for, I am reluctant to say it back.

This chapter is about homelessness, suffering, and Christian spirituality. It is about the relationship between housed Christians who claim to love people who are homeless with a spiritual love and the people who are homeless themselves. I ask three questions. First, what difference do people who are homeless make in the spiritual lives of housed Christians? Second, why do people who are homeless make a difference in the spiritual lives of housed Christians? Finally, what difference does a housed Christian's spiritual love make in the lives of people who are homeless, and what will it take for that love to become more loving?

While I intend to query the relationship between housed Christians and people experiencing homelessness in a broad fashion, these queries are derived

from the limited ethnographic fieldwork I conducted in Seattle over a period of
two and a half years. That fieldwork was done with Christian "street ministers"
who are securely housed at an organization called Operation Nightwatch and
people who are chronically homeless and insecurely housed. I am a Christian
theologian and an ethnographer. What this means is that I spend a lot of time
learning about worlds that are different than my own through, among other
things, participant observation, semi-structured interviews, and historical research. That is the nature of ethnography. As a Christian theologian, I use ethnography while rooted in a tradition that lives, however poorly, in response to a
call from a Palestinian Jew who lived over two thousand years ago. That call is
to love. For this reason, I think Dorothee Sölle best described the task of theology as the imperfect attempt to render life intelligibly so that it can be loved.[2]

At stake in this chapter, then, is a reliable perspective on the relationship
between housed Christians who offer spiritual care to people who are homeless and the people who are homeless themselves. An adequate response to
River is also at stake: a deeply life-giving way of saying, to people experiencing homelessness, if not with words then somehow, "I love you, too."

Outline

This chapter will move in three steps. First, I describe Operation Nightwatch
(ON) and its practice of "street ministry" with people who are homeless in Seattle. While focusing on ON, I note other Christian organizations in Seattle
and beyond that practice related forms of spiritual care with people who are
homeless. Here, I propose that street ministers at ON, and some housed Christians more broadly, have a spiritual relationship to people who are homeless.
In this spiritual relationship, people who are homeless motivate a housed Christian's desire for God and make possible their practice of love. In this unique
and historically significant expression of Christian spirituality, people who are
homeless are, to use a manner of speaking that Christian mystics throughout
history have, "wounds of love."

Second, I explain why people who are homeless motivate a housed Christian's desire for God and make their practice of love possible. I do this by drawing on the work of modern Christian theologians and contemporary social
scientists who study Christianity. Here, I propose that Christians have a problem of presence that people who are homeless help resolve and that many
Christian theologians have increased the likelihood of this particular resolution because of the degree to which they write about how God might be found,
experienced, and pursued in the relationship to the suffering poor.

Third, I consider the difference a housed Christian's spiritual love makes in the lives of people who are homeless and reflect on what it will take for that love to become more loving. Here, I propose that the sense of meaning and belonging that street ministers try to cultivate is likely to help some homeless individuals but may devastate others. In order for a housed Christian's love to become more loving, he or she must help change the alterable conditions in which people experiencing homelessness live. If that does not happen, I fear that homeless individuals are, in the end, little more than a means by which housed Christians save themselves from the poverty of disbelief, meaninglessness, and lovelessness.

Operation Nightwatch

ON was founded in 1967. It began when a young pastor from a small church on Mercer Island named Bud Palmberg heard that a young man from his church ran away from home. Concerned he might begin traveling with hippies, Bud drove from Mercer Island to Seattle's skid row one night after choir practice. The suffering Bud witnessed that night changed his life. The seeming dearth of love, evidenced by rampant homelessness, drug addiction, and prostitution, called out to him as if from the mouth of God. People on the streets, he began to realize, need a minister like the people at his church. Every week after choir practice, even after he found the young man, Bud returned to skid road. He became a street minister.

Since the streets were large and dangerous, Bud started recruiting other street ministers. The problem, however, was that none of the street ministers he knew wanted to do it. Undeterred, Bud picked up a copy of the Yellow Pages and combed through it. "You get some pretty strange guys when you look in the Yellow Pages," Bud recalled in an interview, "but the strange ones were the only ones who were willing to go."[3] In time, a group of street ministers, however strange, was on the streets of Seattle's skid road every night from 10 P.M. until 4 A.M. Their purpose was simple: to accompany people on and off the streets and help them remember, or perhaps discover, that God loves them and has a plan for them. Toward this end, there would be no judging or preaching at people. Only a loving presence.

Not everyone experienced their presence as loving, however. Or even wanted them around. Some worried they might be undercover cops. Since it was the height of the counterculture movement, some didn't want anything to do with people who resembled "the establishment." The first year was not easygoing. A number of street ministers were held up at knife point, there were several visits to the emergency room, and one night Bud was even thrown through the glass windows of a porn shop. Imagine!

Despite these difficulties, however, they kept showing up. And they kept growing. Today, ON is an impressive organization. It provides a warm meal every night at 9 P.M. to over 200 people who are homeless, runs a dispatch center that helps people who might otherwise sleep on the street find emergency shelter, and owns and operates an apartment complex that houses twenty-four low-income seniors. Its budget exceeds a million dollars. After all these years, ON still practices street ministry. Its purpose remains the same: to offer a loving presence to people experiencing homelessness and to help them in and out of their homelessness.

Street Ministry

While ON played an integral role in the development of street ministry in Seattle, it is part of a broader phenomenon. Similar forms of spiritual care, also referred to as "spiritual accompaniment" and "ministries of presence," are practiced by organizations in Seattle, the United States, and even the world. Other organizations in Seattle that practice some form of street ministry include the Union Gospel Mission, New Horizons, Mental Health Chaplaincy, and Seattle Youth Ministry. During my ethnographic fieldwork in Seattle, I interviewed people at all of these organizations. I also got to know Rick and Ben, the current street ministers at Operation Nightwatch, on a personal level. To help me understand what it means to be a street minister and provide spiritual accompaniment to someone who is homeless, they invited me to become a street minister with them for a time.

During my time with ON, I identified five core practices associated with street ministry. The first practice is prayer. Prayer, Ben told me, is the foundation of street ministry. Before street ministers go to the streets, they join hands and pray. The content of their prayers varies. Generally, it consists of asking for God's guidance. Street ministers, for example, might ask God to guide them to the right people to minister to. The intent is to become surrendered and open to God so that, through the street minister, God can love people who are homeless.

After prayer, street ministers show up. Showing up is what I consider the second practice of street ministry. Showing up is just about being there. It is about making their presence known to people who are homeless. It is vital not just to show up, Rick and Ben told me, but to show up consistently. This is how one begins to build trust with people who are homeless, which they find remarkably difficult.

The third practice is greeting people who are homeless. As it turns out, this is also quite difficult. Ben told me that many people develop invisible armor to protect themselves on the streets. This armor makes them guarded. Even saying hello might be experienced as an intrusion—like picking the lock on their front door. To overcome this challenge, Ben offers survival items from a backpack he carries around with him. Rick offers pizza. Once someone's armor is off, it is possible for a relationship to develop.

Building relationship with people who are homeless is the fourth practice I identified at ON. Central here is listening. For street ministers, listening means creating space for someone to share what they are going through. In this space, it is imperative that one be nonjudgmental.

Sometimes a street minister will pray for a person who is homeless or offer a prophecy. To speak prophetically at ON is not about charismatically telling someone her future. It is, rather, simply encouraging someone that she is loved by God and that God has a plan for her. In an interview, Ben told me that sometimes people become so overwhelmed by this prophecy that they begin to cry. He said that love often gets turned off on the streets because of the armor people develop to protect themselves. When there is a chink in the armor, he said, which can come by way of a prophecy, it can overcome someone.

Street Stories

After a long day or night of street ministry, Rick and Ben return to the office. If they have the energy, they sit at their desk and reflect on their experiences. Then they write a story and publish it on their online blog. The goal here is to bring the presence of people who are homeless they have gotten to know to the larger Christian church, and to the world, so that these people can be better loved. Storytelling is what I consider the fifth and final practice of street ministry at ON.

In 2015, a book of Rick's stories was published. It is aptly titled *Street Stories*. By and large, it is a book of frustrated laments. The laments are ecclesial, institutional, and personal. Rick laments how inadequate the Christian church's response to homelessness is, for example: how many churches have the physical space to shelter people who are homeless but don't. He also laments how other institutions, like the city of Seattle, seem, despite their political rhetoric, to lack the political will to solve the problem. Rick laments personal greed and pride: how many housed people hoard unneeded belongings while people without homes have virtually nothing. He laments his own ministry on the streets as well and how, at times, he feels swallowed by his own cynicism and doubt. In *Street Stories*, Rick fashions himself a street minister who gives banal blessings and who feels compelled, perhaps in delirium, to dream an impossible dream.

"Ronnie Kisses Me" is a quintessential street story. It is told not only in *Street Stories* but also at the places Rick is invited to speak. It goes like this. "Ronnie" is an unhoused person in Seattle. Because he causes so much trouble, Ronnie is barred from almost every shelter in Seattle. One night, parting a large crowd, Ronnie approaches Rick. He comes up close and asks Rick if he is beautiful. Uncomfortable and lying, Rick tells Ronnie that he is beautiful. Then Ronnie gets closer to Rick and, with a smile on his face, gives Rick a big kiss on the cheek. Inside, Rick recoils. Ronnie's lips have a distinct taste of homelessness on them; it overwhelms Rick with something he does not want.

The meaning of the stories, Rick told me, changes over time. In his book, for example, Rick writes that Ronnie's kiss helped him realize how ugly and unloving he was being in that situation. He wanted to keep Ronnie and his problems at arm's length. Ronnie's kiss taught him that loving God and other people means embracing what is ugly and uncomfortable. The story ends with this prayer: "Help me love everyone with Your uninhibited joy."[4]

In a video online, the meaning of the story is different. There, Rick says that Ronnie's kiss changed the way he sees people who are homeless. After Ronnie kissed him, Rick said, he no longer sees pain and suffering on the faces of people who are homeless. Instead, he sees their hopes and joys—the hopes and joys everyone, homeless or not, has for his or her life.[5]

Most of the Christian organizations that provide spiritual care to people who are homeless that I observed in Seattle tell stories in this way. In 2009, Craig Rennebohm, founder of Mental Health Chaplaincy, published a widely acclaimed book, *Souls in the Hands of a Tender God: Stories of the Search for Home and Healing on the Streets*. Here is how Craig's book begins: "We begin not in the sanctuary, but on the street. Here in the most unexpected and obscure places, we discover the Spirit at work in the world, *the touch of God* that holds every moment of life with infinite care."[6] The next year, in 2010, Ron Ruthruff, a former director at New Horizons, published a similar book entitled *The Least of These: Lessons Learned from Kids on the Street*. An endorsement of Ron's book suggests that the book is "about how the ministry to young people has broken and shaped Ron's heart for God and for proclaiming the good news in hard places" and how the streets function as a kind of seminary that reveals the face of God.[7] Other books, written from authors outside of Seattle, include *Sometimes God Has a Kid's Face*, by Bruce Ritter, and *Practicing Presence: Insights from the Streets*, by Phyllis Cole-Dai.

In my view, this literature constitutes a historically unique genre in the history of Christian spirituality. There is no one way to read this literature, and there is great variance within it. Yet it seems to me that most stories embody a central dynamic related to the absence and presence of God. On one hand, the stories evoke an absence of God. That absence is articulated in the suffering that people who are homeless experience. On the other hand, the stories evoke a presence of God. God is identified with people who are homeless. In their suffering, God's presence is framed as a question of love. Responding to that question with love is framed as a means of loving God and realizing one's Christianity.[8] This interplay between the absence and presence of God amongst the homeless motivates a housed Christian's relationship with God and makes his practice of love possible.

Wounds of Love

"The wound of love" is a motif that runs through the history of Christian spirituality. Since the third century, Christians have used it to describe the experience of being uniquely and transformatively touched by God.[9] The touch is described as a wound because of what happens in a person's soul. Divine love, the very fount of human desire, becomes immediately, beautifully, and terrifyingly present. In this state, God removes his presence: where once there was a fulfilling touch, now there is a painful absence; there is a wound of love. This absence engenders a painful and yet still beautiful longing, which God uses to draw people closer to herself. With God, the wounded person becomes the shepherd of this longing. It is kept, cultivated, and cared for through prayer and acts of love in the material world.

The actual experience of this wounding and the recovery from it are described by Christians throughout history in similar terms. Interestingly, however, the symbols they say God uses to wound are strikingly different. Precisely *what* God uses to wound a person with love, in other words, is historically unique. Consider Origen of Alexandria, who is the first person in the Christian tradition to use the motif. Origen believed that the Bible, and the Song of Songs in particular, was used by God to wound him with love. In the third century, Origen writes, "Indeed, the soul is led by a heavenly desire and love when once the beauty and glory of the Word of God has been perceived, he falls in love with His splendor and by this receives some dart and wound of love."[10] Julian of Norwich, whose book *Showings* has become more popular of late, is another example of a Christian who wrote about her experience being wounded by God with love. Like many Christians in the medieval world, Julian believed that God used images of Jesus's suffering to wound her with love.[11]

In our time, I propose that people who are homeless wound some housed Christians with love. While I did not hear anyone explicitly refer to homeless

Figure 1. "I Love You, Too" (Photograph by Paul Houston Blankenship)

individuals as "wounds of love," I believe the phenomenon is functionally similar and historically congruent for two reasons. First, the relationship some housed Christians have with people who are homeless is spiritual. The relationship is spiritual because it is where some housed Christians indicate that they find, experience, and pursue God. Second, it is precisely the alternating presence and absence of God's love amongst the homeless that establish, motivate, and enrich the relationship.

The question that I want to turn to now is why. Why, that is, might people experiencing homelessness wound housed Christians with love and make this difference in their spiritual lives?

The Suffering of the Poor: A Place of Divine Encounter in Christian Theology

At the heart of Christianity is a story about a powerful and loving God. Belief in this God threads the garment of Christianity identity. There is a problem with this story, however: it comes apart at the seams when people suffer. For this reason, Christians have long queried: If God is powerful and loving, why is there so much suffering? Is God not powerful enough to prevent people from experiencing homelessness? Is God not loving enough? This line of thinking is referred to as traditional theodicy: it worries itself with explaining suffering, and it has failed.

I consider traditional theodicy a failure because it is, by and large, considered rationally untenable and ethically unsound.[12] In the face of radical suffering, there just aren't good answers for why people suffer, and the bad answers that are available too often make the problem worse. While many Christian theologians agree that radical suffering can no longer be explained, however, they do think that it can be transformed. That has been the main challenge facing Christian theologians since the collapse of traditional theodicy: not to explain suffering but, rather, to transform it.[13]

The collapse of traditional theodicy, then, has changed Christian theology. This change is important to observe because it has made an empirical difference in the world. Theologians speak about God. In doing this, theologians give people language to relate to God and develop their own spiritualities. In the next section of this chapter, I review the work of two influential modern theologians: Dorothee Sölle and Gustavo Gutiérrez. I demonstrate the degree to which they speak about God in relation to the suffering poor. I also propose that this manner of speaking has increased the likelihood that Christians will report having spiritual experiences with the suffering poor. That, then, will be one answer to the question of why people experiencing homelessness wound a housed Christian with love.

Dorothee Sölle

Though lesser known than her German contemporaries Jürgen Moltmann and Johann Baptist Metz, Dorothee Sölle left an indelible mark on Christian theology. *Suffering*, written in the aftermath of Auschwitz and subsequent "death of God," is her most popular work. Much of Sölle's work is an attempt to change the way Christians imagine God. In her view, the conception of God as omnipotent needed to change.

For Sölle, there are two problems that result from belief in divine omnipotence. The first problem is connected to God. She argues that it creates a god whose power is vindicated through human powerlessness.[14] The second problem concerns the effect this god has on individuals. Essentially, this divine imaginary engenders a willingness to suffer and an unwillingness to ask questions about suffering. Ultimate desire is constituted as submission to an alien power. "Why God sends affliction is no longer asked," Sölle writes. "It is sufficient to know he causes it."[15] People become powerless at the hands of an all-powerful God who uses suffering as a disciplinary tactic. No protest against suffering is expressed. "In this particular thought-world," Sölle continues, "the idea does not surface that one should battle suffering and eliminate its causes."[16] Not only does this God alienate a person from herself, he also alienates her from other people. "What this Christian theism has succeeded in producing can be characterized as 'insensitivity to human misery' and thereby 'contempt for humanity,'" Sölle argues.[17] The result is that people end up worshiping their executioner and glorifying their powerlessness.

In effect, Sölle disentangled suffering from God. She argued that suffering and God go together like oil and water: not at all. This did not mean, however, that suffering cannot serve a positive function. To desire a life without suffering is to desire death. The important thing is one's relationship to suffering and whether that relationship produces love, not how a powerful and loving God could allow suffering. "Suffering," Sölle contends, "makes one more sensitive to the pain in the world. It can teach us to put forth a greater love for everything that exists."[18] For Sölle, this requires transforming suffering into a purposeful activity through a kind of mystical openness to it. "It is the mystic sufferer," according to Sölle, "who opens his hands for everything coming his way. He has given up faith in and hope for a God who reaches into the world from outside, but not hope for changing suffering and learning from suffering."[19]

Suffering can be transformed, then, when it teaches one to love. This, however, is contingent upon the poor and those suffering most brutally from abuses of power. In a mystical sense, Christians are called to their suffering. For Sölle, it is, in a sense, where Jesus is being crucified in present time. It is where Christians can hear the sound of God's mourning voice teaching them how to love. "The poor are the teachers," Sölle wrote in a later book, *Theology for Skeptics*. "From them, not from those who have possessions, make decrees, or hold power, we learn what it means to believe in God."[20]

Gustavo Gutiérrez

Gustavo Gutiérrez is a world-renowned theologian and Dominican priest. He is regarded as a founder of liberation theology in Latin America, which is one of the most significant theological movements of our time. For Gutiérrez, liberation theology must be rooted in a concrete spiritual experience with the poor. Like Sölle, he argues that the suffering poor teach us how to love and therefore how to be Christian in the world today.

In *We Drink from Our Own Wells*, for example, Gutiérrez is fundamentally uninterested in the question of how an all-powerful and loving God might permit suffering. Instead, what is at stake for Gutiérrez is an adequate response to the death-dealing poverty in which vast majorities of people in Latin America live. What is at stake is a transformation of the situation that people living in poverty are in so that they may have the option to choose life. Further, what is at stake is the response to Jesus's call in the form of the church's solidarity with the poor in their pursuit of life in the face of death in Latin America. That is, the very possibility of the Christian life is at stake.

The response Gutiérrez develops begins with three rejections. First, he rejects "idealized poverty" in which the suffering of people impoverished are used for pastoral, theological, and spiritual purposes. This spirituality is grounded in the real suffering of real bodies whose lives hang in the balance. Second, his spirituality rejects two prevalent forms of Christian spirituality widely practiced in the church: one that leaves the world behind in the pursuit of God and another that focuses on the interior life of individual Christians. What Gutiérrez seeks, in *We Drink from Our Own Wells*, is a synthesis between action and contemplation.

Gutiérrez is less known for his work on spirituality than theology. The distinction is, for him, however, a vital one. For Gutiérrez, theology is a discursive reflection on spiritual experience. It is secondary. Spirituality, on the other hand, is about a particular experience of Christ. It is what comes first. It is what motivates Christian action and what good theology depends upon. Successful liberation theology, therefore, and an adequate response to the real suffering taking place in Latin America, hinges on spiritual experience. It is the well from which we drink.

While Gutiérrez believes in a universality of spiritual experience, he also argues that the experience of Christ is always particular. "At the root of every spirituality," he writes, "there is a particular experience that is had by concrete persons living at a particular time. The experience is both proper to them and yet communicable to others."[21] For Latin Americans like Gutiérrez, to encounter the poor is to encounter Jesus. To follow Jesus is to be in solidarity with the poor in their pursuit of life. Needed for liberation theology, therefore, is a spiritual experience in which one encounters the face of the poor. He writes, "To be a follower of Jesus is to walk with the poor. When one walks with the poor, one has an experience of Jesus. The Lord is simultaneous revealed and hidden in the face of the poor."[22]

The last point is essential. Jesus is revealed in the poor, but Jesus is not commensurate with the poor. The entities do not collapse into one. Indeed, the encounter with the poor is contingent upon an experience of God's "gratuitous love." A real encounter with the poor is not possible without this. Without it, one will neither be able to actually see the poor nor interact with the poor in an empowering, life-giving way. This gratuitous love, which enables one to love purely and not force an alien will upon someone, is what it means to love authentically and without force. He writes, "The other is our way of reaching God, but our relationship with God is a precondition for encounter and true communion with the other."[23]

It should be clear that Sölle and Gutiérrez are not interested explaining suffering in relation to a powerful and loving God. Instead, their concern is with how suffering can be transformed and replaced with love. It should also be clear that both Sölle and Gutiérrez argue that suffering can be transformed and replaced with love in the context of a spiritual relationship with the suffering poor. Since the death of the theodicy project, this has been an especially strong characteristic in modern Christian theology. To a considerable extent, their theology suggests that God can be discovered, experienced, and pursued in the context of a relationship with the suffering poor. The poor reveal where love is lacking, and therefore where God is, and this lack is used to motivate and materialize Christian love. For many Christian theologians today, the experience of suffering is not a problem in relationship to a powerful and loving God. It is a solution.

Christianity: Why It Works and Its Problem of Presence

In a 2007 essay, the sociologist Christian Smith asked why Christianity has survived for two millennia and what makes it "work" for people. Given all the challenges and problems it has faced over the years, he wanted to know, why do so many people in the world continue to put their faith in it? One reason, Smith argues, is because of the degree to which Christianity meets basic emotional and mental needs that humans have. In Smith's view, Christianity helps people *feel*—not just know—that their lives are meaningful, that they belong, and that they are unconditionally loved.[24] Central to Christianity's capacity to meet these basic human needs is the *belief* in a personal and loving God and a set of *practices* that engage this belief and make it emotionally convincing. Christianity works, in other words, because people feel that a personal and loving God is alive in the universe and because this imbues them with significance, belonging, and love.[25]

Smith's essay answered why Christianity works; it did not, however, answer how it works. The empirical question of precisely how Christians come to feel, in their everyday lives, that a seemingly immaterial God is real and that the universe is charged with meaning, connectedness, and love is left open. In recent years, a number of anthropologists have begun to focus on this question in their own right. Matthew Engelke, for example, refers to the challenge of how a seemingly immaterial God becomes real to people as a "problem of presence." His book A *Problem of Presence* is an ethnographic study in Zimbabwe

on a group of Christians referred to as the Friday Masowe apostolics. The tit-
illating feature of the Masowe apostolics is that they do not read the Bible. In
fact, they consider the Bible a sacrilegious document. It is forbidden in services and, according to their prophets, best used as toilet paper. There are several reasons this is the case. One reason is Africa's colonial history and the
degree to which the Bible was used against them as a weapon of political subjugation. Their approach to the Bible, however, Engelke contends, is not re-
ducible to that. Another reason they reject the Bible is that they desire a live
and direct faith. The Bible, in their view, deadens a live and direct faith. Unlike the presence of God, the Bible can tear, fall apart, and be destroyed. Words
on a page suffocate the breath of God. The Bible traps the Christian in the
past and prevents her from experiencing God in the present. Unlike for other
Christians, where reading the Bible is integral to their relationship with God,
the Bible, in this expression of Christianity, is a limitation.[26] But the problem
of presence does not go away. How the Friday Apostolics respond to it is the
subject of Engelke's book.

His argument is complex. It requires a degree of nuance that I cannot provide in this chapter. In short, however, Engelke's argument is that the Friday
Apostolics' rejection of the Bible creates the possibility for experiencing the
presence of God in different ways. For this group, the voice of their prophet is
considered the True Bible, and sound, experienced within "a community of
practice," is one means through which the presence of God is resolved. The
mediation and experience of the presence of God through sound transpire
within a sophisticated and locally constituted performance and interpretation
(which frequently causes problems to their neighbors).[27]

In *When God Talks Back*, Tanya Luhrmann asks how charismatic evangelicals in the United States resolve the problem of presence. "The problem of
presence," in her words, "is that an immaterial God cannot be seen, heard,
smelled, or felt in an ordinary way, and so worshippers cannot know through
their senses that God is real."[28] For Americans, and people in the West more
broadly, the problem of presence is qualitatively different. In contrast to people
in Africa, fewer people in the West are convinced that gods are real and that
they can make an observable difference in the world. For complex reasons,
about which scholars of secularity debate, our lives in the West appear less
shackled to the gods and their religious traditions. Arguably, this makes it more
difficult to resolve the problem of presence and come to believe that there is
a personally loving God at the center of the universe.[29]

That is one reason evangelicals, one of the most likely religious groups in
the United States to believe in God, are so interesting. Luhrmann's ethnography at various Vineyard churches led her to the conclusion that charismatic

evangelicals resolve their problem of presence through a series of sophisticated practices that teach them to pay attention to their minds in particular and concentrated ways and, in that process, learn to hear the voice of God talking back to them. These practices involve experiencing God in the private space of one's mind, relating to God as a person, and experiencing oneself as unconditionally loved. At the Vineyard, it is in the mind that one waits for God to speak; it is there that one learns to encounter God as present.

In this section of the chapter, I have demonstrated that Christianity works because it meets some of the basic emotional and mental needs that people have. For a number of reasons, many people find the notion that there is a personal and loving God at the center of the universe to be emotionally fulfilling. Precisely how Christians come to feel that this is true and emotionally convincing is a challenge Christians face and an empirical question. Anthropologists refer to it as Christianity's "problem of presence." Because Christianity is diverse and culturally adaptive, as we have seen, the way Christians resolve their problem of presence will vary. According to Engelke, sound is a salient means by which the Friday Apostolics in Africa come to experience God as real. In Luhrmann's study, charismatic evangelicals in the United States use their minds to experience God as real. Based on my fieldwork with street ministers in Seattle, it seems to me that people who are homeless help some Christians resolve their problem of presence as well. People who are homeless, in other words, help make Christianity work. This is because, in the context of a relationship with someone who is homeless, which Christian theology encourages, Christians come to experience that a personally loving God is real and emotionally convincing.

Of course, it is true that people who are homeless do not *invariably* help Christians resolve their problem of presence. No doubt countless Christians have lost their faith by witnessing the abject suffering people who are homeless experience. Notwithstanding, the sentiment that people experiencing homelessness help make Christianity work is captured well in an April 1964 article by Dorothy Day. Day, in a way that seems exaggerated, wrote, "The mystery of the poor is this. That they are Jesus and what you do for them you do for him. It is the only way we have of knowing and believing in our love. It is an act of faith, constantly repeated."[30]

Some may read this chapter and suggest that street ministers and other housed Christians are instrumentalizing people who are homeless: using them, that is, for their own spiritual advantage. That would be a terrible mistake. The street ministers I have gotten to know are deeply and perhaps too painfully concerned about when and how they make their work about themselves and whether they are actually making a positive difference in the lives of people who are homeless. They describe the problem like a temptation to sin and counsel that humility is a necessary disposition for street ministry. Beyond reason and their human frailties, the street ministers I have gotten to know desire to make a real and positive difference in the lives of people who are homeless. They want to love them and for their love to be loving. In the final section of this chapter, I reflect on the difference a street minister's spiritual love for people who are homeless makes, and I join them in struggling with the question of what it will take for their love to become more loving. I begin with a story about Daisy, a woman on the streets of Seattle whom I have gotten to know.

Daisy (and the Limits of Love on the Streets)

Daisy is sitting in a busy street corner in the Capitol Hill district of Seattle. There is a yellow dog in her lap. Behind her a man who looks like Jimi Hendrix is playing guitar. With several young adults who are homeless, I am sitting against a wall: we are listening to the music and watching people walk by and asking them for their spare change.

"Why did you have to go to jail, Wit? Why did you have to leave me alone?" I overhear Daisy ask this question aloud, through fits of tears and rage, to herself, or to Something Out There, over and again.

The police say that Wit hit Daisy. They arrested him for domestic violence and put him in jail. Daisy and Wit claim that is untrue. They say they just like kinky sex and that they don't have a place, being homeless, to go and be human in that way together.

On that same street corner, Daisy practices magic. She describes the old, uneven patch of concrete like it is holy ground; she talks about her finger as a spiritual object. With it, she casts spells. The last spell she cast on the concrete was meant to dispel two men. They were fighting over her, she said, and she wanted them to go away. Sometimes, for at least a little while, the magic seems to work.

Today she is casting a spell on the table we are eating on at Chipotle. We are doing an interview because Daisy is upset and, knowing that I study spirituality on the streets, wants to tell me something that happened to her recently.

A few mornings ago, Daisy remembers, as sunlight spread through the usually cloudy streets of Seattle, a brown sedan drove slowly past her. Then it turned around, drove back, and parked right in front of her. Startled, Daisy watched the man roll down his car window. Smiling, the man told Daisy that Jesus loves her. Then he drove away again. This made Daisy very upset. In protest, she raised her middle finger in the air and spoke softly under her lips, "Asshole."

Later that night, something even more upsetting happened. Her boyfriend became possessed by a demon. Seeing me suspicious, Daisy told me she didn't think it was a bad reaction to the meth they smoke together. What happened, she said, was different, unique, and really scary: he spoke in tongues, his eyes changed color, and then he tried to rape her. None of those things happened before. When Daisy tells me this story her body appears like a teapot about to whistle—as a steel container needing to expel what's been boiling inside.

What really frightened Daisy was not the stranger's remark about Jesus's love in itself or even the sexual assault. What frightened her most had to do with what both events, happening so close together, might signify about the voices she hears.

Before this happened, Daisy thought she had it all figured out: the voices she hears, which she thought were Satan and God, fighting a war for her soul, were not actually real. With some psychiatric care, she came to experience them as parts of herself that need medical care. Today she is no longer so sure. She is afraid that the voices might be real because she thinks the universe might be sending her a message.

On Loving More Lovingly

In the absence of adequate institutional care, a large number of people with serious mental health problems are homeless.[31] Precise numbers are hard to establish, but conservative studies indicate that around one in every four homeless individuals suffers in this way. For some of these people, spirituality is deeply beneficial. One reason for this is that spirituality can help people make meaning out of difficult situations. Meaning, after all, as Leon Anderson and David Snow found in their ethnography of people experiencing homelessness in Texas, is as rudimentary a human need as food and shelter.[32] There are others, however, for whom certain kinds of spirituality, and the meanings they evoke, can be devastating. Daisy is one example. In her case, being told that she is loved by God, something street ministers at Operation Nightwatch frequently do, meant something much different than was intended. Unwittingly, what was said contributed to a frightening psychological experience.

Suffering, we must remember, is not a tame animal. Sometimes it feeds on the things we'd least expect.

A sense of meaning, however, is not the only difference a housed Christian's spiritual love might make in the lives of people who are homeless. I remind the reader of River, with whose story I began this chapter. When she called me from her psychiatric hospital, the one thing she said she needed from me was my company. Presence. Explicitly, she said she didn't want me to be "one of those people" trying to fix her. It is one of the most common sentiments I observed during my fieldwork. Many people who are homeless pine for positive relationships. This should not surprise us. The need to be in personal and loving relationships does not go away on the streets. Housed Christians who provide spiritual care to homeless individuals often meet this need. It is part of the tremendous good they do. Overlooking the good that street ministers do renders our efforts to combat homelessness derelict and inept. Street ministers provide personal, beautiful, and humanizing presence in a crushingly dehumanizing context. They open a door to a reality where hope transcends the radical suffering of the present. As I walked the streets of Seattle with Rick and Ben, I frequently saw the unhoused people they hang out with come alive with the real joy that arises from being in relationship with them.

Building relationships with people who are homeless, however, also poses risks. Many people who are homeless have painful wounds stemming from broken relationships. They also walk a fine line between life and death. Another perceived betrayal, or broken relationship, is enough to push someone off that line. Smokey, another homeless individual in Seattle I got to know, wrote this on Facebook not long after River's husband died: "I told myself that I'd end tonight by either going to a psych ward or putting a bullet in my head. Fuck life. The next friend who betrays me may very well get killed."

Christianity, we must remember, is more than a leap into the absurd; it is also an opening of the heart wide open.[33] As a result, Christianity may require emotional labor that can be exceptionally risky for people under tremendous distress. Asking someone to open his heart, therefore, or putting a chink in the invisible armor he develops to protect himself, as Ben told me is a possible effect of giving someone a prophecy about how he is loved by God, might cause unexpected harm. The summons to become open to love, be it numinous or human, is a solemn risk when the infrastructure needed to support, protect, and nourish that open heart has collapsed. Sigmund Freud's work in *Civilization and Its Discontents* is instructive when he writes that, of all the techniques humans have created for living in the world, nothing leaves one so defenseless against suffering as love.[34]

It is necessary to ask whether a housed Christian's spiritual love for people who are homeless, as we have come to understand that love in the context of my account of street ministry, does more harm than good. Given the risks associated with their love, should housed Christians continue loving people who are homeless? Indeed, is their love actually loving? I do not think Christians should despair the power of love and stop loving people who are homeless. What I think they must continue to do, however, is reflect on what it takes to love someone who is homeless more lovingly. I will conclude this chapter by proposing one suggestion.

For a housed Christian's love toward someone who is homeless to be more loving, it should be able to go on living in the life of the Homeless Other. Love should be able to become more fully alive in the unhoused, in other words, not the housed. That is the difference a housed Christian's love for a person who is homeless must make if it is to become more loving.

This means two things. First, it means that a housed Christian's love for people who are homeless is not fully loving if it exists only in themselves: in the way unhoused persons motivate their relationship with God, for example, or teach them how to become better Christians. If a housed Christian's love cannot become more alive in people who are homeless, then perhaps it is possession and not love. For "love," as Thomas Merton counseled us, "can only be kept by being given away."[35]

If I am right, then I have raised another question. How might a housed Christian's love become more alive in people who are homeless? This is a very difficult question; it is one we should spend more time debating. One answer, however, it seems to me, is without question. To answer it, I turn to the French theologian Simone Weil.

"To be rooted," Weil wrote, "is perhaps the most needed and least recognized need of the human soul." "A human being has roots," she continued, "by virtue of his real, active, and natural participation in the life of a community."[36] Like most Christian theologians, Weil considered love—for God, others, and oneself—to be a paramount challenge that Christians face. In her most popular book, *Waiting for God*, Weil suggests that love is a breath of the human soul and that a soul that goes without love for an extended period of time will likely stop breathing and die.[37] In *The Need for Roots*, however, which is quoted at the beginning of this paragraph, Weil suggests that human love, and this breathing, are contingent upon concrete social conditions: on roots. Without these conditions, love is not fully realizable. Love, we might say, therefore, grows on roots.

By definition, homelessness is a condition of uprootedness. In conditions of uprootedness, as I have suggested in this chapter, the practice of Christian love may be hazardous. To love someone who is homeless lovingly, then, means helping her establish roots. That is what it will take for a housed Christian's spiritual love to be able to go on living in the life of the Homeless Other.

The roots people who are homeless need to establish are many. Not the least among them are housing, adequate health care, and fair-paying jobs. In my view, these roots cannot be dug without the ink of federal legislation. What we need today, therefore, are the kinds of constitutional guarantees that Franklin D. Roosevelt proposed in his State of the Union address in 1944 and that Dr. Martin Luther King Jr. was struggling to achieve in the Poor People's Campaign when he was assassinated: that is, an "economic bill of rights." That will not happen without first developing the political will for it among the public.

For their love to become more loving, housed Christians who provide spiritual care to people who are homeless should leave their houses and accompany people who are homeless to the public spaces where they can generate the political will that is needed to help people establish roots. We must do more than accompany people in their conditions of homelessness, then, and we must do more than accompany people out of homelessness and into housing. We must also help change the conditions that lead to homelessness in the first place: a profound lack of roots. If we won't do this, our love may cause more harm than we intend. If we don't do this, we may have to confess that people who are homeless are little more to us than spiritual capital; little more than suffering bodies that we use to construct our theologies and carry us to heaven. If we are to wound with love, or be wounded by love, may we be led into the dirt.

Notes

1. River's telling of the story was varied and, at times, contradictory. That makes sense given the trauma of her experience. I have tried to render an account that is faithful to her experience.
2. Dorothee Sölle, *Suffering* (Philadelphia: Fortress, 1984), 8.
3. Bob Smietana, "Safe Haven," *Covenant Companion*, January 2009, 6–9.
4. Ibid., 23.
5. See Operation Nightwatch, "Ronnie," Vimeo video, 3:59, October 17, 2013, accessed November 29, 2020, www.vimeo.com/77176392.
6. Craig Rennebohm with David Paul, *Souls in the Hands of a Tender God: Stories of the Search for Home and Healing* (Boston: Beacon, 2008), 1.
7. Ron Ruthruff, *The Least of These: Lessons Learned from Kids on the Street* (Birmingham, Ala.: New Hope, 2010).
8. This stems from the parable of the sheep and goats in Matthew 25.
9. The motif is an allusion to Song of Songs 2:5 and Isaiah 49:2.
10. Origen, *Origen* (New York: Paulist Press, 1979), xi.
11. Julian of Norwich, *Showings* (Mahwah, N.J.: Paulist Press, 1978), 128–30.
12. See Wendy Farley, *Tragic Vision and Divine Compassion* (Louisville, Ky.: Westminster John Knox Press, 1990).
13. See John Swinton, *Raging with Compassion* (Grand Rapids, Mich.: Eerdmans, 2007).

14. Sölle, *Suffering*, 17.

15. Ibid., 18.

16. Ibid.

17. Ibid., 26.

18. Ibid., 125.

19. Ibid., 145.

20. Sölle, *Theology for Skeptics* (Minneapolis: Fortress, 1992), 66.

21. Gustavo Gutiérrez, *We Drink from Our Own Wells* (Maryknoll, N.Y.: Orbis, 2003), 36.

22. Ibid., 38.

23. Ibid., 112.

24. Christian Smith, "Why Christianity Works," *Sociology of Religion* 68, no. 2 (Summer 2007): 167. In the article, Smith addresses other needs as well.

25. By foregrounding the emotional reasons Christianity works, Smith is trying to complement the social-structural reasons it does.

26. Matthew Engelke, *A Problem of Presence: Beyond Scripture in an African Church* (Berkeley: University of California Press, 2007), 78.

27. Ibid., 175.

28. Tanya Lurhmann, *When God Talks Back* (New York: Alfred A. Knopf, 2012), 132.

29. See Charles Taylor, *A Secular Age* (Cambridge, Mass.: Harvard University Press, 2007), 563.

30. Dorothy Day, "The Mystery of the Poor," *Catholic Worker*, April 2, 1964. Again, this is an allusion to the parable of the sheep and the goats in Matthew 25.

31. For a brilliant historical and ethnographic study on how we came to care for the mentally unwell on our streets, see Luhrmann, "Down and Out in Chicago," *Raritan* (Winter 2010): 140–66.

32. David Snow and Leon Anderson, *Down on Their Luck* (Berkeley: University of California, 1993), 230.

33. I thank Jim Spickard for this insight, which came by way of a conversation we had.

34. Sigmund Freud, *Civilization and Its Discontents* (New York: W. W. Norton, 2010).

35. Thomas Merton, *No Man Is an Island* (Boston: Shambala), 1.

36. Simone Weil, *The Need for Roots* (New York: G. P. Putnam's Sons, 1952).

37. Weil, *Waiting for God* (New York: Harper Perennial Modern Classics, 2009), 70.

Making Spirits Whole

Homeless Ministries as a Tool for Integral Development

María Teresa Dávila

Introduction

Do you think God will let me into heaven?
I do not know if I will make it in.
My life . . . I've done some pretty bad things, and I don't know if God
   will take me.
Do you think there is room for me in heaven?
If it is too crowded it doesn't matter.
I can sleep in a corner on the floor as long as it is in heaven.
It doesn't matter.
After all, I'm used to sleeping in corners on the floor.
That wouldn't bother me at all.

These words have haunted me for the past four years. They come from one of the participants (let's call him John) of an outdoor ministry called Chaplains on the Way.[1] He said them when we were saying our goodbyes after sharing in the Way of the Cross, a service we hold every year during Holy Week. At each of the stations different members of the community, both housed and unhoused, share from their heart and soul reflections prompted by the readings and reflection of that station.

We use the text and images from Pope Francis's Way of the Cross celebrated with Eastern churches in 2013.[2] At the eleventh station, "Jesus is Nailed to the Cross," John noticed the image of the soldiers nailing Jesus, ushering in his death. At that moment John felt moved to share with the group how he was a veteran and had, at the order of his superiors, carried out missions that meant killing other people. His grief and guilt over this part of his own story was profound. Whether he had expressed this much grief and guilt before I do not know. But that day John brought up the fact that Jesus on the Cross forgave those whose job at that moment was to kill him, and he began wondering whether or not he would be forgiven for following unjust orders, too.

At that moment I was struck by the spiritual pain that haunted John from his past life experiences. Unable to tell his age, I did not know whether these events had occurred recently or decades ago. This didn't seem to matter. His inability to forgive himself was palpable, as was his desire for some sort of reconciliation with God, however he was defining it at that moment. At a different level I wondered whether his spiritual pain was impinging on his ability to obtain housing. To what extent did he feel that his current situation was a proper punishment for his past life errors? Did he feel his homelessness was atoning for the hurt he had done to others in the past, as so many in homeless ministries share? Can we quantify the effect that homeless ministries have in connecting people with the spiritual healing they seek and how this might relate to gaining stable housing?

The soul work of homeless ministries—attending to the spiritual needs of the unhoused and the housing insecure—must be part of integral human development.[3] According to Catholic Relief Services, "Integral Human Development promotes the good of every person and the whole person: it is cultural, political, social, and spiritual."[4] Efforts to address the material needs of the unhoused, of providing adequate shelter, the sense of permanency and routine that are key to feeling safe and thriving as persons and communities, must go hand in hand with attending to the deep spiritual wounds, both personal and systemic, that accompany the precarious life of homelessness and housing insecurity. Finally, attending to the soul work of homeless ministries challenges and reconceptualizes the Christian understanding of the spiritual works of mercy as they relate to and inform our understanding of the corporal works of mercy in homelessness work and advocacy.[5]

For a really diverse set of reasons, the unhoused or housing-insecure live in a cloud of guilt, shame, feelings of worthlessness, feeling that they have fallen short of the "ideal life," the life that they and their loved ones had hoped would be true, the life that would keep them and their loved ones safe and together. Often their version of themselves does not measure up to their particular ideas of what it means to be a human being, continually revisiting their choices and consequences like an eternal reel of a very tragic movie.

It is in this context that programs such as outdoor or street ministries attempt to bring the healing of forgiveness and reconciliation, the hope that comes from accompaniment and shared prayer and meals, the knowledge of

God's unconditional and solidary love with broken and wounded souls. The soul work of homeless ministries is a key element to bringing wholeness where a combination of life circumstances, choices, and systemic forces has wrought economic and social uncertainty and psychic and spiritual harm, resulting in shame and a lack of self-worth.

A proposal that takes homeless ministries seriously for the task of integral human development must also consider systemic challenges impacting a person's or a community's ability to acquire or access adequate housing. Migration because of war, economic displacement, persecution because of religious, gender, or sexual identity, environmental threats to one's livelihood and land, poor job opportunities combined with wages too low to obtain or sustain housing are some of the systemic elements that impact one's chances at stable and permanent housing. As such, attending to the spiritual needs of those impacted by these forces demands overcoming a deep sense of personal and social dislocation, the sense that all humanity has abandoned one's need for integrity and well-being. It requires breaking through and identifying the damaging political, cultural, and religious rhetoric that targets the unemployed and underemployed, migrants and refugees, the disabled, veterans, and the socially and economically dislocated as enemies, disposable, and rejected.

Finally, a proposal for integral development that takes the spiritual integrity of the unhoused seriously must deal with housing itself. We have learned from Housing First initiatives and advocacy that any attempt at integrity must strive to work in tandem with efforts at providing stable and safe housing conditions for all.[6] Removing or reducing the precariousness that imposes insecurity, fear, and physical vulnerabilities on the unhoused must be an ongoing goal of those who work in homeless ministries. But I would argue that working toward spiritual integrity, while intimately related to being stably housed, must be its own goal, and certainly a work of the church as it strives for integral human development.

Integral Human Development and Homelessness in Catholic Social Teaching

The concept of integral human development in Catholic social teaching provides a view of the material well-being of persons and communities that is intimately related to their spiritual, educational, cultural, mental/intellectual, and social well-being. These factors are ultimately all connected. This view is grounded on the Catholic vision of human dignity, an anthropology centered on the person in community as created by and in God, with rights and dignities that no historical or human condition—imprisonment, homelessness, war, sickness, disability, employment or socioeconomic status—can alter. Human dignity in Catholic social teaching extends beyond a mere floor of basic material and political rights for human survival. It promotes the integrity of the person and her right to flourish economically, culturally, politically, and socially.

As the decolonizing struggles of the first half of the twentieth century were winding down, Catholic social teaching faced the realities of countless populations impoverished by colonial subjugation and the unjust dynamics of global economic exchange seeking to attain economic security and success for their populations.[7] With the World Bank, the International Monetary Fund, and other international trade and finance organization seeking to promote economic development through their own definitions and programs for success, the Catholic Church saw the need to articulate a vision for development that took into consideration the fullness of its vision of the human person. Grounded on a vision of human dignity that promotes the health and flourishing of the whole person, it proposed that development must be measured in dimensions that go beyond material and economic progress.[8]

The concept of integral human development is further developed under the papacy of John Paul II, whose social teaching straddled the end of Soviet communist economies and their transition to liberal capitalist economies. Recalling Paul VI's redefinition of development as a process that "cannot be limited to mere economic growth," the 1987 encyclical *Sollicitudo Rei Socialis* adds that this is a vision that can be shared by all people of good will:

> In this pursuit of integral human development we can also do much with the members of other religions. Collaboration in the development of the whole person and of every human being is in fact a duty of all towards all, and must be shared by the four parts of the world.[9]

For Benedict XVI, integral human development

> requires a transcendent vision of the person, it needs God: without him development is either denied, or entrusted exclusively to man [sic] who falls into the trap of thinking he can bring about his own salvation, and ends up promoting a dehumanized form of development.[10]

The two central Catholic agencies in charge of international aid and development—Caritas and Catholic Relief Services—further develop this concept for their own operations on the ground in cooperation with other development agencies and nongovernmental organizations.[11] Catholic social teaching promotes integral human development as a form of development that acknowledges the transcendental nature of the person: one's relationship with and directionality toward God. At a practical level this transcendental component must be balanced with a diversity of religious traditions among the different populations in which these organizations operate, including those that have no religious affiliation or practice. To this extent the work of these agencies echoes Martha Nussbaum's development of the *capabilities approach*, which includes dimensions such as human participation and a sense of belonging, the exercise of imagination and engagement of emotions, play, and other nonmaterial dimensions as crucial for the development of persons, communities, and nations.[12]

For Catholic social teaching, including the transcendental or spiritual life of a person as part of an effective approach to the development of the whole person is an attempt to be authentic to the truth of the fullness of the person as created by God. In development circles attention to the spiritual and religious life of persons and communities recognizes how religious life can support the economic development and social integration of the poor, providing a sense of belonging, stability, forgiveness, resilience, and other positive markers that greatly impact the material prospects of persons and communities.

Integral development challenges us to view the *corporal works of mercy* (feeding the hungry, visiting the sick and imprisoned, welcoming the stranger, burying the dead), but especially economic development and systemic transformation as intimately connected to the *spiritual works of mercy* (forgiveness, fraternal correction, prayer and liturgy). It points to the goal of attending to the wholeness of the person, seeing sustained relationships with God and others as key elements of personal and communal wholeness. For Catholic Relief Services, for example, integral human development "suggests a state of personal well-being in the context of just and peaceful relationships and a thriving environment."[13]

It is within this vision of integral human development that Catholic social teaching engages the question of the concrete material necessity of housing and shelter for so many of the world's unhoused. In the United States specifically, the United States Conference of Catholic Bishops engaged this question directly in their 1975 document *The Right to a Decent Home: A Pastoral Response to the Crisis on Housing*.[14] As a response to Paul VI's statement that authentic development demands a "transition from less than human conditions to truly human ones,"[15] this pastoral statement clearly described the housing problem prevalent in the United States as an inhuman situation, especially challenging for the integrity of the family. More specifically, it echoes the Catholic understanding of housing and shelter as a human right.[16]

The 1987 document from the Pontifical Commission on Justice and Peace further states that the collective teaching of the church on homelessness considers it to be a matter of structural justice:

Far from being a matter of simple lack or deprivation, to be homeless means to suffer from the deprivation or lack of something which is due. This, consequently, constitutes an injustice. Any ethical consideration of the housing problem must take this as its point of departure.[17]

Housing, then, is not considered a market commodity subject to speculation and price fluctuation in pursuit of the highest profit. Housing is a *social good*— that is, "'a house is much more than a roof over one's head.' It is 'a place where a person creates and lives out his or her life.'"[18] As such it is a human right that ought to be guaranteed for all, over and above the goals of profit maximization and privatization of land and real estate enterprise. In affirming this, the church manifestly takes the side of the poor and advocates for policymaking that attends to housing needs, placing it as essential a need for human flourishing as part of a person's religious and spiritual life.

For Catholic social teaching adequate shelter is essential for spiritual health. These two dimensions must be seen together: the health and flourishing of the human spirit is intimately tied to the well-being and flourishing of an individual's material dimensions. Lack of shelter results in affronts to the spirit, as shelter is considered key to human dignity. Spiritual integrity depends on a person's ability to secure the material goods basic to sustaining life, family, community, and participation in social and political structures. As we will see, however, it is important to consider the ways these two dimensions of human development—the material and the spiritual—have been divorced from one another, resulting in the overspiritualization of homeless ministries and the opposite exclusive focus on providing shelter alone as avenues to restore wholeness to homeless and housing-insecure populations. The concept of integral development pushes us to be watchful of these tendencies as part of our call to love our neighbor.

The Works of Mercy as a Key Christian Feature for Bringing Wholeness to the Unhoused

While integral development is about addressing injustices and advancing the systems responsible for a thriving integral human ecology, the corporal and spiritual works of mercy are mainly prescriptions addressing the path of discipleship for Christ's followers. While these two are not interchangeable concepts, they are deeply interrelated. The works of mercy and integral development both depend on the sense of the inherent worth and dignity of the recipient or participant. In the case of integral development, Catholic social teaching tries to develop an understanding of what is materially, culturally, and spiritually owed each person and communities of persons because of their inherent dignity as bearers of the image of God.

Created in the image and likeness of God (Gn 1:26–31), each person is born with inherent dignity regardless of state in life, mental capacities or other health status, maturity or age, legal status or criminal conviction. As the central concept of Catholic social teaching, human dignity confronts all social, economic, and political dynamics that make the full dignity of the person dependent on human categories, classifications, or processes. In the case of persons experiencing homelessness, they often express feeling that they have lost their dignity because of being excluded from their families, having a prior criminal conviction, making bad choices with respect to substance abuse, or being disabled or mentally ill. Within this framework, which follows the logic of free-market capitalism and a person's worth depending on their economic productivity and ability to consume, the homeless often see their lack of housing or shelter as a deserved consequence of the loss of their human dignity. On this point it is appropriate to bring in a lengthy quote from John Paul II in which the source and depth of human dignity and its inviolability are solidly and definitively expressed as the central element of Catholic social teaching.

> From this point forward it will be necessary to keep in mind that the main thread and, in a certain sense, the guiding principle of Pope Leo XIII's Encyclical, and of all of the Church's social doctrine, is a *correct view of the human person* and of his [sic] unique value, inasmuch as "man . . . is the only creature on earth which God willed for itself." God has imprinted his own image and likeness on man (Gn 1:26), conferring upon him an incomparable dignity, as the Encyclical frequently insists. In effect, beyond the rights which man acquires by his own work, there exist rights which do not correspond to any work he performs, but which flow from his essential dignity as a person.[19]

The requirements for upholding human dignity in Catholic social teaching and the corporal and spiritual works of mercy witness to two different lines of ethical reflection in the Christian tradition. The first is dedicated to exploring political, economic, and sociocultural ways in which our structures and practices nourish or damage human dignity. The second seeks to offer immediate succor to the needs of others because of Jesus's radical identification with them (Mt 25:31–46). These two sets of ethical principles are interrelated in that they both refer to what is owed a person strictly by virtue of his being an echo or reflection of the divine in history. The corporal and spiritual works of mercy are a requirement of discipleship because of who Christ is—both one who spends his ministry performing these works indiscriminately but also who ultimately identifies with those who stand in need of the works of mercy, as in Matthew 25:31–46.[20] Both integral human development and the works of mercy are requirements for building the Beloved Community.

Homeless ministries are often specifically related to the corporal works of mercy. With their emphasis on succoring the needy in the material dimensions of everyday sustenance, including hospitality, the corporal works of mercy offer a ready-made checklist for ministering to the homeless at the local church or parish level. Feeding the hungry, giving drink to the thirsty, clothing the naked, welcoming the stranger and sheltering the homeless, visiting the sick and imprisoned, and burying the dead is a list that appears in various forms throughout the Bible. It was a catalogue of good works with which Jesus's listener in Matthew 25 would be familiar. But in this particular passage the list gets an unexpected twist as Jesus describes how it is he ("The Son of Man") who is directly identified with the hungry, the homeless, and the imprisoned. Listeners at the time might have gone as far as relating the poor and hungry with angels or other emissaries of God in disguise. But Jesus's radical identification with the poor in Matthew 25 and relating these good works to one's possibility of being saved makes the corporal works of mercy a requirement of Christian discipleship, not the optional heroic acts of a moral superhero.

The spiritual works of mercy do not appear in any particular list in scripture, but are found throughout the Hebrew Bible and the New Testament.[21] They center on works that offer wholeness to the soul of our neighbor in need. To admonish the sinner, instruct the ignorant, counsel the doubtful, bear wrongs patiently, forgive offenses willingly, comfort the afflicted, and pray for the living and the dead are practices meant to heal the soul and bring persons closer to God. But they are not without controversy. The first three involve entering the religious journey and narrative of others in ways that presume that one has the wisdom, training, and ecclesial authority to enact judgment as to another's interior practices and state before God.[22] For many, the performance of these very spiritual works of mercy by the untrained or unprepared has sometimes been part of what has driven them away from the support networks of spiritual or church communities essential for stabilization and support. This does not mean that they ought to be done away with completely. Rather, rethinking and redefining these spiritual works of mercy might in fact provide tools that make homeless ministries more targeted toward restoring wholeness and integrity to those it encounters, rather than promoting further judgment, shame, and alienation.

Redefining the spiritual works of mercy as the *soul work* of homeless ministries might look something like this:

Instruction and counsel are turned into fostering opportunities for
   self-reflection and reviewing one's story and journey in a process of
   accompanying each other in the task of learning from our past and
   perhaps our shared vulnerabilities and shared blessings toward
   wholeness in the future;

Admonishing sinners and forgiving offenses could be construed as
   communicating radical welcome, forgiveness, and reconciliation,
   the source of which is God's ever-flowing mercy;

Comforting the afflicted, without judgment;

Offering liturgical and informal opportunities for prayer, mourning,
   and celebration (we make sure that our Way of the Cross liturgy
   includes a station for the Resurrection to remind those gathered
   that we are walking with Jesus toward wholeness from that which
   wounds us and deals unjust death); and

Patience reimagined as ensuring the constancy and continuity of the
   programming needed to attend to the spiritual integrity of the
   unhoused.

The category of integral human development warns us against the overspiritualization of our work with the homeless, even when we acknowledge that religious belonging and spiritual health are essential to the process of obtaining
and sustaining adequate shelter. To emphasize either set of works of mercy at
the expense of the other is reducing the person to categories that do not fully
represent the fullness of their God-given human dignity. Of course, no one
homeless ministry can attend to all dimensions well. Each group must determine its charisms and resources in order to effectively address some of the needs
present in the populations it wishes to serve. My main goal is to present these
categories as interconnected in significant ways such that discernment of how
best to attend the needs of homeless and housing-insecure populations takes the
full spectrum of human development into serious consideration, orienting diverse homeless ministries to work as networks of care and accompaniment for
the full flourishing of persons, rather than individual service providers.

The Soul Work of Homeless Ministries

The soul work of homeless ministries seeks to address the shame, guilt, death,
hope, joy, and faith of the unhoused regardless of their status or source of their
condition. Time is spent, for example, grieving the dead in the community of
the unhoused, something that has become especially urgent and poignant
amidst the drug epidemic facing so many communities in the U.S. Grieving in

community, naming the dead, praying novenas—even among those in the un-housed community who are not Catholic, praying rosaries for the infirmed and the deceased, are all acts that resist the dominant feeling that their lives have zero worth before the eyes of a judging God. Restoring worth through practices of accompaniment aids in restoring hope, and, while not guaranteeing a roof or a physical house, it begins to put in place something close to a spiritual home.

For seven years (2011–18) I taught a course on homeless ministries to sem-inary students in the Boston area. The course placed the students in im-mersion experiences in different settings in the greater New England area (as some students commuted from as far north as Vermont and as far south as Connecticut). Settings included day centers, service agencies with essen-tial needs provided but no shelter or housing aid, overnight shelters, health clinics, women's spaces, recovery houses, trauma centers, worship and prayer settings both indoors and outdoors, long-term housing facilities, and places just for meals. About half of these placements were related to partic-ular religious ministries, while the other half were secular in nature. None of them were government-sponsored.

Students would spend about seven to ten hours at their placement on a weekly basis. We would then meet every two weeks for a two-hour gathering with prayer, discussion, and reflection. Each two-hour session would revolve around a key question such as, What surprised you this week? Can you share one story from the folks you have met? How effective do you think your place-ment is at what it does? What would be one thing you would change about your placement? Because the course was part of the Border Crossing program at my seminary, students were supposed to relate their experience to their over-all seminary education. Further questions included: Which course so far pre-pared you best for the challenges of your placement? How can seminary education take the experiences of your placement's population more seriously in its curriculum? What additional knowledge do you feel you need in order to address the challenges of this placement? Students also had to do a final written and oral reflection on their experience. The written piece placed their experience in the context of their seminary education. The oral piece asked them to communicate their immersion experience to a population that other-wise would not get to know about homelessness or their particular placement if it weren't for listening to their presentation.

A number of placements each year were directly related to homeless min-istries. The two that most frequently hosted our students as part of their work are Chaplains on the Way in Waltham, Massachusetts, and Common Cathe-dral in downtown Boston.[23] Though these are very different ministries that attend to the soul work of homeless ministries, they share some similarities and challenges. Common Cathedral is a large and broad ministry, offering a variety of programming during the week, with a Sunday outdoor communion service held at the Boston Common rain, shine, or snow. It also offers a network of warming centers through the churches of the downtown Boston area, an art program, and city outreach. Sunday communion services at Common Cathedral include a lunch immediately after as well as pastoral counseling for those who seek it.[24] This rather large operation counts on a number of fulltime pastors as well as interns from the different area seminaries who are doing their required experiential learning at Common Cathedral.

Chaplains on the Way defines itself as a ministry of accompaniment. Its main objective is to offer spiritual companionship to those who seek it on the streets in and around the city of Waltham (about fifteen miles from downtown Boston). It is a much smaller operation, working in conjunction with the Waltham Day Center and other area services for the unhoused. Its leadership can be found at various times during the day walking the streets of Waltham, inviting folks to coffee, lunch, or a prayer service. Religious services are designed around the interests and needs of the community and include a meditative labyrinth walk, prayer services during the week, and special services during the seasons of Lent, Holy Week, Advent, and Christmas. The leadership and other volunteers take their ministry of accompaniment quite seriously and visit members of the community in the hospital, try to find rides for them for doctors and other important appointments, and accompany them at court hearings and housing court. While Common Cathedral's religious services tend to follow the Episcopalian tradition, Chaplains on the Way includes a variety of rituals that draw from many spiritual traditions with careful attentiveness to the community members' needs.

A key identifier of both settings—as well as most outdoor and street ministries—is their open and radical welcome. As opposed to many ministries offering shelter and meals indoors, Common Cathedral and Chaplains on the Way have no restrictions on who is able to show up and be welcome at their services. People need not belong to any religious tradition in particular. But most importantly people need not be sober, healthy, employed, seeking housing, or without criminal record. Their services and accompaniment are open to all. This is both part of their gift and a significant challenge. On more than one occasion I had to rearrange the schedule and placements for students who were triggered by the presence of former convicts accused of violent or sexual crimes, or who could not be around folks who were not sober. As part of the course I administered a personal safety checklist for students to determine their level of vulnerability and triggering around the issues most likely to arise from being present and accompanying unhoused and housing vulnerable folk in diverse service settings.

Both settings offer something many unhoused—especially the chronically unhoused—are desperately seeking: a place where their human dignity is upheld regardless of their condition. In particular, participants in these services seek to have that part of their person that is in relationship with God and others acknowledged and honored. For many, judgment, exclusion, and alienation are the most common reactions they receive when trying to access the spiritual communities of support to which they previously belonged. Others might not have had a faith community before becoming unhoused and have come to appreciate the peace and acceptance they receive at these particular ministries. The communal bonds formed during these services are real and deep. And, sadly, they are there for each other when it is their turn to mourn their dead because of either an overdose, or exposure, or violence, or an illness that went untreated. These are spaces where they get to ask crucial questions about what is most important in their lives without feeling judged for their state in life. In these kinds of ministries the unhoused can freely express their faith concerns and enter into community and rituals that are supportive. This does not always lead to them moving forward to finding sustainable permanent housing, but knowing that they are now part of a community of faith positively impacts their mental health and their ability to confront other dimensions of their life that need work and transformation. Most importantly, it is a community to which they can return again and again if they experience ongoing failure or setbacks, whether or not as a result of their own doing. These communities provide avenues for wholeness that the participants would otherwise not have available to them.

Ministering to these communities brings gifts and challenges unique to homeless ministries that are not there in other kinds of spiritual communities. It is often hard to see someone take part in the rituals, liturgies, and other programming one makes available on an ongoing basis and have him suddenly disappear. The connections one makes to participants and members of the community run as deep as within a housed faith community. And yet lives are more transient, with unexpected turns that mean that someone may consistently show up for weeks only to disappear without a trace. The pain of these mysterious losses is real for both the ministerial staff and the other participants who come to see their fellow parishioners as part of a close-knit family.

We work carefully around questions of boundaries, which are important for any community of faith, but which gain a different tonality around issues of housing and homelessness, especially when radical welcome and inclusion might bring participants in in a variety of states of sobriety. Our work, prayers, and hopes are for wholeness for all participants, and this is something that is not guaranteed, as it is often out of our and the participants' control. We rejoice when participants bring their stories of success, or when a space has been created that allows enough room for great diversity or for folks to open up about their experiences, especially around those who are newly unhoused and might be feeling the shame and stigma of their circumstances for the first time. Likewise, we also share in the pain expressed by community members who have lost a loved one (and might not even get to attend their loved one's funeral because of their current situation), end a relationship that is toxic for them, or see their hopes for housing dashed by diverse systemic forces. Building a community where the unhoused and housing-vulnerable can live out some of their most fundamental questions and journeys contributes to feelings of wholeness and integrity, even if briefly, but hopefully in ways that will contribute to their greater material as well as spiritual stability.

The spiritual works of mercy adapted to the situation of homelessness encounter the persons where they are, not judging them for their condition or their journey. Echoing the Quaker saying, "The holy worth in me meets the holy worth in you," the soul work of homeless ministries sees the encounter with the other—especially the poor—as an opportunity to encounter the Holy among us. We become part of a faith community serving unhoused and housing-insecure folk because it satisfies the requirements of the works of mercy, but also because we are able to center on the goal of seeking wholeness together.

Pope Francis's theology of encounter reflects this vision of the Beloved Community—a place where people come together to worship and break bread that is cognizant of all our broken selves—but sees in this brokenness an active God seeking to make us whole once again through each other's compassionate encounter.[25] For Francis, this encounter is not the penitent journey of virtuous saints, but a requirement of human life, created to be in community through compassionate embrace of the other. It acknowledges the human need for connection, but that connection as being part of who God is, and who God is in us, as part of our being made in the image of God. In light of this requirement of encounter for the fullness of our humanity to flourish, the sustaining open and welcoming communities prepared to accompany and walk with the unhoused and housing vulnerable without exclusion become a requirement for Christian churches and communities.

Systemic Challenges: Migration, Economic Dislocation, Violence, and Other Systemic Issues Impacting Housing Security

The spiritual and corporal works of mercy are not to be interpreted as a replacement for the ongoing struggles for the systemic changes necessary to significantly impact the lives of the homeless and housing-insecure. They may be seen in relation to justice as the ongoing work necessary to ensure that justice is also a struggle for wholeness and integrity, both spiritual and material. Spiritual integrity and the soul work of homeless ministries must also seek to help the unhoused find imagery, vocabulary, and resources to name the ways that systemic problems and evils negatively impact their lives. Sharing in prayer, accompaniment, reflection, bible study, and spiritual counseling, as well as pointing out the places where they can engage their own agency, can help them overcome some, if not all, of these affronts to their spiritual dignity and identify the ways external forces impact their life outcomes.

Addiction, war and the war industrial complex, economic migration and dislocation, environmental displacement, and persecution because of gender, sexual orientation, or ethnic or religious identity are some of the systemic forces that force millions of people to be on the move every year, leaving many of them unhoused.[26] Though systemic in nature, each one of these cases is a story of human beings struggling to make the right decisions for themselves and their families.[27]

Spiritually and policy-wise, it is important to recognize the ways in which neoliberal policies and attitudes shape our ability to see these persons as impacted by forces beyond their own making. A dominant anthropology that sees the person as an individual consumer and therefore builder of his own opportunities and destinies in a free market makes the person solely responsible for his material well-being and that of his family. Neoliberal models of economic development, growth, and the good life are grounded on an anthropology opposite that presented by Catholic social teaching's integral human development. Its metrics focus strictly on a person's ability to produce and consume, to take part of economic processes, without really attending whether she has a say in the direction and focus of these processes, the political powers that regulate them, or even whether she does so freely. A neoliberal anthropology is not concerned with whether a person has the ability to enter and nourish meaningful relationships that empower her to be productive in her life, as part of communities of support, faith communities among them.[28]

Spiritually, economic systems grounded on an anthropology of consumption and domination lead to feelings of inadequacy, failing the "norm" of what it means to be a person and a responsible caretaker, ashamed of one's current condition the more removed it is from these destructive measures of being human. Theologically, the unhoused and the housing-vulnerable seek to know how God could have abandoned them so, or worst, whether God would ever forgive them for wrong choices made, choices that in many ways are impacted by the systemic forces discussed earlier.

The soul work of homeless ministries provides language and imagery to more accurately come to describe one's situation, place one's choices in the scope of systemic forces, and place others' indifference to one's condition in the scope of social sin. As they journey toward spiritual integrity the unhoused must consider their own actions balanced by a deeper understanding of social, political, and economic forces that bear down ruthlessly on so many, leaving them without options, even while they benefit the privileged few. For the community member whose quote begins this chapter, a veteran of recent wars, his own destiny is in many ways shaped by the war industrial complex. His spiritual well-being, now part of the work of a ministry of walking with and accompaniment, is shaped by a profound sense of personal guilt.[29] But in seeing himself reflected in the centurion crucifying Jesus, he gathered some imagery and language to see the military industrial complex as an ongoing and historical force of oppression, one that has been creating victims since Jesus's time, but also an evil still within reach of Christ's mercy and therefore able to be transformed through forgiveness and grace, especially that which is expressed within a welcoming and reconciling community.

In my experience with ministries to the unhoused and housing-vulnerable the question remains as to whether there are measurable material outcomes from the soul work of homeless ministries. In effect, participants in these programs receive similar material benefits to those who participate in secular or nonreligious services. Often they will receive clothing, a meal, some medical care, transportation to important appointments, and sometimes even a place to lay their heads, if not overnight, then at least temporarily during a service or gathering. Some homeless ministries bring together housing search with the spiritual services provided. Others find that linking the two really takes away from their ability to be fully present for the soul work described throughout this chapter. Sometimes being accompanied in prayer and liturgy is just the right thing someone needs to stay sober and resist a relapse or to avoid the desperation that leads to suicide. But often that is not enough. What does seem like a measurable outcome is the way in which people are encouraged and assisted in building community where they are, one where they can count on a nonjudgmental hug, coffee, and prayer or simply accompaniment. By using the metrics from integral human development, we can say with more certainty that these kinds of homeless ministries of accompaniment, prayer, and liturgy offer something concrete that provides wholeness where it is often desperately missing.

Conclusion: Housing in the Context of the Journey of the Human Spirit

Catholic social teaching is traditionally much clearer about the meaning of housing in the context of the requirements of justice and the material well-being of persons and communities than it is about its theological and spiritual import. But pronouncements on integral human development clearly state that spiritual integrity is a demand of justice. I contend here that it is also a demand of discipleship as an expression of the spiritual works of mercy, but these need to be refashioned and inculturated to the context of unhoused persons and communities.

The spiritual integrity of the unhoused must also be linked to the spiritual integrity of those of us who are housed as we come to understand shared spiritual and material vulnerabilities, especially in the face of systemic ills such as war, environmental and economic displacement, and persecution of any kind. Stories shared as we build relationships of mutuality foster an environment where the housed come to see the unhoused as having particular worth before God and being full of dignity. To return to the narrative at the beginning of this chapter, the imagery of the Way of the Cross provides rich vocabulary with which both the housed and the unhoused can relate, and through which we can access deep narratives of unconditional love and profound forgiveness from God. It also places personal suffering in the context of a web of shared vulnerabilities. The imagery may not work for everyone, as one really cannot speak of one kind of spiritual life or journey, but, rather, of spiritua*lities* and *journeys*. Through nonjudgmental ongoing accompaniment different forms of ministry learn how best to engage the spiritual life of the particular groups of people they tend to.

By lifting up the spiritual integrity and worth of the unhoused, homeless ministries serve as a way to dismantle the neoliberal anthropology that is soul-crushing for all, but especially for those who feel doubly judged for failing to live up to a model of being human grounded on one's potential or ability to participate in the market as producer, but mainly, as consumer. By providing spiritual accompaniment and being with the unhoused the soul work of homeless ministries serves integral human development by countering deep-seated narratives of shame and replacing them with a renewed sense of sacred worth to all members of the community.

Notes

1. Consult the website of Chaplains on the Way for an overview of its mission, vision, and history, accessed November 29, 2020, www.chaplainsontheway.us.

2. Office for the Liturgical Celebrations of the Supreme Pontiff, *Way of the Cross at the Colosseum: Stations of the Cross Led by the Holy Father Pope Francis* (Vatican City: Libreria Editrice Vaticana, 2013).

3. The term "integral human development" takes shape over time in the Catholic social teaching tradition. In 1967, Pope Paul VI pronounced the first

iteration of such a concept: "The development we speak of here cannot be restricted to economic growth alone. To be authentic it must be well rounded; it must foster the development of every man[sic] and of the *whole* man" (emphasis mine); Paul VI, *Populorum Progressio: Encyclical on the Development of Peoples* (Vatican City: March 26, 1967), no. 14.

4. Catholic Relief Services, *A User's Guide to Integral Human Development (IHD): Practical Guidance for CRS Staff and Partners* (Baltimore, Md.: Catholic Relief Services, 2008), 2.

5. The spiritual works of mercy (counseling the doubtful, instructing the ignorant, admonishing the sinner, comforting the sorrowful, forgiving injuries, bearing wrongs patiently, praying for the living and the dead) complement the corporal works of mercy (feed the hungry, give drink to the thirsty, shelter the homeless, visit the sick, visit the prisoners, bury the dead, give alms to the poor) in the Roman Catholic tradition. See the key primer on these principles of discipleship: James Keenan, S.J., *The Works of Mercy: The Heart of Catholicism*, 3rd ed. (Lanham, Md.: Rowman and Littlefield, 2017).

6. See, for example, Deborah Padgett, Victoria Stanhope, Ben F. Henwood, and Ana Stefancic, "Substance Use Outcomes Among Homeless Clients with Serious Mental Illness: Comparing Housing First with Treatment First Programs," *Community Mental Health Journal* 42, no. 2 (April 2011): 227–32; and Susan E. Collins, Daniel K Malone, Seema L Clifasefi, Joshua A. Ginzler, Michelle D. Garner, Bonnie Burlingham, Heather S. Lonczak, Elizabeth A. Dana, Megan Kirouac, Kenneth Tanzer, William G. Hobson, G. Alan Marlatt, and Mary E. Larimer, "Project-Based Housing First for Chronically Homeless Individuals with Alcohol Problems: Within-Subjects Analyses of 2-year Alcohol Trajectories," *American Journal of Public Health* 102, no. 3 (March 2012): 511–19. However, this and other literature on the subject add the caveat that more data is needed about how Housing First initiatives benefit homeless populations with mental illness and diverse addictions before instituting broad policy prescriptions to put such initiatives in place.

7. Paul VI, *Populorum Progressio*, nos. 7, 52, 63.

8. Ibid., Section I, "Man's Complete Development." Number 13 in particular speaks to this anthropological commitment and duty of the church: "Sharing the noblest aspirations of men [sic] and suffering when she sees these aspirations not satisfied, she wishes to help them attain their full realization. So she offers man her distinctive contribution: a global perspective on man and human realities."

9. John Paul II, *Sollicitudo Rei Socialis: Encyclical on the Twentieth Anniversary of Populorum Progressio* (Vatican City: December 30, 1987, no. 32.

10. Benedict XVI, *Caritas in Veritate: Encyclical on Integral Human Development in Charity and Truth* (Vatican City: June 29, 2009), no. 11.

11. Consult, for example, Duncan MacGregor MacLaren, "A Hermeneutic of Integral Human Development: Bridging the Gap between Magisterial Theory and Catholic Agency Praxis" (Ph.D. diss., University of Glasgow, 2019); and Catholic Relief Services, *User's Guide to Integral Human Development.*

12. See Martha Nussbaum, *Creating Capabilities: The Human Development Approach* (Cambridge, Mass.: Harvard University Press, 2011).

13. Catholic Relief Services, *User's Guide to Integral Human Development*, 2.

14. United States Conference of Catholic Bishops, *Right to a Decent Home: Response to the Crisis in Housing* (Washington, D.C.: USCCB Office of Publishing and Promotion Services, November 1975).

15. Paul VI, *Populorum Progressio*, no. 20.

16. United States Conference of Catholic Bishops, *Right to a Decent Home*, 7: "We begin with the recognition that decent housing is a right. Our Catholic tradition, eloquently expressed by Pope John XXIII and Pope Paul VI, insists that shelter is a basic right of the human person. The Second Vatican Council has said with great directness: 'There must be made available to all men [sic] everything necessary for leading a life truly human, such as food, clothing, and shelter.'"

17. Pontifical Commission on Justice and Peace, *What Have You Done to Your Homeless Brother: The Church and the Housing Problem*, (Washington, D.C.: USCCB Office of Publishing and Promotion Services, December 1987), III.2.

18. United States Conference of Catholic Bishops, *Homelessness and Housing: A Human Tragedy, A Moral Challenge* (Washington, D.C.: USCCB Office of Publishing and Promotion Services, March 1988), 5, quoting from John Paul II's introduction to *What Have You Done to Your Homeless Brother*.

19. John Paul II, *Centesimus Annus: Encyclical on the Hundredth Anniversary of Rerum Novarum* (Vatican City: May 1, 1991), 11, quoting from the Second Vatican Council, *Gaudium et Spes: Pastoral Constitution of the Church in the Modern World* (Vatican City: December 7, 1965), 24. Italics in original.

20. The corporal and spiritual acts of mercy are a recurring theme in the Bible. In the New Testament they are called forth as a sign of faithfulness in Jesus the Christ, a mark that one follows the Way of Jesus (see, for example, James 2 and 1 John 3). In Hebrew scripture they are included in the ordinances of the people of Israel after they are delivered from bondage in Egypt (for example in Deuteronomy 5, 14, and 24).

21. Consult "The 7 Spiritual & 7 Corporal Works of Mercy," unpublished document, n.d., available on the website of the Catholic Diocese of Fort Worth, accessed November 29, 2018, www.fwdioc.org.

22. Ibid., 2: "Though ideally applicable for all faithful, not everyone is considered capable or obligated to perform the first three spiritual works of mercy before they possess the proper tact, knowledge, or canonical training to do so."

23. Consult, for example, "We Are Common Cathedral," available on the website of Chaplains on the Way, accessed November 29, 2020, www.commoncathedral.org.

24. Pastoral counseling is also available at other times during the week.

25. Thomas J. Eggleston, "What Pope Francis Means by a Culture of Encounter," July 1, 2015, available on the website of *Houston Catholic Worker*, accessed November 29, 2020, www.cjd.org.

26. A current primer on push factors on migrations, statistics on sending and receiving nations, and general flows of peoples is available in this report by Eduardo

Porter and Karl Russell, "Migrants Are on the Rise Around the World, and Myths About Them Are Shaping Attitudes," *New York Times*, June 20, 2018, accessed November 29, 2020, www.nytimes.com.

27. Pope Francis, "Message of His Holiness Pope Francis for the World Day of Migrants and Refugees (2014)" (Vatican City: August 5, 2013): "Migrants and refugees are not pawns on the chessboard of humanity. They are children, women and men who leave or who are forced to leave their homes for various reasons, who share a legitimate desire for knowing and having, but above all for being more."

28. Pope Francis, *Apostolic Exhortation Evangelii Gaudium: On the Proclamation of the Gospel in Today's World* (Vatican City: November 24, 2013), ch. 2, sec. 1; and ch. 4, sec. 2.

29. Tori DeAngelis, "More PTSD among Homeless Vets," *Monitor on Psychology: American Psychological Association* 44, no. 3 (March 2013): 22.

"And I Saw Googleville Descend from Heaven"

Reading the New Jerusalem in Gentrified Latinx Communities of Silicon Valley

Roberto Mata

And I saw the holy city, the new Jerusalem, descending from heaven, from God, prepared as a bride adorned for her husband.

— REVELATION 21:2

Introduction

Mayor Liccardo's Googleville

In recent months, Mayor Sam Liccardo announced Google's plan to build its second headquarters in San Jose, California. Googleville, as the project has been wittingly dubbed, will occupy forty acres of land near Diridon Station in central San Jose and generate thousands of jobs. Beyond employment opportunities, Mayor Liccardo anticipates that Googleville will help address three major issues facing the city of San Jose: traffic, housing, and homelessness. The tech giant intends to expand the train station in central San Jose, a hub for the city's public transportation.[1] Googleville will also include multiple housing units, with a share earmarked for low-income housing. Yet, long-time residents and Latinx advocacy groups in the area have warned that Googleville will consummate the gentrification of Latinx communities by increasing already high housing prices, contribute to the exodus of long-time residents to more affordable cities in the United States, and exacerbate the problem of homelessness. Using the Latinx community's critique as a reading lens, I turn to interrogate the rhetoric of revitalization embedded within another utopian vision.

Current Interpretations of the New Jerusalem

Reminiscent of Mayor Liccardo's rhetoric of revitalization, John of Patmos introduces the New Jerusalem as the solution to the problems facing his communities in Asia Minor and the ancient world as a whole. In Revelation 21, he beholds a vision of the New Jerusalem as a city that descends from heaven to revitalize struggling communities and eradicate the various evils afflicting the ancient world. The city's size is of gargantuan proportions and stands to occupy most of the ancient Roman Empire, but it is also incredibly wealthy. According to John, the New Jerusalem is made of pure gold "clear as glass," each of its twelve gates is a pearl, and its foundations are decorated with all kinds of precious stones (Rv 21:16–21). Considering John's rhetorical portrait of the New Jerusalem, scholars have cast the New Jerusalem as a symbol of new creation, spiritual salvation, and liberation of marginalized peoples. As G. K. Beale has suggested, the New Jerusalem emerges as a new (καινός) creation for the redeemed people of God and constitutes the antithesis of Babylon and its concomitant economic corruption, idolatry, and immorality.[2] While Jürgen Roloff views the New Jerusalem as the salvation community that is now reunited with its Savior,[3] Elisabeth Schüssler-Fiorenza sees it as a symbol of liberation of the marginalized peoples who have been liberated by the Lamb.[4] While these interpretations are attentive to John's rhetoric of revitalization insofar as they highlight the positive dimensions of the New Jerusalem's descent, they hardly critique its negative implications and risk embracing the author's point of view, as well as his silencing of the inscribed marginalized voices. The implicit paradigms of interpretation account, to a large extent, for the oversight or lack of interest in liberationist readings.

Mapping John's Rhetoric of Revitalization

For Latinx communities experiencing gentrification and dealing with the eminent descent of Googleville, John's rhetorical portrait of the New Jerusalem raises critical questions. While John presents the New Jerusalem as the solution to his community's problems and as embodying the revitalization of the ancient world, one must interrogate the rhetorical intent of the author. What is the goal of John's rhetoric of revitalization? Why is this reading from the margins critical for communities dealing with gentrification? And how does his presentation of the New Jerusalem reinforce or denounce the exclusion of marginalized peoples? This reading seeks to bring these questions to the forefront, as well to discuss the role of biblical texts in struggles for social justice and liberation. Drawing from the struggles of gentrified Latinx communities, this chapter will map the double-sided nature of John's portrayal of the New Jerusalem. In my view, the heavenly city may be seen as a gentrifying project that operates on a type of rhetoric of revitalization and its concomitant contradiction. On the one hand, like Googleville, the city embodies the hopes for liberation, renewal, and justice for the people of God. On the other, the New Jerusalem will gentrify the ancient world insofar as it displaced the "old creation," becomes an exclusive and patrolled space, and brings in a new cadre of people who stand to replace those deemed unfit to inhabit the city.

Transgressing the Paradigm of Biblical Studies

Eurocentric Paradigms

A reading that takes seriously societal concerns such as gentrification and homelessness and uses them as lenses to interpret biblical texts must transgress the boundaries of Eurocentric methods of interpretation. Certainly, locating texts in their sociohistorical context is of utmost importance for reconstructing the marginalized voices and their struggles, as well as for sidelining facile correlations between the modern and ancient world. Yet, modern readers should consider how their social location shapes their interests, questions, and approaches to the text, while interrogating the idea of neutrality and universality. This shift calls for an analysis of the various paradigms for doing biblical studies and their concomitant stakes and implications. In her work *Rhetoric and Ethic*, Elisabeth Schüssler-Fiorenza offers an insightful discussion of four current paradigms in biblical studies, as well as of the ways in which they foster or hinder readings for liberation and well-being. These include the Doctrinal-Theological, Scientific-Positivist, Cultural Studies, and Emancipatory-Rhetorical paradigms.

The theological paradigm sees biblical texts as divinely inspired. Insofar as it follows the biblical author's line of argumentation, this paradigm could reinforce the silencing of his opponents and potentially spiritualize oppression and domination.[5] Thus, one could see the bright side of the rhetorical presentation of the New Jerusalem simply as hope, but neglect to unpack the reproduction of an imperializing vision of power and exclusion.

The scientific-positivist paradigm of biblical interpretation claims the ability to retrieve the original meanings of the text through the rigorous application of various "scientific" tools of interpretation, from historical criticism to source criticism. Through it, we might consider how John uses various Hebrew Bible understandings of the New Jerusalem, invokes ignominious figures from the history of Israel to represent his opponents, or borrows from the book of Ezekiel, particularly the description of the measuring of the temple. Nevertheless, insofar as this paradigm reduces the text to a window into the world of ancient Christianity and sidelines the concerns of the modern reader or caricatures them as subjective parodies and as bad scholarship, it masks the sociopolitical location of the interpreters.[6] Thus, it is not only unable to speak to the theo-ethical concerns of modern readers, but would misrepresent a reading such as this as a hermeneutics of correlation, where one makes a one-to-one comparison between the inscribed audience of Revelation and the marginalized communities of San Jose.

While the cultural studies paradigm has made significant contributions to the development of contextual biblical studies, largely through its emphasis on the social location of rooted readers, it must still grapple with the repro-duction of imperial power embedded in its vision of liberation.

Emancipatory-Rhetorical Paradigm

The emancipatory rhetorical paradigm enables scholars to speak ethically to the variegated social concerns in the public sphere while acknowledging the particularities of biblical texts in their sociohistorical and rhetorical situation. Most importantly, this paradigm problematizes the notion of the universal and disinterested subject and opens a new space for the excluded others of "elite Western history" and their concerns.[7] As Schüssler-Fiorenza observes, the purpose of this paradigm is threefold. First, it seeks to redefine the self-understanding of biblical scholarship in ethical and political terms. Second, it encourages scholars of religion to engage responsibly in public discussions about biblical texts and their interpretations. Furthermore, its overall goal is to foster bibli-cal scholarship that promotes justice and well-being in societies throughout the globe.[8]

These objectives outline the intersection between knowledge and power inso-far as the objective "man of reason" is constructed vis-à-vis the colonized irra-tional other who "does not know how to think." Overall, this paradigm seeks to accentuate the public character and political responsibility of scholarly inter-pretations. It encourages scholars to "contribute to the advent of a society and religion that are free from all forms of kyriarchal inequality and oppression" by critically dismantling oppressive texts in their rhetorical strategies of persua-sion. Through its application, then, one must only view the New Jerusalem as a vision of hope, but also consider how it reinscribes the rhetoric of power and imperialism of its antithesis (Rome), along with the oppression and exclusion of those deemed unworthy to inhabit within it. Because this paradigm calls for a type of biblical scholarship that is liberating in its reconstruction of biblical texts and ethical in its applications to contemporary struggles, I locate my contextual reading of the New Jerusalem in its broader umbrella.

Reading from Gentrified Barrios

The Descent of Googleville

The proponents of Googleville strategically position its arrival as a key step toward solving San Jose's major problems, including traffic, housing shortages, and homelessness. Because Googleville will entail the creation of at least 20,000 jobs, supporters are hopeful about its power to eradicate disinvestment and revive the local economy. Furthermore, Google has also promised to expand Diridon Station, the local train station, by adding lines for the Bay Area Rapid Transit (BART) to San Francisco. In anticipation of California's high-speed rail, Google will also include a stop for the route connecting the Bay area with the San Joaquin Valley. Considering the recent increase in homeless populations in Silicon Valley, Googleville proponents have underscored its impact on housing. Apart from including multiple units, supporters have pointed out that at least 20 percent of those units will be marked as "affordable." The project is also of gargantuan proportions and stands to sit on forty acres of land, whose purchase is already under negotiation. In view of the socioeconomic struggles of Latinx communities in San Jose, the advent of Googleville generates mixed responses.

Gentrification and the Rhetoric of Revitalization

From its inception, a rhetoric of revitalization has characterized the various understandings of gentrification. According to *The Encyclopedia of Housing*, gentrification is a "process by which central urban neighborhoods that have undergone disinvestments and economic decline experience a reversal, reinvestment, and the immigration of a relatively well-off, middle- and upper-middle-class population."[9] Embedded in this definition is the early optimism of the 1960s that gentrification had the power to revitalize marginalized communities through redevelopment stemming from private investors and hardly any state involvement. It also casts the immigration of "well-off" residents as extremely positive while neglecting to map out the repercussions on longtime residents, and particularly ethnic minorities. Indeed, the rhetoric of revitalization characterizes subsequent waves of gentrification in the U.S., each with varying degrees of involvement from local and state stakeholders. The first wave (1973–77) rallied local and state authorities under the banner of redressing per-

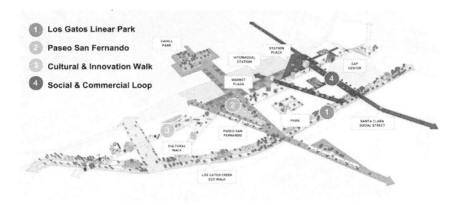

- 1 Los Gatos Linear Park
- 2 Paseo San Fernando
- 3 Cultural & Innovation Walk
- 4 Social & Commercial Loop

Figure 1. Proposed Plan for Google Village in Downtown San Jose (Source: Bay Area News Group, 2018; see George Avalos, "Google Village in Downtown San Jose Would Connect Local Neighborhoods, Company Vows," *Mercury News*, May 23, 2018, accessed December 7, 2020, www.mercurynews.com)

ceived urban decline. Confident in gentrification as a solution to urban disinvestment, the second wave (1970–87) saw more private market enterprises with less state intervention. Despite the market crash of 1987, the prevailing idea of gentrification as revitalization initiated a third wave with three distinctive traits: (1) gentrification expanded beyond the inner city; (2) the increased involvement of large developers; and (3) the decimation of resistance efforts. As Mayor Liccardo's presentation of Googleville demonstrates, the understanding of gentrification as a revitalizing force for urban areas maintains its appeal among the power holders in San Jose. However, for struggling Latinx communities, the rhetoric of revitalization entails a different and less exciting reality.

Googleville Coming to Diridon Neighborhoods

Despite the characterization of Googleville as a revitalizing force for the city of San Jose, community advocates have warned of its potential to displace the Latinx community and other low- and middle-income residents in the area surrounding Diridon Station. The St. Leo neighborhood located in tract 5003, for instance, is home to a resilient Latinx community and thriving ethnic minority businesses. The neighborhood is currently experiencing the pressures of rising property values and gentrification. In 2004, a housing development project known as Georgetown Place, which included ninety-four housing units, was completed in St. Leo. While housing developers welcomed this initiative to "revitalize" the neighborhood, it is also causing those residents who owned a

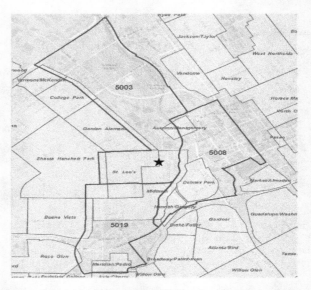

Figure 2. Neighborhoods around Diridon Station (Source: City
of San Jose, Planning Services Division, 2004)

home to sell to younger, white, and upper-middle-class buyers. In 2013, the median
household income in tract 5003, where St. Leo is located, was $106,307 compared
to $81,829 in the city of San Jose. Similarly, Buena Vista is another neighborhood
composed primarily of Latinx immigrants and low-income renters who are facing
threats of eviction that would be directly affected by Googleville. Hence, city
planners are worried about the threat of displacement as well as closure of locally
owned businesses because of the opening of chain stores in the area.

Indeed, demographic and educational attainment changes in the neighborhoods near Diridon Station confirm that, in anticipation of Googleville's arrival, gentrification is no longer a threat but a reality. Census figures show that
the number of Latinx residents between 2000 and 2013 decreased from 4,236
to 3,945 residents, whereas the number of Asian residents increased from 679
to 2,075. The number of white residents also increased from 2,374 to 3,876.
Unsurprisingly, the percentages of residents with college degrees has increased, while the number of residents without college degrees has decreased
significantly, which points to an exodus of long-term Latinx residents. This
dark side of gentrification of Latinx communities in Silicon Valley calls for an
interrogation of the rhetoric of revitalization embedded in biblical texts.[10] On
the one hand, the utopian visions set themselves as the solution to a community's problems, but on the other, they reproduce their own sets of exclusion.

Revelation and the Rhetoric of Revitalization

The Descent of the New Jerusalem

In chapter 21, John presents the New Jerusalem as a massive project for revitalizing not just the seven cities in which the *ekklēsia* are located, but the rest of the inhabited world, as well. In chapter 21, he describes the city as a symbol of a new creation and world order that replaces the decrepit and old creation:

> Then I saw a new heaven and a new earth; for the first heaven and the first earth had passed away, and the sea was no more. And I saw the holy city, the New Jerusalem, coming down out of heaven from God, prepared as a bride adorned for her husband.[11]

Unlike Googleville, the New Jerusalem will be much larger than forty acres. To keep readers in awe of such a magnificent place, John makes sure to give us the measurements of both the wall and the city. A perfect cube, the city's length, breadth, and height are equal, each measuring something over 1,200 miles, a dimension exceeding all human imagination.[12] Furthermore, the height of the walls is 144 cubits, or about 200 feet.

Three major characteristics of John's utopian vision is that the city is cast as the dwelling place of God and mortals and as eradicating all the evils afflicting the community, including suffering, mourning, and death (Rv 21:3–4). Most importantly, the city has the glory of God and the radiance of precious stones. An inescapable element, too, is the fact that the New Jerusalem is an overly wealthy, healthy, and secure place. According to John, the entire city is made of gold pure as crystal, and the foundations of its walls are adorned with every precious stone possible, including jasper, sapphire, agate, emerald, onyx, carnelian, the chrysotile, beryl, topaz, caryopses, the eleventh jacinth, the twelfth amethyst. Furthermore, each of its twelve gates is a pearl! (Rv 21:19–21).

The city also embodies the promise of health for its residents and the nations. In chapter 22, John describes the healing power of the city's water and fruit trees:

> Then the angel showed me the river of the water of life, bright as crystal, flowing from the throne of God and of the Lamb through the middle of the city's street. On either side of the river is the tree of life with its twelve kinds of fruit, producing its fruit each month; and the leaves of the tree are for the healing of the nations.[13]

Yet, what also makes the New Jerusalem stand out is the situation of crisis, poverty, and turmoil in which the faithful of the *ekklēsia* find themselves.

The Crisis Situation

The Crisis Situation "Calling" for Googleville

Mayor Liccardo's vision of Googleville as a revitalizing project hinges on the situation of crisis it is supposed to address and that in turn legitimates its vision of renewal and transformation. In a recent interview, the mayor noted that San Jose, the largest city of the Bay Area, has often been "the bridesmaid and not the bride for large tech companies."[14] The mayor's rhetoric of crisis is primarily evident in the three major problems currently afflicting the city: traffic, housing, and homelessness.

Commutes within Silicon Valley that should take between twenty and thirty minutes are now taking between one and two hours, driving some commuters to tears and to desperately call for a solution. According to a recent survey by the Bay Area city council, the traffic crisis is so bad that residents want it addressed as an emergency situation. As for housing, prices have spiked so much that a median home in the metropolitan area of San Jose is now priced at $1.2 million. California officials estimate that while 80,000 houses are built per year, there is a need for at least 180,000 in order to keep with the growth of the population.[15] And in terms of homelessness, according to the U.S. Department of Housing and Urban Development, at least 43 percent of the unhoused population in the city identified themselves as Hispanic or Latino.[16] In short, the rhetorical construction and articulation of the city's problems constitute a rhetorical situation that is the problem that both elicits and frames the solution intended to address them. Hence, we should expect to see this reflected in the ways in which John presents the New Jerusalem as the solution to the problems afflicting the ancient world.

The Crisis of Calling for a New Jerusalem

As with Googleville, the exigency framing the rhetorical situation of Revelation is one of crisis, at least from John's point of view. The problems that the seven cities of Revelation face, however, have more to do with harassment of believers and exploitative structures of Roman imperial power. John himself writes to the assemblies from Patmos, an island off the coast of ancient Anatolia, where he resides "on account of the word of God and the testimony of Jesus" (Rv 1:9). He also claims to be sharing the oppression (τῇ θλίψει) and consistent resistance (ὑπομονῇ) of Jesus Christ.[17] The traditional translation of θλῖψις as "persecution" seems to reinforce the view that John was banished to Patmos by Roman authorities and that he wrote to Christian churches suffering an imperial persecution under Domitian.[18]

Because Leonard L. Thompson has convincingly shown the lack of historical evidence to accuse Domitian of persecuting Christians,[19] scholars have posited other alternatives. Adela Yarbro-Collins suggests that the crisis John faced arose out the contradiction between his expectation of the kingdom of God and the reality of his political situation.[20] On the other hand, Paul B. Duff suggests that the crisis may be understood as a prophetic rivalry over power to determine how to relate to "pagan" Greco-Roman society.[21] Regardless of the exact nature of the crisis or historical evidence for or against it, the rhetoric of crisis frames the New Jerusalem as a response to the situation of John and the so-called Seven Churches. The heavenly city is supposed to eradicate all these evils and offer believers a new and secure space where there will be no more sickness, suffering, or death, for as John of Patmos points out, "the first things have passed away" (Rv 21:4). Yet, the irony behind the rhetoric of revitalization is that the anticipated solution to the issues John raises stands to replicate the othering and poverty he has just critiqued.

The Others of "Googleville"

The Residents of the Other "Googleville"

Although the rhetoric of revitalization gives the impression that everyone has access to its promises and projects, it actually exacerbates the creation of a homeless population of Others. Access to Googleville and its benefits, for instance, are set for a select few. Apart from the free tech gadgets and free food, the purported 20,000 jobs that Googleville intends to bring to San Jose will be likely accessible to people with high educational achievement. While Google claims to have earmarked 20 percent of the units as "affordable," it has not yet released the total of housing units it plans to build. Thus, community advocacy groups have complained about the lack of detail on this issue during city council meetings.

The gentrification of Latinx neighborhoods near Diridon Station will likely translate into demographics changes in the area. The profile of Googlers in Mountain View suggests that they are often single, educated, upper middle class, and largely white or Asian. As community advocacy groups have observed, the poor, low-income, and unskilled laborers can hardly aspire to have a future in a neighborhood affected by Googleville. Anticipating the effects of Google's project near Diridon Station on the city's homeless population, some advocacy groups have named an encampment near highway 101 and Story road "Googleville." Accordingly, to Sandy Perry, a representative of the Affordable Housing Network of Santa Clara County, observed, there is a correlation between the millions Google makes and the increase of the homeless populations in Silicon Valley. For Luis Mares, a resident of the "Googleville encampment" and former business owner, the arrival of an affluent and white population to his neighborhood became the "writing on the wall." In contrast to the future residents of the Googleville set to descend near Diridon Station, the residents of the homeless "Googleville" are often portrayed as lazy, polluted disease carriers, prone to crime, and as drug addicts.

The Residents of the New Jerusalem

As gentrifying entities of sorts, both the New Jerusalem and Googleville are set to replace the residents associated with "the old creation," so to speak, with a new cadre of peoples. In Revelation, the New Jerusalem triggers an eschatological gentrification that will enable a select few to live inside the city and have access to the wealth, health, and security that the city offers, even as it excludes and creates a population of Others. John refers to the inhabitants of the New Jerusalem as the conquering ones (νικῶντας)—namely, those who have abstained from the morality, idolatry, and corruption of Roman imperial society.[22] But the construction of self often implies a construction of the other.

In Revelation, John contrasts the conquering ones with those he deems unworthy to reside in the apocalyptic city:

> But as for the cowardly, the faithless, the polluted, the murderers, the
> fornicators, the sorcerers, the idolaters, and all liars, their place will be
> in the lake that burns with fire and sulfur, which is the second death.[23]

In the epilogue to this Revelation, John once again suggests that while the conquering ones will enjoy the benefits of the New Jerusalem, the rest, whom he vilifies, will be excluded from the city: "Outside are the dogs and sorcerers and fornicators and murderers and idolaters, and everyone who loves and practices falsehood" (Rv 22:15). The contrast between the conquering ones and those John deems as cowardly evokes what Albert Memmi describes as a "portrait of wretchedness," which is the depiction of the Others as backward, lazy, immoral, and violent in order to legitimate their domination and exclusion.[24]

Policed Space

Revitalizing the City

As gentrifying entities, both Googleville and the New Jerusalem include the policing, systemic and otherwise, of their space. Redevelopment and the arrival of a more affluent population also entails the policing of the spaces they inhabit, which at times translates into a systemic boundary that keeps former residents away or under pressure to leave. During his time as New York's mayor, Rudy Giuliani introduced the "broken windows" style of policing gentrified neighborhoods. This approach suggests that ticketing and arresting people for minor crimes, including littering, jaywalking, or parking in wrong spaces, helps prevent more serious crimes and overall reduces the levels of criminality in the city. However, as Peter Moskowitz notes, "This style of policing, predictably, disproportionally impacts people of color and the poor."[25]

As an attempt to ban homeless populations from certain areas, the city of San Jose has also started to police its central spaces more closely. St. James Park, near downtown San Jose, for instance, has long been a space where the homeless gather and where church groups often congregate to feed the poor and offer other items such as clothes. Because of a "revitalization plan" for the park dating to 2014, the city has opted to "crack down" on "unauthorized" food distributions in the park. According to Matt Cano, assistant parks and recreation director, the city is trying to make the park more accessible to everyone and reactive its social life by offering yoga, movie nights, and running clubs. However, as Pastor Scott Wagers, founder and director of CHAM Deliverance Ministry, says, this constitutes yet another attempt to build systemic walls around the city and exclude its poor and homeless populations. He regards feeding the poor at St. James as not only a constitutional right, but a Christian duty. Yet, what happens when the very texts we use to offer hope reinscribe the kinds of exclusions we fight against? The "broken windows" style of policing is also evident in the multiple sweeps of homeless encampments around the city, including the other "Googleville."

The Walls of the New Jerusalem

As a gentrifying entity, the New Jerusalem's walls offer a certain security but also entail the policing of its space. In his description of the New Jerusalem, John is keen to point out that the city has walls:

> It has a great, high wall with twelve gates, and at the gates twelve angels, and on the gates are inscribed the names of the twelve tribes of the Israelites; on the east three gates, on the north three gates, on the south three gates, and on the west three gates. And the wall of the city has twelve foundations, and on them are the twelve names of the twelve apostles of the Lamb."[26]

Because the rhetoric of revitalizations paints the New Jerusalem as the ideal polis, some scholars explain away its exclusive components. According to Roloff, "It would be wrong to conclude that the city had the character of a fortification and that its walls were to serve as a defense against enemies, for in the new creation there will be no more enemies of God and his own."[27] In order to calm the already skeptic reader, Robert H. Mounce suggests, tongue in cheek, that "the wall is simply part of the description of an ideal city, just as it was conceived by people in antiquity who were used to the strong protection that external walls provided."[28] Conversely, the rhetorical portrait of the other clearly suggests that the walls are in place to embody a boundary between the conquering and the conquered. As a gentrification project for the ancient world, the New Jerusalem includes heavy policing of its boundaries, systemic and otherwise. More akin to homeless bans, the city excludes those it regards as others and unfit to live in the city and reveals the dark side of the rhetoric of revitalization.

Conclusion

In this essay I have explored the rhetoric of revitalization embedded within the visions and rhetorical constructions of both Googleville and the New Jerusalem. Situating this project within emancipatory rhetorical paradigm of biblical studies, which calls scholars to be engaged in societal issues and the discussion about religion in the public square, I have explored the ways in which both Googleville and the New Jerusalem emerge as gentrifying projects that hinge on a rhetoric of revitalization. As the case studies from Latinx communities in process of gentrification show, such rhetoric includes an idealized space/project that promises to revitalize the community and solves some its major projects.

However, as the dark side of the rhetoric of revitalization, there is a situation of crisis, the construction of an "unwanted population" of others, as well as the policing of gentrified spaces. While they are often cast as a solution to the world's problems and overly wealthy and secure spaces, projects of revitalization also contain their own sets of exclusions. As with the New Jerusalem, the rhetorical construction of Googleville as a solution to the city's problems with traffic, housing, and homelessness is hardly neutral. The vision of Googleville may mask the interests of city officials, real estate investors, and Google itself. Thus, its supporters strategically deployed its rhetoric of revitalization, which seeks to persuade residents that the gentrification of their city is in their own interest.

Notes

1. George Avalos, "Google Village in Downtown San Jose Would Connect Local Neighborhoods, Company Vows," *Mercury News*, May 24, 2018, accessed November 30, 2020, www.mercurynews.com.

2. Gregory K. Beale, *The Book of Revelation: A Commentary on the Greek Text* (Grand Rapids, Mich.: Eerdmans and Paternoster Press, 1999), 1064.

3. Jürgen Roloff, *A Continental Commentary: The Revelation of John* (Minneapolis: Fortress, 1993), 242.

4. Elisabeth Schüssler-Fiorenza, *Revelation: Vision of a Just World* (Minneapolis: Fortress, 1998), 103.

5. While the patristic iteration presupposes a fourfold sense of scripture, Schüssler-Fiorenza notes that this paradigm insists on a literalist reading of scripture and promotes its own cultural readings as divine revelation.

6. Interestingly enough, this paradigm is often invoked only to mine insights or historical "facts" that might be used to reinforce a theological position.

7. See Schüssler-Fiorenza. *Rhetoric and Ethic: The Politics of Biblical Studies* (Minneapolis: Fortress, 1999), 45.

8. Ibid., 44.

9. Willem van Vliet, *The Encyclopedia of Housing* (Thousand Oaks, Calif.: Sage, 1988), 198.

10. See Logan Rockefeller Harris, Mitchell Crispell, Fern Uennatornwaranggoon, and Hannah Clark, "San Jose: Urban Redevelopment around Diridon Station," Center for Community Innovation, University of California, Berkley (June 2015). Considering the already high cost of living in the area and the stagnant wages of low-income Latinx workers, fears about a forced migration to the Central Valley or affordable cities in the nation are quite realistic.

11. Rv 21:1–2.

12. Roloff, *A Continental Commentary*, 243.

13. Rv 22:1–2.

14. While in the past seven years Silicon Valley produced nearly three million jobs, it has not received the attention from tech giants such as Apple or Facebook as nearby cities of Palo Alto and Mountain View.

15. In 2017, the median rent in San Jose was $1,983 for a studio (476 sq. ft.); $2,367 for a 1-bedroom (715 sq. ft.); $2,800 for a 2-bedroom (1,006 sq. ft.); and $3,429 for a 3-bedroom (1,305 sq. ft.).

16. See United States Census Bureau data profiles for Santa Clara County, California (2015–17), available at data.census.gov. Consult also, Applied Survey Research, *City of San José 2017 Homeless Census & Survey: Comprehensive Report* (San José, Calif.: 2017).

17. The word θλῖψις derives from the verb θλίβω, which means to press, oppress, or afflict. The NRSV's translation of θλῖψις as "persecution" evidences proclivities toward the imperial persecution view.

18. Giancarlo Biguzzi, "John of Patmos and the 'Persecution' in the Apocalypse," *Estudios Biblicos* 56 (1998): 201–20.

19. Leonard L. Thompson, *The Book of Revelation: Apocalypse and Empire* (New York: Oxford University Press, 1990), 191. Thompson alludes to the lack of historical and archeological evidence and the unreliability of historians such as Suetonius,

Tacitus, and Pliny, who demonized the Flavians to negotiate their status under the Antonians. Instead, he suggests "Christians, for the most part, lived alongside their non-Christian neighbors, sharing peacefully in urban Asian life."

20. Adela Yarbro-Collins, *Crisis and Catharsis: The Power of the Apocalypse* (Philadelphia: Westminster, 1984), 105–6. In her view, such crisis was created by the incompatibility of John's world context with his vision of God's kingdom: "A new set of expectations had arisen as a result of faith in Jesus as the Messiah and of belief that the kingdom of God and Christ had been established."

21. Paul B. Duff, *Who Rides the Beast? Prophetic Rivalry and the Rhetoric of Crisis in the Churches of the Apocalypse* (New York: (Oxford University Press, 2001), 15.

22. The author deliberately contrasts the warnings to the unfaithful with a series of seven promises to the victors that include: (1) access to the tree of life in the paradise of God or the New Jerusalem (Rv 2:7); (2) immunity from the second death (Rv 2:11); (3) access to the hidden manna or heavenly food meant sustain the people of God (Rv 2:17); (4) authority to rule the nations (2:26–27); (5) a white robe and a place in the book of life (3:5); (6) access to the New Jerusalem and the mark of Jesus's name (3:12); and a place at the right hand of Jesus (3:21).

23. Rv 21:8.

24. Albert Memmi, *The Colonizer and the Colonized* (New York: Routledge, 2013), 126.

25. Peter Moskowitz, *How to Kill a City: Gentrification, Inequality, and the Fight for the Neighborhood* (New York: Nations, 2017), 55.

26. Rv 21:12–14.

27. Roloff, *Continental Commentary*, 242.

28. Robert H. Mounce, *The Book of Revelation*, The New International Commentary on the New Testament, rev. ed. (Grand Rapids, Mich.: Eerdmans, 1997), 391.

Offensive Wisdom

Homeless Neighbors, Bible Interpretation, and the
Abode of God in Washington, D.C.

Sathianathan Clarke

Among the commandments that Moses receives from Yahweh to be
transmitted to his people, we find—in simple and expressive terms—
the one that says we must be concerned about where those who have
nothing with which to cover themselves will sleep. (cf. Exodus 22:26)
—GUSTAVO GUTIÉRREZ, *ON THE SIDE OF THE POOR:*
THE THEOLOGY OF LIBERATION

Once Jesus was asked by the Pharisees when the kingdom of God was
coming, and he answered, "The kingdom of God is not coming with
things that can be observed; nor will they say, 'Look, here it is!' or
'There it is!' For, in fact, the kingdom of God is among [ἐντὸς: within,
in the midst of, in-between] you."
—LUKE 17: 20–21, NRSV

Introduction

A country's greatness is directly proportional to the welfare of its marginalized
peoples. Security of minorities, care for the poor, well-being of the laboring
class, gender equality, and protection for persons who slip to the bottom are
thus realistic measures that indicate the state of the union, which we call the
United States of America. Indeed, "the least of these" (Matthew 25:40, 45) in
our communities will decide if America is great again!

In this essay, I focus on one segment of the least that also lives with acute
loss of human dignity: our homeless neighbors in this wannabe great country.
It is a national shame that the country that has the largest amount of private

wealth in the world ($63.5 trillion) also has the largest wealth inequality gap.[1]
A 2018 report published by the United Nations highlights what would rather
be hidden from the world about the extent and extremity of poverty in the
United States despite its incredible wealth:

> The United States is a land of stark contrasts. It is one of the world's
> wealthiest societies, a global leader in many areas. . . . But its immense
> wealth and expertise stand in shocking contrast with the conditions in
> which vast numbers of its citizens live. About 40 million live in poverty,
> 18.5 million in extreme poverty, and 5.3 million live in Third World
> conditions of absolute poverty. It has the highest youth poverty rate in the
> Organisation for Economic Co-operation and Development (OECD),
> and the highest infant mortality rates among comparable OECD States.[2]

Structural inequality and extreme poverty expose a nation-state's moral failure, and they have dire consequences. No wonder then that one of the richest countries in the world cannot give its own inhabitants the basics
enshrined in the Universal Declaration of Human Rights. Article 25 (1) of
the Declaration states, "Everyone has the right to a standard of living adequate for the health and well-being of himself and of his family, including
food, clothing, *housing* and medical care and necessary social services, and
the right to security."[3]

In spite of all the rhetoric of greatness, the United States of America, which
also projects itself as a good nation, is failing its own people. We do not provide everyone "the right to . . . housing." A statement issued by the Administrative Board of the United States Conference of Catholic Bishops puts it well:
"A great and good nation cannot turn away as people wander our streets looking
for a decent home."[4] By its own admission, the U.S. Department of Housing
and Urban Development acknowledged:

> On a single night in 2018, roughly 553,000 people were experiencing
> homelessness in the United States. About two-thirds (65%) were
> staying in sheltered locations—emergency shelters or transitional
> housing programs—and about one-third (35%) were in unsheltered
> locations such as on the street, in abandoned buildings, or in other
> places not suitable for human habitation.[5]

This means, "For every 10,000 people in the country, 17 were experiencing
homelessness." What is most alarming, according to the same study, was the
fact that "homelessness increased (though modestly) for the second year in a
row. The number of homeless people on a single night increased by 0.3 percent
between 2017 and 2018."[6]

One would think that the capital city of the United States has the backs of *all* those who live in a city where senators, congressmen, congresswomen, and the president and his cabinet spend most of their time. Regrettably, this is hardly the case. A December 2016 study published by the United States Conference of Mayors highlighted the grim fact that the rate of homelessness in Washington was a staggering 124 people per 10,000, embarrassingly higher than the national rate of homelessness, which was 17 per 10,000. The capital city of the United States of America had the dishonor of leading the country that year in the rate of homelessness.[7] Even if there has been a decrease in homeless people in Washington, D.C., over the last three years, 2019 still posts unacceptably high numbers. In the shadow of the regal White House, the stately Capitol, the Treasury building, and the elegant Washington Memorial, the annual point-in-time (PIT) count carried out by the District of Columbia on January 23, 2019, "found that 6,521 people were experiencing homelessness in the District on that night."[8]

Autoethnography through Over-Hearing

It is in the gloominess of this imagined "city set on a hill" that I read the Bible with a small community of homeless neighbors early on many Sunday mornings. Since 2010, I have participated in the Welcome Table Bible study at the Church of the Epiphany located at 1317 G Street, N.W., Washington, D.C., just a stone's throw from the White House.[9] Most times this is a humbling, enlightening, challenging, stretching, and profound experience. Between eight and sixteen homeless men and women (the women are in the minority, between one and three) come together at 7:00 A.M. on Sundays for about fifty minutes to read and discuss the Bible Readings for the Week from the Revised Common Lectionary. Mostly, we stay with the gospel text for the day. Because of my extensive travels outside of the D.C. area, my role has gradually transformed from being a facilitator to becoming a participant.

A brief word on method is appropriate at this juncture. In this essay, I am doing theology and biblical interpretation from below. Yet such embedded theology is also indebted to a version of the autoethnography method, which brings together personal and social dimensions of qualitative research.[10] Autoethnography, according to Thomas Schwandt, "now commonly refers to a particular form of writing that seeks to unite ethnographic (looking outward at a world beyond one's own) and autobiographical (gazing inward for a story of one's self) intentions."[11] In this self-conscious yet self-critical mode of research and writing, subjectivity is readily conceded without sacrificing commitment to the rigorous, adequate, and reliable representation of the others who are also the subjects of the narrative. Cheryl Le Roux sums up key aspects of the method employed in this essay: "Autoethnography offers a way of giving voice to personal experience for the purpose of extending sociological understanding" even as it "provides opportunities to help people interrogate and challenge aspects of their worlds and themselves" with a view "to work towards reshaping these worlds—often in the interest of social justice."[12]

Through the many Bible studies that I was part of over the years, I listened carefully to the explicit comments of the small gathered community on Sunday mornings, along with my own inner musings, which I jotted down later during the day. No doubt, my autobiography ("story of one's self") is responsible for how these complex conversations are deciphered and for construing an interpretive frame through which these interactions emerge as a cogent narrative. So, what follows in this essay arises from a process of autoethnography through "over-hearing": a method of listening into conversations with and among homeless neighbors (ethno-graphy) while simultaneously stretching that which is heard to make sense of the Christian gospel as experienced by the author (auto-graphy).

But why am I searching for a Word from God by reading the Bible in the company of folk pushed to the economic, social, and political margins of the national capital of the self-christened "great" United States of America? Some biographical disclosure may be needed to throw light on these reflections. I am a naturalized U.S. citizen born into a Christian family in India in 1956. I lived and worked in India for three decades until I came to the United States for graduate study in 1987. By then, however, I had completed two masters, in Social Work and Theology, and had spent three years working among impoverished communities in rural India (the State of Tamil Nadu). While in India, I discovered the importance of sifting and shaping conventional knowledge about God, the world, and human beings dispensed to me at first-rate educational institutions through the wisdom freely offered by marginalized communities not represented in the orbit of formal education. I did some of this by living among and serving fourteen extremely poor and socially marginalized Dalit.[13] Previously referred to as "Untouchables," Dalits numbered about 201 million, according to the 2011 government census, and estimates put their numbers at between 225 and 230 million in 2018.

Partly to pursue an in-depth study of the religious wisdom of the Dalits and partly to escape my father, who was my boss as the Church of South India (CSI) bishop in Madras, I moved to the U.S. for nine years, combining graduate study and pastoral ministry in the Episcopal Church (1987–96). In the United States, my research focused on the resistant and emancipatory religious resources of one specific Dalit/Untouchable community (*"Paraiyar,"* from whom derives the English word "pariah"). It deliberately incorporated the wisdom of the outcast/e Dalits into the domain of religious knowledge. After completing my doctorate, I returned to India for the next eight years (1996–2004) to teach theology, study the knowledge systems of Dalits, collaborate with nongovernmental organizations advancing Dalit human rights, and work in local churches. I kept alive my practice of interrogating formal knowledge through the lived wisdom of the poor and the marginalized. Much was published from the weighty knowledge I gleaned from planting my feet on the ground alongside marginalized peoples in the area of Dalit theology[14] and Bible interpretation[15] from the underside.

After I returned to the U.S. in 2005, it took me a few years to find the community I might submit my library-accumulated knowledge to for needed scrutiny and potential reconfiguration. Over the last nine years, I have found my dialogical reading of the Bible with the homeless collective at my church in Washington, D.C., a laboratory for both testing acquired scholarship and discovering fresh insights. This essay is inspired and informed by my engagement with this segment of the "fragile classes" in the United States of America.[16] It unfolds in three sections.

The first section reflects upon the dialogical alternate space of biblical meaning-seeking and the ways in which the Bible functions within this interpretive event. At a time when the U.S. has been unwilling to provide homeless neighbors with the security of shelter, I note how this space functions as a relational one, forging a *kinship around the Word of God* to practice equality and experience human dignity. The second section gleans and collates truth from the collaborative Bible study. I elaborate upon two themes that emerge as I reflect upon the conversations: the identity and mission of Jesus and the subjectivity of homeless neighbors. In their offensive wisdom, one notices traces of the *kingdom of God* as a structural domain in the real world. In the final section, I constructively work with the wisdom gleaned from our homeless neighbors. I reflect upon three themes that might be instructive in our common objective to care for homeless neighbors even while we move toward a world in which no one needs to "wander our streets looking for a decent home": integrating the mission of extending personal relationship spaces (kinship) with the vocation of advancing just social structures (kingdom); deploying the Bible differently for cultivating critical and creative agency among the homeless poor; and invoking "the abode of God" as a translation of the *Basileia tou Theou* (the Kingdom or reign of God) within a nation neglectful of its homeless neighbors and a world teeming with refugees displaced from their homes.

Community Bible Study as Dialogical Alternate Space

The Bible study that meets early every Sunday morning at the Church of the Epiphany carves out an alternate space of relationship between those on the cold, hazardous, and anonymous street and those within the warm, secure, and intimate home. The group of mostly vulnerable persons made homeless and some securely housed ones meet in this optional setting. In a space that is not as cozy as the home but not as hostile as the street, this intentional group gathers to sift out a Word from God by sharing insights about the Bible. The egalitarian and dialogical nature of the community Bible study forges a kinship around the Word of God. Such solidarity, which is transitory, imagined, and symbolic, can be detected in three distinct practices.

The circular seating arrangement means that members sit close to each other. The circle conveys the message to the participants that this exercise involves a collective and cooperative search for meaning from the Bible. Another reason for this intimate huddle is functional. To hear each other in the large parish hall, in which other activities take place, members need to draw together in a tight circle. Second, every participant at the Bible study has a printed copy of the three Bible readings assigned for the week. The text is in the hand of each participant so that it can be read aloud to start with and then referred to as she or he offers an interpretation. Often, the gospel text is read more than once to remind the group of the specifics of the narrative, even as such repetitive readings benefit those who might have limited reading ability. Third, through the course of the community Bible study, every participant is invited to offer what he or she considers to be the meaning of the text. Now and then, what is shared is inchoate and circuitous. Sometimes, experiences are shared among the group that have very little to do with the biblical narratives. Yet, mostly, participants interrogate and explain the meaning of the passage from their own marginalized situation. The facilitator works patiently and pleadingly to bring the group back to the gospel text even while lifting up what is offered as commentaries on the passage.

The Bible functions in a distinctive way within this gathered community. The participants, I discovered, have a strong sense of affinity with the Bible. At least three-fourths of the participants on any given Sunday are African Americans, and they often talk about biblical teachings from the churches in which they grew up or quote a family member who is a minister of the gospel. Members of the Bible study enter into its contents with familiarity, ease, and a sense of ownership. It is as if the sacred book belongs to them. The self-assurance that the Bible is their book comes through in the confidence with which each member comments on the various texts discussed. There are many occasions in which participants have quoted from other passages in the Bible to draw parallels with the text being discussed. Through the dynamics of the study, the Bible performs a complex role: on the one hand, it relativizes all the readers as being equally under its sole authority, and, on the other hand, the Bible legitimizes each one's interpretation. There seems a covenanted assumption that the Bible democratizes every interpretation offered concerning its meaning. Yet each participant also feels confident that his or her respective perspective is valid and true and beneficial for the well-being of the whole group.

The Bible, in the hands of this community, is not viewed as a finished portrait; rather, biblical texts are regarded as sketchy outlines onto which artists add their bit to complete the painting. The Bible thus in this context is not pedestalized as the church's canon that can only be interpreted by the scholarly experts. Rather it is the people's sacred Word that can be grasped and explained by all God's people. I learned in my early months of leading the Bible study that in the view of those gathered there was no distinction between participants and facilitators. Whether the facilitators (usually securely housed) like it or not, the voice of the unhoused neighbors determines the direction and subject matter of the dialogue.

The Content of Offensive Wisdom: Biblical Insights on the Identity and Mission of Jesus and the Subjectivity of Homeless Neighbors

So, what was the content generated from the collaborative Bible lab, which functioned as a provisional, egalitarian, dialogical, and eclectic alternate space to help participants live out dignity with freedom? In order to be truthful about the process out of which I construe a coherent narrative for this book project, I must admit that, at times, the interchange of ideas was confusing and contentious, even as it was sometimes illuminating. While articulation was circuitous, it was always strident: raw, sometime crude, but always bold. In what follows, I shall lift up insights that I have assembled and elucidated from the Bible study sessions that brought dignity to the unhoused neighbors and injected their wisdom into the conversation.[17]

Biblical Insights on the Identity and Mission of Jesus

It was at a Bible study on Matthew 11:2–11 that the term "offensiveness of Jesus" and his mission came up in our discussion.[18] In the passage for study, John the Baptist, the one who introduces Jesus as the inaugurator of the kingdom,

338 THEOLOGICAL INSIGHTS FOR HOMELESS MINISTRIES

sends his disciples to Jesus with the question, "Are you the one who is to come, or are we to wait for another?" Notably, Jesus does not go into a logical exposition about his divine identity, whether he is the Son of God or the Messiah. Instead, Jesus tells them to go and report all that they "hear and see": "the blind receive their sight, the lame walk, the lepers are cleansed, the deaf hear, the dead are raised, and the poor have good news brought to them" (11:5). Jesus then ends the conversation with the words, "And blessed is anyone who takes no offense at me" (11:6).

Offense was taken because Jesus brought eruptions of the kingdom of God into the world that were transformative for the afflicted in health (the blind, the lame, the deaf), the outcast (the leper and the dead), and the poor. The offensive nature of the kingdom mission was that it destabilized the security of those at the center and effected change for those pushed to the margins. There was a diverse and large group pushed to the edges by the temple, the social and economic elite, and the Empire. Those afflicted with illness, because of the association of sickness with sin, were sidelined by the temple; lepers, because they were the symbol of impurity, were ostracized by the community; and the poor, because they were dispensable for the regimes of the world, were marginalized by the whole society.

In the Bible study, it was noted that often Christian mission among the afflicted, the outcast, and poor simply doles out teaching and doctrine. This is safe and easy distribution of the gospel. The mission of the kingdom of God rooted in Jesus, according to this text, needs to be much more offending to the status quo, which is sustained by soothing knowledge about the soul being kept safe forever. The offensive truth of God in Jesus is let loose by healing and freeing action on behalf of the afflicted, the outcast, and the poor, which is a sign that the kingdom of God "has come near." This is what would offend people even as it transforms the lives of those on the margins of society.

Interestingly, this passage from Matthew is quite different from the "I Am" statements that disclose the identity of Jesus in the Gospel of John.[19] Here the focus for Jesus is not on who "I am" but on what "I do." "I am what I do" may be a good way of stating the point of the Matthean passage, which also has resonance in Luke, where Jesus says, "But I am among you as one who serves" (Luke 22:27b). This calls for a new way of thinking about the offense of Jesus's mission as related to the kingdom of God. Optimally, communities are called by Jesus to join in his mission by transforming the lives of the afflicted in health, the outcast, and the poor, which will be offensive to the world. If not, at least modestly, this passage calls us not to take offense at the drawing near of the kingdom of God among the blind, lame, lepers, deaf, the dead, and the poor who have "good news brought to them." Mission that does not offend the elite and dominant classes even as it benefits the sick, outcast, and poor is not Christian. Structures also need altering if the kingdom of God must become good news to the poor.

The offensiveness of Jesus in terms of engendering transformative practices for the outcast and poor, I had learned from another member of the Bible study, was indebted to John the Baptist. He was, as it were, the patron saint of the homeless community.[20] No wonder then that John the Baptist was checking on whether Jesus was indeed the hoped-for divine agent whom he had baptized after pronouncing that the "one who is more powerful than I is coming after me" (Matthew 3:11). Let me get back to the word of wisdom about John the Baptist that was offered to me. After a service in which I preached from Mark 1:1–8, which talks about John the Baptist, one member of the Bible study came up to talk with me.[21] When he approached me, I was feeling good about myself as an interpreter of scripture based on the numerous compliments on my sermon that morning. He got straight to the point. "You missed an important aspect of the Gospel passage," he said, and then went on to point out that "John the Baptist is the closest there is to a homeless man in all of the scriptures." "Like many of us," he continued, "John lived in the wilderness, wore camel hair for clothes and ate locus and honey."[22] I was amazed at the correlation he had made between the unhoused prophet living in the wilderness, who ate whatever was available to him from the largess of nature, and the homeless men and women, who live on the harsh streets eating whatever they could get from whichever source was available to them. "But that was not all," he went on to say. "It must also be mentioned," he concluded, "that Jesus came to this homeless man. John did not go to Jesus. Jesus sought him out and came to him for baptism."

I was amazed and humbled by this wisdom. I had learned something new and noteworthy about the forerunner of offensive wisdom, who screamed for action rather than acclamation and whose endorsement Jesus sought. The one who embodied the unhoused in that time lived on the edges on purpose. "To live there [unhoused in the wilderness] was to ignore the boundaries of civilization, to act with a certain air of defiance."[23] Recall that the prophetic Word of John the Baptist was harsh in tone, incisively critical, and structural in focus. Let me draw from the Gospel of Luke. "You brood of vipers!" John rails. "Who warned you to flee from the wrath to come?" (Luke 3:7b). He goes on challenge them to "bear fruit worthy of repentance" (3:8a). He then warns them that if such transformation does not happen there will be disastrous consequences: "Even now the axe is lying at the root of the trees; every tree therefore that does not bear good fruit is cut down and thrown into the fire" (3:9). And, finally, John counsels the social and economic demands of such a repentance:

> Whoever has two coats must share with anyone who has none; and
> whoever has food must do likewise. . . . Collect no more than the
> amount prescribed for you. . . . Do not extort money from anyone by
> threats or false accusation, and be satisfied with your wages.[24]

Even Flavius Josephus (37/38 C.E.–100 C.E.), in his brief historical jottings
of events in the First Century, connects John the Baptist with the pursuit of
social justice. Let me quote his words:

> For Herod had him [John called the Baptist] killed, although he was a
> good man and had urged the Jews to exert themselves to virtue, both
> as to justice toward one another and reverence towards God, and
> having done so join together in washing.[25]

The authenticity of this offensive word from God is, I contend, connected
to the unhoused prophet's independence from the social, political, and economic system. His decision to live in the wilderness and eat food not under
the control of the economic production system could well have been the
reason that he was able to speak the prophetic word of denouncement to the
powerful elite.[26] In a way, this is an indictment of my own role as an interpreter of offensive wisdom. I am obliged to the economic system that controls
the arrangement and distribution of labor, capital, and goods and services for
the benefit of some rather than all. At the same time, this is also an attestation
to the wisdom of the homeless neighbors. Stinging and radical prophetic
criticism of the kingdoms of this world might only come from those who do
not benefit from the system of production supporting our unjust economy.

The other twist in the interpretation offered on this narrative of John the
Baptist involves Jesus seeking out the homeless prophet to endorse his kingdom mission. The interpretation involves a striking reversal. Jesus desires to
be endorsed (in academic language, we might say "accredited") by the unhoused prophet, who is a representative of homeless neighbors. Of course,
Jesus was commissioned by God to announce and advance the kingdom of
God. Yet he seeks an attestation to such a commissioning by publicly seeking
out the initiation rite offered by John the Baptist. Notably, soon after this
baptism by John-of-the-wilderness, Jesus is "led by the Spirit in the wilderness" (Luke 4:1) to prepare for a life in which "the Son of Man has nowhere to
lay his head" (Luke 9:58). It is worth pointing to the irony of much Christian
service to our unhoused neighbors. In a context that generally thinks of service to the unhoused neighbor as compassionate Christian mission, the insight
that "John did not go to Jesus" but rather "Jesus sought" out this homeless
prophet "and came to him for baptism" puts the homeless community as the

instruments of validating the kingdom mission. But this is not how homeless neighbors feel valued by most churches and by society at large.

Biblical Insights on the Subjectivity of Homeless Neighbors

So, what are ways in which our homeless neighbors utilized the dialogical space of collective Bible study to enhance their own subjectivity? To answer this question, let me turn to three pointers that I heard and saw at these Bible studies, each of which offers wisdom into its own subjectivity. I use the term "subjectivity" to hold together the sense of worth and power of agency manifest in individuals and the collective.

First, homeless neighbors want to be part of forging the narratives, which become the conceptual tents under which communities live both as Christians and as human beings. An example comes to mind. One participant was concerned that, as a facilitator, I was invoking the metaphor of sheep far too uncritically while discussing John 10, especially in relation to the group of mostly unhoused neighbors. He was direct and categorical: "We [homeless folk] are considered sheep but it must be said that we are not dumb."[27] Like most other human collectives, unhoused persons were not willing to live under a theological or ideological scaffolding erected for them. In fact, there were numerous occasions in which participants rejected aspects of the biblical text because it was written by those who did not know their reality or who wrote universal truths from their own particular social and economic situation. Let me quote one such pushback. During the Bible study, one member who was cautioning us on the evils of wealth referred to the Bible passage from the Second Letter of Timothy to make his point. It says, "For the love of Money is the root of all evil" (6:10). Another member disagreed with this general axiom. "The Bible does not speak to my experience," he stated. And then he went on to say, "What is truer is, 'For the lack of money is the root of all evil.'" After giving the group an example of how he once had to cheat someone to get some money to pay for food and medication, he finished by saying, "Most of the evil in the world stems from people not having enough to maintain a basic standard of living. That is my experience."[28]

Along with refusing to live under a theological narrative that did not include their worldview and distinctive experience, the homeless neighbors had suspicion that church leaders were trying to woo them to live under the interpretations the leaders were weaving as universal ones. While talking about the signs in heaven and earth that can be noted to herald the return of "the Son of Man" (Mark 13:24–37), one member warned the group, "We look too much to human beings who manipulate us. Jesus gives us independent signs from the cosmos—independent of personalities."[29] When another participant asked him to elaborate on his caution, he went on to set up the example of Jesus over and against present-day church leaders. "So many pimp God for a paycheck," he said, "as a poor man I see it so often. But I cannot fight back." He then went on to lift up Jesus: "We need persons like Jesus. He reached out to others selflessly."[30]

Second, homeless neighbors want to be agents in the kingdom of God. They do not want to be thought of as only receiving from others' acts of mercy; they also want to be dispensers of such acts of compassion. In fact, there are many instances in which it was mentioned that the numerous biblical exhortations to serve the poor must also have corresponding urgings to serve the rich. But one long discussion stemming from a Bible study on John 15:1–8 drove this point home poignantly. The first part of the Bible study went deep into the text because there is a wonderful sense of mutuality that Jesus communicates in his invitation, "Abide in me as I abide in you" (15:4). In thinking together about this image of mutual abiding, the group was struck by the fact that while Christ never ceases to abide in us we may choose not to abide in Christ: "Those who abide in me and I in them bear much fruit, because apart from me you can do nothing. Whoever does not abide in me is thrown away like a branch and withers" (15:5–6). What stood out for the group was that one cannot use Christ only for self-preservation; fruit is the purpose of mutual abiding. When we only want him to abide in us, but we do not want to live for Christ's ends, which is the main purpose of the vine, we will "wither" and be "thrown away."

When we were talking about what these fruits are that we might bear for the good of the vine and the vineyard, most pushed toward an interpretation from Matthew 25. We show forth fruit when we feed the hungry, give water to the thirsty, welcome the stranger, cloth the naked, care for the sick, and visit those thrown into prison. It all seemed to be going quite smoothly when one participant intervened with his alternate insight:

> Most of these acts mentioned in Matthew 25 are relevant to people that have food and water and clothes to give away and those who have homes in which to care for the sick and welcome people into. But what about many of us who do not have all these things? Can we not also be fruitful? For me fruits must not be associated only with physical gifts such as food, water, shelter, and clothing. I do not have these to give away. I take fruits to be gifts that come from positive thoughts within that can be shared with others. These are free and abide in each of us. This passage calls me to give a word of encouragement to people that I meet. This is a fruit coming from abiding in Christ that I can manage to produce.[31]

Finally, homeless neighbors are keenly aware that both voice and act are tandem expressions of kingdom agency. I have dedicated most of this essay to pinpointing and highlighting the voice of our homeless neighbors as evidence of their subjectivity. However, I have also pointed out that Jesus's offensive mission of the kingdom of God was also manifest in deeds. Something along the lines of "I am what I do" is the report sent back to John the Baptist. The agency of living out what you are thinking up was sometimes observable among the participants in the Bible study. One instance was deeply moving. The text of our study was Matthew 10:40–42, which contained Jesus's teaching about welcoming:

> And whoever welcomes you welcomes me, and whoever welcomes me welcomes the one who sent me . . . and whoever gives even a cup of cold water to one of these little ones in the name of a disciple—truly I tell you, none of these will lose their reward.

There was much talk about the coffee that was offered at the Welcome Bible Study as a step up from a cup of water. There were also depressing comments made about the lack of welcome in shelters. One participant asked, "In the United States people come to the shelter to adopt dogs but how many have been to a shelter to give us a 'cup of cold water?'" While we were deeply engrossed in discussing this passage on giving someone a cup of water, I noticed one of our regular participants walk in late. He walked with some difficulty and slowly plopped his body on the chair. Without any fuss another participant quietly got up and gave him a cup of hot coffee before rejoining the Bible study. We were talking about welcome; one of us was doing it. As the facilitator, I noted this action that showed us the meaning of this Bible passage, to which another member quipped, "Don't just think about it; be about your thinking."[32]

What emerges as a hope from the kinship around the Word (collective Bible study) was a more systemic vision of the kingdom of God, a domain that would spill over into the real world. No doubt, this kingdom would be offensive to the elite of this world, but it is one that promises to bring healing to the sick and outcast and good news to the poor. The kingdom of God is announced by the unhoused prophet John the Baptist, from whom Jesus seeks endorsement before he himself inaugurates and advances the gospel. Yet this kingdom hope, which animates the thoughts and acts from kinship around the Word, cannot be complete without the subjectivity of the homeless neighbors, their worldviews, their gifts, and their acts of mercy.

Becoming a Good Nation in a World Where There Is a Place for Everyone to Call Home

In the concluding section of this essay, reflecting upon the twists and turns of biblical interpretation gleaned from the wisdom of community Bible study, let me offer three constructive comments even as we seek to be a good nation in a hospitable world where there is a place for everyone to call home.

One key takeaway from this exposition of offensive wisdom urges that faith-based organizations (FBOs) adopt a complementary approach. While keeping one eye on cultivating personal dignity and individual transformation, the other eye must pay attention to critically disassembling a system that creates homelessness while putting together a social and political order in which no one will be unsheltered. After all, one needs transformed individuals among those made homeless to fully enjoy a restructured social system that is more equitable, just, and hospitable to "the least" among us. Such a bifocal analysis and course of action takes homeless neighbors as distinct persons with intrinsic worth even as it deals with transforming societal structures that create homelessness. Compassion for homeless neighbors as inherently valuable human beings needs to be accompanied with passion for co-creating a social system that will allow for food, shelter, health, security, and dignity for every member, especially "the least of these" in our communities. Laura Stivers makes this point forcefully:

> It is vitally important that we disrupt the causes of poverty and home-lessness and advocate for alternate visions and policies that promote flourishing lives for all. Neither [prophetic] disruption nor [political] advocacy will help individuals or communities to flourish, however, if we do not have a deep level of compassion for *all* of our neighbors. Christian communities can and should offer a strong moral voice and commitment to the movement for a just and compassionate world, but just as important, individual Christians and communities must *practice* hospitality, compassion, and justice.[33]

The either-or option that often divides collectives working on the problem of homelessness creates an unhelpful breach between those charged with the mission of serving the body, mind, and spirit of human beings and those called to the mission of transforming the structures of society so that no one will be without adequate "food, clothing, *housing*, and medical care." The theological content of offensive wisdom generated from the practice of sharing insights on scripture commends a more integrated way of working with homeless neighbors and eradicating homelessness. FBOs need to both nurture relational spaces, however provisional, that help affirm and express human dignity in a spirit of freedom and pursue structural transformation, however fractional, that expands positive right in our society so that no one is hungry, naked, home-less, or a stranger. In the long road toward adequate "food, clothing, *housing*, and medical care," which is the structural promise of a hospitable nation, we need to offer interim spaces for kinship formation to experience human dignity and freedom.

Another learning comes from the manner in which the Bible is employed by homeless neighbors. They insert themselves as subjects into what God is doing for them and through them in the world. In my discussion in the previous sections, I have collated many of the theological insights from the homeless neighbors that affirmed their human dignity and asserted their freedom by means of this platform for Bible interpretation. In what follows, let me point to the method of interpreting the Bible, which reveals the critical and constructive agency of this community.

The method that the homeless neighbors utilized for interpreting the Bible subverted conventional hermeneutical categories and yet reconfigured them creatively. Let me explain. One can generally divide Christian interpretations of the Bible into the biblicist, constructivist, and liberationist camps. *Biblicists* take the Bible to be "authoritative by virtue of its supernatural origin" in such a manner that "the direct identity of its words" discloses "the Word of God."[34] The meaning of scripture is derived from the plain sense of exactly what is written. *Constructivists*, partly in reaction to biblicists, are averse to freezing meaning within ageless texts or inside the mind of ancient authors of such texts. Constructivists mainly extend biblical truths by interlocking them with the truths known from contemporary experience.[35] Biblical meaning, for the constructivists, arises from the words of scripture (Bible) living on because of becoming entangled with the body of flesh (community) seeking to appropriate the Word. *Liberationists* reflect on the things from above (revealed texts) by starting from below (context of human beings). There is also a prior commitment to read the Bible from the perspective of the poor and excluded. Not only does such interpretations of the Bible reveal "the preferential option" of God for the outcast, but it also engenders hope by "bringing good news to the poor" (Luke 4:18).[36]

I had assumed that our homeless neighbors would readily interpret the Bible as liberationists. However, this was not predictably the case. They were much less willing to be confined to any one interpretive bloc. On several occasions, I received challenges for my own propensity to downplay literal explanations for the miraculous and interventionist acts of God. There seemed a distrust of human agency even if, as in the case of many FBOs, such effort was executed on behalf of the homeless neighbors. There was a need among the homeless for God to act in mighty ways. Yet at other times, when literalist interpretations were put forth, there were objections that these supernatural acts of God never seemed to envelop the poor and excluded today. "Where do we see such mighty works of God acting for us to provide manna to eat and a dwelling place to rest?" they wondered. And yet, whatever reading approach was utilized in the dialogue, there was always a push to make the Word come down to become entwined with their struggles and strivings for human dignity and freedom. I suggest that we think of the interpretive mode in these reading events as *collectively interested eclecticism*. In such an approach, mostly homeless neighbors with some securely housed collaborators participate in a process of biblical meaning-seeking and meaning-making by shrewdly and calculatingly employing all modes of interpretation while keeping an eye on how such interpretations can enhance the worth and dignity of all human beings, especially those who are cast out by society.

This critical and creative method of reading the Bible suggests a more general principle for FBOs working with the homeless communities: trust homeless neighbors to bring their own agency into reworking shared resources and incorporate such real-life wisdom for solving the common predicament that binds them in solidarity with us. Like most resources shared between representatives of FBOs and homeless communities, the Bible too can be utilized as an instrument of co-option or empowerment. Often, the Bible is used to discipline (sometimes under the guise of discipling) communities on the margins to live within an orderly world that arises from the imaginary of the elite and dominant in society. However, the Bible can also be used as cannon fire against such kingdoms of the world and as a people's canon that suggests alternative visions of a more just, inclusive, and God-willed world.

A final comment stems from the opportunity of FBOs to transfigure theological language, which, while being faithful to the good news announced by Jesus, must also animate his disciples to advance that gospel in the world. I have already captured this good news as articulated by the homeless neighbors. Their theological insights from the Bible study, emanating from the experience of kinship around the Word, boldly visualize the systemic prospects of the kingdom of God in the world. Such a divine vision, in their view, was rooted in an offensive Jesus, who was endorsed by the homeless one (John the Baptist). Jesus and his mission offered hope to poor and outcast communities, the hope that the kingdom of God was close at hand.

The terminology of "kingdom of God," though, has often hidden the concrete dimensions of this hope, which involves food, clothing, and shelter for all God's children. Instead, the concept of God's reign has either been transported to another realm outside of the earth (heavenly kingdom) or been transposed into God's rulership over the hearts of the faithful (personal governance). In a wealthy nation such as the United States, which neglects to provide its populace with a dwelling place, claiming the notion of "the abode of God" may reveal the tangible characteristic of *Basileia tou Theou*, since an abode brings to mind house, residence, shelter, and habitat. Perhaps yearning and praying for "the abode of God" will make the Christian community work toward God's transformed world that provides the "least of these" among us with "the right to a standard of living adequate for the health and well-being of himself and of his family, including food, clothing, *housing* and medical care and necessary social services, and the right to security."[37]

The good news of the *Basileia tou Theou* (the abode of God), however, must not be confined to national aspirations alone. It is a vision that encompasses the universal human family. Understanding "the abode of God" as a transnational divine project keeps the universal ramifications of shelter for all human beings in our faith-based cosmovision. Even while it experiments with strategies to remain "great" or become "great" again as an economic and military power in our globalized world, the United States certainly cannot stake its claim to be the most equitable and just nation in the world. There may even be a correlation between how badly the United States treats its homeless and how poorly it responds to the millions of displaced peoples in the world.

In a predominantly Christian nation "the abode of God" as a translation of the *Basileia tou Theou* both indicts and spurs on a nation neglectful of its homeless neighbors even as it invites us to work toward securing shelter for the millions of refugees displaced from their homes (even homelands). May the Abode of God come on earth as it is in heaven, both to shelter the whole human family and to sustain each one's God-given right to live with dignity and in freedom!

Notes

I must offer my gratitude to the homeless neighbors, lay leadership, and clergy of the Church of the Epiphany in Washington, D.C., who have welcomed me over the last nine years into a meaningful community. I still serve there as Assisting Clergy. A draft of this essay was presented at a symposium on homelessness organized at Seattle University in April of 2018. I am indebted to Manuel Mejido and the rest of the scholars who contributed to this volume for their pointed and valuable comments. A version of this essay was also presented at the Australian Centre for Christianity and Culture (ACCC) in Barton, Australia, on August 2, 2018. I am thankful to the Director of ACCC, Right Reverend Dr. Stephen Pickard, and the Centre scholars for their critical and constructive suggestions.

1. Kathrin Brandmeir, Michael Grimm, and Arne Holzhausen, *Allianz Global Wealth Report 2015* (Munich: Allianz SE Economic Research, August 2015).

2. United Nations General Assembly, "Report of the Special Rapporteur on Extreme Poverty and Human Rights on His Mission to the United States of America," A/HRC/38/33/Add.1, Human Rights Council Thirty-Eighth Session, New York, June 18–July 6, 2018.

3. United Nations General Assembly, "Universal Declaration of Human Rights," A/RES/217(III), Hundred and Eighty-Third Plenary Meeting, Paris, December 10, 1948.

4. United States Conference of Catholic Bishops, *Homelessness and Housing: A Human Tragedy, A Moral Challenge* (Washington, D.C.: USCCB Office of Publishing and Promotion Services, March 1988).

5. United States Department of Housing and Urban Development, "The 2018 Annual Homeless Assessment Report (AHAR)," by Meghan Henry, Anna Mahathey, Tyler Morrill, Anna Robinson, Azim Shivji, and Rian Watt, Abt Associates (Washington, D.C.: December 2018), 1.

6. Ibid.

7. Homeless Research Institute, "The U.S. Conference of Mayors' Report on Hunger and Homelessness: A Status Report on Homelessness and Hunger in America's Cities" (Washington, D.C.: National Alliance to End Homelessness, December 2016).

8. Patrick Geiger, "A Closer Look at the District's Point-in-Time Count," *Street Sense Media*, May 21, 2019, accessed November 30, 2020, www.streetsensemedia.org.

9. The Church of the Epiphany states the following in its website to introduce the ministry of the "Welcome Table Bible Study": "Approximately 15 participants share insights into how the Gospel impacts daily living and calls us to transformation. Community building is an important component of the study group. Parishioners facilitate the conversations"; accessed November 30, 2020, www.epiphanydc.org.

10. For a concise essay on the differences between "analytic autoethnography" and "evocative autoethnography" and their commonality and divergence from grounded theory, see Steven Pace, "Writing the Self into Research: Using Grounded Theory Analytic Strategies in Autoethnography," *TEXT Special Issue: Creativity, Cognitive, Social and Cultural Perspectives* 13 (2012): 1–15.

11. Thomas A. Schwandt, *The Sage Dictionary of Qualitative Inquiry*, 3rd ed. (Thousand Oaks, Calif.: Sage, 2007), 16.

12. Cheryl S. Le Roux, "Exploring Rigour in Autoethnographic Research," *International Journal of Social Research Methodology* 20, no. 2 (2017): 198.

13. The government census does not include Christians and Muslims from Dalit backgrounds. Thus, these numbers are not a full count of Dalits in India. The National Campaign on Dalit Human Rights (NCDHR) estimates the global Dalit population to be 260 million. Consult, for example, Asia Dalit Rights Forum, *Post-2015 Sustainable Development Goals: Agenda of Dalits in South Asia* (New Delhi: UNDP and Asia Dalit Rights Forum, November 2014), 1.

14. For example, see Sathianathan Clarke, *Dalits and Christianity: Subaltern Religion and Liberation Theology in India* (New Delhi: Oxford University Press, 1998).

15. For example, see Clarke, "Viewing the Bible through the Eyes and Ears of Subalterns in India," *Biblical Interpretation* 10, no. 3 (2002): 245–66.

16. This is a term from Stephen Pimpare, *A People's History of Poverty in America* (New York: New Press, 2008), 6.

17. Of course, in designing and executing this essay I have picked the interpretations that I found appealing and valuable. When participating in this interpretive exercise, I

made it a regular practice to make notes while the Bible study was in progress, which I then transposed onto my laptop. I also recorded the name of the person who made the comment, along with the date and passage of the Bible study. However, because I do not have written permission from them to use their comments, I do not furnish the names of the authors of such offensive wisdom.

18. This took place on December 15, 2013.

19. The "I Am" sayings of Jesus in the Gospel of John are as follows: John 6:48 ("I am that bread of life"); John 8:12 ("I am the light of the world"); John 10:9 ("I am the gate"); John 10:11 ("I am the good shepherd"); John 11:25 ("I am the resurrection, and the life"); John 14:6 ("I am the way, and the truth, and the life"): and John 15:1 ("I am the true vine").

20. While the Protestant and Roman Catholic churches tend to confine John to the season of Advent, the Orthodox Church places great emphasis on John the Baptist in its theology. As Sergius Bulgakov puts it, "The holy Orthodox Church honors and venerates St. John, Forerunner and the Baptist of the Lord, above all saints . . . he comes right after Virgin Mary"; Bulgakov, *The Friend of The Bridegroom: On the Orthodox Veneration of the Forerunner* (Grand Rapids, Mich.: Eerdmans, 2003), 1.

21. This conversation took place on December 4, 2011.

22. "The description of John's clothing and food serves to separate him from the elegant society and to identify him with the wilderness that was to be the scene of eschatological renewal"; M. Eugene Boring, "Matthew," *New Interpreter's Bible*, vol. 8 (Nashville, Tenn.: Abington Press, 1995), 156; also see an explanation of this claim in Boring, *Mark: A Commentary* (Louisville, Ky.: John Knox Westminster Press, 2006), 37–43.

23. Carl R. Kazmierski, *John the Baptist: Prophet and Evangelist* (Collegeville, Minn.: Liturgical Press, 1996), 35.

24. Luke 3:10–14.

25. Josephus, *Antiquities of the Jews*, Books XVIII–XIX, Loeb Classical Library, trans. Louis H. Feldman (Cambridge, Mass.: Harvard University Press, 1965), Book XVIII, chapter 5.

26. Such freedom from the economics of the production system is hinted at by Robert H. Smith in his commentary on Matthew: "John's diet was locust and wild honey, food provided by the Creator, not produced by human labor or effort of cultivation"; quoted by James A. Kelhoffer, *The Diet of John the Baptist: "Locusts and Wild Honey" in Synoptic and Patristic Interpretation* (Tubingen: Mohr Siebeck, 2005), 32.

27. Bible study on May 15, 2011.

28. Bible study on December 18, 2011.

29. Bible study on November 27, 2011. The text being explained was, "But in those days, after that suffering, the sun will be darkened, and the moon will not give its light, and the stars will be falling from heaven, and the powers in the heavens will be shaken. Then they will see 'the Son of Man coming in clouds' with great power and glory" (Mark 13:24–26).

30. Bible study on November 27, 2011.

31. Bible study on May 6, 2012.

32. Bible study on June 29, 2014.

33. Laura Stivers, *Disrupting Homelessness: Alternative Christian Approaches* (Minneapolis: Fortress, 2011), 123.

34. Daniel L. Migliore, *Faith Seeking Understanding: An Introduction to Christian Theology*, 3rd ed. (Grand Rapids, Mich.: Eerdmans, 2014), 49.

35. Constructivists must be distinguished from the liberal interpretive school, which is influenced by post-Enlightenment's erosion of confidence in the biblical worldview combined with embarrassment with the mythological and miraculous inherent in it.

36. Even if influenced by Latin American liberation theology in general, I am mostly indebted to Gerald O. West from KwaZulu-Natal, South Africa, for my liberationist biblical strategies and commitments. See the following: *Biblical Hermeneutics of Liberation: Modes of Reading the Bible in the South African Context*, 2nd rev. ed. (Maryknoll, N.Y.: Orbis, 1995); "Contending with the Bible: Biblical Interpretation as a Site of Struggle in South Africa," in *The Bible in the Public Square: Reading the Signs of the Times*, ed. Cynthia B. Kittredge, Ellen B. Aitken, and Jonathan A. Draper (Minneapolis: Fortress, 2008), 101–15; and "Reading the Bible with the Marginalized: The Value/s of Contextual Bible Reading," *Stellenbosch Theological Journal* 1 and 2 (2015): 235–61.

37. United Nations General Assembly, "Universal Declaration of Human Rights," Article 25:1.

Acknowledgments

The contributors to this volume gathered at Seattle University in 2017 and 2018 to develop and discuss the ideas presented here. Grants from the Henry Luce Foundation and the Arthur Vining Davis Foundations made this initiative possible. Hannah Hunthausen provided important editorial support. I am grateful to Richard Morrison of Fordham University Press for his invaluable guidance throughout the publication process.

Contributors

Paul Houston Blankenship has served as an adjunct professor of religion and theology at Fordham University and Seattle University and a visiting scholar at the University of Washington. His doctoral dissertation at the Graduate Theological Union (Berkeley) provided an ethnographic account of the spiritual lives of people experiencing homelessness in Seattle. Prior to entering the academy, Blankenship was a social worker in San Diego and Santa Ana, California. His scholarship has appeared in collected volumes like *Street Homelessness and Catholic Theological Ethics* (Orbis, 2019).

Margaret Breen is Research and Development Director at the Renton Ecumenical Association of Churches. She has been coordinating faith-based responses to homelessness and housing insecurity in the Puget Sound region for over a decade. Originally from Scotland, Breen is an ordained minister of the Presbyterian Church (U.S.A.). Her publications include "Faith-Based Responses to Homelessness in Greater Seattle: A Grounded Theory Approach" (*Social Compass*, 2020).

Jeremy Phillip Brown is an Assistant Professor of Theology at the University of Notre Dame specializing in medieval Judaism. He has taught at the University of San Francisco and served as Simon and Ethel Flegg Postdoctoral Fellow in Jewish Studies at McGill University in Montreal. His research focuses on the Zohar, the penitential discourses of Jewish mysticism and pietism, Jewish-Christian polemic in medieval Iberia, and the dissemination of Kabbalah in Latin America. Brown's recent publications include "Gazing into Their Hearts: On the Appearance of Kabbalistic Pietism in Thirteenth-Century Castile" (*European Journal of Jewish Studies*, 2020); and "From Nacionalista Anti-Kabbalistic Polemic to Aryan Kabbalah in the Southern Cone" (*Journal of Religion*, 2019).

Sathianathan Clarke is Bishop Sundo Kim Chair in World Christianity and Professor of Theology, Culture, and Mission at Wesley Theological Seminary. A presbyter of the Church of South India, he started his ministry serving as a social worker and priest for the Diocese of Madras among Dalit communities in rural India. Clarke is the author of two books: *Dalits and Christianity: Subaltern Religion and Liberation Theology in India* (Oxford University Press, 1998); and *Competing Fundamentalisms: Violent Extremism in Christianity, Islam, and Hinduism* (Westminster John Knox, 2017).

John A. Coleman, S.J., has been an associate pastor at Saint Ignatius Parish in San Francisco since 2009. Previously, he was the Charles Casassa Professor of Social Values at Loyola Marymount University (1997–2009); Professor of Religion and Society at the Jesuit School of Theology and the Graduate Theological Union, Berkeley (1974–1997); and the Thomas More Chair, The University of Western Australia (2005 and 2007). Coleman has edited, coauthored, or authored eighteen books, including *The Evolution of Dutch Catholicism, 1958–1974* (University of California Press, 1978); *An American Strategic Theology* (Paulist Press, 1982); *One Hundred Years of Catholic Social Teaching* (Orbis, 1991); and *Christian Political Ethics* (Princeton University Press, 2007). He has also contributed over seventy chapters to collected volumes such as *Civil Society and Government* (Princeton University Press, 2002); *Religion Returns to the Public Square: Faith and Policy in America* (The Johns Hopkins University Press, 2003); *The True Wealth of Nations* (Oxford University Press, 2010); *Modern Catholic Social Teaching* (Georgetown University Press, 2018); and *American Parishes: Remaking Local Catholicism* (Fordham University Press, 2019).

María Teresa (MT) Dávila is Associate Professor of practice at Merrimack College in North Andover, Massachusetts. Previously, she was Associate Professor of Christian Ethics at Andover Newton Theological School, teaching at the intersection of Christian ethics and public theology. Her publications and courses focus on immigration, racism and racial justice, class and inequality, Catholic social teaching, and the ethics of the use of force. She is coeditor of *Living With(out) Borders: Catholic Theological Ethics and the Movement of Peoples* (Orbis, 2016). Dávila has served as the president of the Academy of Catholic Hispanic Theologians of the United States (ACHTUS).

Michael R. Fisher Jr. is an Assistant Professor of African American Studies in the College of Social Sciences at San José State University. He has served as a Postdoctoral Fellow in the Department of Public Administration and Policy and an Affiliate Scholar at the Metropolitan Policy Center in the School of Public Affairs at American University. He has also served as a Smithsonian Postdoctoral Research Fellow at the National Museum of African American History and Culture. Before his career as an educator, Fisher was a public policy advocate in Washington, D.C. His policy portfolio included immigration reform and federal welfare programs for those struggling in poverty.

Nancy A. Khalil is an Assistant Professor in Arab and Muslim American Studies at the Department of American Culture of the University of Michigan. Previously, she served as an Instructor of Muslim Ministry at Harvard Divinity School and was a Postdoctoral Fellow at Yale University's Center for the Study of Race, Indigeneity, and Transnational Migration. One of Khalil's recent projects explored the politics of American Islam through in-depth ethnographic research on Islamic higher education institutes and religious clerics—imams—in the United States.

Lauren Valk Lawson is the Lead for the Community/Public Health Track of the Seattle University College of Nursing's Graduate Program. Since 2008, Lawson and her nursing students have worked in partnership with Seattle Mennonite Church's Community Ministry in their provision of services to people experiencing homelessness in Lake City, Washington. She has conducted community-based participatory research to build capacity and design recuperative care services for those experiencing homelessness in the neighborhood. She lives in Seattle with her family and is a member of the Bahá'í Faith. Lawson's publications include contributions to collected volumes like *Nursing Research: Using Participatory Action Research* (Springer, 2015).

Roberto Mata is an Assistant Professor of Religious Studies at Santa Clara University specializing in the book of Revelation and contextual biblical interpretation. He is a recipient of Harvard University's Derek Bok Center Award for teaching excellence and the prestigious William's Fellowship. He has also received fellowships from the Hispanic Theological Initiative and the Forum for Theological Exploration. Mata has published in a number of volumes, including *Latinx's, the Bible, and Migration* (Palgrave, 2018); and *Transforming Graduate Biblical Education: Ethos and Discipline* (Society of Biblical Literature, 2010).

Manuel Mejido Costoya has worked for the United Nations in Geneva and Bangkok and has held teaching and research appointments in Chile, Switzerland, and the United States. He has been the lead author of a number of U.N. technical reports, such as *Time for Equality: The Role of Social Protection in Reducing Inequalities in Asia and the Pacific* (ESCAP, 2015); has contributed to several collected volumes, including *Latin American Liberation Theology: The Next Generation* (Orbis, 2005); and has published in journals like *Social Compass, Philosophy and Theology,* and the *European Journal of Development Research.*

Bruce Granville Miller is a Professor of Anthropology at the University of British Columbia and author of eight books concerning Indigenous peoples, law, culture, and relations to the state, including *Invisible Indigenes: The Politics of Nonrecognition* (University of Nebraska Press, 2008); *The Problem of Justice: Tradition and Law in the Coast Salish World* (University of Nebraska Press, 2001); *Oral History on Trial: Recognizing Aboriginal Narratives in the Courts* (University of British Columbia Press, 2012); and *Be of Good Mind: Essays on the Coast Salish* (University of British Columbia Press, 2008). Miller has worked with Coast Salish people and communities over the last forty years and has served as an expert witness in courts and human rights tribunals.

James V. Spickard is Professor Emeritus of Sociology and Anthropology at the University of Redlands, where he taught courses on homelessness and social inequality, religion, social theory, and research design. His homelessness course, which won the university's 2014 Innovative Teaching Award, sent students on analytic internships with local social service agencies. Spickard has published widely on religion in contemporary society, human rights, social research methods, social theory, and the social foundations of ethics. His textbook on research design—*Research Basics: Design to Data Analysis in*

Six Steps (Sage, 2017)—has a chapter on homeless counts. His most recent book, *Alternative Sociologies of Religion: Through Non-Western Eyes* (New York University Press, 2017), reimagines what sociologists might notice about religion if they began from Navajo, Confucian, and Khaldunian starting points rather than from Western Christian ones. He has served as president of the Association for the Sociology of Religion and the Research Committee on the Sociology of Religion of the International Sociological Association.

Laura Stivers is Dean of the School of Liberal Arts and Education and Professor of Social Ethics at Dominican University of California. She received her Ph.D. from the Graduate Theological Union in Berkeley, her M.Div. from Pacific School of Religion, and her B.A. from Saint Olaf College. Stivers was a past president of the Southeast Commission for the Study of Religion and served on the Board of the Society of Christian Ethics. She is the author of *Disrupting Homelessness: Alternative Christian Approaches* (Fortress Press, 2011); coauthor of *Earth Ethics: A Case Method Approach* (Orbis, 2015) and *Christian Ethics: A Case Method Approach* (Orbis, 2020); and coeditor of *Justice in a Global Economy: Strategies for Home, Community, and World* (Westminster John Knox, 2006).

Index

Abode of God, 24, 335, 346–47. See also
  Basileia tou Theou; kingdom of God
Ackerman, Bruce, 240
action research, 28, 73, 87
adverse childhood experience, 177
affordable housing, 4, 23, 49, 60, 64, 66, 75,
  79, 82, 93, 94, 95, 97, 98, 140, 142, 147–48,
  153, 165, 168, 169, 241. *See also* eviction(s);
  financialization of housing; housing crisis;
  housing insecurity; real estate investment
  trust(s); rental housing; single-family
  rental housing industry; social good(s);
  unaffordable housing
Affordable Housing Network of Santa Clara
  County, 325
African Methodist Episcopal Church, 28, 231
Alexander, Michelle, 150n52
American Episcopal Church, 216
Ammerman, Nancy, 75, 235
Amster, Randall, 118, 120
Associated Ministries of Tacoma-Pierce
  County, 80, 83–85
Augustine, 229
autoethnography, 29, 333–36, 348n10

Basileia tou Theou, 24, 335, 346–47. *See also*
  Abode of God; kingdom of God
Baylor Institute for Studies of Religion,
  38n69, 39n72, 241–42
Beale, G. K., 317
Beloved Community, 134, 156, 304, 309.
  See also kingdom of God

Bible, 239, 283, 289, 304, 333; Hebrew, 304
  (*see also* Hebrew scripture); interpretation
  (*see* interpretation, biblical); New Testa-
  ment, 304 (*see also* Revelation); study, 21,
  27, 310, 335–37, 343
Black Seed Café and Grill, 29, 216, 219
Black Seed Writers Group, 223–24
blockbusting, 146
boosterism, 124
Boston, 19, 29, 166, 214–20, 306–7
Bread for the World, 20, 28, 231, 236–37, 239
Briggs, Xavier de Souza, 79
British Columbia, 194, 207, 209
British Columbia Human Rights Tribunal,
  196
Brogan, Denis W., 229
Brown Douglas, Kelly, 154, 156
Burawoy, Michael, 50
Bush, George W., 234

capabilities approach, 23, 301. *See also*
  human capability framework
Caritas, 300
Carter, Stephen, 240
Casanova, José, 75
Cathedral Church of St. Paul, 216
Catholic Charities U.S.A, 9, 20, 226, 236,
  241, 243–44
Catholic Community Services of Western
  Washington, 81–83
Catholic Housing Services, 81
Catholic Relief Services, 298, 300

CPSIA information can be obtained
at www.ICGtesting.com
Printed in the USA
JSHW041230130421
13534JS00001B/66